COMPUTER SCIENCES

COMPUTER SCIENCES

Second Edition
Volume 1
Foundations: Ideas and People

K. Lee Lerner
Editor-in-Chief

Brenda Wilmoth Lerner
Managing Editor

MACMILLAN REFERENCE USA
A part of Gale, Cengage Learning

GALE
CENGAGE Learning

Detroit • New York • San Francisco • New Haven, Conn • Waterville, Maine • London

Computer Sciences
2nd Edition

Editor-in-Chief: K. Lee Lerner

Managing Editor: Brenda Wilmoth Lerner

Product Manager: Douglas A. Dentino

Project Editor: Kimberley A. McGrath

Rights Acquisition and Management: Margaret
    Chamberlain-Gaston

Composition: Evi Abou-El-Seoud

Manufacturing: Wendy Blurton; Dorothy Maki

Imaging: John Watkins

Product Design: Kristine Julien

For product information and technology assistance, contact us at
Gale Customer Support, 1-800-877-4253.
For permission to use material from this text or product,
submit all requests online at **www.cengage.com/permissions.**
Further permissions questions can be emailed to
permissionrequest@cengage.com

Cover photographs courtesy of the following: Technician working on server rack;
© Yurchyks/ShutterStock.com. Screens with program web code; © Taiga/ShutterStock.com.
Three business people working at meeting; © Dmitriy Shironosov/ShutterStock.com.
Hands holding a tablet or a Pad; © Luis Louro/ShutterStock.com. Computer classroom;
© sixninepixels/ShutterStock.com. Wireless computer mouse; © AlexGul/ShutterStock.com.

While every effort has been made to ensure the reliability of the information presented
in this publication, Gale, a part of Cengage Learning, does not guarantee the accuracy of the
data contained herein. Gale accepts no payment for listing; and inclusion in the publication
of any organization, agency, institution, publication, service, or individual does not imply
endorsement of the editors or publisher. Errors brought to the attention of the publisher and
verified to the satisfaction of the publisher will be corrected in future editions.

LIBRARY OF CONGRESS CATALOGING-IN-PUBLICATION DATA

Computer sciences / K. Lee Lerner, editor-in-Chief, Brenda Wilmoth Lerner,
managing editor. -- Second edition.
    v. cm
Summary: "Computer Sciences, 2nd Edition reviews the history of the discipline and
concepts, as well as profiles contributors in the field. The impact of computers on the
economy and society is explored, with examples in literature, film, and science provided
to illustrate and support trends. These illustrated volumes also include sidebars,
bibliographies, a timeline, charts, and a glossary. This title is organized in four separate
topical volumes, although articles in each volume will be in an A-Z arrangement; the
set's comprehensive cumulative index is found in each volume"-- Provided by publisher.
    Includes bibliographical references and index.
    Contents: v. 1. Foundations : ideas and people
    ISBN-13: 978-0-02-866220-6 (set : hardback)
    ISBN-10: 0-02-866220-2 (set : hardback)
    ISBN-13: 978-0-02-866221-3 (v. 1 : hardback)
    ISBN-10: 0-02-866221-0 (v. 1 : hardback)
[etc.]
    1. Computer science. I. Lerner, K. Lee. II. Lerner, Brenda Wilmoth.
QA76.C572 2013
004--dc23

                                                                          2012037340

Gale
27500 Drake Rd.
Farmington Hills, MI, 48331-3535

ISBN-13: 978-0-02-866220-6 (set)   ISBN-10: 0-02-866220-2 (set)
ISBN-13: 978-0-02-866221-3 (vol. 1)   ISBN-10: 0-02-866221-0 (vol. 1)
ISBN-13: 978-0-02-866222-0 (vol. 2)   ISBN-10: 0-02-866222-9 (vol. 2)
ISBN-13: 978-0-02-866223-7 (vol. 3)   ISBN-10: 0-02-866223-7 (vol. 3)
ISBN-13: 978-0-02-866224-4 (vol. 4)   ISBN-10: 0-02-866224-5 (vol. 4)

This title is also available as an e-book.
ISBN-13: 978-0-02-866225-1 ISBN-10: 0-02-866225-3
Contact your Gale, a part of Cengage Learning, sales representative for ordering information.

Printed in China
1 2 3 4 5 6 7 17 16 15 14 13

Table of Contents

Table of Contents

Volume 2: Software And Hardware

Volume 3: Social Applications

Table of Contents

· ·

Volume 4: Electronic Universe

Preface

....

Computer Sciences, 2ⁿᵈ Edition is devoted to providing younger students and general readers with a foundation upon which to build an understanding of modern computer science. Because applications of technology now invigorate almost all fields of study, topics in *Computer Sciences* are carefully selected to present insightful information related to topics in the news. Both updated and new entries, for example, help explain both technical and ethical dimensions of issues related to social media and online privacy. Special entries on digital photography and digital filmmaking highlight applications of computer science that enhance how we view and understand our world.

The articles in *Computer Sciences* are meant to be understandable by anyone with a curiosity about basic computer science. When topics move into highly technical research and development areas, every effort has been taken to explain concepts clearly and simply, without sacrifice of fundamental accuracy. Accordingly, entries in *Computer Sciences* include treatments of topics designed to excite less-experienced students while simultaneously providing a solid reference for students preparing for more specialized studies. The editors have taken special care to provide treatment of topics that foster essential critical thinking skills that will enable students and readers to tackle emerging issues.

We live in an increasingly digital world where an understanding of basic computer science principles and applications is essential. The Internet, for example, is now a global network connecting, with more than a billion computers used by billions of people. Personal information, medical records, opinions, industrial secrets, military communications, financial transactions, messages between conspirators, orders for goods and services, and many other types of communications travel over the Internet. *Computer Sciences* enables students and readers to understand how the digital world works.

Equally as important, however, for citizens of the digital age, *Computer Sciences* enables students and readers to understand how increases in computing capacity relate to the capacity to wage cyberwarfare; how viruses transform from annoyances to instruments of covert operations and computer crime; and how breakthroughs in technology enable online activism that contributes to social and political change.

Contributors and Advisors

In addition to engineers specializing in computer science, *Computer Sciences* contributors include scientists, journalists, artists, teachers, and writers who explain the practical applications of computer science.

In this and the previous edition of *Computer Sciences*, a number of experts have written and advised on topics related to their expertise. We would like to express our sincere appreciation to:

Tom Abel: Penn State University, University Park, PA.

Martyn Amos: University of Liverpool, United Kingdom.

Richard Archer: Pittsburgh, PA.

Pamela Willwerth Aue: Royal Oak, MI.

William Atkins: Independent research consultant, Normal, IL.

Nancy J. Becker: St. John's University, New York.

Mark Bedau: Reed College, Portland, OR.

John Micheal Bell: LMG research associate. Harvard DCE Graduate Professional Program in Journalism. Harvard University, Cambridge MA.

Mercy Bell: LMG research associate. Nashville, TN.

Pierfrancesco Bellini: University of Florence, Italy.

Gary H. Bernstein: University of Notre Dame, Noire Dame, IN.

Anne Bissonnette: Kent State University Museum, Kent, OH.

Kevin W. Bowyer: University of Notre Dame, Notre Dame, IN.

Stefan Brass: University of Giessen, Germany.

Barbara Britton: Windsor Puttie Library, Windsor, Ontario, Canada.

Kimberly Mann Bruch: San Diego Supercomputer Center, University of California, San Diego.

Ivan Bruno: University of Florence, Italy.

Dennis R. Buckmaster: Pennsylvania State University, University Park, PA.

Dan Burk: University of Minnesota, Minneapolis, MN.

Guoray Cai: Pennsylvania State University, University Park, PA.

Shirley Campbell: University of Pittsburgh, Pittsburgh, PA.

Sara V. Castillo: Independent media consultant. Dubai, United Arab Emirates.

Siddharth Chandra: University of Pittsburgh, Pittsburgh, PA.

J. Alex Chediak: University of California, Berkeley, CA.

Kara K. Choquette: Xerox Corporation.

John Cosgrove: Cosgrove Communications, Pittsburgh, PA.

Cheryl L. Cramer: Digimarc Corporation, Tualatin, OR.

Anthony Debons: University of Pittsburgh, Pittsburgh, PA.

Salvatore Domenick Desiano: NASA Ames Research Center (QSS Group, Inc.).

Ken Doerbecker: Perfection Services, Inc.; WeirNet LLC; and FreeAir Networks, Inc.

Judi Effis: KPMG, LLP, Pittsburgh, PA.

Karen E. Esch: Karen Esch Associates, Pittsburgh, PA.

Ming Fan: University of Notre Dame, Notre Dame, IN.

Jim Fike: Ohio University, Athens, OH.

Ida M. Flynn: University of Pittsburgh, Pittsburgh, PA.

Roger R. Flynn: University of Pittsburgh, Pittsburgh, PA.

H. Bruce Franklin: Rutgers University, Newark, NJ.

Thomas J. Froehlich: Kent State University, Kent, OH.

Chuck Gaidica: WDW-TV, Detroit, MI.

G. Christopher Hall: PricewaterhouseCoopers.

Gary Hanson: Kent State University, Kent, OH.

Shaquilla T. Harrigan, Production intern at LernerMedia Global, Summer 2012. Harvard College (Class of 2016), Cambridge, MA.

Karen Hartman: James Monroe Center Library, Mary Washington College, Fredericksburg, VA.

Melissa J. Harvey: Carnegie Mellon University, Pittsburgh, PA.

Albert D. Helfnck: Embry-Riddle Aeronautical University, Daytona Beach, PL.

Angelia Herrin: Harvard Business Publishing, Cambridge, MA.

Stephen Hughes: University of Pittsburgh, Pittsburgh, PA.

Joseph Patterson Hyder: Hyder Law Group, Jacksonville, FL.

Bruce Jacob: University of Maryland, College Park, MD.

Radhika Jain: Georgia State University, Atlanta, GA.

Wesley Jamison: University of Pittsburgh at Greensburg.

Sid Karin: San Diego Supercomputer Center, University of California, San Diego.

Declan P. Kelly: Philips Research, The Netherlands.

Betty Kirke: New York, NY.

Mikko Kovalainen: University of Jyväskylä, Finland.

Paul R. Kraus: Pittsburgh, PA.

Prashant Krishnamurthy: University of Pittsburgh, Pittsburgh, PA.

Marina Krol: Mount Sinai School of Medicine, New York, NY.

Susan Landau: Sun Microsystems Inc., Mountain View, CA.

Nicholas C. Laudato: University of Pittsburgh, Pittsburgh, Pennsylvania.

George Lawton: Eutopian Enterprises.

Cynthia Tumilry Lazzaro: Pinnacle Training Corp., Stonebam, MA.

Joseph J. Lazzaro: Massachusetts Commission for the Blind, Boston, MA.

John Leaney: University of Technology, Sydney, Australia.

Robert Lembersky: Ann Taylor, Inc., New York, NY.

Adrienne Wilmoth Lerner: Hyder Law Group, Jacksonville, FL.

Terri L. Lenox: Westminster College, New Wilmington, PA.

Joyce H-S Li: University of Pittsburgh, Pittsburgh, PA.

Michael R. Macedonia: USA STPJCOM, Orlando,.

Dirk E. Mahling: University of Pittsburgh, Pittsburgh, PA.

Cynthia J. Martincic: St. Vincent College, Latrobe, PA.

Michael J. McCarthy: Carnegie Mellon University, Pittsburgh, PA.

Ann Mclver McHoes: Carlow College, Pittsburgh PA.

Genevieve McHoes: University of Maryland, College Park, MD.

John McHugh: CERTTM Coordination Center, Software Engineering Institute, Carnegie Mellon Pittsburgh, PA.

Donald M. Mclver: Northrop Grumman Corporation, Baltimore, MD.

Maurice Mclver: Integrated Databases, Inc., Honolulu, HI.

William J. Mclver, Jr.: University at Albany, State University of New York.

Trevor T. Moores: University of Nevada, Las Vegas.

Christopher Morgan: Association for Computing Machinery, Nero York, NY.

Bertha Kugelman Morimoto: University of Pittsburgh, Pittsburgh, PA.

Tracy Mullen: NEC Research Inc., Princeton, NJ.

Paul Munro: University of Pittsburgh, Pittsburgh, PA.

Stephen Murray: University of Technology, Sydney, Australia.

Carey Nachenberg: Symantec Corporation.

John Nau: Frank R. Rusch.

Paolo Nesi: University of Florence, Italy.

Kai A. Olsen: Molde College and University of Bergen, Norway.

Evan Austin Ott: University of Texas, Austin, TX.

Ipek Ozkaya: Carnegie Mellon University, Pittsburgh, PA.

Bob Patterson: Perfection Services, Inc.

Robert R. Perkoski: University of Pittsburgh, Pittsburgh, PA.

Thomas A. Pollack: Duquesne University, Pittsburgh, PA.

Guylaine M. Pollock: IEEE Computer Society; Sandia National Laboratories, Albuquerque, NM.

Wolfgang Porod: University of Notre Dame, Notre Dame, IN.

Anwer H. Puthawala: Park Avenue Associates in Radiology, P.C., Binghamton, NY.

Mary McIver Puthawala: Binghamton, NY.

Sudha Ram: University of Arizona, Tucson, AZ.

Edie M. Rasmussen: University of Pittsburgh, Pittsburgh, PA.

Robert D. Regan: Consultant, Pittsburgh, PA.

Allen Renear: University of Illinois, Urbana-Champaign.

Sarah K. Rich: Pennsylvania State University, University Park, PA.

Mike Robinson: Sageforce Ltd., Kingston on Thames, Surrey, United Kingdom.

Elke A. Rudensteiner: Worcester Polytechnic Institute, Worcester, MA.

Frank R. Rusch: University of Illinois at Urbana-Champaign.

William Sherman: National Center for Supercomputing Applications, University of Illinois at Urbana-Champaign.

Marc Silverman: University of Pittsburgh, Pittsburgh, PA.

Munindar P. Singh: North Carolina State University, Raleigh, NC.

Cindy Smith: PricewaterhouseCoopers, Pittsburgh, PA.

Barry Smyth: Smart Media Institute, University College, Dublin, Ireland.

Amanda Spink: Pennsylvania State University, University Park, PA.

Michael B. Spring: University of Pittsburgh, Pittsburgh, PA.

Savitha Srinivasan: IBM Almaden Research Center, San Jose, CA.

Maria Stenzel: Photojournalist. *National Geographic*, Washington, D.C.

Igor Tarnopolsky: Westchester County Department of Laboratories and Research, Valhalla, NY.

George A. Tarnow: Georgetown University, Washington, DC.

Lucy A. Tedd: University of Wales, Aberystwyth, Wales, United Kingdom.

Umesh Thakkar: National Center for Supercomputing Applications, University of Illinois at Urbana-Champaign.

Richard A- Thompson: University of Pittsburgh, Pittsburgh, PA.

James E. Tomayko: Carnegie Mellon University, Pittsburgh, PA.

Christinger Tomer: University of Pittsburgh, Pittsburgh, PA.

Upkar Varshney: Georgia State University, Atlanta, GA.

Jonathan Vos Post: Magic Dragon Multimedia, http://magicdragon.com.

Tom Wall: Duke University, Durham, N.

Brett A. Warneke: University of California, Berkeley, CA.

Patricia S. Wehman: University of Pittsburgh, Pittsburgh, PA.

Isaac Weiss: University of Maryland, College Park, MD.

Martin B. Weiss: University of Pittsburgh, Pittsburgh, PA.

Jeffrey C. Wingard: Leesburg, VA.

Victor L. Winter: University of Nebraska, Omaha.

Charles R. Woratschek: Robert Morris University, Moon Township, PA.

Peter Y. Wu: University of Pittsburgh, Pittsburgh, PA.

William J. Yurcik: Illinois State University, Normal, IL.

Gregg R. Zegarelli: Zegarelli Law Group, P.C.

Acknowledgments

The editors offer special thanks to: Angelia Herrin and Maria Stenzel for bringing their expertise in modern practice of journalism and photojournalism to, respectively, the *Computer Sciences*. Herrin, a former Knight Fellow in Journalism at Stanford University reporter for Knight-Ridder newspapers, served as Washington, D.C., editor of *USA Today*. Herrin is now an editor at Harvard Business School

Publishing. Stenzel, a frequent and long-time contributor to *National Geographic* served as a Knight Fellow in Science Journalism at MIT.

Writing on tight deadlines from Dubai in the United Arab Emirates, Sara V. Castillo contributed the article on digital filmmaking.

Evan Ott at the University of Texas offered invaluable assistance in advising and updating topics related to on emerging applications of computer science.

The editors thank Shaquilla T. Harrigan, our summer 2012 production intern at LernerMedia Global. Ms. Harrigan, a member of the class of 2016 at Harvard College in Cambridge, Massachusetts, assisted in photo selection and captioning.

This book would not have been possible without the efforts of project manager Kim McGrath. Her perspectives, patience, and penchant for asking good questions across a broad spectrum of topics added significantly to the quality of all aspects of *Computer Sciences*.

K. Lee Lerner and Brenda Wilmoth Lerner, editors
Cambridge, MA

December, 2012

For Your Reference

This section provides information that may be of assistance in understanding the entries that make up this book: definitions for SI terms and symbols, and; conversion tables for SI measurements to other measurement systems. Also included are examples from various base numbering systems and their equivalents, as well as the relative sizes of objects.

SI BASE AND SUPPLEMENTARY UNIT NAMES AND SYMBOLS

Physical Quality	Name	Symbol
Length	meter	m
Mass	kilogram	kg
Time	second	s
Electric current	ampere	A
Thermodynamic temperature	kelvin	K
Amount of substance	mole	mol
Luminous intensity	candela	cd
Plane angle	radian	rad
Solid angle	steradian	sr

Temperature

Scientists commonly use the Celsius system. Although not recommended for scientific and technical use, earth scientists also use the familiar Fahrenheit temperature scale (°F). 1°F = 1.8°C or K. The triple point of H_2O, where gas, liquid, and solid water coexist, is 32°F.

- To change from Fahrenheit (F) to Celsius (C):
  °C = (°F-32)/(1.8)
- To change from Celsius (C) to Fahrenheit (F):
  °F = (°C x 1.8) + 32
- To change from Celsius (C) to Kelvin (K):
  K = °C + 273.15
- To change from Fahrenheit (F) to Kelvin (K):
  K = (°F-32)/(1.8) + 273.15

UNITS DERIVED FROM SI, WITH SPECIAL NAMES AND SYMBOLS

Derived Quantity	Name of SI Unit	Symbol for SI Unit	Expression in Terms of SI Base Units
Frequency	hertz	Hz	s^{-1}
Force	newton	N	$m \cdot kg \cdot s^{-2}$
Pressure, stress	pascal	Pa	$m^{-1} \cdot kg \cdot s^{-2}$
Energy, work, heat	joule	J	$m^2 \cdot kg \cdot s^{-2}$
Power, radiant flux	watt	W	$m^2 \cdot kg \cdot s^{-3}$
Electric charge	coulomb	C	$s \cdot A$
Electric potential, electromotive force	volt	V	$m^2 \cdot kg \cdot s^{-3} \cdot A^{-1}$
Electric resistance	ohm	Ω	$m^2 \cdot kg \cdot s^{-3} \cdot A^{-2}$
Celsius temperature	degree Celsius	°C	K
Luminous flux	lumen	lm	Cd
Illuminance	lux	lx	$m^{-2} \cdot cd$

UNITS USED WITH SI, WITH NAME, SYMBOL, AND VALUES IN SI UNITS

The following units, not part of the SI, will continue to be used in appropriate contexts (e.g., angtsrom):

Physical Quantity	Name of Unit	Symbol for Unit	Value in SI Units
Time	minute	min	60 s
	hour	h	3,600 s
	day	d	86,400 s
Plane angle	degree	°	$(\pi/180)$ rad
	minute	'	$(\pi/10,800)$ rad
	second	"	$(\pi/648,000)$ rad
Length	angstrom	Å	10^{-10} m
Volume	liter	l, L	$1\ dm^3 = 10^{-3}\ m^3$
Mass	ton	t	$1\ Mg = 10^3$ kg
	unified atomic mass unit	u	$\approx 1.66054 \times 10^{-27}$ kg
Pressure	bar	bar	$10^5\ Pa = 10^5\ N\ m^{-2}$
Energy	electronvolt	eV (= e X V)	$\approx 1.60218 \times 10^{-19}$ J

CONVERSIONS FOR STANDARD, DERIVED, AND CUSTOMARY MEASUREMENTS

Length

1 angstrom (Å)	0.1 nanometer (exactly) 0.000000004 inch
1 centimeter (cm)	0.3937 inches
1 foot (ft)	0.3048 meter (exactly)
1 inch (in)	2.54 centimeters (exactly)
1 kilometer (km)	0.621 mile
1 meter (m)	39.37 inches 1.094 yards
1 mile (mi)	5,280 feet (exactly) 1.609 kilometers
1 astronomical unit (AU)	1.495979×10^{13} cm
1 parsec (pc)	206,264.806 AU 3.085678×10^{18} cm 3.261633 light-years
1 light-year	9.460530×10^{17} cm

Area

1 acre	43,560 square feet (exactly) 0.405 hectare
1 hectare	2.471 acres
1 square centimeter (cm^2)	0.155 square inch
1 square foot (ft^2)	929.030 square centimeters
1 square inch (in^2)	6.4516 square centimeters (exactly)
1 square kilometer (km^2)	247.104 acres 0.386 square mile
1 square meter (m^2)	1.196 square yards 10.764 square feet
1 square mile (mi^2)	258.999 hectares

MEASUREMENTS AND ABBREVIATIONS

Volume

1 barrel (bbl)*, liquid	31 to 42 gallons
1 cubic centimeter (cm^3)	0.061 cubic inch
1 cubic foot (ft^3)	7.481 gallons 28.316 cubic decimeters
1 cubic inch (in^3)	0.554 fluid ounce
1 dram, fluid (or liquid)	$1/8$ fluid ounce (exactly) 0.226 cubic inch 3.697 milliliters
1 gallon (gal) (U.S.)	231 cubic inches (exactly) 3.785 liters 128 U.S. fluid ounces (exactly)
1 gallon (gal) (British Imperial)	277.42 cubic inches 1.201 U.S. gallons 4.546 liters
1 liter	1 cubic decimeter (exactly) 1.057 liquid quarts 0.908 dry quart 61.025 cubic inches
1 ounce, fluid (or liquid)	1.805 cubic inches 29.573 milliliters
1 ounce, fluid (fl oz) (British)	0.961 U.S. fluid ounce 1.734 cubic inches 28.412 milliliters
1 quart (qt), dry (U.S.)	67.201 cubic inches 1.101 liters
1 quart (qt), liquid (U.S.)	57.75 cubic inches (exactly) 0.946 liter

Units of mass

1 carat (ct)	200 milligrams (exactly) 3.086 grains
1 grain	64.79891 milligrams (exactly)
1 gram (g)	15.432 grains 0.035 ounce
1 kilogram (kg)	2.205 pounds
1 microgram (µg)	0.000001 gram (exactly)
1 milligram (mg)	0.015 grain
1 ounce (oz)	437.5 grains (exactly) 28.350 grams
1 pound (lb)	7,000 grains (exactly) 453.59237 grams (exactly)
1 ton, gross or long	2,240 pounds (exactly) 1.12 net tons (exactly) 1.016 metric tons
1 ton, metric (t)	2,204.623 pounds 0.984 gross ton 1.102 net tons
1 ton, net or short	2,000 pounds (exactly) 0.893 gross ton 0.907 metric ton

Pressure

1 kilogram/square centimeter (kg/cm^2)	0.96784 atmosphere (atm) 14.2233 pounds/square inch (lb/in^2) 0.98067 bar
1 bar	0.98692 atmosphere (atm) 1.02 kilograms/square centimeter (kg/cm^2)

---

* There are a variety of "barrels" established by law or usage. For example, U.S. federal taxes on fermented liquors are based on a barrel of 31 gallons (141 liters); many state laws fix the "barrel for liquids" as $31 1/2$ gallons (119.2 liters); one state fixes a 36-gallon (160.5 liters) barrel for cistern measurment; federal law recognizes a 40-gallon (178 liters) barrel for "proof spirts"; by custom, 42 gallons (159 liters) comprise a barrel of crude oil or petroleum products for statistical purposes, and this equivalent is recognized "for liquids" by four states.

Base 2 (Binary)	Decimal (Base 10) Equivalent	Approximations to Powers of Ten
2^0	1	
2^1	2	
2^2	4	
2^3	8	
2^4	16	
2^5	32	
2^6	64	
2^7	128	10^2; 100; one hundred; 1 followed by 2 zeros
2^8	256	
2^9	512	
2^{10}	1,024	10^3; 1,000; one thousand; 1 followed by 3 zeros
2^{11}	2,048	
2^{12}	4,096	
2^{13}	8,192	
2^{14}	16,384	
2^{15}	32,768	
2^{16}	65,536	
2^{17}	131,072	
2^{18}	262,144	
2^{19}	524,288	
2^{20}	1,048,576	10^6; 1,000,000; one million; 1 followed by 6 zeros
2^{21}	2,097,152	
2^{22}	4,194,304	
2^{23}	8,388,608	
2^{24}	16,777,216	
2^{25}	33,554,432	
2^{26}	67,108,864	
2^{27}	134,217,728	
2^{28}	268,435,456	
2^{29}	536,870,912	
2^{30}	1,073,741,824	10^9; 1,000,000,000; one billion; 1 followed by 9 zeros
2^{31}	2,147,483,648	
2^{32}	4,294,967,296	
2^{33}	8,589,934,592	
2^{34}	17,179,869,184	
2^{35}	34,359,738,368	
2^{36}	68,719,476,736	
2^{37}	137,438,953,472	
2^{38}	274,877,906,944	
2^{39}	549,755,813,888	
2^{40}	1,099,511,627,776	10^{12}; 1,000,000,000,000; one trillion; 1 followed by 12 zeros
2^{50}	1,125,899,906,842,624	10^{15}; 1,000,000,000,000,000; one quadrillion; 1 followed by 15 zeros
2^{100}	1,267,650,600,228,229,401,496,703,205,376	10^{30}; 1 followed by 30 zeros
2^{-1}	1/2	
2^{-2}	1/4	
2^{-3}	1/8	
2^{-4}	1/16	
2^{-5}	1/32	
2^{-6}	1/64	
2^{-7}	1/128	1/100; 10^{-2}; 0.01; 1 hundredth
2^{-8}	1/256	
2^{-9}	1/512	
2^{-10}	1/1,024	1/1000; 10^{-3}; 0.001; 1 thousandth

Base 16 (Hexadecimal)	Binary (Base 2) Equivalent	Decimal (Base 10) Equivalent	Approximations to Powers of Ten
16^0	2^0	1	
16^1	2^4	16	
16^2	2^8	256	2×10^2; 2 hundred
16^3	2^{12}	4,096	4×10^3; 4 thousand
16^4	2^{16}	65,536	65×10^3; 65 thousand
16^5	2^{20}	1,048,576	1×10^6; 1 million
16^6	2^{24}	16,777,216	
16^7	2^{28}	268,435,456	
16^8	2^{32}	4,294,967,296	4×10^9; 4 billion
16^9	2^{36}	68,719,476,736	68×10^9; 68 billion
16^{10}	2^{40}	1,099,511,627,776	1×10^{12}; 1 trillion
16^{-1}	2^{-4}	1/16	
16^{-2}	2^{-8}	1/256	
16^{-3}	2^{-12}	1/4,096	$1/4 \times 10^{-3}$; 1/4-thousandth
16^{-4}	2^{-16}	1/65,536	
16^{-5}	2^{-20}	1/1,048,576	10^{-6}; 1 millionth
16^{-8}	2^{-32}	1/4,294,967,296	$1/4 \times 10^{-9}$; 1/4-billionth
16^{-10}	2^{-40}	1/1,099,511,627,776	10^{-12}; 1 trillionth

Base 10 (Decimal)	Equivalent	Verbal Equivalent
10^0	1	
10^1	10	
10^2	100	1 hundred
10^3	1,000	1 thousand
10^4	10,000	
10^5	100,000	
10^6	1,000,000	1 million
10^7	10,000,000	
10^8	100,000,000	
10^9	1,000,000,000	1 billion
10^{10}	10,000,000,000	
10^{11}	100,000,000,000	
10^{12}	1,000,000,000,000	1 trillion
10^{15}	1,000,000,000,000,000	1 quadrillion
10^{-1}	1/10	1 tenth
10^{-2}	1/100	1 hundredth
10^{-3}	1/1,000	1 thousandth
10^{-6}	1/1,000,000	1 millionth
10^{-9}	1/1,000,000,000	1 billionth
10^{-12}	1/1,000,000,000,000	1 trillionth
10^{-15}	1/1,000,000,000,000,000	1 quadrillionth

Sizes of and Distance to Objects	Equivalent	Additional Information
Diameter of Electron (classical)	5.6×10^{-13} centimeters	5.6×10^{-13} centimeters; roughly 10^{-12} centimeters
Mass of Electron	9.109×10^{-28} grams	roughly 10^{-27} grams (1 gram = 0.0353 ounce)
Diameter of Proton	10^{-15} meters	10^{-13} centimeters
Mass of Proton	1.67×10^{-24} grams	roughly 10^{-24} grams (about 1,836 times the mass of electron)
Diameter of Neutron	10^{-15} meters	10^{-13} centimeters
Mass of Neutron	1.673×10^{-24} grams	roughly 10^{-24} grams (about 1,838 times the mass of electron)
Diameter of Atomic Nucleus	10^{-14} meters	$\sim 10^{-12}$ centimeters (10,000 times smaller than an atom)
Atomic Mass (Atomic Mass Unit)	1.66×10^{-27} kilograms	one atomic mass unit (amu) is equal to 1.66×10^{-24} grams
Diameter of Atom (Electron Cloud)	ranges from 1×10^{-10} to 5×10^{-10} meters	$\sim 10^{-10}$ meters; $\sim 10^{-8}$ centimeters; $\sim 3.94 \times 10^{-9}$ inches (roughly 4 billionth of an inch across or 1/250 millionth of an inch across)
Diameter of (standard) Pencil	6 millimeters (0.236 inches)	roughly 10^{-2} meters
Height (average) of Man and Woman	man: 1.75 meters (5 feet, 8 inches) woman: 1.63 meters (5 feet, 4 inches)	human height roughly 2×10^0 meters; 1/804.66 miles; 10^{-3} miles
Height of Mount Everest	8,850 meters (29,035 feet)	~ 5.5 miles; roughly 10^4 meters
Radius (mean equatorial) of Earth	6,378.1 kilometers (3,960.8 miles)	$\sim 6,400$ kilometers (4,000 miles); roughly 6.4×10^6 meters
Diameter (polar) of Earth	12,713.6 kilometers (7,895.1 miles)	$\sim 12,800$ kilometers (8,000 miles); roughly 1.28×10^7 meters (Earth's diameter is twice the Earth's radius)
Circumference (based on mean equatorial radius) of Earth	40,075 kilometers (24,887 miles)	$\sim 40,000$ kilometers (25,000 miles) (about 8 times the width of the United States) (Circumference = $2 \times \pi \times$ Earth's radius)
Distance from Earth to Sun	149,600,000 kilometers (92,900,000 miles)	$\sim 93,000,000$ miles; ~ 8.3 light-minutes; roughly 10^{11} meters; roughly 10^8 miles
Distance to Great Nebula in Andromeda Galaxy	2.7×10^{19} kilometers (1.7×10^{19} miles)	~ 2.9 million light-years; roughly 10^{22} meters; roughly 10^{19} miles

Timeline: Significant Events in the History of Computing

· ·

The history of computer sciences has been filled with many creative inventions and intriguing people. Here are some of the milestones and achievements in the field.

c. 300-500 BCE	The counting board, known as the ancient abacus, is used. (Babylonia)
1200 CE	The modern abacus is used. (China)
1500	Leonardo da Vinci drafts a design for a calculator. (Italy)
1614	John Napier suggests the use of logarithms. (Scotland)
1617	John Napier produces calculating rods, called "Napier's Bones." (Scotland)
	Henry Briggs formulates the common logarithm, Base 10. (England)
1620	Edmund Gunter devises the "Line of Numbers," the precursor to slide rule. (England)
1623	Wilhelm Schickard conceives a design of a mechanical calculator. (Germany)
1632	William Oughtred originates the slide rule. (England)
1642	Blaise Pascal makes a mechanical calculator which can add and subtract. (France)
1666	Sir Samuel Morland develops a multiplying calculator. (England)
1673	Gottfried von Leibniz proposes a general purpose calculating machine. (Germany)
1777	Charles Stanhope, 3rd Earl of Stanhope, Lord Mahon, invents a logic machine. (England)
1804	Joseph-Marie Jacquard mechanizes weaving with Jacquard's Loom, featuring punched cards. (France)
1820	Charles Xavier Thomas (Tomas de Colmar) creates a calculating machine, a prototype for the first commercially successful calculator. (France)
1822	Charles Babbage designs the Difference Engine. (England)
1834	Charles Babbage proposes the Analytical Engine. (England)
1838	Samuel Morse formulates the Morse Code. (United States)
1842	L. F. Menabrea publishes a description of Charles Babbage's Analytical Engine. (Published, Italy)
1843	Ada Byron King, Countess of Lovelace, writes a program for Babbage's Analytical Engine. (England)
1854	George Boole envisions the Laws of Thought. (Ireland)

1870	William Stanley Jevons produces a logic machine. (England)
1873	William Thomson, Lord Kelvin, devises the analog tide predictor. (Scotland)
	Christopher Sholes, Carlos Glidden, and Samuel W. Soule invent the Sholes and Glidden Typewriter; produced by E. Remington & Sons. (United States)
1875	Frank Stephen Baldwin constructs a pin wheel calculator. (United States)
1876	Alexander Graham Bell develops the telephone. (United States)
	Bell's rival, Elisha Gray, also produces the telephone. (United States)
1878	Swedish inventor Willgodt T. Odhner makes a pin wheel calculator. (Russia)
1884	Dorr Eugene Felt creates the key-driven calculator, the Comptometer. (United States)
1884	Paul Gotlieb Nipkow produces the Nipkow Disk, a mechanical television device. (Germany)
1886	Herman Hollerith develops his punched card machine, called the Tabulating Machine. (United States)
1892	William Seward Burroughs invents his Adding and Listing (printing) Machine. (United States)
1896	Herman-Hollerith forms the Tabulating Machine Company. (United States)
1901	Guglielmo Marconi develops wireless telegraphy. (Italy)
1904	John Ambrose Fleming constructs the diodevalve (vacuum tube). (England)
	Elmore Ambrose Sperry develops the circular slide rule. (United States)
1906	Lee De Forest invents the triode vacuum tube (audion). (United States)
1908	Elmore Ambrose Sperry produces the gyrocompass. (United States)
1910	Sperry Gyroscope Company is established. (United States)
1912	Frank Baldwin and Jay Monroe found Monroe Calculating Machine Company. (United States)
1914	Leonardo Torres Quevado devises an electromechanical calculator, an electromechanical chess machine (End Move). (Spain)
	Thomas J. Watson Sr. joins the Computing Tabulating Recording Company (CTR) as General Manager. (United States)
1919	W. H. Eccles and F. W. Jordan develop the flip-flop (memory device). (England)
1922	Russian-born Vladimir Kosma Zworykin develops the iconoscope and kinescope (cathode ray tube), both used in electronic television for Westinghouse. (United States)
1924	The Computing Tabulating Recording Company (CTR), formed in 1911 by the merger of Herman Hollerith's Tabulating Machine Company with Computing

Scale Company and the International Time Recording Company, becomes the IBM (International Business Machines).

1927   The Remington Rand Corporation forms from the merger of Remington Typewriter Company, Rand Kardex Bureau, and others. (United States)

1929   Vladimir Kosma Zworykin develops color television for RCA. (United States)

1931   Vannevar Bush develops the Differential Analyzer (an analog machine). (United States)

1933   Wallace J. Eckert applies punched card machines to astronomical data. (United States)

1937   Alan M. Turing proposes a Theoretical Model of Computation. (England)

George R. Stibitz crafts the Binary Adder. (United States)

1939   John V. Atanasoff devises the prototype of an electronic digital computer. (United States)

William R. Hewlett and David Packard establish the Hewlett-Packard Company. (United States)

1940   Claude E. Shannon applies Boolean algebra to switching circuits. (United States)

George R. Stibitz uses the complex number calculator to perform Remote Job Entry (RJE), Dartmouth to New York. (United States)

1941   Konrad Zuse formulates a general-purpose, program-controlled computer. (Germany)

1942   John V. Atanasoff and Clifford Berry unveil the Atanasoff-Berry Computer (ABC). (United States)

1944   The Colossus, an English calculating machine, is put into use at Bletchley Park. (England)

Howard Aiken develops, the Automatic Sequence Controlled Calculator (ASCC), the Harvard Mark I, which is the first American program-controlled computer. (United States)

Grace Hopper allegedly coins the term "computer bug" while working on the Mark I. (United States)

1946   J. Presper Eckert Jr. and John W. Mauchly construct the ENIAC (Electronic Numerical Integrator and Computer), the first American general-purpose electronic computer, at the Moore School, University of Pennsylvania. (United States)

J. Presper Eckert Jr. and John W. Mauchly form the Electronic Control Company, which later becomes the Eckert-Mauchly Computer Corporation. (United States)

1947   John Bardeen, Walter H. Brattain, and William B. Shockley invent the transistor at Bell Laboratories. (United States)

1948   F. C. Williams, Tom Kilburn, and G. C. (Geoff) Tootill create a small scale, experimental, stored-program computer (nicknamed "Baby") at the University of Manchester; it serves as the prototype of Manchester Mark I. (England)

1949	F. C. Williams, Tom Kilburn, and G. C. (Geoff) Tootill design the Manchester Mark I at the University of Manchester. (England)
	Maurice V. Wilkes develops the ED SAC (Electronic Delay Storage Automatic Calculator) at Cambridge University. (England)
	Jay Wright Forrester invents three-dimensional core memory at the Massachusetts Institute of Technology. (United States)
	Jay Wright Forrester and Robert Everett construct the Whirlwind I, a digital, real-time computer at Massachusetts Institute of Technology. (United States)
1950	J. H. Wilkinson and Edward A. Newman design the Pilot ACE (Automatic Computing Engine) implementing the Turing proposal for a computing machine at the National Physical Laboratory (NPL). (England)
	Remington Rand acquires the Eckert-Mauchly Computer Corporation. (United States)
1951	Engineering Research Associates develops the ERA 1101, an American commercial computer, for the U.S. Navy and National Security Agency (NSA). (United States)
	The UNIVAC I (Universal Automatic Computer), an American commercial computer, is created by Remington Rand for the U.S. Census Bureau. (United States)
	Ferranti Mark I, a British commercial computer, is unveiled. (England)
	Lyons Tea Co. announces Lyons Electronic Office, a British commercial computer. (England)
1952	UNIVAC I predicts election results as Dwight D. Eisenhower sweeps the U.S. presidential race. (United States)
	Remington Rand Model 409, an American commercial computer, is originated by Remington Rand for the Internal Revenue Service. (United States)
	Remington Rand acquires Engineering Research Associates. (United States)
1953	The IBM 701, a scientific computer, is constructed. (United States)
1954	The IBM 650 EDPM, electronic data processing machine, a stored-program computer in a punched-card environment, is produced. (United States)
1955	Sperry Corp. and Remington Rand merge to form the Sperry Rand Corporation. (United States)
1957	Robert N. Noyce, Gordon E. Moore, and others found Fairchild Semiconductor Corporation. (United States)
1957	Seymour Cray, William Norris, and others establish Control Data Corporation. (United States)
	Kenneth Olsen and Harlan Anderson launch Digital Equipment Corporation (DEC). (United States)

1958   Jack Kilby at Texas Instruments invents the integrated circuit. (United States)

1959   Robert N. Noyce at Fairchild Semiconductor invents the integrated circuit. Distinct patents are awarded to both Texas Instruments and Fairchild Semiconductor, as both efforts are recognized. (United States)

1960   The first PDP-1 is sold by Digital Equipment Corporation, which uses some technology from the Whirlwind Project. (United States)

            The UNIVAC 1100 series of computers is announced by Sperry Rand Corporation. (United States)

1961   The Burroughs B5000 series dual-processor, with virtual memory, is unveiled. (United States)

1964   The IBM/360 family of computers begins production. (United States)

            The CDC 6600 is created by Control Data Corporation. (United States)

1965   The UNIVAC 1108 from Sperry Rand Corporation is constructed. (United States)

1965   The PDP-8, the first minicomputer, is released by Digital Equipment Corporation. (United States)

            Robert N. Noyce and Gordon E. Moore found Intel Corporation. (United States)

1969   The U.S. Department of Defense (DoD) launches ARP ANET, the beginning of the Internet. (United States)

1970   The PDP–11 series of computers from Digital Equipment Corporation is put into use. (United States)

            The Xerox Corporation's Palo Alto Research Center (PARC) begins to study the architecture of information. (United States)

1971   Ken Thompson devises the UNIX Operating System at Bell Laboratories. (United States)

            Marcian E. (Ted) Hoff, Federico Faggin, and Stanley Mazor at Intel create the first microprocessor, a 4-bit processor, 4004. (United States)

1972   Seymour Cray founds Cray Research Inc. (United States)

            Intel releases the 8008 microprocessor, an 8-bit processor. (United States)

1974   Intel announces the 8080 microprocessor, an 8-bit processor. (United States)

            Motorola Inc. unveils the Motorola 6800, its 8-bit microprocessor. (United States)

            Federico Faggin and Ralph Ungerman co-found Zilog, Inc., a manufacturer of microprocessors. (United States)

1975   Bill Gates and Paul Allen establish the Microsoft Corporation. (United States)

The kit-based Altair 8800 computer, using an 8080 microprocessor, is released by Ed Roberts with MITS (Model Instrumentation Telemetry Systems) in Albuquerque, New Mexico. (United States)

MITS purchases a version of the BASIC computer language from Microsoft. (United States)

The MOS 6502 microprocessor, an 8-bit microprocessor, is developed by MOS Technologies, Chuck Peddle, and others, who had left Motorola, (United States)

1976 Gary Kildall creates the CP/M (Control Program/Monitor or Control Program for Microprocessors) Operating System of Digital Research; this operating system for 8-bit micro-computers is the forerunner of DOS 1.0. (United States)

Steven Jobs and Stephen Wozniak found Apple Computer, Inc. and create the Apple I. (United States)

Seymour Cray devises the Cray-1 supercomputer. (United States)

Commodore Business Machines acquires MOS Technologies. (Canada)

1977 The Commodore PET (Personal Electronic Transactor) personal computer, developed by Jack Tramiel and Chuck Peddle for Commodore Business Machines, features the 6502 8-bit Microprocessor. (Canada)

The Apple II personal computer from Apple Computer, Inc., is released featuring a 6502 microprocessor. (United States)

The TRS-80 personal computer from Tandy Radio Shack, equipped with the Zilog Z80 8-bit microprocessor from Zilog, is unveiled. (United States)

Intel announces the 8086 16-bit microprocessor. (United States)

1978 Digital Equipment Corporation launches the VAX 11/780, a 4.3 billion byte computer with virtual memory. (United States)

1979 Intel presents the 8088 16-bit microprocessor. (United States)

Motorola Inc. crafts the MC 68000, Motorola 16-bit processor. (United States)

1980 Tim Patterson sells the rights to QDOS, an upgrade operating system of CP/M for 8088 and 8086 Intel microprocessors, 16-bit microprocessor, to Microsoft. (United States)

1981 The IBM Corporation announces the IBM Personal Computer featuring an 8088 microprocessor. (United States)

The Microsoft Operating System (MS-DOS) is put into use. (United States)

The Osborne I, developed by Adam Osborne and Lee Felsenstein with Osborne Computer Corporation, invent the first portable computer. (United States)

1982 Scott McNealy, Bill Joy, Andy Bechtolsheim, and Vinod Khosla found Sun Microsystems, Inc. (United States)

1984	The Macintosh PC from Apple Computer Inc., running with a Motorola 68000 microprocessor, revolutionizes the personal computer industry. (United States)
	Richard Stallman begins the GNU Project, advocating the free use and distribution of software. (United States)
1985	The Free Software Foundation is formed to seek freedom of use and distribution of software. (United States)
	Microsoft releases Windows 1.01. (United States)
1986	Sperry Rand and the Burroughs Corporation merge to form Unisys Corporation. (United States)
1989	SPARCstation I from Sun Microsystems is produced. (United States)
1991	Tim Berners-Lee begins the World Wide Web at CERN. (Switzerland)
	Linus Torvalds builds the Linux Operating System. (Finland)
	Paul Kunz develops the first Web server outside of Europe, at the Stanford Linear Accelerator Center (SLAG). (United States)
1993	Marc Andreesen and Eric Bina create Mosaic, a Web browser, at the National Center for Supercomputing Applications (NCSA), University of Illinois-Urbana Champaign. (United States)
1994	Marc Andreesen and James H. Clark form Mosaic Communications Corporation, later Netscape Communications Corporation. (United States)
	Netscape Navigator is launched by Netscape Communications Corporation. (United States)
1995	Java technology is announced by Sun Microsystems. (United States)
1996	World chess champion Garry Kasparov of Russia defeats Deep Blue, an IBM computer, in a man vs. computer chess matchup, four to two. (United States)
1997	IBM's Deep Blue defeats world chess champion Garry Kasparov in a rematch, 3.5 to 2.5. (United States)
	An injunction is filed against Microsoft to prohibit the company from requiring customers to accept Internet Explorer as their browser as a condition of using the Microsoft operating system Windows 95. (United States)
1998	America OnLine (AOL) acquires Netscape. (United States)
	Compaq Computer Corporation, a major producer of IBM compatible personal computers, buys Digital Equipment Corporation. (United States)
	America OnLine (AOL) and Sun form an alliance to produce Internet technology. (United States)

1999	Shawn Fanning writes code for Napster, a music file-sharing program. (United States)
1998	The Recording Industry Association of America (RIAA) files a lawsuit against Napster for facilitating copyright infringement. (United States)
2000	Zhores I. Alferov, Herbert Kroemer, and Jack Kilby share the Nobel Prize in Physics for contributions to information technology. Alferov, a Russian, and Kroemer, a German-born American, share half the prize for their contributions to semiconductor-based technology used in high speed circuits. Kilby is awarded the other half of the prize for invention of the integrated circuit.
	Google becomes the first search engine to index one billion pages. (United States)
2001	Wikipedia, a free online user originated encyclopedia, comes online. (United States)
	Windows XP is introduced. (United States)
	Dell becomes the world's top computer systems provider. (United States)
2002	Hewlett Packard purchases Compaq. (United States)
2003	Apple creates and opens iTunes, an online music-buying application. (United States)
2004	Mark Zuckerberg creates and launches the online social network, Facebook. (United States)
	Google introduces Gmail, an Internet service. (United States)
2005	Video-sharing Web site, YouTube, comes online. (United States)
	Chinese company, Lenovo, acquires IBM's Personal Computing Division, making it the world's third-largest PC purveyor. (China)
2006	Apple switches all computers to Intel core processors. (United States)
	The first Twitter post is posted by co-founder Jack Dorsey at Twitter.com. (United States)
2007	Steve Jobs and Apple release the iPhone.
	Microsoft releases Windows Vista to the public. (United States)
	Apple announces that it will discontinue the use of the word "computer" in its title as it was working with products other than computers. It is now known as Apple, Inc. (United States)
2008	Bill Gates steps down as chairman of Microsoft to focus on philanthropic work. (United States)
2009	Intel unveils the "iA32 processor single-chip cloud computer," a CPU with 48 processing cores on a single chip. (United States)
2010	2010 Cyber-warfare and cyber-counterterrorism goes public: Stuxnet worm disrupts Iran's centrifuges dedicated to uranium enrichment.

2011   Social media, especially Facebook and Twitter, are credited with helping organizers form Arab Spring protests across Middle East. Revolution in Egypt results in resignation of President Hosni Mubarak and first free elections in Egypt's history.

              IBM's Watson supercomputer defeats human champions on the game show "Jeopardy."

2012   Facebook begins trading on NASDAQ as a private company (IPO).

              Facebook Facebook announces 'Graph Search' tool.

Timeline: The History of Programming, Markup, and Scripting Languages

. . . .

The history of computer sciences has been filed with many creative inventions and innovations. Here are some of the milestones and achievements in the field of computer programming and languages.

c. 800 al-Khowarizmi, Mohammed ibn-Musa develops a treatise on algebra, his name allegedly giving rise to the term, algorithm.

1843 Ada Byron King, Countess of Lovelace, programs Charles Babbage's design of the Analytical Engine.

1945 Plankalkul is developed by Konrad Zuse.

1953 Sort-Merge Generator is created by Betty Holberton.

1957 FORTRAN is devised for IBM by John Backus and team of programmers.

FLOW-MATIC is crafted for Remington-Rand's UNIVAC by Grace Hopper.

1958 LISP is produced by John McCarthy at Massachusetts Institute of Technology.

1959 COBOL is formulated by the CODASYL Committee, initiated by the U.S. Department of Defense (DoD)

1960 ALGOL is the result of work done by the ALGOL Committee in the ALGOL 60 Report.

1961 JOSS is originated by the RAND Corporation.

GPSS (General Purpose Simulation System) is invented by Geoffrey Gordon with IBM.

RPG (Report Program Generator) is unveiled by IBM.

APL (A Programming Language) is designed by Kenneth Iverson with IBM.

1963 SNOBOL is developed by David Farber, Ralph Griswold, and Ivan Polonsky at Bell Laboratories.

1964 BASIC is originated by John G. Kemeny and Thomas E. Kurtz at Dartmouth.

PL/I is announced by IBM.

Simula I is produced by Kristen Nygaard and Ole-Johan Dahl at the Norwegian Computing Center.

1967 Simula 67 is created by Kristen Nygaard and Ole-Johan Dahl at the Norwegian Computing Center.

LOGO is devised by Seymour Papert at the MIT Artificial Intelligence Laboratory.

1971 Pascal is constructed by Niklaus Wirth at the Swiss Federal Institute of Technology (ETH) in Zurich.

1973	C developed by Dennis Ritchie at Bell Laboratories.
	Smalltalk is invented by Alan Kay at Xerox's PARC (Palo Alto Research Center).
1980	Ada is developed for the U.S. Department of Defense (DoD).
1985	C++ is created by Bjarne Stroustrup at Bell Laboratories.
1986	SGML (Standard Generalized Markup Language) is developed by the International Organization for Standardization (ISO).
1987	Perl is constructed by Larry Wall.
1989	HTML (HyperText Markup Language) is proposed by Tim Berners-Lee at CERN (Organization européenne pour la recherche nucléaire).
1991	Visual Basic is launched by the Microsoft Corporation.
1993	Mosaic is created by Marc Andreesen and Eric Bina for the National Center for Computing Applications (TSTCCA) at the University of Illinois-Urbana Champaign.
1994	A written specification of VRML (Virtual Reality Markup Language) is drafted by Mark Pesce, Tony Parisi, and Gavin Bell.
1995	Java is crafted by James Gosling of Sun Microsystems
1996	Javascript is developed by Brendan Eich at Netscape Communications co-announced by Netscape and Sun Microsystems.
1997	VRML (Virtual Reality Modeling Language), developed by the Web3D Consortium, becomes an international standard.
1998	XML (Extensible Markup Language) is originated by a working group of the World Wide Web Consortium (W3C).
2000	Microsoft publicly introduces the programming language C#.
2002	Perl 5.8 is released to the public.
2008	HTML5 is first introduced to the public as a working draft.

A

Abacus

The abacus, an ancient calculating device, originated in Babylon around 2400 BC as a counting device. It was one of the earliest calculators, and contemporary versions are still in use today.

An abacus is a wooden or metal rectangular frame with vertical or horizontal bars containing movable beads. Prior to the advent of the abacus, stones were used as computational tools. This had two major disadvantages: it was easy to lose track while figuring, and finding or transporting large numbers of stones was difficult. By contrast, the abacus was a highly portable, easy-to-use device that proved to be an excellent alternative to a bag of stones.

The abacus was used extensively in the development of culture and mathematics in the Middle East and as far eastward as Japan. The number of vertical bars, as well as the number of beads on each bar, varied from culture to culture, but the basic function of the abacus—calculating the costs and quantities of goods—remained the same.

The Chinese abacus, the most familiar form today, divides the frame with a horizontal bar. The classic version, known as *suan-pan*, or the "2/5 abacus," is thought to have developed around AD 1200. The area above the horizontal bar, heaven, contains two beads per vertical rod; each has a value of five. In the lower area, or earth, each vertical rod contains five beads, each with a value of one. Each vertical rod represents a unit of ten. Calculating is accomplished by moving beads toward or away from the horizontal divider. In the mid–1800s, the 2/5 abacus was replaced by the 1/5 abacus, and, by the 1930s, the most widely used form of abacus was the Japanese-made *soroban*, or 1/4 abacus.

Although pocket calculators and other devices have replaced the abacus in most parts of the world, many shopkeepers and schoolchildren in Asia, the Middle East, and in parts of Africa still use some form of abacus for basic arithmetic functions (i.e., adding, subtracting, multiplying).

 See also **Napier's Bones** • **Slide Rule**

Resources

Books

Berlinghoff, William P., and Fernando Q. Gouvea. *Math Through the Ages: A Gentle History for Teachers and Others.* Classroom resource materials. Washington, D.C.: Mathematical Association of America, 2004.

Aztec Abacus

Archaeologists discovered that the Aztec culture used a counting device similar to the Asian abacus. The Aztec abacus (c.900–1000) consisted of a wooden frame with mounted strings threaded with kernels of maize (corn).

School children competing in an abacus contest. © *YOSHIKAZU TSUNO/AFP/ Getty Images.*

* **bit** a single binary digit, 1 or 0—a contraction of Binary digIT; the smallest unit for storing data in a computer

Burton, David M. *The History of Mathematics: An Introduction.* New York: McGraw-Hill, 2007.

D'Angelo, Frank, and Nevin Iliev. *Teaching Mathematics to Young Children Through the Use of Concrete and Virtual Manipulatives.* 2012.

Kojima, Takashi. *Advanced Abacus Theory and Practice.* New York: Tuttle Publishing, 2012. http://public.eblib.com/EBLPublic/PublicView. do?ptiID=953082.

Rooney, Anne. *The History of Mathematics.* New York: Rosen Pub, 2013.

Analog Computing

Humans have always desired mechanical aids to computations. There is evidence of "computing" devices, such as the present-day abacus, from as early as the thirteenth century. The first computing devices were accumulators only capable of adding or subtracting. Even "adding machines," which were made well into the twentieth century, could only perform that one function. Subtraction is nothing more than adding a negative number.

Nearly all modern computers are digital, which means that all the internal machine states are either on or off, a one or a zero, true or false, or other nomenclature. There is nothing between a zero and a one such as one-half or one-third etc. The number of bits* used to define a quantity sets the number of different values that the quantity can have. As an example, a quantity represented by an 8-bit binary

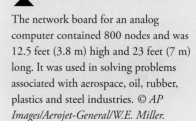

number can only be one of 256 values. The least significant of a binary number is the least amount by which two binary numbers can differ. If, in the example, the least significant were 1, an 8-bit binary number would define integers from 0 to 255.

Analog computing, on the other hand, uses physical characteristics to represent numerical values. For example, the slide rule* uses distance to represent the logarithms* of numbers, and an oscilloscope* uses electric current to show the amplitude and frequency of waves. In an analog computer, the internal signals of the computer can assume any value. As an example, a voltage can vary from zero to one volt where there are an infinite number of values between the minimum of zero and a maximum of one volt. In a mechanical machine, voltage would be replaced with distance, or displacement such as the turning of a shaft. A pointer could be attached to the shaft, which will be a part of a mechanical dial to display an answer.

Many of the early computing devices are digital, such as the previously mentioned abacus. Only one bead could be pushed along the wire. It was not possible to move a fraction of a bead to be used in calculations. These historic adding machines were well suited to accounting where the monetary system was inherently digital. If the least significant bit of an accounting machine were also the smallest unit of currency, the machine would be adequate for most calculations.

The Slide Rule

For accounting, addition, subtraction, multiplication, and division are usually the only mathematical operations required. Scientists and engineers routinely perform much more sophisticated calculations involving mathematics using trigonometric functions, logarithms, exponentiation, and many others. The ubiquitous* tool of the engineer and scientist for calculations until the development of the hand-held scientific calculator in the early 1970s was the slide rule. The slide rule was invented in the 1600s and uses logarithms.

The slide rule is an example of a mechanical analog computer while the adding machine is an example of a mechanical digital computer.

The slide rule could do any common mathematical function except add and subtract. The interesting characteristic of the slide rule was the device actually added and subtracted but it added and subtracted logarithms. When using logarithms to multiply, the logarithms are added. To determine the answer, the "anti" logarithm of the resulting sum is found. Division involved subtracting logarithms. Trigonometric functions were shown on the slide rule by simply transferring the "trig tables" found in a mathematics handbook to the slide rule.

The major problem of the slide rule was it was only accurate to about three decimal places, at best. When the hand-held scientific calculator appeared, the use of the slide rule disappeared, virtually overnight.

The network board for an analog computer contained 800 nodes and was 12.5 feet (3.8 m) high and 23 feet (7 m) long. It was used in solving problems associated with aerospace, oil, rubber, plastics and steel industries. © *AP Images/Aerojet-General/W.E. Miller.*

* **slide rule** invented by Scotsman John Napier (1550-1617), it permits the mechanical automation of calculations using logarithms

* **logarithm** the power to which a certain number called the base is to be raised to produce a particular number

* **oscilloscope** a measuring instrument for electrical circuitry; connected to circuits under test using probes on leads and having a small screen that displays the signal waveforms

* **ubiquitous** to be commonly available everywhere

Analog Thrives

Much of the world is analog and it would be no surprise that many early computers used analog techniques. Despite the development of extremely powerful digital microprocessors, analog computing still plays an important role in the modern world.

Early Calculators and Computers

The slide rule and the adding machine are "calculators." Fixed numbers are entered and fixed answers result. One requirement for engineers and scientists is to solve problems where the numbers are always in a state of change. Mathematician Isaac Newton (1642–1727) in his study of mechanical motion discovered the need for a math that would solve problems where the numbers were changing. Newton invented what he called "fluxions," which are called "derivatives" in modern calculus. Think of fluxions as describing something in the state of flux. Equations written using variables that are in a constant state of change are called "differential equations." Solving these equations can be very difficult particularly for a class of equations called "nonlinear." Solving these equations requires a nonlinear algebra and can be very complicated. The most effective way to solve this type of equation is to use a computer.

Some of the first true computers, meaning they were not calculators or accounting machines, were invented for the purpose of predicting tides. Later machines solved difficult differential equations. These machines used electric motors, gears, cams, and plotting devices to draw the solution of a differential equation. These early mechanical devices were called "differential analyzers." These machines were "programmed" by installing various gears, shafts, and cams on a large frame. These machines were actually used for solving equations up until the end of World War II.

Similar mechanical computers were used to control various machines such as naval guns. An analog computer would receive information relative to the ship's location, heading, speed, wind direction, and other parameters as well as operator-entered data concerning the type of projectile, the amount of explosive charge and, most important, the location of the target. The mechanical analog computer would then control the aiming of the gun. Perhaps the most well known analog computer was the computer used for controlling anti-aircraft guns from radar data during World War II.

Mechanical computers were initially very heavy and slow. After the war, engineers took advantage of the rapidly growing field of electronics to replace the mechanical components of the analog computer. Special amplifiers can add, subtract, and perform calculus operations such as differentiation and integration. The amplifiers were placed in what is called a "feedback" circuit where some of the output signal is fed back to the input. The nature of the feedback circuit would determine the mathematical operation performed by the amplifier. These amplifiers were called "operational amplifiers" because they perform mathematical operations. Feedback circuits can perform exponentiation, multiplication, and division, taking logarithmic and trigonometric functions. Replacing the bulky, massive mechanical components of the analog computer with electronic circuits resulted in a much faster analog computation. In the early days of the electronic computer, analog computers were faster than digital computers when solving complex differential equations.

Longevity of Analog Computers

Analog computation is still used long after digital computers achieved very high levels of performance. Universities still research analog computing: The Harvard Robotics Laboratory, for example studies the way analog computing fits into the modern world. The physical world is mostly analog. Parameters such as distance, angles, speed, and so on are all analog quantities. If a simple calculation is required of an analog function where both the input and output are analog, it is often not worth the expense of a digital microprocessor to perform the task that an operational amplifier can provide. If the calculation is complicated, the advantages of the digital computer will justify the use of a microprocessor.

One of the more common modern applications of analog computers is in process control. As an example, a simple analog circuit using a few operational amplifiers may be used to control the temperature of an industrial process where the use of a digital computer is not warranted.

The stand-alone analog computer does not exist at the time of this writing. The stored-program digital computer has the distinct advantage that the computer is completely programmed by software and does not require any external feedback components. Very powerful software exists for solving differential equations and systems based on differential equations, both linear and nonlinear. Even though the stand-alone "analog computer" no longer exists, operational amplifiers are standard electronic components and are used in a large number of applications still performing mathematical operations.

 See also **Abacus • Binary Number System • Digital Computing • Napier's Bones • Slide Rule**

Resources

Books

Aspray, William, ed. *Computing before Computers.* Ames: Iowa State University Press, 1990.

Cortada, James W. *The Computer in the United States: From Laboratory to Market, 1930 to 1960.* Armonk, NY: M. E. Sharpe, 1993.

Roy, Michael R. *A History of Computing Technology.* 2nd ed. Los Alamitos, CA: IEEE Computer Society Press, 1997.

Web Sites

Harvard Robotics Laboratory "Analog Computation" http://hrl.harvard. edu/research/index.html#analog (accessed November 3, 2012).

▲

Two experimental models for Babbage's analytical engine, about 1870. © *SSPL via Getty Images.*

* **punched card** a paper card with punched holes which give instructions to a computer in order to encode program instructions and data

* **binary code** a representation of information that permits only two states, such as on-or-off, one-or-zero

Analytical Engine

Modern inventions have often been preceded by prototypes that foreshadowed the modern version's development. Sometimes such prototypical ideas arise before they can be carried out in any practical way. Such is the case of the analytical engine, which may be considered the great-grandfather of the modern computer. The analytical engine is widely recognized as the first conceptual device that incorporated principles found in contemporary computing.

What makes the Analytical Engine so truly extraordinary is that it was conceptualized well before electricity was in use. In the early 1800s, English mathematician, inventor, and mechanical engineer Charles Babbage (1791–1871) conceived of the idea of a computational device that would store numbers and process them with mathematical accuracy. The first working general-purpose, electronic, digital computer was the U.S.-built Electronic Numerical Integrator And Computer (ENIAC); but ENIAC was not in operation until the mid–1940s, roughly 120 years after Babbage's work began on the Analytical Engine. Nevertheless, Babbage's Engine set the blueprint for the modern computer.

The Analytical Engine was developed to meet the mathematical needs of the time, and it contained most of the features found in modern computers. There was a way to input data, a place for storing data, a place for processing data, a control unit to give directions, and a way to receive output. Babbage used punched cards* for data input, which were also used for input into early electronic computers until the early 1970s. The systems were actually derived from the textile industry; the Jacquard Loom of the early 1800s used punched cards to control color and pattern coordination in the weaving of textiles. Similarly, punched cards were employed in calculating machines of the nineteenth century, including the prototypical Analytical Engine.

Like modern computers, the Analytical Engine included programming capabilities. The first programmer was Ada Byron King, Countess of Lovelace (1815–1852), daughter of English poet Lord George Gordon Byron (1788–1824). Using punched cards, she entered data in binary code* to automate mathematical processes. The binary code reduces all computed equations, images, and other related items to a code using only zeros (0) and ones (1). Data are coded onto the punched cards and entered into the computing device. In this way, the processes are automated. For Babbage's machine, the process was automated by a series of clicks that were the equivalent of counting. Many of these processes are still used today, and remains the groundwork of all programming.

The Analytical Engine was never made operational, although much of Babbage's life work revolved around the design and construction of calculating machines. The Analytical Engine was, in fact, a theoretical construct that coincided with the onset of the Industrial Revolution, which began in England in the late eighteenth century. Western society as a whole was moving away from a farming-based economy to one in which the sources of capital depended less on working the land and more on the manipulation of raw materials with machinery. Events in the late nineteenth century would give rise to full-scale industrialization with steel mills, railroads, and other mechanized means of production and delivery of goods. The historical significance of the Analytical Engine lies in the fact that it was not only a product of the Industrial Revolution, but also a forerunner to the foundation of the Information Age, namely, the computer.

Babbage created several other calculating machines in addition to the Analytical Engine. Most of his machines did not actually work; however, this is probably because they, like Babbage and King, were ahead of their time. Quite simply, the Analytical Engine contained all the theoretical components of the modern computer; but the technological precision required to construct Babbage's Engine were probably insufficient at the time, nor in any case was there sufficient funding to complete such a formidable project. Still, as the first attempt at a digital computational device possessing features such as a variable data input method (punched cards), as well as data storage, processing, control, and output, the Analytical Engine is considered the great-grandfather of the computer of today.

Due to Babbage's enormous influence in the modern computer world, several institutions and locations have been named in his honor. Some of them include a crater on the Moon (Babbage Crater, located near the northwestern limb of the Moon), the Charles Babbage Institute at the University of Minnesota, a lecture theatre at Cambridge University, and the Babbage Building at the University of Plymouth.

 See also **Babbage, Charles • King, Ada Byron**

Resources

Books

Babbage, Charles. *The Works of Charles Babbage: The Analytical Engine and Mechanical Notation, Vol. 3.* Edited by Martin Campbell-Kelly. New York: New York University Press, 1989.

Collier, Bruce. *The Difference Engine: Charles Babbage and the Quest to Build the First Computer.* New York: Penguin, 2002.

Synder, Laura J. *The Philosophical Breakfast Club: Four Remarkable Friends Who Transformed Science and Changed the World.* New York: Broadway Paperbacks, 2011.

Web Sites

Charles Babbage Institute, University of Minnesota. "Who Was Charles Babbage?" http://www.cbi.umn.edu/about/babbage.html (accessed January 24, 2012).

Animation

Animation is the art by which two-dimensional (2-D) drawings or inanimate objects are turned into moving visual representations of three-dimensional (3-D) life. Computer animation uses computer hardware and software to make the animation process easier, faster, and executable by less skilled and fewer creators. Although a clear division used to exist among cartoon and feature film animation, visual effects, gaming software, 3-D animation, and GIF animation*, these related forms of animation now often overlap.

Animation can be described as the creation of the illusion of motion through a rapid sequence of still images. Although the quality of the original images is important, equally important is the quality of the sequence through which action, character, and story development are portrayed. There must be a coherent pattern to the action. A common story structure introduces characters, a source of conflict, the development of this conflict, a climax, and finally a resolution. But an animated story can also be more fluid, including the creation of forms or simple images, some interaction of them, and then a transformation or transmutation*, such as a smiley face turning into a frown or dissolving into the background.

Creating an Animated Story

Although the process of animation takes many forms depending on the medium used, the following is typical. A preview or rough overview of the story, termed a pencil test, is created. This is a sample sequence of pencil drawings created on paper to present a rough overview of the story. In the early days of animation, these were then recorded on an animation stand, but now they are placed on film or videotape. Sometimes, after a story

Cartoonist using computer animation.
© *AP Images/Elaine Kurtenbach.*

idea is conceived, a treatment—a brief narrative description of the proposed film or video—is created instead of a pencil test. Both pencil tests and treatments are often used to solicit sponsors. The action of the story and its development are conveyed through the use of storyboards, which are used to compose, organize, and deploy the animation.

A storyboard is a series of visual sketches that the story creator uses when developing the narrative and depicting the action of the animation. This is done so that everyone involved in the animation project can literally sketch out what is happening, making sure that important details are not overlooked. The storyboard details the sequence of actions necessary to convey the story line, character development, and point of view. This would include the background, action, and camera movement of the scene, but also each change of scene, each change in perspective, the timing and length of each scene, sound requirements, and the timing of the whole work.

With the storyboard in place, the dialog or music for the animation is recorded, and the sound length is determined in terms of the number of frames that it can handle. This information is entered on a dope sheet—a document detailing the nature of the music clips, their times, and the number of frames per clip. A layout is drawn up for each scene and the director uses the layout and dope sheet to plan the action and its timing. Next a background is created and the movement is created by a sequence of drawn images, which is then also entered on the dope sheet.

The image drawings for movement are then tested; if there are discrepancies, corrections are made to the timing or the drawings. In traditional animation, hand-drawn or cel animation is the most common technique. The cleaned-up drawings are inked and colored by hand on acetate overlays termed cels. The cels are placed on the background, which is then placed under the camera. The camera operator, using the dope sheet, assembles the background and movement cels, and shoots each frame, after which the film is sent for processing and printing. The printed scenes are then edited to integrate all the sound tracks, including music and dialogue. The result of this integration is termed a work or cut print. The lab makes a final print that can be projected to an audience or is transferred to film.

Computers are now used for many or all parts of this process. With current technology, the completed computer file is sent directly to digital tape, which will be transferred to film or broadcast on DVD or videotape.

Types of Animation

Many types of animation exist but there is no common classification scheme to describe them. The *Encyclopedia of Animation Techniques* (2003) lists drawn animation and model animation, but there are also cutout animation, 3-D animation, virtual reality (VR)* animation, and animatronics*, to name a few other types. The hand-drawn or cel animation, mentioned earlier, is the most common traditional technique. Hundreds of examples of hand-drawn animation were generated by

* **virtual reality (VR)** the use of elaborate input/output devices to create the illusion that the user is in a different environment

* **animatronics** the animation (movement) of something by the use of electronic motors, drives, and controls

American film producer Walt Disney (1901–1966) and his studios, such as *Snow White and the Seven Dwarfs* (1937) and *Bambi* (1942). Hand-drawn animation in pencil form and cels is no longer used in modern animation. Drawings are often made with computer software, and foregrounds and backgrounds are now generated through the use of digital files.

Model animation follows a process similar to hand-drawn animation, using models such as puppets (sometimes referred to as puppet animation) or clay figures (sometimes referred to as claymation). Set workers create movement by physically modifying the clay figures or changing the positions of the puppets. Each time this is done, a new scene is recorded on film or videotape. Because motion is captured through the position-by-position image of the models on single frames, model animation employs a technique known as stop-motion animation. The Christmas favorite *Rudolph the Red-Nosed Reindeer* (1964) is a classic example of stop-motion animation.

One of the well-known creators and directors of claymation is British filmmaker Nicholas "Nick" Park (1958–), who created the characters Wallace and Gromit in *A Grand Day Out* (1990), which won a British Academy Award. He also created *Creature Comforts* (1990), featuring interviews with inmates of a zoo, which won an Academy Award, as did three more adventures of Wallace and Gromit: *A Close Shave* (1995), *The Wrong Trousers* (1998), and *The Curse of the Were Rabbit* (2005). In 2010, the Park creation *Wallace & Gromit: A Matter of Loaf and Death* was nominated for an Oscar for Best Animated Short Film.

Cutout animation has been made notable by American-born British filmmaker and writer Terry Gilliam (1940–) in *Monty Python's Flying Circus* and by American screenwriters and producers Matthew "Matt" Stone (1971–) and Trey Parker (1969–) in *South Park*. To create cutout animation, an artist cuts actors and scenes out of paper, overlays them, and moves them, and captures their images frame by frame, again using stop-motion animation. In Gilliam's work, the animation was done frame by frame, but Stone and Parker quickly abandoned the physical work of generating the figures and turned instead to advanced computer workstations that create the same effect.

Three-dimensional animation is similar to hand-drawn animation, but it involves thinking in 3-D space and working with objects, lights, and cameras in a new way. This type of animation requires the use of computers to model a 3-D space and calculate how it would look from a specific point and angle. The movie *Toy Story* (1995) and its sequels, *Toy Story 2* (1999) and *Toy Story 3* (2010), are each examples of 3-D computer animation.

Virtual reality animation is created through such technologies as VR and Virtual Reality Modeling Language (VRML) or its successor X3D, which is an ISO-standard, XML-based file-formatting style that represents 3-D computer graphics (where ISO stands for International

* **interpolation** estimating data values between known points but the values in between are not and are therefore estimated

Organization for Standardization and XML is short for Extensible Markup Language). These make it possible to create 3-D environments, accessible through websites, within which viewers can feel fully immersed in the animated surroundings. Quicktime VR uses photographic images or pre-rendered art to create the inside of a virtual environment that is downloaded to the viewer's own computer. VRML uses 3-D models and real-time interaction that puts the viewer inside 3-D environments.

Animatronics entails the use of computer-controlled models that can be actuated in real-time. These models have electronic and mechanical parts including motion-enabling armatures covered with a synthetic skin. These models, often used in conjunction with live actors, form the foundation for animation sequences. Films featuring animatronics include *Jaws* (1975), *Star Wars* (1977), and *Jurassic Park* (1993).

Animation Techniques

Two basic animation techniques are *keyframing* and *in-betweening*. Keyframing is derived from key moments of still frames in the animation sequence. A keyframe is defined by its particular moment in the animation sequence, its timeline, parameters, and characteristics. In traditional pencil drawings, these would be keyframe drawings; in claymation or puppet animation, these would be key poses. Once the keyframes are established, then the sequences of animations between these keyframes have to be done. This technique is termed in-betweening; it involves creating the frames that fill the gaps between the key frames. In computer environments, the technique is referred to as interpolation*, of which there are several varieties. Keyframe interpolation provides the frames that are required, but how this is done depends on the kind of interpolation used, linear or curved. Linear interpolation provides frames equally spaced between the key frames, based on an averaging of the parameters of the key frames and employing a constant speed. Curved interpolation is more sophisticated and can accommodate changes in speed.

History of Animation

Most basic animation principles and techniques were developed in the first twenty years of the twentieth century, and were perfected by the 1940s, particularly by Walt Disney, whose studios popularized the form through full-length feature films. Disney's impact on animation and the entertainment industry was profound. Ironically, his first attempt at an animated film production was a failure. In 1922, as a twenty-one-year-old commercial artist, he launched Laugh-O-Gram films in Kansas City, Missouri. The company went bankrupt after a year. Fortunately, his creditors permitted him to retain one of his short features, which provided the basis for the launch of Disney Brothers Cartoon Studio in Hollywood, California. It produced the *Alice Comedies*, which featured a combination of animation and live action.

Disney In 1928, Walt Disney teamed with his brother, Roy O. Disney (1893–1971), and American animator Ub Iwerks (1901–1971) to produce *Steamboat Willie* (1928), the first cartoon that was synchronized with sound. *Steamboat Willie* gave the world Mickey Mouse, one of the long line of popular characters—such as Donald Duck, Goofy, Pluto, Cinderella, and Simba—that made Disney famous and on which the Disney empire is built. Then, Disney made a series of animated short films set to classical music, named the Silly Symphonies (1929–1939), in which he introduced Technicolor into animation. Disney held the Technicolor patent for two years. Disney won an Oscar for the first cartoon and full-Technicolor feature named *Flowers and Trees* (1932).

In 1937, Disney released *Snow White and the Seven Dwarfs*, the first full-length animated feature film. In order to produce this film, Disney invented the multiplane animation camera. With this invention, for which he was inducted into the National Inventors Hall of Fame, he changed the animation industry. Disney's camera made it possible to have cartoon characters move through many layers of scenery.

Disney always pushed the limits in his use of new technologies: for example, he produced *Fantasia* (1940) in Fantasound, a forerunner of current movie sound systems; *Lady and the Tramp* (1955) in CinemaScope, an innovative movie viewing experience with a wide screen and stereophonic sound; and *101 Dalmations* (1961) using Xerox technology to make cels from animated drawings.

Following the success of *Snow White*, Disney produced a series of animated films, now regarded as classics, that secured his reputation. Among them are: *Fantasia* (1940), *Pinocchio* (1940), *Dumbo* (1941), *Bambi* (1942), *Song of the South* (1946), *Cinderella* (1950), *Alice in Wonderland* (1951), *Peter Pan* (1953), *Lady and the Tramp* (1955), and *Sleeping Beauty* (1959). Starting in 1961, Disney found additional success in the rapidly growing medium of television with what came to be known as *Walt Disney's Wonderful World of Color*, which included many animated components or productions. During his lifetime, Walt Disney won thirty-two personal Academy Awards, and the Walt Disney Studios during the same time won an additional twenty-three Oscars in categories such as in animation (e.g., *Pigs Is Pigs* in 1953) and original musical compositions or songs (e.g., *Pinocchio* in 1941).

After the death of Walt Disney in 1966, his studios continued to garner awards and to produce commercial animation successes such as *The Little Mermaid* (1989), *Beauty and the Beast* (1991), *Aladdin* (1992), *The Lion King* (1994), *Pocahontas* (1995), *Mulan* (1998), *Atlantis* (2001), *Lilo & Stitch* (2002), *Treasure Planet* (2002), *Brother Bear* (2003), *Home on the Range* (2004), *Chicken Little* (2005), *Meet the Robinsons* (2007), *The Princess and the Frog* (2009), *Tangled* (2010), *Winnie the Pooh* (2011), and *Wreck-It Ralph* (2012). In 2013, the Walt Disney Animation Studios planned to release the musical-fantasy-comedy film *Frozen*, which is loosely based on Hans Christian Andersen's fairy tale, "The Snow Queen."

The company also produces many live-action films and television series. Disney's animations are also on display throughout the company's popular theme parks.

MGM Metro-Goldwyn-Maycr (MGM) was an early promoter of animated films. Two of their in-house animators, Americans William Hanna (1910–2001) and Joseph Barbera (1911–2006), launched the *Tom and Jerry* films in 1940 that subsequently won five Academy Awards. They later created such familiar characters as the Jetsons, Scooby Doo, the Flintstones, and the Smurfs.

Pixar Pixar is an animation studio which has made its name with highly-acclaimed computer-generated animation films and advanced rendering technology. Pixar was founded in 1986 when American businessperson Steve Jobs (1955–2011), one of the founders of Apple, Inc., bought the Graphics Group from Lucasfilm. Originally focused on selling specialized computer hardware and software for animation, today Pixar specializes in creating its own animated content. Pixar has produced numerous animated films, such as *Toy Story* (1995), *Finding Nemo* (2003), *Cars* (2006), *WALL-E* (2008), and *Cars 2* (2011). Pixar uses enormous amounts of computer resources to create their films. They have custom software, such as Marionette, to help animators create digital content and large numbers of computers in compute farms to help render content into its final form. The final form is a series of frames, which, like traditional animation, are rapidly switched to give the appearance of movement. Frames are generated from computer models, lighting effects, and programmed movement of characters. A single frame, which represents about one twenty-fourth of a second, takes approximately six hours to render but some frames have taken up to ninety hours, 7.7 million times longer than the time it will be shown on screen.

Trends Major growth in animation productions started in the 1960s prompted by the growth of mass media, particularly with visual effects in films (e.g., *Mary Poppins* (1964)) and animated cartoon series on television (e.g., *The Flintstones*). In the 1970s, the growth of computer animation was facilitated by the invention of minicomputers, particularly by Digital Equipment Corporation's PDP and VAX computers. Because of cost and complexity, computer-assisted animation was still the domain of commercial companies. While personal computers (PCs), such as the Macintosh and the IBM-PC, were introduced in the mid–1980s, it was only in the 1990s that their power and available software were adequate for personal computer animation authorship. The diversity of developments and inventions and increasing use of technologies for computer animation are presented in a timeline (1960–1999) in Isaac Victor Kerlow's *The Art of 3-D Computer Animation and Imaging* (2009).

Principles of Animation

Around 1935, some animators at Walt Disney Productions wanted to develop lessons that would refine the basic animation techniques that had been in use from the earliest days of animation. These became the fundamental principles of traditional animation, though most can also be applied to Internet and 3-D graphics environments. American animator and director John Lasseter (1957–), in "Principles of Traditional Animation Applied to 3D Computer Animation," provides a list:

1. *Squash and Stretch*, in which distortion is used in animated action to convey the physical properties of an object;

2. *Timing*, in which actions are spaced so that they help portray the personal or physical characteristics of characters or objects;

3. *Anticipation*, meaning that actions are foreshadowed or set up;

4. *Staging*, through which the animator conveys ideas clearly through background, foreground, and action;

5. *Follow-Through and Overlapping Action*, wherein the end of one action builds a bridge to the next action;

6. *Straight-Ahead and Pose-to-Pose Action*, which are two primary ways of creating action;

7. *Slow In and Out*, which refers to the animator's placement of the in-between frames to create various levels of sophistication in timing and motion;

8. *Arcs*, a visual representation of movement that appears natural;

9. *Exaggeration*, wherein an idea is emphatically represented through design and action that is not restricted to representing reality;

10. *Secondary Action*, which refers to the action of an animated object or character that is caused by the action of something or someone else;

11. *Appeal*, or audience-pleasing action, stories, and visuals.

Web Animation

Several software formats have been used for producing animation on the Internet. One of the first was Netscape Navigator 2's GIF89, which allowed a user to animate Graphic Interchange Format (GIF) images. It was not intended as a medium for full animation, however. Partly as a response to this, dynamic Hypertext Markup Language (dHMTL) was born. It is a hybrid of JavaScript, HTML, and Cascading Style Sheets, but the disparity between Internet Explorer and Navigator platforms made it difficult to use.

When CD-ROMs (Compact Disk-Read Only Memory) became common, Macromedia distinguished itself with Director, a multimedia authoring system. In 1995, the company released the Shockwave Internet browser plug-in for Director, which allowed users to see online content created by Director. Macromedia later produced a plug-in designed specifically for Web browsers, termed Flash. Adobe Systems acquired Macromedia in 2005, and the company continued to improve and support Flash into 2012. Adobe has enhanced Flash to be used as a tool for Rich Internet Applications (RIAs), which provide for richer Internet experiences.

Game Animations

Games began to appear almost as soon as computers appeared. In the late 1960s, *Spacewar!* was created, partly as a way of experimenting with one of the earliest computers, the PDP-1, developed by Digital Electronic Corporation. Many two-dimensional games began to follow, including *Pac-Man*. In 1984 Atari's *I, Robot* appeared. Loosely based on Russian-born American author and biochemist Isaac Asimov's (1920–1992) book by the same name, it foreshadowed the movement to three-dimensional games. At the same time, Nintendo was working on a video game console, Famicom, which later emerged as the Nintendo Entertainment System in the United States.

Part of the success of these systems was the structure of the computer they used: the computer had chips for the central processing unit (CPU), audio, and video which permitted better efficiency and looser control. This was the case with Commodore's Amiga and Atari's ST computer series. Before long, PC peripheral manufacturers started producing more powerful video cards (e.g., graphics accelerator cards with their own chips and memory, such as the ATI series), and sound cards (e.g., SoundBlaster). These eventually posed a challenge to the units designed specifically for games because they could handle the graphics and sound requirements necessary for games. Examples include Nintendo's Wii, Sony's Playstation 3, and Microsoft's X-Box 360.

Animation in the early games was basic, relying on simple movement and graphics, but current games embrace sophisticated animation. There are many genres of games, including electronic versions of traditional games like *Monopoly, Solitaire, Hearts*, and *Jeopardy!* Early maze games, such as *Pac-Man*, and puzzle games, like *Tetris*, paved the way for more sophisticated action games like *Street Fighter* and *Mortal Kombat* (fighting games); *Castle Wolfenstein* and *Doom* (first-person shooter games); and third-person 3-D games, such as *Tomb Raider*. Animated computer games also include racing games such as *Need for Speed* and 3-D vehicle-based games, such as *Dead Reckoning*; flight simulators, such as *Wing Commander*, and other popular simulations (e.g., *Sim City, Sim Ant*); role-playing games, such as *Dungeon Hack*; and adventure games, such as *The Hitchhiker's Guide to the Galaxy*. Sports video games have been present from the original Nintendo system, *Tecmo Bowl*, to modern game systems with titles like the Madden Franchise. At the pinnacle are full-motion video games, like *Halo* and *Metal Gear Solid*. Two new types of games have become popular in recent years. Massively Multiplayer Online Games (MMOGs), like *World of Warcraft*, put the player in a persistent virtual world with other players from around the globe. On October 21, 2011, the fourth edition of the game, called *Mists of Pandaria*, was announced. Unlike other genres, the world continues to exist even if the player is not playing. Rhythm games require the player to coordinate actions with rhythm presented by the game. Games like *Guitar Hero* present the player with a song, and using a guitar-shaped controller, challenges the user to play the right notes at the right time to score points. Software, including *The Games Factory* and *PIE 3D Game Creation*, has emerged to cope with the demands of creating animated games.

 See also **Games • Music • Music, Computer**

Resources

Books

Byrne, P. *Computer Game and Film Graphics.* Art off the wall. Chicago: Heinemann Library, 2007.

Dowling, Jennifer Coleman. *Multimedia Demystified.* New York: McGraw-Hill, 2012.

Faber, Liz. *Computer Game Graphics.* New York, NY: Watson-Guptill, 1998.

Gabler, Neal. *Walt Disney: The Triumph of the American Imagination.* New York: Vintage Books, 2007.

Jenisch, Josh. *The Art of the Video Game.* Philadelphia, PA: Quirk Books, 2008.

Kerlow, Isaac Victor. *The Art of 3-D Computer Animation and Effects.* Hoboken, NJ: John Wiley & Sons, 2009.

Paik, Karen. *To Infinity and Beyond!: The Story of Pixar Animation Studios.* San Francisco: Chronicle Books, 2007.

Parent, Rick. *Computer Animation: Algorithms and Techniques.* San Francisco, CA: Morgan Kaufmann, 2008.

Price, David A. *The Pixar Touch: The Making of a Company.* New York: Alfred A. Knopf, 2008.

Taylor, Richard. *Encyclopedia of Animation Techniques.* Edison, NJ: Chartwell Books, 2003.

Web Sites

Science Daily. "Computer Animation." http://www.sciencedaily.com/articles/c/computer_animation.htm (accessed September 25, 2012).

Apple Computer, Inc.

Apple, Inc., formerly Apple Computer, Inc., was founded by American businessman Steven Jobs (1955–2011) and American computer engineer Stephen Wozniak (1950–) in Jobs's garage in Los Altos, California, in 1975. Their goal was to change the world by developing an easy-to-use computer that everyone could own.

In November of 1975, Wozniak finished assembling the Apple I—a modest device that consisted of a motherboard*, a keyboard, and a display. The advantages to the Apple I were simplicity, price, neatness, and reliability. The disadvantage was that it used the 6502 MOS Technologies microprocessor chip, a cheaper alternative to the popular Intel 8080 chip. This chip fundamentally set the Apple I apart from Intel-based machines. However, Jobs first proved his marketing skills with this computer when he found backers willing to supply the cash and personnel to incorporate the company.

For the Apple II, which was released in 1977, Wozniak switched to a Motorola microprocessor, then gave the personal computer a color display. In doing so, Wozniak redesigned the way the computer utilized the microprocessor. He engineered the software to allow the microprocessor to do multiple tasks at the same time, including driving the color display. This simplified the machine so much that personal computers became cooler in temperature, lighter, more durable, cheaper, and easier to assemble. As a result, computer hardware could be mass-marketed, resulting in an affordable product for the consumer and better profit for the manufacturer.

The Apple II computer was so successful that several versions of it remained on the market for ten years. During a time when the word

* **motherboard** the part of the computer that holds vital hardware, such as the processors, memory, expansion slots, and circuitry

Unveiling a new operating system at Apple. © *David Paul Morris/Bloomberg via Getty Images.*

Steven Jobs

At the age of twenty-one, American businessman Steven Jobs (1955–2011) was persuaded by his friend American computer engineer Stephen Wozniak (1950–) to help him create an "insanely great" personal computer that anyone could use. When the stock of their company went public five years later, Jobs made $256.4 million.

After ten years with Apple, Jobs left to start a new computer company, NeXT. He also bought Pixar, Inc., a small computer animation company, from George Lucas. Pixar produced *Toy Story* (1995), the first feature-length computer animated film, using computers from SGI, Hewlett-Packard, and Sun. When Pixar's stock went public in January 1995, thirty-year-old Jobs became a billionaire.

In 1997 Jobs returned to Apple and shortly thereafter assumed the role of CEO, a title he also held at Pixar. Jobs is credited with the development of the very popular iMac computer and a string of successful multi-touch-interface products including the iPod, iPhone, and iPad. Jobs's personal wealth consistently placed him in the ranks of the world's wealthiest individuals.

* **mainframe computer** large computer used by businesses and government agencies to process massive amounts of data; generally faster and more powerful than desktop computers but usually requiring specialized software

computer evoked images of huge commercial, or mainframe, machines, Apple outsold all others in the budding personal computer market, dominating the competition from Atari, Zenith, Commodore, and Tandy.

In 1980 the Apple III was released. It proved unsuccessful. Shortly thereafter, IBM, the mainframe computer* manufacturer and Apple's main competitor, introduced its PC in 1981. The IBM-PC used Microsoft's DOS operating system and the Intel 8088 chip. This opened the door to a more competitive market for personal computers during the 1980s.

In 1983, Apple's sophisticated Lisa failed to meet expectations. However the Macintosh, introduced in 1984 with a Motorola 68000 microprocessor chip, added a versatility that put the machine many years ahead of its competition. In addition to its technical superiority, the Macintosh also was the first commercially available computer to feature a mouse as a primary input device and a graphical user interface (GUI). This also marked the division of the personal computer market into two primary segments: the Macintosh platform of hardware and software vs. the IBM or IBM-compatible PC platform.

In 1985 both Wozniak and Jobs left the company they had cofounded ten years earlier. Throughout the 1980s and 1990s, Apple declined to make the Macintosh operating system compatible with Intel-based PCs. With few exceptions, the company declined to license either its hardware or software, as well, making it difficult or impossible for other companies to create software and hardware peripherals that would be compatible with Macintosh systems.

Instead of continuing to dominate the industry it helped establish, Apple became the classic illustration of non-conformity and incompatibility in a marketplace that rewards compatibility. For example, a sixty-watt light bulb of any brand is compatible with a lamp from any manufacturer. By the late 1980s, people had come to expect such compatibility between software and computers as well. Some industry experts believe that if Apple had agreed to license its products, the industry would have matched its peripheral hardware and software to Apple products. Instead, the establishment of computer industry standards fell to IBM, Intel, and Microsoft.

From its inception, Apple grew steadily into a multi-billion dollar company. However the dominant market share it once held shrank to less than four percent by 1997. Furthermore, it was not until the Internet was established that Apple made its products compatible with Intel-based computers. Before long, Apple Computer's decline appeared to be irreversible. Compatibility problems with PCs, low market share, persistent dismal sales, the frequent turnover of its top executives, the loss of talented personnel, and successive layoffs sent the value of the company stock to a record low of less than $13 per share in 1997, well short of its break-even point.

However, in 1997, then-CEO Gil Amelio (1943–) recruited Jobs back to Apple. Jobs brokered an agreement between Apple and Microsoft. The contract provided Apple with a much-needed cash infusion, Microsoft software specific to the Macintosh, and new credibility. With the subsequent introduction of the iMac, PowerBook G3 laptop computer, and the PowerMac G4, Apple stock was revived. By December of 1999, the iMac was the best-selling personal computer brand in the retail market, and Apple's market share had increased to 11.3 percent.

In 2001, Mac OS X, an operating system based on NeXT's OPENSTEP and BSD Unix, was released. Later in 2001, Apple, Inc. opened its first two retail stores and introduced the iPod portable digital audio player. The iTunes Store, launched in 2003, revolutionized and reinvigorated digital music sales. The store enables users to download music, eBooks, movies, television shows, podcasts, and university lectures. In 2006, Apple, Inc. began manufacturing computers with Intel processors.

Apple announced the Apple TV in 2006 and made the first generation of the device available in 2007. Apple TV enables users to stream media content such as music, movies, and television shows to their televisions. In July 2008, Apple released a compatible app called Remote that allows user iPhones and other devices to control content on Apple TV much like a traditional television remote control except it utilizes wi-fi instead of RF signals. With AirPlay mirroring, added in 2012, users could mirror their computer to their television screen through Apple TV.

Apple's multi-touch interfaces, which allow users to manipulate the device with various combinations of finger-based movement, are a contrast to traditional touch screen interfaces that mimic the point and click concept of a desktop computer. The multi-touch interface provide a richer method of interaction and enable navigation controls to be omitted from the screen, thus saving space on an already limited display. Apple's iPod Touch, iPhone, iPad, and iPad Mini lines all use a multi-touch, touch-screen interface. The company's laptop computers employ a similar multi-touch interface through trackpads.

Under the direction of Jobs, Apple created a string of innovative and successful multi-touch-interface products including the iPod (music player), iPhone, and iPad (tablet). The MacBook Pro and MacBook Air lines of computers became iconic standards in laptop technology. After his return in the 1990s, Apple went on to become one of the world's most valuable companies. Just weeks before his death on October 5, 2011, Jobs resigned as CEO of Apple, choosing Tim Cook (1960–) as his replacement. Jonathan Ive (1967–), who has worked with Apple since 1992 and overseen many of the company's iconic product designs, continues to lead industrial design for Apple.

 See also **Intel Corporation • Microcomputers • Microsoft Corporation**

Resources

Books

Isaacson, Walter. *Steve Jobs.* New York: Simon & Schuster, 2011.

Kahney, Leander. *Inside Steve's Brain.* New York: Portfolio, 2008.

McFedries, Paul. *Macs.* Hoboken, NJ: Wiley, 2008.

Stephen Wozniak

Apple cofounder Stephen Wozniak (1950–), an American computer engineer, was in his mid–20s, working for Hewlett Packard, when he and American businessman Steven Jobs (1955–2011) began to build the first Apple computer. When their company went public in 1980, Wozniak made $135 million.

In February of 1981, Wozniak sustained serious injuries in a plane crash. After recovering, he intermittently worked at Apple, and briefly ran his own company making universal remote controls. He has become well known for his philanthropy and interest in lifelong learning. In 1990 Wozniak hired teachers to help him collaborate with the Los Gatos School District to teach computer science to middle school students in his own computer lab.

* **polynomial** an expression with
more than one term

O'Grady, Jason D. *Apple Inc.* Westport, CT: Greenwood Press, 2009.

Wozniak, Steve, and Gina Smith. *IWoz: Computer Geek to Cult Icon:
How I Invented the Personal Computer, Co-Founded Apple, and Had
Fun Doing It.* New York: W.W. Norton & Co, 2006.

Young, Jeffrey S., and William L. Simon. *ICon: Steve Jobs, the Greatest
Second Act in the History of Business.* Hoboken, NJ: Wiley, 2005.

Artificial Intelligence

Artificial intelligence (AI) is a field of study based on the premise that
intelligent thought can be regarded as a form of computation—one that
can be formalized and ultimately mechanized. To achieve this, however,
two major issues need to be addressed. The first issue is knowledge representation, and the second is knowledge manipulation. Within the intersection of these two issues lies mechanized intelligence.

History

The study of artificial intelligence has a long history, dating back to the
work of British mathematician Charles Babbage (1791–1871) who developed a special-purpose "Difference Engine" for mechanically computing
the values of certain polynomial* functions. Similar work was also done
by German mathematician Gottfried Wilhem von Leibniz (1646–1716),
who introduced the first system of formal logic and constructed machines
for automating calculation. George Boole (1815–1864), the Countess of
Lovelace Ada Byron King (1815–1852), Gottlob Frege (1848–1925),

AI researchers and their robot. © *AP
Images/Laurent Cipriani.*

and Alfred Tarski (1901–1983) have all significantly contributed to the advancement of the field of artificial intelligence.

Knowledge Representation

It has long been recognized that the language and models used to represent reality profoundly impact one's understanding of reality itself. When humans think about a particular system, they form a mental model of that system and then proceed to discover truths about the system. These truths lead to the ability to make predictions or general statements about the system. However, when a model does not sufficiently match the actual problem, the discovery of truths and the ability to make predictions becomes exceedingly difficult.

A classic example of this is the pre-Copernican model in which the Sun and planets revolved around the Earth. In such a model, it was prohibitively difficult to predict the position of planets. However, in the Copernican revolution this Earth-centric model was replaced with a model where the Earth and other planets revolved around the Sun. This new model dramatically increased the ability of astronomers to predict celestial events.

Arithmetic with Roman numerals provides a second example of how knowledge representation can severely limit the ability to manipulate that knowledge. Both of these examples stress the important relationship between knowledge representation and thought.

In AI, significant effort has gone into the development of languages that can be used to represent knowledge appropriately. Languages such as LISP, which is based on the lambda calculus*, and Prolog, which is based on formal logic, are widely used for knowledge representation. Variations of predicate calculus* are also common languages used by automated reasoning systems. These languages have well-defined semantics and provide a very general framework for representing and manipulating knowledge.

Knowledge Manipulation

Many problems that humans are confronted with are not fully understood. This partial understanding is reflected in the fact that a rigid algorithmic solution—a routine and predetermined number of computational steps—cannot be applied. Rather, the concept of search is used to solve such problems. When search is used to explore the entire solution space, it is said to be exhaustive. Exhaustive search is not typically a successful approach to problem solving because most interesting problems have search spaces that are simply too large to be dealt with in this manner, even by the fastest computers. Therefore, if one hopes to find a solution (or a reasonably good approximation of a solution) to such a problem, one must selectively explore the problem's search space.

The difficulty here is that if part of the search space is not explored, one runs the risk that the solution one seeks will be missed. Thus, in order

* **lambda calculus** important in the development of programming languages, a specialized logic using substitutions that was developed by Alonzo Church (1903–1995)

* **predicate calculus** a branch of logic that uses individuals and predicates, or elements and classes, and the existential and universal quantifiers, "all" and "some," to represent statements

to ignore a portion of a search space, some guiding knowledge or insight must exist so that the solution will not be overlooked.

Heuristics* is a major area of AI that concerns itself with how to limit effectively the exploration of a search space. Chess is a classic example where humans routinely employ sophisticated heuristics in a search space. A chess player will typically search through a small number of possible moves before selecting a move to play. Not every possible move and countermove sequence is explored. Only reasonable sequences are examined. A large part of the intelligence of chess players resides in the heuristics they employ.

A heuristic-based search results from the application of domain or problem-specific knowledge to a universal search function. The success of heuristics has led to focusing the application of general AI techniques to specific problem domains. This has led to the development of expert systems capable of sophisticated reasoning in narrowly defined domains within fields such as medicine, mathematics, chemistry, robotics, and aviation.

Another area that is profoundly dependent on domain-specific knowledge is natural language processing. The ability to understand a natural language such as English is one of the most fundamental aspects of human intelligence, and presents one of the core challenges for the AI community. Small children routinely engage in natural language processing, yet it appears to be almost beyond the reach of mechanized computation. Over the years, significant progress has been made in the ability to parse text to discover its syntactic structure. However, much of the meaning in natural language is context-dependent as well as culture-dependent, and capturing such dependencies has proved highly resistant to automation.

The Turing Test

At what point does the behavior of a machine display intelligence? The answer to this question has raised considerable debate over the definition of intelligence itself. Is a computer capable of beating the world chess champion considered intelligent? Fifty years ago, the answer to this question would most likely have been yes. Today, it is disputed whether or not the behavior of such a machine is intelligent. One reason for this shift in the definition of intelligence is the massive increase in computational power that has occurred over the past fifty years, allowing the chess problem space to be searched in an almost exhaustive manner.

Two key ingredients are seen as essential to intelligent behavior: the ability to learn and thereby change one's behavior over time, and synergy, or the idea that the whole is somehow greater than the sum of its parts.

In 1950 British mathematician Alan Turing (1912–1954) proposed a test for intelligence that serves as a litmus test for intelligent behavior. Turing suggested that the behavior of a machine could be considered intelligent if it was indistinguishable from the behavior of a human. In this imitation game, a human interrogator would hold a dialogue via a terminal with both a human and a computer. If, based solely on the content of the dialogue, the interrogator could not distinguish between the human and the computer, Turing argued that the behavior of the computer could be assumed to be intelligent.

In 2011, Leslie Valiant (1949–), a British professor at Harvard University, received the $250,000 Turing Award for advances in artificial intelligence, including his work in computer-based handwriting recognition, computer simulated vision, and natural language processing.

The same year, IBM's Watson, an AI computer system, competed on *Jeopardy!*, a U.S. quiz show. Watson had to analyze natural language clues before searching four terabytes of databases and formulating a natural language response. The computer used thousands of language analysis algorithms to analyze key words from each clue before searching for related terms in its databases to devise answers. Watson competed against, and defeated, former *Jeopardy!* champions during the week-long competition.

Opponents of Turing's definition of intelligence argue that the Turing Test defines intelligence solely in terms of human intelligence. For example, the ability to carry out complex numerical computation correctly and quickly is something that a computer can do easily but a human cannot. Given that, is it reasonable to use this ability to distinguish between the behavior of a human and a computer and conclude that the computer is not intelligent?

 See also **Assistive Computer Technology For Persons With Disabilities • LISP • Optical Character Recognition • Robotics • Robots**

Resources

Books

Luger, George F. *Artificial Intelligence: Structures and Strategies for Complex Problem Solving.* 6th ed. Reading, MA: Addison Wesley, 2009.

Olsen, Dan R. *Building Interactive Systems: Principles for Human-Computer Interaction.* Boston: Course Technology, 2010.

Russell, Stuart J., and Peter Norvig. *Artificial Intelligence: A Modern Approach.* 3rd ed. Upper Saddle River, NJ: Prentice Hall, 2010.

Artificial Intelligence: AI

As technology becomes more common in today's society, many questions are raised regarding its social and moral consequences. Often filmmakers tap into the high-tech market for ideas about family values and virtues. One such effort is Steven Spielberg's 2001 movie *Artificial Intelligence: AI.* The story revolves around David, a human-like robot, and his desire to experience real love and emotions, like other humans. The real question the film poses to its viewers is: Can humans love an artificial being?

Association for Computing Machinery

The Association for Computing Machinery (ACM) is the world's oldest and largest educational and scientific computing society. It was founded in 1947 by a group of computer pioneers, including American physicist John Mauchly (1907–1980), co-inventor of the first electronic computer. The new professional society would foster the science and art of computing.

More than 65 years later, the ACM, headquartered in New York City, is the nucleus for the ever-changing science of information technology. It plays a key role in leveraging the remarkable growth of the profession. Its membership comprises more than one-hundred thousand computing and information technology (IT) professionals and students in more than one hundred countries, working in all areas of industry, academia, and government. The ACM also has over 170 local chapters, more than 500 university and college chapters, and numerous special interest group chapters. In addition, it sponsors over 170 conferences annually around the world, including the Design Automation Conference, Distributed Event Based Systems Conference, and Federated Computing Research Conference. For its members, the ACM offers a vital forum for the exchange of information, ideas, and discoveries.

Since its inception, the ACM has chronicled the key developments in computer technology through its publications. Each year the ACM formally recognizes the accomplishments of the people responsible for these advances by awarding prizes such as the ACM Turing Award, named after British mathematician Alan Turing (1912–1954), who conceived of

Moshe Vardi (left), editor-in-chief of Communications of the Association for Computer Machinery, moderates a panel discussion during the 2012 ACM Turing Centenary Celebration in San Francisco. *© AP Images/Ryan Anson/Association for Computing Machinery.*

* **artificial intelligence (AI)**
a branch of computer science
dealing with creating computer
hardware and software to
mimic the way people think and
perform practical tasks

a theoretical computing machine in 1936 and thus set the stage for the development of computers in the twentieth century. The A. M. Turing Award is one of the leading honors in computing presented yearly by the ACM. It is widely regarded as the Nobel Prize within computing. Its famous recipients include American computer scientist Donald Knuth (1938–), author of *The Art of Computer Programming*; American computer scientist and LISP creator John McCarthy (1927–2011); American computer scientists and UNIX co-inventors Ken Thompson (1943–) and Dennis Ritchie (1941–2011); American inventor and mouse developer Doug Engelbart (1925–); American computer scientist and graphics pioneer Ivan Sutherland (1938–); American computer scientist and inventor of TCP/IP Vinton "Vint" Cerf (1943–); and Indian-American computer scientist and artificial intelligence (AI)* expert Dabbala Rajagopal "Raj" Reddy (1937–). In 2011, the Turing Award went to Israeli-American computer scientist Judea Pearl (1936–) for "fundamental contributions to artificial intelligence through the development of a calculus for probabilistic and causal reasoning."

The ACM bestows many other awards for excellence, including an award named for American computer scientist Grace Murray Hopper (1906–1992), the Allen Newell (1927–1992) award, the Paris Kanellakis (1953–1995) Theory and Practice Award, the Gordon Bell Prize, the Eugene L. Lawler Award, and the Karl V. Karlstrom Outstanding Educator award.

Education and Curriculum Recommendations

A key mission of the ACM is the education of computer and information specialists. Volunteer committees under the Education Board develop and recommend computer curricula for all educational levels and provide self-assessment procedures, home study courses, and professional development seminars for professionals already in the field. Through its participation in the Computer Sciences Accreditation Board, the ACM is instrumental in evaluating and accrediting computer science programs in colleges and universities.

The ACM has won worldwide recognition for its published curriculum recommendations, both for colleges and universities and for secondary schools that are increasingly concerned with preparing students for advanced education in the information sciences and technologies.

Member Products, Services, and Programs

The ACM provides many products and services to its membership. These include student activities, publications, special events, and a digital library, among others.

Student Activities The ACM's vital electronic community offers high school and college students the opportunity to network with noted computer experts and access a wide range of activities and services, including free searching of its acclaimed Digital Library (http://

www.acm.org/), the world's largest online resource for information about computing. Students can also take advantage of the many services available at more than 500 ACM student chapters located in colleges, universities, and high schools throughout the United States and worldwide. These local chapters publish their own newsletters and meet regularly to hear lectures and conduct workshops and conferences. Other ACM services for students include networking at conferences, the International Programming contest, and the ACM's *Crossroads* magazine, published by and for students. The ACM has also established many ACM-W (women's) chapters. ACM-W chapters seek to increase the recruitment of women to computing fields and educational programs and provide support to female students and professionals. The representation of women in computing fields has dropped dramatically since a peak in the 1980s, and the ACM-W serves an important role in disproving misconceptions about the role of women in computing and to encourage women to pursue computer-related careers.

ACM Publications The ACM publishes, distributes, and archives original research and firsthand perspectives from the world's leading thinkers in computing and information technologies. ACM offers more than forty publications that help computing professionals negotiate the strategic challenges and operating problems of their work. The ACM Press Books program covers a broad spectrum of interests in computer science and engineering. The ACM also publishes many professional journals, including the *Communications of the ACM*, the *Journal of the Association for Computing Machinery, Computing Surveys*, and more than a dozen additional titles.

ACM Events and Services

The ACM is the driving force behind many key events in the computing world, including SIGGRAPH, the annual computer graphics show that attracts tens of thousands of people to see the latest developments in this fast-changing field. Over the years, the ACM has produced such high-profile events as the computer chess match between Russian chess player Garry Kasparov (1963–) and the IBM Deep Blue computer, and the annual ACM International Collegiate Programming Contest, in which thousands of student teams compete worldwide. It also produces a special exposition and conference every four years dealing with the future of computing. The 1997 event attracted more than twenty thousand attendees.

Special Activities The ACM sponsors scores of special committees, boards, and forums dealing with a wide variety of special topics, including:

- The ACM's Committee on Women in Computing, dealing with all aspects of computing as it affects the lives and careers of women and girls;

- The online *Risks* forum, which deals with risks to the public associated with computers and related systems;
- The Membership Activities Board, which encourages the development of programs that enhance the value of membership in ACM.

The ACM Digital Library   The ACM's Digital Library is the world's most comprehensive online collection of information about the world of computing. It features an archive of journals, magazines, and conference proceedings online, as well as current issues of the ACM's magazines and journals. The ACM's online services included a lively IT-related opinion magazine and forum termed *Ubiquity*, and the popular *Tech News* digest containing information about the latest events in the IT world.

Volunteerism and Special Interest Groups (SIGs)   The ACM is built on a strong base of volunteerism. Volunteers serve on the ACM Council, boards, committees, task forces, and other subgroups that comprise ACM's governing structure. They are also at the heart of the ACM's thirty-eight Special Interest Groups (SIGs), each covering a defined computing discipline. SIGs* write their own newsletters and are governed by their own elected officers. SIGs come in many forms, including Electronic Forums, which promote the electronic exchange of ideas and information about one special interest area; Conference, which produce ongoing technical meetings and conferences; Newsletter, and so on.

ACM Fellows   The ACM Fellows Program was established by the ACM's Council in 1993 to recognize and honor outstanding ACM members for their achievements in computer science and information technology and for their significant contributions to the mission of the ACM. The ACM Fellows serve as distinguished colleagues to whom the ACM and its members look for guidance and leadership as the world of information technology evolves. More than 500 people have been recognized as ACM Fellows.

Code of Ethics

The ACM has developed a code of ethics for its members based on the following seven major tenets:

1. Contribute to society and human well-being.
2. Avoid harm to others.
3. Be honest and trustworthy.
4. Be fair and take action not to discriminate.
5. Honor property rights including copyrights and patent.
6. Give proper credit for intellectual property.
7. Respect the privacy of others.

> *See also* **Institute of Electrical and Electronics Engineers (IEEE) • Turing, Alan M.**

Resources

Web Sites

Association for Computing Machinery (ACM). "Judea Pearl." http://www.acm.org/about (accessed September 20, 2009).

Association for Computing Machinery (ACM). "What is ACM?" http://www.acm.org/about (accessed September 20, 2009).

B

Babbage, Charles
British Inventor and Mathematician
1791–1871

A mathematician, philosopher, and inventor, Charles Babbage is best remembered for his concept of the Analytical Engine—a calculating machine that was not actually built during his lifetime.

Being born into a wealthy family on December 26, 1791, allowed Babbage to pursue his interests free from financial worries through most of his life. The oldest child of a successful Devonshire banker, Babbage spent the greater part of his early childhood relieved of study due to poor health. Deprived of formal study, the young Babbage used experiments to find answers to his questions. For example, he would take toys apart to see what was inside. On another occasion, he tried, unsuccessfully, to summon the devil to confirm the creature's existence. His failure to do so led him to reason that devils and ghosts were not real.

Babbage's formal education began at a boarding school in London, England. Algebra interested him to such an extent that he and another student would wake at 3 A.M. to study for a few hours. In 1814 Babbage entered Cambridge University to study mathematics. As a result of his late-night algebra studies and knowledge of European mathematical advances, he knew more than his tutors. Babbage and his equally mathematically talented friends, John Herschel and George Peacock, formed the Analytical Society to promote European mathematics as a more advanced subject than the mathematics of English physicist Isaac Newton (1642–1727). On the lighter side, he joined friends to form the Ghost Club.

Upon completing a master of arts, Babbage continued to work for mathematical reform through the translation of a paper by Sylvestre François Lacroix. This and further works on calculus were recognized by Cambridge University in 1828 when Babbage was elected as Lucasian Professor of Mathematics. During his ten years as professor, Babbage gave no lectures; however he participated in the examination of students for the Smith prizes given for excellence in mathematics.

A major outcome of his mathematical studies was the idea for a calculating machine—the Difference Engine—which would calculate and print numbers in a sequence based on the principle of differences. The sequences of the calculations can be described by a theorem or as a polynomial* and the succeeding values are calculated by addition and subtraction rather than by multiplication. The Difference Engine produced tables of logarithmic and trigonometric functions to six decimal

Charles Babbage. © *SSPL via Getty Images.*

* **polynomial** an expression with more than one term

places. This machine would have a mechanical memory and the capability of producing printed tables. To get funding to build a large Difference Machine, Babbage used a small working model to demonstrate the machine's potential to the British government. The machine was designed to a second-order difference and six decimal places. All parts of the machine were hand tooled or cast. Babbage built a foundry and forge on his land to facilitate and oversee the creation of the components.

In 1824 Babbage was awarded a grant to build his machine. As work progressed on the machine, he was making changes on the design and eventually scrapped the original model for a more complex one, the Analytical Engine. He again petitioned the government for more funding but was denied. Despite the lack of funding, he continued to design and construct parts for the Analytical Engine using his own funds.

The Analytical Engine design incorporated the following functions. Variables and detailed instructions would be read into the machine from punched cards. These cards were based upon the card coding method used in Jacquard weaving. The variables would be placed in a 'store,' memory, as would intermediate calculations. The 'mill,' processor, would carry out the instructions thereby performing the calculations. Based on calculation results, the engine could determine which instruction should be used next. Babbage had developed a decision function. The results would be printed out. This design has all the characteristics of a computer.

Despite his accomplishments, Babbage could not get financial support for the Analytical Engine and did not have the resources to complete a working model. He did leave detailed drawings for the internal mechanism and notes for the design and construction.

In the early 1840s, Babbage came in contact with Ada Byron King, Countess of Lovelace, a female contemporary mathematician and theoretician. King had translated a summary of Babbage's achievements from an original Italian account. When she showed Babbage her translation, he suggested that she add her own notes, which turned out to be three times the length of the original article. Letters between Babbage and King raced back and forth. When King eventually published the article in 1843, it included her predictions that Babbage's machine might be used to compose complex music and to produce graphics, and it might be used for both practical and scientific use. She was correct. It was King who also suggested to Babbage the idea of writing a plan on how his engine might calculate Bernoulli numbers*. This plan is now regarded as the first "computer language."

When not completely involved with the calculating engines, Babbage turned his attention to other pursuits. He was avidly interested in all kinds of statistics, from the heartbeat of a pig, to the quantity of wood that a man could saw in a specific amount of time. Babbage would put himself into danger to learn more. Once he spent time in a large drying machine to test the human body's reaction to heat. On another occasion, he spent five to six minutes inside a 129°C (265°F) oven, noting his pulse and the quantity of his perspiration. Another venture was to explore the inside of an active volcano. Babbage descended into Italy's Mount Vesuvius to observe the occurrence of mini eruptions. Having determined that the time between eruptions was about ten minutes, Babbage proceeded to descend further and closer to the eruption site to see liquid lava and note its movement. He remained for six minutes allowing four minutes to retreat from his position before the next eruption.

In 1837 Babbage conducted experiments which determined that the Brunel wide gauge track (railway) was safer and more efficient than narrower gauge tracks. Plus, his calculations of mail delivery showed that the most costly aspect of the mailing process was the distance traveled, and not the time or labor involved. This analysis resulted in the introduction of uniform postal rates.

Babbage's book, *Economics of Manufactures and Machinery,* set out the mathematics for the manufacturing processes. The book became a basis for operations research. Babbage published numerous papers covering a wide range of topics, from science to religion. He founded the British Association's Statistical Society and the British Association for the Advancement of Science; was elected a fellow of the Royal Society; and was a member of the Astronomical Society. Babbage's *The Ninth Bridgewater Treatise* details his ideas that science could explain religion. Babbage died in London on October 18, 1871.

▶ *See also* **Analytical Engine • King, Ada Byron**

Resources

Books

Morrison, Philip, and Emily Morrison, eds. *Charles Babbage and his Calculating Engines.* New York: Dover Publishing Inc., 1961.

Web Sites

Charles Babbage Institute. http://www.cbi.umn.edu/ (accessed November 2, 2012)

The Babbage Pages. http://www.ex.ac.uk/BABBAGE/welcome.html (accessed November 2, 2012)

Bell Labs

Bell Telephone Laboratories Inc., was founded in 1925 as the research and development (R&D) branch of the Bell System. Until the early 1990s, Bell Labs as it is commonly referred to, was owned and supported by American Telephone & Telegraph Company (AT&T), the Bell System's parent company, and by the Western Electric Company (WECo), the Bell System's manufacturing branch, which was owned by AT&T. WECo paid the salaries of Bell Labs personnel who developed new products that WECo manufactured;

The Cowcatcher

In 1830 Babbage was a passenger on the opening run of the Manchester and Liverpool railroad line. His interest in rail travel led to the invention of the cowcatcher. This plow-shaped device was mounted on the front of the steam engine for the purpose of rapidly removing any obstruction on the rails, particularly cows.

Alcatel Lucent's Bell Labs in Villarceaux, France. © *Balint Porneczi/Bloomberg via Getty Images.* ▶

* **transistor** a contraction of TRANSfer resISTOR; a semiconductor device, invented by John Bardeen, Walter Brattain, and William Shockley, which has three terminals; can be used for switching and amplifying electrical signals

* **automata theory** the analytical (mathematical) treatment and study of automated systems

AT&T paid the salaries of Bell Labs personnel who performed research and systems engineering (R&SE). The Bell System's customers provided R&SE revenue via their monthly telephone bills, and Bell Labs systems engineers ensured that the United States had the world's best telephone system. Bell Labs had its headquarters in Berkeley Heights, New Jersey, but had research and development facilities located throughout the world.

The research performed at Bell Labs was the world's best, especially between the 1940s and the 1970s. The people at Bell Labs developed such groundbreaking technologies as the transistor, the laser, radio astronomy, information theory, the UNIX operating system, the C programming language, and the C++ programming language. Over the years, many Bell Labs employees received prestigious awards in their fields, including a number of Nobel Prizes. During the three decades that followed the 1947 invention of the transistor* at Bell Labs, scientists and engineers at Bell Labs contributed many other advances to the technologies that underlie digital communications and digital computing—electronics, magnetic and semiconductor memories, digital circuit design, and integrated circuits.

Although federal regulation precluded AT&T from participating in the commercial computer industry until the 1980s, Bell Labs personnel also contributed directly and significantly to computer architecture and software science—partly to find better ways to control telephone switching systems and partly through basic research. Bell Labs researchers contributed to digital design, automata theory*, databases, operating systems, programming languages, coding, speech processing, and other fields of computer science.

Early Computing and Bell Labs

An early computer was built at Bell Labs in the late 1930s using electro-mechanical relays. This research project was a generalization of the special-purpose computers termed markers that controlled telephone calls. Markers were used from the 1930s to the 1950s in the electro-mechanical telephone systems that were manufactured by WECo and operated by the Bell System's telephone companies. An even more significant contribution to computing came in the 1960s with a telephone switching system termed the No. 1 Electronic Switching System (1E).

During the early 1960s, three significant commercial software systems were developed concurrently at different places in the United States: the first database (for airline reservations), the first operating system (for IBM's 7090 computer), and the first real-time process control software (at Bell Labs, for the 1E). Software similar to that found in the 1E thirty years ago still controls factories and operates automobile engines.

During the 1970s and 1980s, the UNIX operating system was developed at Bell Labs. Even though AT&T could not sell computer products like operating systems, it was able to license the use of UNIX source code to universities, corporations, and the U.S. government. The use of UNIX source code by universities as a teaching aid and an open research platform led to its rise in popularity.

American computer scientists Kenneth Thompson (1943–) and Dennis Ritchie (1941–2011), two engineers who also contributed to the creation of UNIX, created the C programming language in 1972. At the time, C was considered a higher-level programming language and encouraged architecture independent programming. This enabled programs to be written that could easily be retargeted for other computers, not just for the computers for which they were originally designed. Given the rapidly changing hardware landscape of the day, this was an important feature, which drove adoption. After its development, UNIX was rewritten in the C language. Danish computer scientist Bjarne Stroustrup (1950–), another Bell engineer, enhanced the C language in 1979 in what would be termed C++ in time. C++ has grown to be one of the most popular programming languages every created, and is still in wide use.

In the early 1980s, the Bell System was broken up, with a dramatic effect on Bell Labs. Since Bell Labs (and WECo) remained with AT&T, a new R&D company termed Bell Communications Research (Bellcore) was created for the seven new Baby Bells (Ameritech, Bell Atlantic, Bell South, Nynex, PacTel, Southwest Bell, and US West). Many Bell Labs personnel were transferred to Bellcore before Bellcore split from Bell Labs in 1984.

Afterward, the phone companies' R&SE revenue went to Bellcore, and R&D at Bell Labs (now supported fully by WECo) gradually became more product-oriented. In the 1990s, Bellcore's seven owners sold their R&D company, now known as Telcordia, and AT&T split up again. WECo was divested as a separate company, termed Lucent Technologies, and since Bell Labs went with Lucent, AT&T formed a new internal R&D

Bell's Famed Employees

Many famous scientists and engineers have been employed at Bell Labs. They have contributed to many branches of science: physics, chemistry, electronics, cognition, communications, computing, and even cosmology. Among the famous scientists who worked at Bell labs were Edward "Ed" Moore (1925–2003), who contributed to automata theory, and Richard "Dick" Hamming (1915–1998), who developed error-correcting codes. Unix was developed by a group of computer scientists including Canadian Brian Kernighan (1942–), American Dennis Ritchie (1941–2011), and American Ken Thompson (1943–). In 1956, John Bardeen (1908–1991), Walter H. Brattain (1902–1987), and William Shockley (1910–1989) were awarded the Nobel Prize in Physics for inventing the first transistors. But perhaps the most remarkable scientist who ever worked at Bell Labs was American electronic engineer and mathematician Claude Shannon (1916–2001), who (besides his famous work on Information Theory) proved that any digital function could be implemented using only two levels of elementary logic operations. Since this theory underlies modern digital design using electronic and-gates and or-gates, Shannon could be referred to as the father of digital design. Shannon also contributed greatly to the field of cryptography while supporting the war effort during World War II.

* **base-2** a number system in which each place represents a power of 2 larger than the place to its right (binary)
* **base-10** a number system in which each place represents a power of 10 larger than the place to its right (decimal)

division, termed AT&T Labs. Some Bell Labs personnel were transferred to AT&T Labs before that split occurred. In 2006, Lucent merged with Alcatel, a foreign firm also with ties to the telecommunication industry since the late 1800s.

Now the remnants of Bell Labs are spread across three different companies, one of which still uses the Bell Labs name. Although all three companies still perform outstanding R&D, the golden age of Bell Labs research is over. As of 2012, Bell Labs was the research and development subsidiary of the French-owned company, Alcatel-Lucent.

▶ *See also* **Shannon, Claude E • Telecommunications • Transistors**

Resources

Books

Dodd, Annabel Z. *The Essential Guide to Telecommunications.* Upper Saddle River, NJ: Prentice Hall, 2012.

Casson, Herbert N. *The History of the Telephone.* Gardners Books, 2007.

Gertner, Jon. *The Idea Factory: Bell Labs and the Great Age of American Innovation.* New York: Penguin Press, 2012.

Lojek., Bo. *History of Semiconductor Engineering.* Berlin: Springer, 2007.

Web Sites

AT&T Research. "Biography of Claude Elwood Shannon" http://www2.research.att.com/~njas/doc/shannonbio.html (accessed September 25, 2012).

PBS. "Transistorized!" http://www.pbs.org/transistor/album1/index.html (accessed September 25, 2012).

Binary Number System

The binary number system, also called the base-2* number system, is a method of representing numbers that counts by using combinations of only two numerals: zero (0) and one (1). Computers use the binary number system to manipulate and store all of their data including numbers, words, videos, graphics, and music.

The term bit, the smallest unit of digital technology, stands for "BInary digiT." A byte is a group of eight bits. A kilobyte is 1,024 bytes or 8,192 bits.

Using binary numbers, 1 + 1 = 10 because "2" does not exist in this system. A different number system, the commonly used decimal or base-10* number system, counts by using 10 digits (0,1,2,3,4,5,6,7,8,9) so 1 + 1 = 2 and 7 + 7 = 14. Another number system used by computer programmers is the hexadecimal system, base-16*, which uses 16 symbols (0,1,2,3,4,5,6,7,8,9,A,B,C,D,E,F), so $1 + 1 = 2$ and $7 + 7 = E$. Base-10 and base-16 number systems are more compact than the binary system. Programmers use the hexadecimal number system as a convenient, more compact way to represent binary numbers because it is very easy to convert from binary to hexadecimal and vice versa. It is more difficult to convert from binary to decimal and from decimal to binary.

The advantage of the binary system is its simplicity. A computing device can be created out of anything that has a series of switches, increasingly in the form of programmable microchip circuits, each of which can alternate between an "on" position and an "off" position. These switches can be electronic, biological, or mechanical, as long as they can be moved on command from one position to the other. Most computers have electronic switches.

When a switch is "on" it represents the value of one, and when the switch is "off" it represents the value of zero. Digital devices perform mathematical operations by turning binary switches on and off. The faster the computer can turn the switches on and off, the faster it can perform its calculations.

Each numeral in a binary number takes a value that depends on its position in the number. This is called positional notation. It is a concept that also applies to decimal numbers.

For example, the decimal number 123 represents the decimal value $100 + 20 + 3$. The number one represents hundreds, the number two represents tens, and the number three represents units. A mathematical formula for generating the number 123 can be created by multiplying the number in the hundreds column (1) by 100, or 10^2; multiplying the number in the tens column (2) by 10, or 10^1; multiplying the number in the units column (3) by 1, or 10^0; and then adding the products together. The formula is: $1 \times 10^2 + 2 \times 10^1 + 3 \times 10^0 = 123$.

This shows that each value is multiplied by the base (10) raised to increasing powers. The value of the power starts at zero and is incremented by one at each new position in the formula.

This concept of positional notation also applies to binary numbers with the difference being that the base is 2. For example, to find the decimal value of the binary number 1101, the formula is $1 \times 2^3 + 1 \times 2^2 + 0 \times 2^1 + 1 \times 2^0 = 13$.

Binary Operations

Binary numbers can be manipulated with the same familiar operations used to calculate decimal numbers, but using only zeros and ones. To add two numbers, there are only four rules to remember:

$0 + 0 = 0$

$0 + 1 = 1$

$1 + 0 = 1$

$1 + 1 = 10$

Binary code on a video screen at a technology fair. © *AP Images/Ronny Hartmann.*

* **base—16** a number system in which each place represents a power of 16 larger than the place to its right (hexadecimal)

Therefore, to solve the following addition problem, start in the right-most column and add $1 + 1 = 10$; write down the 0 and carry the 1. Working with each column to the left, continue adding until the problem is solved.

```
  10101
+   101
-------
  11010
```

To convert a binary number to a decimal number, each digit is multiplied by a power of two. The products are then added together. For example, to translate the binary number 11010 to decimal, the formula would be as follows:

In base-2, we have the representation 11010.

To convert to base-10, we need to use the place value of each digit of the binary representation: $(1 \times 2^4) + (1 \times 2^3) + (0 \times 2^2) + (1 \times 2^1) + (0 \times 2^0)$

So in the base-10 representation, we have: $16 + 8 + 0 + 2 + 0 = 26$

To convert a binary number to a hexadecimal number, separate the binary number into groups of four starting from the right and then translate each group into its hexadecimal equivalent. Zeros may be added to the left of the binary number to complete a group of four. For example, to translate the number 11010 to hexadecimal, the formula would be as follows:

In binary, again, we have the representation 11010.

In groups of four, we have 0001 and 1010.

In hexadecimal, these groups are 1 and A.

Thus, the hexadecimal representation of the number is 1A.

Digital Data

Bits are a fundamental element of digital computing. The term "digitize" means to turn an analog* signal, or a range of voltages, into a digital signal, or a series of numbers representing voltages. A piece of music can be digitized by taking very frequent measurements of it, called sampling, and translating it into discrete* numbers, which are then translated into zeros and ones. If the samples are taken very frequently, the music sounds like a continuous tone when it is played back.

A black and white photograph can be digitized by laying a fine grid over the image and calculating the amount of gray at each intersection of the grid, called a pixel*. For example, using an 8-bit code, the part of the image that is purely white can be digitized as 11111111. Likewise, the part that is purely black can be digitized as 00000000. Each of the 254 numbers that fall between those two extremes (numbers from 00000001 to 11111110) represents a shade of gray. When it is time to reconstruct the photograph using its collection of binary digits, the computer decodes the image, assigns the correct shade of gray to each pixel, and the picture appears. To improve resolution, a finer grid can be used so the image can be expanded to larger sizes without losing detail.

A color photograph is digitized in a similar fashion but requires many more bits to store the color of the pixel. For example, an 8-bit system uses eight bits to define which of 256 colors is represented by each pixel (2^8 equals 256). Likewise, a 16-bit system uses sixteen bits to define each of 65,536 colors (2^{16} equals 65,536). Therefore, color images require much more storage space than those in black and white.

▶ *See also* **Early Computers • Memory**

Resources

Books

Ammari, Habib, and Hyeonbae Kang, eds. *Imaging Microstructures: Mathematical and Computational Challenges: Proceedings of a Research Conference, June 18–20, 2008, Institut Henri Poincaré, Paris, France.* Providence, RI: American Mathematical Society, 2009.

Badiou, Alain. *Number and Numbers.* Cambridge, UK, and Malden, MA: Polity Press, 2008.

Reid, Constance. *From Zero to Infinity: What Makes Numbers Interesting.* 5th ed. Wellesley, MA: A.K. Peters, 2006.

Yin and Yang

There is some evidence (although not undisputed) that the binary number system has its roots in the concept of *yin* and *yang*—the ancient Confucian belief in two forces of nature that are separate, yet equal, which when combined represent the whole of existence. In the Chinese language, *yang* is represented as a solid line, whereas *yin* is shown as a broken line. As with the binary numbers of "1" and "0," the symbols for *yin* and *yang* can be combined to make many more characters.

CD

Census Bureau

The United States Census Bureau has a long history. The Census Bureau collects data about the people and economy of the U.S. every ten years. The first census was taken in 1790 by U.S. marshals who were told to visit every dwelling place and count the individuals living there. Taking about a year to complete the count, census clerks determined the population to be 3.9 million inhabitants. The most recent census, in 2010, counted more than 308 million Americans

As the country grew, an increasing need developed for statistics to help the government understand the current situation and to make plans for the future. The content of the census changed accordingly. In 1810, the first inquiry about manufacturing was included. Questions about fisheries were added in 1840. In 1850, the census included questions about crime, taxation, churches, and other social issues. In 1870, the Census Bureau used a wooden machine invented by American colonel Charles W. Seaton (1831–1885) to help keep the columns of figures aligned. By 1880, the census undertaking was so complex that it took almost eight years to tabulate.

American inventor Herman Hollerith (1860–1929) was employed by the U.S. Census Bureau to help tabulate the 1880 census. He left the Census Bureau for a succession of jobs and eventually he devised a punched card* tabulating machine to track health statistics. After testing Hollerith's machine against two other inventions, the Census Bureau agreed to rent fifty-six Hollerith machines to speed up the tabulation of the 1890 census. Clerks used a hand punch to enter data into cards slightly larger than a dollar bill. The cards were then read and sorted by Hollerith's machine and later summarized on numbered tabulating dials. The 1890 census took just two and a half years to complete and the Census Bureau saved more than $5 million.

Many researchers believe that the 1890 census was the first time that a large data collection and analysis problem was handled by machines. Because of the agency's need to process large amounts of data in a timely and cost-efficient fashion, the Census Bureau has been in the forefront of the data processing revolution.

The Census Bureau was instrumental in securing funding for American physicist John Mauchly (1907–1980) and American electrical engineer J. Presper Eckert, Jr. (1919–1995), through the National Bureau of Standards, to develop a practical electronic digital computer. In 1951, the Census Bureau installed the Universal Automatic Computer

* **punched card** a paper card with punched holes which give instructions to a computer in order to encode program instructions and data

Mobile Census Bureau. © *AP Images/The Santa Fe New Mexican, Natalie Guillen.*

(UNIVAC) I, which was developed by Mauchly and Eckert's company, Remington-Rand Corporation. It was the first commercially viable electronic digital computer.

Use of the UNIVAC I computer to tabulate the 1950 census did not yield great improvement over past tabulating methods, due to general inexperience with the computer and the awkwardness of this early computer technology. However, several surveys were tabulated using the UNIVAC I computer after the 1950 census. Improved performance on these surveys indicated to the bureau that increased use of electronic computing technology would continue to enhance survey productivity and expand the Census Bureau's ability to collect new types of data.

With the 1954 Economic Census, use of the electronic computer greatly reduced the bureau's reliance on the time-consuming and manually intensive punched card tabulating machines that had been in place since 1890. The new computer-based data processing system allowed the bureau to calculate sophisticated statistics that were previously impractical to use. The UNIVAC I computer also allowed the bureau to check for inconsistencies in the census data and correct them, thereby increasing accuracy. The electronic computer allowed longer records to be stored, sorted, and tabulated, which greatly increased the amount and types of data that could be analyzed. From this point, the Census Bureau focused much of its research and development efforts on auxiliary computer equipment to improve input and output operations and thus increase productivity.

For the 2010 census, 500,000 handheld computers were used for data collection. These computers were initially used in a testing phase to verify addresses in 2007. Problems with the handheld computers, which affected the productivity of field staff, were reported, including issues with data transmission and collecting mapping coordinates, device freezing, and problems when canvassing large blocks. The Government Accountability Office (GAO) issued recommendations to address these issues for optimal Field Data Collection Automation for the official address verification taking place in 2009.

The Census Bureau has developed a wide range of interactive tools to help people analyze and understand the statistics generated by the bureau. For example, the Data Extraction System is used to extract data from the current population survey and public use census data. The Data Extraction System is now available via the Internet, as are many other access and analysis tools. The TIGER system, which is short for Topologically Integrated Geographic Encoding and Referencing system, is another analysis and application tool; it integrates maps with information about highways, parks, railroads, streets, and population statistics. When a user enters a ZIP code (ZIP is short for Zone Improvement Plan), a map is displayed. The user can request various levels of detail, as desired.Internet users, makes a variety of applications available, including a street locator, business patterns for each county, surveys of manufacturers, international trade information, and more.

The U.S. Census Bureau is part of the Department of Commerce, and its director is appointed by the president of the United States. As of September 2012, American sociologist and research professor Robert Martin Groves (1948–) was the Census Bureau's director, a position he assumed starting on July 15, 2009. With its generation of the census every ten years (decennial), as directed by the U.S. Constitution (article I, section II), the bureau is the only comprehensive, statistical source of social and economic data in the United States. The huge volume of data from the census is published and the statistics that are generated filter into almost every aspect of life in the United States. Population statistics are used to help determine each state's number of seats in the House of Representatives, funding for school districts, and money for road and bridge repairs. Census numbers are used directly or indirectly by the federal government to allocate more than $400 billion each year for education programs, housing and community development, healthcare services for the elderly, and numerous other state and federal programs and services. In addition, businesses use the statistics to decide where to locate factories, shopping malls, movie theaters, banks, and offices.

Some people are concerned that the individual answers they provide in a census can be seen by others. For instance, the American Community Survey (ACS) is a statistical survey that annually samples a small percentage of the U.S. population for information that can be used on the local, state, and federal level. However, by law, confidentiality in census information is rigorously enforced. Individual answers cannot be shared with anyone, including other government agencies.

interconnectivity the ability
of more than one physical
computer to operate with
one or more other physical
computers; interconnectivity is
usually accomplished by means
of network wiring, cable, or
telephone lines

Since the first census in 1790, the U.S. Census Bureau has been a
source of data about who American citizens are, where they live, and what
they need to do to grow and prosper as a country. The Bureau has been
instrumental in developing new ways to collect, analyze, and distribute
this data—first, through the use of mechanized tabulating machines, then
through computer technology, and now through the Internet.

▶ See also **Early Computers** • **Eckert, J Presper, Jr, and Mauchly, John W** •
Hollerith, Herman • **Tabulating Machines**

Resources

Books

Anderson, Margo, Constance F. Citro, and Joseph J. Salvo, editors.
*Encyclopedia of the U.S. Census: From the Constitution to the American
Community Survey.* Thousand Oaks, CA: CQ Press, 2012.

Gaquin, Deirdre, and Gwenavere, W. Dunn. *The Who, What, and Where
of America: Understanding the American Community Survey.* Lanham,
MD: Bernan Press, 2012.

Web Sites

United States Census Bureau. "About the American Community
Survey" http://www.census.gov/acs/www/about_the_survey/
american_community_survey/ (accessed September 27, 2012).

United States Census Bureau. "About Us" http://www2.research.att.
com/~njas/doc/shannonbio.html (accessed September 27, 2012).

Washington Post and Carol Morello. "Groves Brings Scholarly
Depth to Bear in Leading Census, Winning Over Critics" http://
www.washingtonpost.com/wp-dyn/content/article/2010/03/30/
AR2010033003675_pf.html (accessed September 27, 2012).

Computer Fraud and Abuse Act of 1986

Prior to the mid-1980s, few laws existed to regulate the usage of computers. In the 1970s and early 1980s, users of business computers were generally operating networked computers in a highly supervised and controlled employment setting. Computer hobbyists and home users were generally limited to computers that were neither as technologically advanced as business computers, nor as interactive or interconnected with other computers.

By the mid-1980s, however, technological advances brought personal computers into widespread use in homes, high schools, colleges, and businesses. Interconnectivity* of computers via telephone lines and modems grew rapidly. Valuable, often confidential, information could now be stored on systems that were increasingly vulnerable to outside interference.

Legislating Computer Activity

The United States Computer Fraud and Abuse Act of 1986 (referred to in this article as the Act) was an amendment to the Counterfeit Access Device and Computer Fraud and Abuse Act of 1984 (the 1984 Act). It was the first comprehensive legislation in the United States to identify and provide for the prosecution of crimes committed through and against computer systems.

The 1984 Act was limited in scope and provided for only three categories of computer-related crime: (1) unauthorized access to and use of certain federal data; (2) unauthorized access to or use of consumer credit-related information; and (3) unauthorized access to a computer used for, or on behalf of, the U.S. government. Thus, the 1984 Act only addressed crimes related to government computers, as well as government data and consumer credit data. Because of its limited scope, the 1984 Act was amended and superseded in 1986. The new Act was the first comprehensive federal legislation regarding computer crimes that affected non-government computers, as well.

Offenses and Penalties

The centerpiece of the Act was the creation of the concept of the "federal interest computer." Under the Commerce Clause of Article 8 of the U.S. Constitution, the government has the right to regulate commerce between or among the several states. The government exercised this power to make it a crime if an unauthorized act occurred with a "federal interest computer," the definition of which includes one of two or more computers not in the same state, even if the computers and data accessed were not owned by, or related to, the government. This means that, for the first time, unauthorized access to virtually any Internet connected computer could be a federal crime.

It became illegal if someone knowingly or intentionally, and without authorization, attempted to:

1. Obtain protected information relating to national defense or foreign relations;

2. Obtain financial information;

3. Access a government-related computer;

4. With the intent to defraud, access a federal interest computer and obtain anything of value;

5. Access a federal interest computer and alter, damage, or destroy information or prevent the authorized use of the computer or information, if the resulting loss is $1,000.00 or more or if the information relates to medical records;

6. Traffic in passwords with the intent to defraud.

Penalties for violation of the Act included fines as well as prison terms as long as 10 years. Prison terms could more than double for subsequent convictions, which is the result of amendments to the Act as contained in the National Information Infrastructure Protection Act of 1996.

Viruses and Worms

The term virus is often used generically to identify any harmful migrating computer program. However, more strictly defined, a worm is a program that travels from one computer to another, usually over a network, but does not attach itself to the operating system of the computer it infects. It replicates itself until the host computer runs out of memory or disk space. A Trojan horse is a piece of computer software that acts as if it has a benign purpose, but is actually performing an ulterior malicious command, such as erasing files. A virus insidiously attaches itself to the operating system of any computer it enters and can infect any other computer that uses files from the infected computer.

Intellectual Property

Intellectual property is something that the law recognizes as existing and capable of ownership, but which is not physical in its nature. The four common intellectual properties are patents, copyrights, trademarks, and trade secrets. Depending upon its purpose, function, and use, a computer software product can be or contain any combination of the four intellectual properties.

Necessity of the Act

To understand why the Act became necessary, one must study the then-current state of the computer industry. In 1965, Digital Equipment Corporation (DEC) introduced the Programmable Data Processor 8 (PDP-8), the first commercially successful mini-computer, which despite its name was large enough to require its own room and air conditioner. It was marketed to large enterprises, sparking a new era in business computing. In 1977, three mass-market personal computers opened up the consumer market: The Apple II, the Radio Shack TRS-80, and the Commodore PET. These computers were generally affordable but were purchased primarily by hobbyists for games and simple programming activities.

In 1981 the International Business Machines Corporation (IBM) introduced its personal computer—the IBM-PC, where PC stands for personal computer. Because of IBM's significant size and presence in the marketplace, it was uniquely able to mass-market and mass-produce personal computer hardware and software at a reasonable price. IBM had earned a reputation in the business community for traditional business machines, and other businesses became comfortable following IBM's lead in the new industry. From a technical perspective, and quite importantly, IBM allowed other companies to create products such as software, modems, and printers that would work with IBM personal computers. This was sometimes called an open architecture and provided consistent and predictable standards required by the business community. Apple Computer, by comparison, did not have an open architecture for its computer hardware. By 1986, barely five years after the IBM-PC had been introduced, personal computers were being used for mainstream business purposes, and the computing power that had once been available to large businesses was now accessible to classrooms and homes, as well.

The Act Becomes Law

In the 1980s, because personal computers were so new, knowledge of computer programming techniques was primarily in the hands of people of high school and college age, who were the first to adopt and be formally trained in the new technology. As a result, for the first time, sophisticated computer systems containing sensitive economic, military, and other types of confidential information became uniquely vulnerable to the technological pranks, curiosities, and experiments of relatively young high school and college students. Existing laws were no longer adequate to address the trespassing and theft that could occur with the new technologies. For instance, using a computer, a person could now perform a million crimes in a split-second, take something that is valuable even if it is not tangible, perform the act without actually being there physically or leaving any tangible evidence, and perform the act on any other computer anywhere in the world.

It was time for the U.S. Congress to begin debating what would become known as intellectual property in the vast new virtual territory called cyberspace. The result was the U.S. Computer Fraud and Abuse Act of 1986, which continues to provide the foundation for prosecuting those whose actions breach the accepted standards of privacy and security in the world of electronic communication.

The Morris Worm

The first person convicted of violating the Federal Computer Fraud and Abuse Act of 1986 was Robert T. Morris (1965–), a Harvard graduate and graduate student in Cornell University's computer science doctor of philosophy (PhD) program. He was found guilty of distributing an Internet worm. Morris was working on a computer program to demonstrate security flaws on computer networks. On November 2, 1988, he anonymously released a self-replicating computer program, also known as a worm, on to the Internet from a computer he was authorized to use at the Massachusetts Institute of Technology. The worm, now often called the Morris worm, was not intended to interfere with normal computer operations. It consisted of two parts: a probe and a corpus. The probe attempted to penetrate computers through flaws in network security systems, and if successful, compiled itself on the host computer and then sent for its computer corpus, or pieces of a computer language or program that is encoded in a standardized way for open-ended retrieval tasks.

Despite the precautions Morris tried to build into the worm, which was not intended to cause malicious harm, as many as 6,000 computers (6 percent of all computers on the Internet at the time) were infected within hours of the worm's release, causing widespread computer failure. When Morris discovered what was happening, he sent an anonymous message over the Internet instructing programmers how to kill the worm. But, the Internet routes were so clogged by his worm replication that the message did not get through in enough time to be meaningful.

Despite much debate to determine whether Morris intended to cause harm, it was ultimately decided that he intended unauthorized access, and that was enough for a conviction under the Act. Morris was sentenced to three years of probation, fined $10,000 plus the costs of probation, and ordered to perform 400 hours of community service. U.S. Attorney Frederick J. Scullin, Jr. commented: "Among other things, the *Morris* case should put the would-be hacker on notice that the Department of Justice will seek severe penalties against future computer criminals, whether or not they are motivated by a venal or malicious intent."

As of October 2012, the Act has been amended in 1989, 1994, 1996, and 2001, by the Patriot Act of 2002 (which is a shortened form for Uniting and Strengthening America by Providing Appropriate Tools Required to Intercept and Obstruct Terrorism Act of 2001), and in 2008, by the Identity Theft Enforcement and Restitution Act of 2007.

 See also **Association of Computing Machinery • Security**

Resources

Books

Computer Fraud and Abuse Act, P.L. 98–473, Title II, Section 2102, 98 Stat. 2190, October 12, 1984, as amended by P.L. 99–474, 100 Stat. 1213, October 16, 1986; 18 U.S.C. Chapter 47, Section 1030.

Probe and Corpus

A probe is a computer program that operates on its own but is intended to operate with another (generally a larger and principal) computer program, and the purpose of which is to perform some preliminary inquisitive technical matter and report the result thereof to the other principal computer program with which it operates. The corpus is the principal portion of a computer program (or group of computer programs intended to operate together) that may or may not be capable of operating in a self-sufficient manner, but usually intended to operate in conjunction with a probe or other minor computer software product.

Cyber Crime: Updating the Computer Fraud and Abuse Act to Protect Cyber Space and Combat Emerging Threats (Hearing before the Committee on the Judiciary, United States Senate, One Hundred Twelfth Congress, First Session, September 7, 2011). Washington, DC: U.S. GPO, 2011.

Dumortier, Jos. *CCH International Encyclopaedia of Laws: Cyber Law.* St. Paul, MN: Thomson/West, 2009.

Dunne, Robert. *Computers and the Law: An Introduction to Basic Legal Principles and Their Application in Cyberspace.* Cambridge: Cambridge University Press, 2009.

Web Sites

Department of Computer Science, North Carolina State University and Edward F. Gehringer. "Morris Worm." http://ethics.csc.ncsu.edu/abuse/wvt/worm/ (accessed October 1, 2012).

Internet Law Treatise. "Computer Fraud and Abuse Act (CFAA)." http://ilt.eff.org/index.php/Computer_Fraud_and_Abuse_Act_(CFAA) (accessed October 1, 2012).

Computer Scientists

The title computer scientist encompasses a variety of jobs in which people work to design computers and to discover new applications for them. Their work often involves using theory, research, and scientific concepts to solve problems. A strong background in computer science, mathematics, or a similar scientific area is necessary to work in the field.

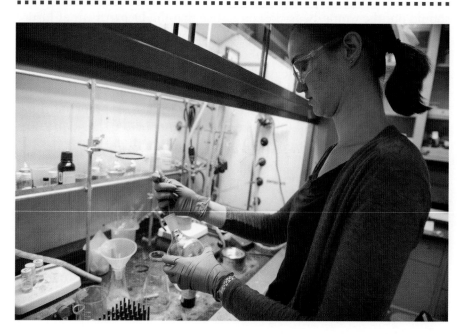

A research scientist for IBM Research works in the lab at the IBM Research - Almaden in San Jose, California.
© *David Paul Morris/Bloomberg via Getty Images.*

Computer usage has expanded dramatically due to the development of the Internet, faster processors, cheaper prices, and better user interfaces. As a result, computers can be found in homes, companies, and educational institutions. They are used for business, scientific, and artistic applications. These applications have become increasingly complex, requiring sophisticated software and very fast processors. Computer scientists create the software and hardware products and concepts that fuel this technological progress.

Some computer scientists choose to work with hardware and explore new chip designs or design and build internal components that make computers work faster and more efficiently. Other computer scientists may specialize in creating new programming languages and writing software that expands the way people use computers. Because the process of creating software has become more complex, there is also a need for computer scientists to create better software development tools to assist programmers in writing error-free computer code.

Today, computers are linked so that they can communicate with each other. These networks of computers may be small and occupy an office building, or they may be very large, as the Internet is. Computer scientists develop and test new methods for designing networks and improving the speed of transmitting data, voice, images, and video. Wireless networks similar to the ones used to provide cellular telephone communication have increased in popularity; their widespread use presents many technical challenges for computer scientists.

As computers become more powerful, computer scientists look for ways to help people interact with them more easily. Research is being done to increase the ability of computers to respond to voice commands as well as keyboard commands. This is a demanding task for computers and the effort requires computer scientists with specialized backgrounds in mathematics, software engineering, linguistics, and hardware design. An area of research growing in importance is how to efficiently make use of the growing number of processors within modern computers. Since its introduction, the desktop computer has traditionally had one processor. This has ceased to be the norm, with new processors bundling multiple cores into one chip. Given the tradition of a single processor, most computer scientists have been trained on how to program a computer with a single processor. Making efficient use of multiple processors is not always as simple as just running multiple programs to keep each processor busy. Some computer scientists are exploring how to design tools which will help parallelize programs such that a single program can make use of multiple processors.

Robotics* is another area in which computer scientists conduct research. Robots have a variety of uses in industrial, manufacturing, and medical areas. Robots present special challenges since they integrate computer technology with mechanical movement. Computer scientists specializing in robotics usually work in teams with professionals who have expertise in engineering and physics.

Knowledgeable professionals are also needed to help computer users learn to operate and work effectively with various hardware and software,

*robotics the science and engineering of building electromechanical machines that aim to serve as replacements for human laborers

Common Bond

Computer scientists may work in different areas. However, they all work with scientific theory to solve complex computer problems with new and innovative techniques.

and also to help workers solve problems that arise. In this consulting capacity, computer scientists play an important role.

There are many other areas, including database design, information retrieval, simulation, and modeling, in which computer scientists perform research and develop their ideas into product prototypes.

Education, Skills, and Job Outlook

Computer research scientists generally need to have a college degree and in most cases they also need an advanced degree due to the complexity of their work. They need to think logically and apply scientific theory to real world problems. Hardware and software designers who work on discovering new ways to use computers must be creative and possess an innovative style of thinking. Computer scientists often work as part of a team, so they need good communication skills. Because the field of computer science changes rapidly, computer scientists are always updating their skills and staying abreast of new developments. They read scientific journals, attend conferences, and enroll in professional development classes.

A strong demand exists for computer scientists because computer usage is increasingly common at home, at work, and at school. Computer scientists can work at universities, companies, or research centers. They spend a large amount of time working with the computer and may work in an office or a laboratory. Because they need to stay current with changes in technology, they may find their jobs require some travel to attend conferences, trade shows, and training seminars.

 See also **Association of Computing Machinery • Institute of Electrical and Electronics Engineers (IEEE) • National Aeronautics and Space Administration (NASA) • Robotics**

Resources

Books

Farr, J. Michael. *Top 100 Computer and Technical Careers: Your Complete Guidebook to Major Jobs in Many Fields at All Training Levels.* 4th ed. JIST's top careers series. Indianapolis, IN: JIST Publishing, 2009.

Henderson, Harry. *Career Opportunities in Computers and Cyberspace.* 2nd ed. New York: Checkmark Books, 2004.

Knee, Michael. *Computer Science and Computing: A Guide to the Literature.* Westport, CT: Libraries Unlimited, 2006.

Shannon, Susan, ed. *Leading-Edge Computer Science Research.* New York: Nova Science, 2006.

Tucker, Allen B. *Computer Science Handbook.* 2nd ed. Boca Raton, FL: Chapman & Hall/CRC, 2004.

Wyckoff, Claire. *Computers and Information Technology.* New York, NY: Ferguson, 2008.

Digital Computing

Digital computing, which encompasses the system of the ancient abacus in modern computers and calculators, enables people to perform complicated functions and calculations quickly and with great precision. There are two basic data transfer and communication systems in computing technology—digital and analog. Analog systems have continuous input and output of data, while digital systems manipulate information in discrete chunks. Although digital devices can use any numeric system to manipulate data, they currently only use the binary number system, consisting of ones and zeros. Information of all types, including characters and decimal numbers, are encoded in the binary number system before being processed by digital devices. In mixed systems, where sensors may deliver information to a digital computer in analog form, such as a voltage, the data have to be transformed from an analog to digital representation (usually binary also).

The chief difference between digital and analog devices is related to accuracy and speed. Since encoding is generally necessary for digital systems, it is not possible to exactly represent things like data from sensors*, oscilloscopes, and other instruments. The information is numeric, but changes constantly. Therefore, what goes into a digital computer is an approximation. An example is the use of floating-point arithmetic to process large numbers in digital devices. Conversion from their complete form to floating-point representation (which is usually some power of ten) may result in some inaccuracy as a few figures of the least significant digits may be lost in trying to fit the mantissa (or fraction part) in the registers of a digital device. When floating-point numbers are used in calculations, the inherent errors in each succeeding step grow larger. As for speed, digital devices work on the coded representations of reality, rather than the analog model, which works from reality. This makes digital devices inherently slower due to the conversions and discrete nature of the calculations involved.

Analog devices can work on a continuous flow of input, whereas digital devices must explicitly sample the data coming in. Determination of this sample rate is an important decision affecting the accuracy and speed of real-time systems. One thing that digital computers do more easily is to include the evaluation of logical relationships. Digital computers use Boolean arithmetic and logic. The logical decisions of computers are probably as important as their numerical calculations.

The first instance of digital computing was the abacus*. In fact, the word "digital" may originate from the "digits" of the hand that is used to manipulate the counters of the abacus, although the name may also have come from the tradition of finger counting that pre-dated it. The origins of the abacus are too ancient to have been recorded, but it made its appearance in China c. AD 1200 and other parts of East Asia within a few hundred years. The abacus is not just a toy. Evidence of this was clearly presented when a Japanese arithmetic specialist, using an abacus,

* **sensors** devices that can record and transmit data regarding the altitude, flight path, attitude, etc., so that they can enter into the system's calculations

* **abacus** an ancient counting device that probably originated in Babylon around 2,400 B.C.E.

beat a U.S. Army soldier, who was using an electrical calculator, in a series of calculations in 1946. The abacus is digital, with five ones on one side of each post, and a five on the other side, the posts being the tens columns.

In 1642 French mathematician and philosopher Blaise Pascal (1623–1662) built a machine that was decimal in nature. Each dial of his calculator represented a power of ten. Each tooth of the gears represented a one. He also invented an ingenious carry mechanism, moving beyond the abacus, which required "carry overs" to be done mentally.

The first digital computer of the modern sort was the programmable calculator designed, but never built, by British mathematician Charles Babbage (1791–1871). This Analytical Engine* used base-10* numbers, with each digit a power of ten and represented by a gear tooth. When the first electronic computers appeared in the late 1930s and 1940s, some utilized the binary number system to perform calculations, while others used the decimal number system.

The machine built by American physicist John Vincent Atanasoff (1903–1995) and his graduate student Clifford E. Berry (1918–1963) in the late 1930s could only solve a restricted class of problems, but it used digital circuits in base-2.*

The Electronic Numerical Integrator and Computer (ENIAC), designed by American engineers J. Presper Eckert (1919–1995) and John W. Mauchly (1907–1980), is considered the first general purpose, electronic digital computer. It used base ten to represent and calculate numbers, thereby simplifying its input and output interfaces. The first truly practical programmable digital computer, the Electronic Delay Storage Automatic Calculator (EDSAC), designed by Maurice V. Wilkes (1913–) in Cambridge, England, in 1949, used binary representation. Since then, all digital devices of any practicality have been binary at the machine level, and octal (base 8) or hexadecimal (base 16) at a higher level of abstraction.

Digital computers are forgiven their small inaccuracies because of their speed. Consider, for instance, the integral calculation used in figuring out the area under a curve. The digital solution is to "draw" a large number of rectangles below the curve approximating its height. Each of these rectangles has tiny lines representing two sides—the larger the number of rectangles, the smaller the lines. These tiny lines approximate the curved line at many points, so if one adds up the areas of each rectangle, he obtains an estimate of the integral. The faster the machine, the more rectangles one can program it to create, and the more accurate the calculation.

There is also a time lag inherent in analog-to-digital conversion and vice versa. Many aircraft flight control systems have sensors that generate analog signals. For instance, one might transmit a voltage, the magnitude of which is indicative of some important parameter related to the aircraft's flight, such as airspeed. The magnitude of the voltage (which is representative of airspeed) is then converted to a number in digital form, which can then be processed by the (digital) flight computer. Conversions occur in the opposite manner: digital outputs from the flight computer are converted into analog signals in order to command mechanical components such as actuators and stepper motors, which in turn control the flight characteristics of the aircraft. These flight control systems can typically calculate new values fifty times a second.

The speed improvements in digital computers became common when the entire processor was integrated on one chip. Data transfers between the components on the chip are quite fast due to the small distances between them. Analog-to-digital and digital-to-analog converters can also be chip-based, avoiding the need for any speedup.

Digital computers are made of up to more than 1,000 of these processors working in parallel. This makes possible the very fast processing speeds that are the chief strength of digital computers. High processing speeds enable them to accomplish tasks that are impossible for humans. At first, digital computers performed calculations faster, if not better, than people. Then computers controlled other devices, some digital themselves, some analog, almost certainly better than people could. Finally, the greatly increased speed processing power of modern digital computers perform extremely complicated calculations and functions, such as the modeling of wind flowing over a wing, the first microseconds of a thermonuclear explosion, or the deciphering of a supposedly unbreakable code.

 See also **Abacus • Analog Computing • Binary Number System**

Resources

Books

Givant, Steven R., and Paul R. Halmos. *Introduction to Boolean Algebras.* New York: Springer, 2009.

Pelgrom, Marcel J. M. *Analog-to-Digital Conversion* New York: Springer Publishing, 2010.

Speed Over Accuracy

Digital computers are actually less accurate than the older analog machines because they deal in larger numbers of approximations over the range of a problem while analog computers model reality continuously. However, modern electronic digital machines can perform calculations so quickly, consume such low power, and can take up such little space (as compared to the first digital computers), that they have nearly taken over all tasks requiring machine-based computation, decision-making, and control functions.

E

Early Computers

The development of the computer industry began with a demand for computing power before and during World War II. Wartime computing was a means to a very specific and urgent end. Between 1935 and 1945 there was a great need for ballistics* computations and other statistical work in support of military efforts; this was time-consuming work carried out by people using rudimentary calculators. During this time, there was a rush to invent single-purpose digital computing machines to speed up the calculation of the problems, firing tables, and code-breaking calculations. Governmental organizations, industrial companies, and office machine companies in the United States, Great Britain, and Germany created several such machines.

Differential Analyzer

Although there were a number of calculators available for business use in the 1920s, they were not powerful enough to solve scientific computational problems. The first serious attempt at building a computer for scientists was made by Vannevar Bush (1890–1974), an engineer at Massachusetts Institute of Technology (MIT). In the 1930s, Bush and one of his students, Harold Locke Hazen, built an analog* computer called the "differential analyzer." It was a collection of gears, shafts, and wires. It was better than the calculators of the time, but it was still slow and cumbersome, often needing two or three days of set-up time before it could solve a problem.

A faster and more accurate differential analyzer was built in 1935, but it, too, required adjustments with screwdrivers and hammers to prepare it for a run. It weighed 110 metric tons (200,000 pounds), had 2,000 vacuum tubes* and several thousand relays, took up several hundred square feet (where one square meter equals about 10.8 square feet), and had about 150 motors and 322 kilometers (200 miles) of wires. Duplicates of the differential analyzer were set up at the U.S. Army's Ballistics Research Laboratory and at the Moore School of Electrical Engineering, at the University of Pennsylvania.

Bell Telephone Laboratories Model 1

Other computing devices were being built to serve purposes beyond what the differential analyzer was designed to do. The telephone company needed computing power to help set up telephone connections. At that time, when a rotary telephone was dialed, a number was transmitted to a

* **ballistics** the science and engineering of the motion of projectiles of various types, including bullets, bombs, and rockets

* **analog** a quantity (often an electrical signal) that is continuous in time and amplitude

* **vacuum tube** an electronic device constructed of a sealed glass tube containing metal elements in a vacuum; used to control electrical signals

* binary number system a number system in which each place represents a power of 2 larger than the place on its right (base-2)

machine that converted each digit to a four-pulse code. This was not fast enough for telephone switching demands, so Bell Telephone Laboratories engineers and scientists, including American engineer George R. Stibitz (1904–1995), began studying the binary number system*. Stibitz felt that the binary system would be suited for the computation since a relay, called a flip-flop, had been developed. The relay could detect the presence or absence of a current (a binary system).

Stibitz built his "Complex Number Computer" in 1937. It converted decimal digits to binary, then converted them back to decimal for the answers. Push buttons were used to make it easier to operate, and in October 1939 it was sent to Bell Labs' New York office under the name of "Model 1."

The Model 1 may have been the world's first time-sharing computer, because several departments from Bell Labs accessed it remotely, with teletype machines. It may also have been the first remote job-entry computer. Mathematicians at Dartmouth College, in New Hampshire, accessed it through a teleprinter to submit problems to the computer in New York City. The answers came back on a telephone line hook-up in about one minute.

Harvard Mark I

In 1937 American mathematician Howard H. Aiken (1900–1973), then a Harvard graduate student, proposed building a machine based on the work of early computer researchers Charles Babbage and Herman Hollerith. He intended it to be an electromechanical Analytical Engine (an acknowledgement of Babbage's proposed—but never completed—Analytical Engine). The project was called the IBM Automatic Sequence Controlled Calculator (ASCC), or the Harvard Mark I. It was begun in 1939, and like the vast majority of the other computers of its day, it was huge. The Mark I was 15.2 meters (50 feet) long and 2.4 meters (8 feet) tall. Many of its 800,000 components were taken from IBM punched-card machines. It had 805 kilometers (500 miles) of wire, required an enormous amount of energy to run, and weighed about 4.5 metric tons (10,000 pounds). Every day, tons of ice were required to keep the machine cool.

Mark I's memory had 72 adding registers made of 24 wheels each, and 60 special purpose registers using manual switches. The registers held 23-digit numbers plus the computational sign. Electric contacts were used to sense the number from the wheels. Clutches were used to transfer the number to another wheel for the calculation. Addition could be done in three-tenths of a second, multiplication in five seconds, and division in 11 seconds.

The machine input came from paper tape. Data was punched on three tapes and instructions on a fourth. It used two electric typewriters for output. There was no keyboard, and it was set up for a run by adjusting 1,400 switches. The Mark I computer was presented to Harvard in 1945. IBM had financed the research and construction costs of approximately half a million dollars. The Harvard Mark I was the first fully automatic

* **capacitor** a fundamental electrical component used for storing an electrical charge

* **Bakelite** an insulating material used in synthetic goods, including plastics and resins

computer to come into operation. It was already obsolete, however, as scientists and engineers would soon replace the electromechanical components with fully electronic models.

The Z1 in Germany

While Aiken was working on his computers at Harvard, a young engineering student in Germany was also thinking of computing machines that could perform long series of calculations. This person was German inventor Konrad Zuse (1910–1995), who decided on a design similar to Babbage's Analytical Engine, consisting of a storage unit, an arithmetic unit, and a control unit. The control unit would be directed by punched tape to deliver instructions to a selection mechanism, which connected the storage and arithmetic units.

Zuse decided to make it a binary device with a mechanical memory unit, using movable pins in slots to indicate zeroes and ones. This resulted in a compact memory that used only about 0.8 cubic meters (27 cubic feet), which was connected to a crude mechanical calculating unit. The machine was called the Z1 and was produced in 1938.

In 1941, Zuse completed the Z3. It had 2,000 relays and could multiply and divide, as well as extract square roots, in only three seconds. It was a compact machine that acted under program control. Push buttons were used on the control panel. One could push a button to convert decimal numbers into binary and then push again to convert them back. The Z3 was destroyed when an Allied bomb fell on Zuse's apartment building in 1944. The fundamental conceptual components of Zuse's Z-machines—such as the use of a storage unit, an arithmetic unit, and a control unit—were not too different from those employed by microcomputers in use today.

Atanasoff-Berry Computer (ABC)

In 1939, John Vincent Atanasoff (1903–1995), a mathematician and physicist at Iowa State College (now Iowa State University), and a graduate student he recruited, Clifford Berry (1918–1963), began working on the machine that would be called the ABC (Atanasoff-Berry Computer). It used a binary number system and would use electronic technology. Numbers were stored on electric capacitors* on two Bakelite* drums and were read off as the drums rotated. Each drum could store 30 binary numbers of up to 50 binary digits.

Data were input through punched cards in decimal, five 15-digit numbers and a sign. This was converted to binary before doing the calculations. The computer was manually operated, with an operator pushing a button to show where the numbers should go, then putting a card in a holder and activating it by closing a contact. The card was read by rows of brushes, similar to the card readers developed later for computer use. To store intermediate results, Atanasoff designed a system to burn the cards with electric sparks. The burnt areas had less resistance than the rest of the card, so the numbers could be read by applying electric current to the card and reading the voltage.

The memory was to be bigger than the 300 bits available on commercial calculating machines, so they needed units that would be cheaper and smaller than vacuum tubes. Their choice was paper electrical condensers, which looked like miniature cigarettes. A memory built of condensers would have saved money but would have required recharging from time to time. Atanasoff developed a procedure for recharging that he called "jogging." The computer's memory would be regularly "jogged" by the computer by resetting the data as they were read out. This was similar to a person "jogging" his or her own memory by repeating some phrase or word. The concept of "jogging" influenced the design of later computers built after World War II.

The prototype of the ABC contained what Atanasoff called an "abacus," a plastic disc mounted on a shaft turned by an electric motor. Each side of the disc had 25 condensers arranged as spokes on a wheel, which gave it the capacity of 25 binary digits. It proved to Atanasoff and Berry that an electronic machine using binary numbers with a condenser memory was possible. It also showed that the "jogging" technique was feasible. However, Atanasoff and Berry were unable to complete the ABC as their work was interrupted by World War II.

Developments in Great Britain

As the Germans advanced across Europe during the first phase of World War II, a team of scientists and engineers came together in a mansion north of London at the Government Code and Cipher School. Their goal was to design machines that would break the codes generated by the Enigma, the cryptographic* machine that the Germans used to encode and send messages.

The German Enigma used two typewriters. The original message was typed on one machine, a key was selected for encoding, and the coded message was automatically typed on the other electric machine. Every message could be sent with a different key, giving about a trillion possible code combinations. The key was changed three times a day, to make it more difficult to break the code.

British mathematician Alan Turing (1912–1954), one of the scientists on the project, developed an algorithm* to sift through all the possible combinations and find the key. This was implemented on a special purpose computer called the Bombe. It was an electromechanical relay machine with wheels similar to those of the Enigma. Its goal was to work out the solution of the cipher as quickly and accurately as possible. It did not decode the messages, but found the key. The messages were then decoded by people. The Bombe, of which there were several individual machines, is credited with saving many lives during World War II.

When the Germans replaced the Enigma with a more sophisticated machine, known to the British as Fish, the British also attempted to build a better machine. The result was the Heath Robinson, an electronic machine using vacuum tubes. The Heath Robinson was named after a British cartoonist whose drawings of far-fetched machines were well known. For input, Heath Robinson used two synchronized photoelectric paper tape readers that could read 2,000 characters per second. This is the equivalent of a 300-page book being read in just over five minutes. Its output was a primitive printer that could print 15 characters per second. An adder carried out binary calculations used to break the codes of the German machine. It proved how fast and powerful electronic computing could be, but it still could not keep up with the demands being placed on it.

This led to the development of Colossus. The Colossus is considered to be an electronic computer, but it was a special purpose computer, unsuited for anything else other than deciphering codes. It was completed in December 1943. It had 1,800 vacuum tubes that counted and compared numbers and performed simple arithmetic calculations. It was fed information on paper tape at a rate of 5,000 characters per second, more than twice the rate of the Heath Robinson. It had no internal memory, but the users adjusted its operation as it came close to deciphering a message. The program was fed into it by an array of switches and phone jacks. Data were entered separately on tape.

Yet 5,000 characters per second was still not fast enough, so several machines were used in parallel, which today is called parallel processing. The parallel processing machine, of which there are different types, speeds up computing by performing tasks together, in parallel, instead of doing them sequentially.

Colossus had five different processors working in parallel. Each processor read a tape at 5,000 characters per second, so the total was 25,000 characters per second. This was made possible by the addition of shift registers, which allowed Colossus to read the tapes in parallel, and an internal clock that kept the parts of the machine working in synch. It was the best code breaker of its day.

Electronic Numerical Integrator and Computer (ENIAC)

John Mauchly (1907–1980), an American meteorologist interested in doing weather calculations, set out to build an inexpensive digital computer. He wanted to replace the calculators that were not fast enough for his needs. In 1941, he discussed his ideas with American engineer J. Presper Eckert (1919–1995) and in April 1943, the Moore School of Engineering received a contract from the Ballistics Research Laboratories to build a computer to calculate shell (munitions) trajectories. Mauchly and Eckert started work on the Electronic Numerical Integrator and Computer (ENIAC).

ENIAC had 18,000 vacuum tubes, 70,000 resistors, 10,000 capacitors, 6,000 switches, and 1,500 relays. It took up 162 square meters (1,800 square feet) and weighed 30 short tons (60,000 pounds; or about 27 metric tons). It required 160 kilowatts of power and was 30.5 meters (100 feet) long, 3.1 meters (10 feet) high and 0.9 meters (3 feet) deep. It required two great 20-horsepower blowers to cool it. It generated 150 kilowatts of heat and its cost was more than $486,000.

Demonstrations of Computing Power

To make sure that the ENIAC gave the correct answers, two women were employed to work out a problem, using desk calculators, over a year's time. ENIAC solved the problem in an hour. At its dedication ceremony, it computed an artillery shell's trajectory in 20 seconds. It took the shell 30 seconds to reach the target in real life.

ENIAC was 500 times faster than the Harvard Mark I and could perform 5,000 operations per second. It did an addition in two-tenths of a millisecond*, a multiplication in 2.8 milliseconds, and a division in 24 milliseconds, which was extraordinary for that time.

ENIAC was a decimal machine working with numbers up to 20 digits long. The numbers were sent to the central processing unit by a transmitter made of relays connected to an IBM card reader. They were fed through the card reader at 125 cards per minute. Earlier machines, like the Harvard Mark I, were programmed with punched cards or paper tape so the program could be changed easily. This worked because their computational speed, being electromechanical, matched that of the paper tape readers and card readers. However, ENIAC's speed of 5,000 operations per second outstripped that of the card and tape readers. For that reason, Mauchly and Eckert decided to wire the machine specifically for each problem. This was similar to the plug boards used in electronic business machines or punched card equipment.

Each of ENIAC's problems was set up on a plug board similar to that used by punched card machines. If the program was complicated, it could take several days to set up. The later idea of creating a computer that could use a stored program came from this time-consuming effort. ENIAC became operational in November 1945, too late to help with the war effort, but it was a model for computers to come. It was highly regarded for its simplicity and carefully planning. The ENIAC was dismantled in October 1955.

Electronic Discrete Variable Automatic Computer (EDVAC)

When Hungarian mathematician John von Neumann (1903–1957) was told of the work on the ENIAC, he arranged to become a consultant to the project. He played a key role in the design of the subsequent EDVAC, starting in 1944. This new machine was to remember its instructions in an internal memory. This would remove the need to plug and unplug and replug, as in the ENIAC. The instructions could be changed internally.

EDVAC was given delay-line storage instead of vacuum tubes. The delay lines used the binary number system. With 1,024 bits, which was their capacity, they could be used to store data consisting of 32 words, with each word encoded using 32 bits (32 words multiplied by 32 bits per word yields the total storage capacity of 1,024 bits). It was estimated that the EDVAC would require between 2,000 and 8,000 words of data storage, necessitating between 64 and 256 delay lines. This was a large amount of equipment, but it was still smaller than the ENIAC. When completed in 1951, the EDVAC had some 3,500 vacuum tubes, but its importance lies in the fact that it embodied the stored-program concept and the "von Neumann machine," two ideas that would greatly influence the design of computers. The stored-program computer is still in use today. A stored-program computer allows the instructions to be fed in with the data. Earlier computers, such as the Bell Labs Model 5 and Heath Robinson, had separate tapes for the data and the instructions.

A von Neumann machine is the model on which most machines are built today. It executes the instructions sequentially, as opposed to a parallel processor, which supports multiple operations at the same time. EDVAC became operational at the end of 1951 and was active until 1962. Its separate components—memory, central control, arithmetic unit, and input and output—were introduced by von Neumann.

Manchester Mark I and Electronic Delay Storage Automatic Calculator (EDSAC)

After security was lifted from the ENIAC project, the dean of the Moore School organized a summer school to make sure that those outside of the project would know of its results. The lectures took place in July and August of 1946. They attracted many of the leading scientists of the day. Among them were British computer scientists, including Maurice V. Wilkes.

ENIAC was explained in detail during the lectures, but the EDVAC was not discussed since it was still a classified project. In retrospect, one can see the connection between these lectures and various projects carried out by the governments, universities, and industrial laboratories in Great Britain and the United States. Great Britain was the only European country not so devastated by the war that it could carry out a computer project.

British mathematician Max Newman (1897–1984), one of the researchers of the Colossus computer, launched the computer project at Manchester University in England. One of his university colleagues, British engineer Sir Frederic Williams (1911–1977), developed a memory system based on the cathode ray tube (CRT)*. A primitive machine using this memory was developed in 1947, but it did not have input or output devices. The program was entered using push buttons; the results were read from the tubes. Williams' project prevailed over Newman's original plans. The university's Manchester Mark I was completed in 1948, incorporating the stored-program concept. It proved that the idea was achievable. It stored 128 40-bit words on the tubes and had additional memory in the form of magnetic drums.

Inspired by the Moore School lectures, Cambridge University professor Maurice V. Wilkes (1913–) started work on a stored-program computer. By February 1947 he had built a successful delay line storage that could store bit patterns for long periods of time. Encouraged by this, he went on to construct the full machine. Despite the short supply of electronic components in postwar Britain, the Electronic Delay Storage Automatic Calculator (EDSAC) began to take shape. Its control and arithmetic units were stored in three long racks, each 1.8 meters (6 feet) tall. The vacuum tubes were exposed to keep them from overheating. Input was a tape reader, output was on a teleprinter, and the programs were punched on telegraph tape.

Pioneering Computer Software

On May 1949, before EDVAC was completed, a slim ribbon of paper containing the instructions to compute the squares of integers was fed into it. Thirty seconds later it began to print the numbers 1, 4, 9, 16, 25… The first program in a stored-program computer had been born.

* **cathode ray tube (CRT)** a glass enclosure that projects images by directing a beam of electrons onto the back of a screen

De-Bugging the System

The Mark I's successor, Mark II, was run without air-conditioning in a room with open windows. One hot summer day in 1945, the Mark II stopped. Grace Hopper (1906–1992) and her coworkers investigated and found that the source of the trouble was a moth that had been killed by a relay closing. The dead moth was removed and the incident was recorded in the logbook. Before long, Aiken came in to ask whether they were "making any numbers"—which was his phrase for computing. His team explained that they were "debugging" the Mark II. The word "bug" had been in existence for more than a century to describe mechanical system failures, appearing first in the writings of Thomas Edison, but this was allegedly the first use of "debugging" as a computing term.

Although EDSAC was very large—it had 3,000 tubes and consumed 30 kilowatts of electric power—it was smaller than the ENIAC and had one-sixth the tube count. It could perform an addition in 1.4 milliseconds, and its users developed one of the first assembly languages, as well as a library of programming procedures called subroutines.

Whirlwind

In the early 1950s, the United States and the Soviet Union were engaged in the Cold War. MIT engineers were working on a computer to help the U.S. military with its computational needs. After considering an analog machine, it was finally decided that the machine would be digital, and would require a large memory to store the information needed to control an aircraft trainer, a "real-time" exercise. The requirements of the memory were beyond the capabilities of the CRTs and delay-lines of the day.

Jay Wright Forrester (1918–), an engineer working on the project, thought of alternative designs. He eventually settled on a three-dimensional design, the "core memory." He also experimented with different media from which to construct the memory. He tried rolled-up bits of magnetic tape, then he tried iron-bearing ceramics that were molded in the shape of tiny rings and mounted on grids. These became the magnetic "cores" of the powerful computer that would be named Whirlwind. The Whirlwind began working in 1951. It helped to coordinate New England military radar units in scanning the skies for Soviet planes during the Cold War.

Two decades after Whirlwind debuted, times had changed. At the time of Aiken and his colleagues, there were only a handful of computer designers and engineers, and most knew each other. By the 1960s and 1970s, the field was replete with practitioners, enough to populate a small city, and the pioneer computers seemed almost forgotten.

 See also **Babbage, Charles • Digital Computing • Early Pioneers • Memory • Vacuum Tubes**

Resources

Books

Campbell-Kelly, Martin, and William Aspray. *Computer: A History of the Information Machine.* 2nd ed. New York: Westview Press, 2004.

Lavington, Simon H. *Moving Targets: Elliott-Automation and the Dawn of the Computer Age in Britain, 1947–67.* London and New York: Springer, 2011.

Web Sites

Bletchley Park. "The History of Bletchley Park." http://www.bletchleypark. org.uk/content/hist/history.rhtm (accessed November 1, 2012).

ENIAC at the U.S. Army Research Lab. "History of Computing Information." http://ftp.arl.army.mil/%7Emike/comphist/ (accessed November 1, 2012).

Early Pioneers

The evolution of computer technology between 1930 and 1950 was strongly influenced first by mathematical theoreticians and then by military needs during World War II. During this twenty-year span, the early pioneers of modern computer science found ways to create machines that harnessed the power of electronics, moving beyond strictly mechanical computational devices and laying the foundation for the transistor-based computers that would follow in the 1950s and 1960s.

Conceptual Foundations

In 1931, electrical engineer Vannevar Bush (1890–1974) designed a mechanical calculator that solved complex differential equations. Although its gears and other moving and stationary parts made the machine difficult to use, Bush's invention was considered significant in mathematical circles because mathematicians and scientists could use it to solve equations long thought to be virtually unsolvable. Bush's greater contribution to modern computer science came in 1945 with the publication of an article that described a conceptual device for linking and accessing information that he called a memex*. His device was never built, but the ideas underlying his concept later influenced the developers of what is now known as hypertext.

In the 1930s, British mathematician and cryptographer Alan Turing (1912–1954) developed the concept of a mechanical machine by which mathematical statements could be either proved or disproved. Although the Turing Machine was a concept, rather than a device, Turing's principles were part of the foundation upon which early mechanical computational devices were designed. In addition, his work toward speeding up the process of breaking German military codes during World War II was influential in the development of the Colossus (1943), a code-breaking computer that is the first known programmable logic calculator to use electronic valve technology (i.e., vacuum tubes). Whereas the Colossus was significant in the Allied war effort, it did not have as much influence on the development of computer science because it was designed for a single purpose and its existence was kept secret as classified military information until 1975.

During the 1940s, the mathematical and theoretical work that would later be incorporated into modern computer technology was overshadowed by focused efforts to create machines designed for specific military purposes. Just as there was a wartime need to increase the code-breaking capabilities of the Allied military forces, there was an urgent need for the accurate creation of artillery firing charts. This was a repetitive task performed by large numbers of people using mechanical computing devices not specifically designed for the purpose. The need to compile these essential military charts, which consisted of tabulated data such as firing angles, ranges, and so forth, quickly led to government-funded efforts to invent machine solutions to the problem. Scientists in the

* **memex** a device that can be used to store personal information, notes, and records that permits managed access at high speed; a hypothetical creation of Vannevar Bush

* **base-2** a number system in which each place represents a power of 2 larger than the place to its right (binary)

* **binary** existing in only two states, such as "on" or "off," "one" or "zero"

United States and Great Britain, who had already been studying various means of creating electromechanical computing devices, then turned their energies specifically toward devising one-of-a-kind machines to meet this need.

From Concepts to Machines

The computing devices developed between 1941 and 1951 represent the first generation of modern computer technology, and their inventors are considered the true early pioneers of computer science. The physical implementation of a variety of concepts by men such as Howard H. Aiken, John V. Atanasoff, John Presper Eckert, John W. Mauchly, and German engineer Konrad Zuse set the stage for the business computers built during the 1950s and 1960s.

Howard H. Aiken Working in partnership with IBM, Harvard engineer Howard H. Aiken (1900–1973) produced an electronic calculator for military use in 1944. The machine, which required 804 kilometers (500 miles) of internal wiring, was 15.2 meters (50 feet) long and 2.44 meters (8 feet) high. It was used by the U.S. Navy to calculate and create ballistics charts. The electro-mechanical computer, known as the Harvard Mark I, was controlled by a punched tape paper roll. Its mechanical parts responded to electromagnetic signals. The five-ton machine was slow and time-consuming to program, and its components were vulnerable to damage from the heat generated by the unit. Despite its drawbacks, however, the Harvard Mark I represented a significant point of development in computing technology.

Aiken was a graduate student at Harvard in 1937 when he first conceptualized a machine that would combine and implement the ideas of Charles Babbage (1791–1871) and Herman Hollerith (1860–1929). The development of the machine that would be known as the Mark I began in 1939. This electronic relay computer was followed in 1947 by an electronic computer known as the Mark II. Aiken also opened the Harvard Computational Laboratory in 1947, creating the world's first computer science academic program. He later founded a company, Aiken Industries, and continued to influence the development of computer electronics through research and writing.

John V. Atanasoff A mathematician at heart and an electrical engineer and theoretic physicist by education, John V. Atanasoff (1903–1995) began his career teaching mathematics and physics at Iowa State College in 1930. Fascinated by the prospect of finding ways to perform mathematical computations more quickly and accurately, Atanasoff studied the existing machines available for computation, and believed that they could be improved. Categorizing devices such as the Monroe calculator and the IBM tabulator as analog machines, Atanasoff envisioned an electronic, digital device based on base-2* numbers (the binary* system).

During the 1930s, Atanasoff worked with graduate student Clifford E. Berry (1918–1963) to design and build an electronic digital computer that would be introduced in 1939 as the Atanasoff-Berry Computer (ABC). This is widely considered to be the world's first all-electronic digital computing device. Atanasoff filed patent applications for his invention, but the process was slow. Before he could be granted patent protection for his work, and thus historic credit as the creator of the first machine of its kind, patents would be released for the ENIAC as the first electronic digital computer. Atanasoff, who was one of the first computer scientists to understand the potential of digital computing, went on to receive patents for 32 other inventions. Eventually, credit for his best known innovation would revert to him, as well.

J. Presper Eckert, Jr.   In November 1945, another pivotal computing device was put into use, although its presence was not announced publicly until February 1946. The Electronic Numerical Integrator and Computer (ENIAC) was designed to perform mathematical calculations for military purposes. It began to take shape in 1943 at the Moore School of Electrical Engineering at the University of Pennsylvania, in response to the U.S. Army's need for new ways to produce trajectory tables used for precision targeting of large artillery. As the chief engineer on the ENIAC project, J. Presper Eckert, Jr. (1919–1995) shared credit for the computer's success with the ENIAC's architect, John W. Mauchly (1907–1980). Although it was finished too late to contribute to the war effort, the ENIAC was used to design hydrogen bombs, predict weather, and provide calculations related to military-sponsored studies of wind tunnels, thermal ignition*, and other phenomena.

The ENIAC was 500 times faster than the Harvard Mark I computer. It cost a few hundred thousand dollars to develop, it weighed 30 short tons (60,000 pounds; or about 27 metric tons), and its dimensions were gargantuan (3.0 meters [10 feet] tall, 0.9 meters [3 feet] deep, 30.5 meters [100 feet] long). Even as the ENIAC was being built, Eckert began working on the problem of creating a stored-program computer, in part because the ENIAC, which had to be rewired for each computational task, proved to be limited by the lack of stored-program capabilities. The result of this next project would be known as the EDVAC (Electronic Discrete Variable Automatic Computer), which was completed in 1951, without the continued involvement of Eckert, who resigned from the Moore School in 1946. Eckert took out patent applications for more than 80 more electronic devices between 1948 and 1966. His pioneering work on the ENIAC and later computer developments earned him many awards, including the U.S. National Medal of Science in 1969.

John W. Mauchly   The ENIAC computer, from which the modern electronic computer is said to have evolved, was conceived by John W. Mauchly (1907–1980), a physicist at the Moore School of Electrical

* **thermal ignition** the combustion of a substance caused by heating it to the point that its particles have enough energy to commence burning without an externally applied flame

* **cathode ray tubes (CRTs)** glass enclosures that project images by directing a beam of electrons onto the back of a screen

Engineering, University of Pennsylvania. Mauchly and chief engineer John Presper Eckert gained notice for their creation of the first general-purpose computer that could perform 5,000 operations per second, a previously unimaginable speed.

During the early part of his career, Mauchly taught at Ursinis College near Philadelphia. After attending an electronics seminar at the Moore School, he ended up joining its staff. The U.S. Army's Ballistics Research Laboratory was familiar with earlier research Mauchly had performed involving the use of motors and vacuum tubes to design and build calculating equipment. In 1943 Mauchly was selected by the military to design a unit capable of writing programs to calculate the trajectories of artillery under multiple conditions. The result was the ENIAC computer, which was completed too late to be of use during World War II.

Although Mauchly and Eckert began collaborating on the EDVAC even as the ENIAC was still being built, they were both forced to resign from the Moore School before the EDVAC was operative due to their desire to be recognized in patent records as inventors of the ENIAC, which breached University of Pennsylvania protocol for patents. Mauchly continued to work with Eckert until 1959, during which time they established the first commercial computer company and built the Universal Automatic Computer (UNIVAC). Despite disputes over patent rights and the origin of certain computer design ideas, Mauchly can rightly be considered a major innovator in the development of practical computing machines designed for flexible use.

British Computer Pioneers

During the years preceding and during World War II, American and British mathematicians and engineers joined forces to support their countries' military efforts, seeking ways to automate such tasks as the compilation of artillery firing tables and the deciphering of enemy coded communications. Much of this work led to the post-war development of electronic computing devices. Manchester University in Manchester, England, was the site of one of these developments, which was known as the Manchester Mark I.

Manchester Mark I Following World War II, mathematician Maxwell Newman (1897–1984) joined Manchester University as professor of pure, rather than applied, mathematics. In 1946 he acquired funding and other resources to build a stored-program computer at the university specifically to investigate its use in the study of pure mathematics. His plan was similar to one being developed at Cambridge University by Maurice V. Wilkes (1913–2010).

At the same time, Freddie C. Williams (1911–1977), a professor in the electrical engineering department at Manchester University, was investigating the use of cathode ray tubes (CRTs)* for program storage. As the work of the Williams team progressed, Newman's team at Manchester encountered difficulties. Ultimately, Newman decided to suspend work on his computer, pending the results of Williams' efforts. By October of 1949, the Williams group had successfully demonstrated an operational version of the Manchester Mark I, a computing machine with true stored program functionality.

EDSAC At Cambridge University, meanwhile, Wilkes was working on a project known as the Electronic Delay Storage Automatic Calculator (EDSAC). In 1946, he studied electronic computer design at the Moore School of Electrical Engineering at the University of Pennsylvania, the home of ENIAC. Wilkes's research over the next few years resulted in the first operations stored-program computer; the EDSAC was introduced in May of 1949, barely five months before the Manchester Mark I was completed.

Konrad Zuse Although American and British mathematicians, physicists, and engineers are credited with many of the innovations in early computer design and manufacturing, German engineer Konrad Zuse (1910–1995) is also considered one of the early pioneers of modern computer science. By 1941, Zuse had designed and built what became known as the Z3, the world's first electromechanical digital computer controlled by programming. Unlike the British and American efforts that were heavily funded by Allied money, Zuse's work was largely independent of government control or interest.

Between 1936 and 1938, Zuse used recycled parts and donations from friends and family members to assemble his first computer, which he called the Z1. This was the world's first binary computer. It is significant that Zuse's innovations took place outside the mainstream of computer development then going on in other parts of the world. Drafted for military service in 1939, Zuse tried in vain to persuade the Nazi/German Army military establishment of the value of his inventions. When he was reassigned from active duty to work as a structural aircraft engineer, Zuse resumed his computer-building activities, incorporating telephone relays in the construction of the Z2 and electromagnetic relays in the Z3.

Zuse's model Z4 was the only one of his original inventions to survive the bombing of Germany during World War II. By the end of the war, Zuse and his family were refugees in southern Germany. Between 1945 and 1950, Zuse continued his research when it was possible, and in 1947 he jointly founded the Zuse Engineering Company to design and build computers for scientific and business applications. Over the next several decades, Zuse and his company began interacting with computer-development interests worldwide, and his early innovations received the recognition they deserved. He received numerous awards and honors for his contributions to the field of modern computer technology.

Early Computer Programmers

In 1945 the U.S. Army hired eighty mathematicians whose high security, top-secret work no one had performed before. All of them were women. Their job was to program the ENIAC to calculate artillery firing trajectories, in order to increase the accuracy of military war efforts.

An Unclear View of the Future

The early computer pioneers may have been dedicated to their work, but perhaps they had little idea how their inventions would revolutionize the worlds of business and communication. In 1947 Harvard engineer Howard H. Aiken, who is credited with producing two of the first electronic computing machines in the mid-1940s, was quoted as saying he believed that "the computing needs of the entire United States" could be met with no more than "six electronic digital computers."

Credit Where Credit Is Due

In 1940 John W. Mauchly met with John V. Atanasoff, who had recently introduced the Atanasoff-Berry Computer (ABC). Atanasoff demonstrated the ABC to Mauchly, who later implemented some of Atanasoff's ideas as he designed the ENIAC. Because Atanasoff's work had not yet been granted patent protection, the ENIAC received early recognition as the world's first electronic digital computer. Later on, Mauchly's reputation as a major contributor to the ENIAC's successor, EDVAC, would be undercut by the publication of a report by John von Neumann, who received credit for the design of the first stored-program computer.

Carpal Tunnel Syndrome

Ergonomic workstations are intended to relieve repetitive stress injuries that cause problems such as carpal tunnel syndrome (CTS), which causes pain, numbness, tingling, and loss of muscle control in the hands and wrists. Women are more likely to develop the problem than men, especially those who work as secretaries, keyboard users, or office assistants.

As the first wave of computer programmers, these women laid the foundation for all later computer programming. They had to become familiar with the mechanics of the ENIAC and then figure out how to give the computer directions to carry out specific actions. The women, many of whom had recently graduated from college as mathematics majors, were recruited because there was a scarcity of male mathematicians available.

In October of 1998, four of these pioneers—Jean Kathleen McNulty Mauchly Antonelli, Jean Jennings Bartik, Frances Snyder Holberton, and Marlyn Wescoff Meltzer—were honored by Women in Technology International for their contributions to the computer industry. At the ceremony, Antonelli pointed out that the capabilities of the ENIAC were considered more remarkable during its decade of operation than were the achievements of the women who programmed the machine to perform as it did. Holberton, who compared their wartime work to that of construction engineers, would later be among the programmers who helped develop the programming languages known as COBOL and FORTRAN.

Computer Pioneers, 1930–1950

As the 1940s drew to a close, the early pioneers of modern computing continued to pursue new avenues of research in the growing field of computer science. Other engineers made new contributions. In 1947 came the invention of the transistor, which replaced vacuum tube technology in the design of computers and revolutionized the computer and electronic communications industries. The inventors of the transistor, John Bardeen (1908–1991), William Shockley (1910–1989), and Walter Brattain (1902–1987), would jointly share the 1956 Nobel Prize in physics. Their 1947 innovation rounded out two decades of pioneering work that took computing from mechanical calculating machines to the brink of the digital age.

 See also **Computer Scientists • Digital Computing • Early Computers**

Resources

Books

Campbell-Kelly, Martin, and William Asprey. *Computer: A History of the Information Machine.* 2nd ed. Boulder, CO: Westview Press, 2004.

Lavington, Simon. *Moving Targets: Elliott-Automation and the Dawn of the Computer Age in Britain, 1947–67.* London and New York: Springer, 2011.

Web Sites

ENIAC at the U.S. Army Research Lab. "History of Computing Information." http://ftp.arl.army.mil/%7Emike/comphist/ (accessed November 1, 2012).

E-commerce

E-commerce (sometimes termed Web-based commerce) is the term used to describe the activity of doing business on the Internet. It includes business-to-business, business-to-consumer, and even consumer-to-consumer transactions that involve the buying and selling of goods and services, the transfer of funds, and even the exchange of ideas. E-commerce includes functions such as marketing, manufacturing, finance, selling, and negotiations. The phrase can also refer to downloading software, accessing games, or downloading content such as journal articles and books.

Business-to-business transactions are commonly accomplished through Electronic Data Interchange (EDI). This protocol* is now used by most Fortune 1,000 companies. EDI enables large organizations to transmit information over private networks; it has also found a role on internal corporate Web sites (termed intranets*).

Business-to-consumer e-commerce can provide customers with convenience and access to a wide range of goods and services, while allowing businesses to reach large or unique markets. Components of business-to-consumer e-commerce include security measures, shopping carts, payment options, and marketing.

Security

A business web site must be secure if it is going to handle financial transactions. A standard option is to make the website available over HTTPS, a security extension to the Hypertext Transport Protocol (HTTP) which allows HTTP requests and responses to be encrypted before transmission. HTTPS uses Secure Sockets Layer (SSL), a security protocol which performs authentication and encryption* of network participants and transactions, respectively. Authentication using HTTPS allows the client (the Web browser) to verify that the Web sites is who they claim to be. This is accomplished by the Web sites providing an HTTPS certificate to prove their identity. This certificate contains the Web sites's name, HTTP address, and other information to verify identity. The most important information, however, is the name of the Certificate Authority (CA), which provides the certificate to the Web sites and the certificate signature, which is a cryptographic hash* of the contents of the certificate. This hash is generated by the CA and encrypted using public key*. Once a client receives the certificate, they can verify the signature by calculating the hash of the certificate, decrypting the signature with the CA's public key, and comparing the computed value with the decrypted value. If the values differ, then something has caused the certificate to change and implies the website cannot be trusted. The type of algorithms involved with hashing and encrypting the certificate guarantee that even a single character change to the certificate will create a different hash value. If the website's certificate appears valid, then the remaining communication is encrypted with SSL using a key, which is created by the Web sites and

* **protocol** an agreed understanding for the sub-operations that make up a transaction, usually found in the specification of inter-computer communications

* **intranet** an interconnected network of computers that operates like the Internet, but is restricted in size to a company or organization

* **encryption** also known as encoding; a mathematical process that disguises the content of messages transmitted

* **cryptographic hash** Either a mathematical function, which produces a unique value for a given input, with the property that solely the output cannot be used to calculate the input, or the output of a cryptographic hash function

* **public key** A type of encryption in which two different keys are used to encrypt and decrypt a message. The nature of the algorithm used to create the keys guarantees that knowledge of one key cannot be used to help guess or calculate the value of the other key. Typical use involves publishing the public key and encrypting outgoing messages with the private key. Incoming messages are encrypted by others with the public key and can be decrypted with the private key.

An E-trader at work. © *HOANG DINH NAMAFP/Getty Images.*

client specifically for that session. This helps prevent hackers from intercepting communication and replaying the same messages in order to act as one of the parties.

This seemingly complicated process takes place almost instantaneously over broadband connections, and ensures that private information—such as passwords, credit card numbers, and customer profile data—is secure and encrypted as it is transmitted. Consumers will know they are using secure sites when they see closed padlock icons on the status bars of their Web browsers. It is important to note that HTTPS and SSL can ensure that information is transmitted safely across a public network like the Internet, but cannot ensure that the recipient of the information will keep it secure. Companies with poor security practices have had consumer information stolen even though their e-commerce Web site was itself secure. Additionally, a thief could create an e-commerce Web site and obtain a valid HTTPS certificate for this Web site. If they could convince consumers to send their personal or credit card information to the Web site, the thief would have unencrypted access to this information. This underscores the point that online security can only protect information while in transit, and e-commerce should only be done with reputable companies.

Another security protocol is termed Secure Electronic Transactions (SET). SET encodes the credit card numbers on a business server. Created by Visa and MasterCard, SET is very popular in the banking community.

Shopping Carts

The electronic shopping cart is a popular feature that allows consumers simply to click on a button to select one or more products for purchase. When the customer has finished shopping, the cart system allows the consumer to check out.

Payments

Various payment options exist to facilitate business-to-consumer e-commerce. These include digital or electronic cash, electronic wallets, and micropayments.

Digital or Electronic Cash (E-cash) With digital cash, a consumer can pay for goods or services by transmitting a number. The numbers, similar to those on a dollar bill, are issued by a bank and represent specific sums of real money. Key features of digital cash are that it is anonymous and it can be reused, just like real cash. Various forms of e-cash have been around for awhile but consumers seem to prefer to use their credit cards. Federal laws provide credit card users the right to dispute any payments charged to their cards and limit theft losses to $50.

Electronic Wallets These wallets store credit card numbers on personal computers in encrypted forms. Consumers can make purchases using their credit cards at websites that support one of these wallets. A secure transaction is created by the electronic wallet company's server.

Micropayments These transactions are in amounts up to $10, usually made in order to download or gain access to games or graphics. Micropayments can also be accumulated over a period of time and billed to the consumer as one larger transaction. This method of paying for online content is not as widespread as others.

Marketing

Because e-commerce allows businesses to reach a worldwide market and to compete around the globe, creative marketing and promotion of a website is crucial to the success of an Internet-based business. This must be balanced with sound business practices, however. Although many of the dot.com* businesses that were heavily marketed to consumers during the late 1990s and into the new millenium managed to acquire good name recognition, a significant number were unable to stay in business, in part because they failed to provide the level of service consumers had been led to expect.

E-Commerce vs. Traditional Commerce

The Internet has changed the nature and structure of competition. In the past, most businesses had to compete within a single industry (such as groceries) and often within a specific geographic area, but the Internet is blurring those boundaries. An example is Amazon.com. The company began as an online bookstore but quickly expanded into new products and markets such as music, videos, home improvement supplies, apparel, furniture, toys, and even groceries with the launch of AmazonFresh (only available in the Seattle area as of 2009). Amazon Marketplace allows customers to sell new and used merchandise. Retail stores and individuals can be affiliated with Amazon, which allows them

*** dot.com** a common term used to describe an Internet-based commercial company or organization

* **overhead** the expense or cost involved in carrying out a particular operation

* **disintermediation** a change in business practice whereby consumers elect to cut out intermediary agencies and deal directly with a provider or vendor

to sell their products as merchants through the Amazon.com website for a fee. Through the Internet, customers can purchase products from virtually anywhere in the world.

A traditional business may have large overhead* costs associated with maintaining a storefront. But a Web-based business does not necessarily have that type of overhead, which may mean that continued growth becomes easier. With e-commerce, businesses can move more quickly and usually less expensively to reach a worldwide audience. For example, the cost of reaching a consumer in Minneapolis, Minnesota, is the same as reaching one in Clifton, Colorado.

An important difference between traditional business and e-commerce is the elimination of the middleman, known as disintermediation*. Businesses and consumers can communicate directly to carry out transactions, which can help entrepreneurs market their products or services without the cost of salespeople or product representatives. Although e-commerce is still a developing part of the economy, some people believe that traditional stores and mail-order companies may eventually go out of business. Other observers believe that traditional and electronic commerce will find new ways to work together.

Despite some consumer wariness, due in part to reports of hackers breaking into allegedly secure websites and downloading credit card information, businesses have found that financial transactions on the Internet can actually be more secure than traditional retail environments. A great deal of credit card fraud is caused by store employees who mishandle card numbers. Most consumers do not seem to realize their credit card numbers are vulnerable every time they hand their cards to waiters, place orders by phone, or toss out receipts. The encryption of card numbers for online transactions protects both the consumer and the business from credit card fraud.

Finally, the Internet is revolutionizing competition in the area of pricing. At any point, a business may choose to simply give away a service, free of charge, that others sell. One example was when Microsoft began to include a free browser with Windows software. Such businesses generate income through other means, such as by selling ads or products and services related to the give-away item. Such strategies can help business attract customers. In addition, when products do not require manufacturing and packaging, as is the case with software downloaded via the Internet by a user, the reduction in business costs can be passed on to customers.

The Influence of the Internet

Research by Jupiter Media Metrix showed that 13.4 million households banked online from July 2000 to July 2001, a 77.6 percent increase in one year alone. Of the 88.2 million Americans with Internet access, 69.7 million households currently use online banking services, with 64.4 million households paying at least one bill online. According to the U.S. Census data, online sales reached $106.6 billion in 2006.

Online shopping also has skyrocketed in recent years. During the 2011 holiday season, American shoppers spent $32 billion online, a 15 percent increase from 2010.

Statistics aside, the Internet has made strong inroads into the lives of people in virtually all demographic groups. Computer businesses, telephone companies, cable retailers, Internet providers, public libraries, and even coffeehouses have made Internet access available to almost anyone. School children are taught how to access the Internet, but so are patrons of libraries, community centers, and senior citizen centers. Readily available Internet access has opened the door wide for the world of e-commerce.

The Future of E-Commerce

Many analysts believe that e-commerce will reshape the business world. Some predict that the huge growth of virtual communities—people getting together in ad hoc interest groups online—promises to shift the balance of economic power from the manufacturer to the consumer, eroding the marketing and sales advantages of large companies. A small company with a higher quality product and better customer service can use these communities to challenge larger competitors—something it might not be able to do in the traditional world of commerce.

Non-business organizations are using lessons learned in the early years of e-commerce. An example of what the future may hold is edu-Commerce, a concept combining online course offerings with advertising content. Some experts believe that universities may eventually face stiff competition from organizations that offer their courses at no charge, counting on sales generated from ads to make their profits and draw new customers. Other forms of e-commerce will surely emerge as consumers explore the vast reaches of doing business via the Internet.

 See also **Internet • Intranet • World Wide Web**

Resources

Books

Adams, F. Gerard. *The E-Business Revolution & the New Economy: E-Conomics after the Dot-Com Crash.* Mason, OH: Thomson/ South-Western, 2004.

Bajaj, Kamlesh K., and Debjani Nag. *E-Commerce: The Cutting Edge of Business.* 2nd ed. New Delhi: Tata McGraw-Hill Publishing, 2005.

Cheeseman, Henry R. *The Legal Environment of Business and Online Commerce: Business Ethics, E-Commerce, Regulatory, and International Issues*, 7th ed. Upper Saddle River, NJ: Pearson Prentice Hall, 2013.

Competitive Edge

One concern that consumers express about making their purchases online is the high cost of shipping and handling. As such, some online stores run free shipping campaigns, especially around the holidays, to entice customers to buy from them. Other methods of shipping discounts to promote purchases include offering free shipping after spending a minimum amount or free shipping for new customers. E-sellers note that ordering online saves consumers from having to wait in long lines around the holidays.

Hypertext Markup Language (HTML) an encoding scheme for text data that uses special tags in the text to signify properties to the viewing program (browser) like links to other documents or document parts

Internet Service Providers (ISPs) commercial enterprises which offer paying subscribers access to the Internet (usually via modem) for a fee

Funabashi, Matohisa, and Adam Grzech. *Challenges of Expanding Internet: E-Commerce, E-Business, and E-Government: 5th IFIP Conference on E-Commerce, E-Business, and E-Government (13E'2005), October 28–30, 2005, Poznan, Poland.* New York: International Federation for Information Processing, 2005.

Khosrowpour, Mehdi. ed. *Cases on Electronic Commerce Technologies and Applications.* Cascs on information technology series. Hershey, PA: Idea Group Publishing, 2006.

Li, Feng, ed. *Social Implications and Challenges of E-Business.* Hershey, Pa.: Information Science Reference, 2007.

MacGregor, Robert C., and Lejla Vrazalic. *E-Commerce in Regional Small to Medium Enterprises.* Hershey, PA: IGI Publishing, 2007.

Napier, H. Albert. *Creating a Winning E-Business.* 2nd ed. Boston: Thomson Course Technology, 2006.

Web Sites

Newyorktimes.com and Claire Cain Miller. "How People Shopped Online This Holiday Season" http://bits.blogs.nytimes.com/2011/12/22/how-people-shopped-online-this-holiday-season/ (accessed November 3, 2012).

E-mail

E-mail, which is short for electronic mail, offers virtually instant, one-way communication around the world via computer. It was one of the first methods of person-to-person communication made available through the information superhighway. In the early days of e-mail, simple text messages were sometimes difficult to manage, and adding pictures or documents was possible only if other software was available to make transmission from e-mail to computer possible. Current e-mail software generally provides easy-to-use options for attaching photos, sounds, video clips, complete documents, and Hypertext Markup Language (HTML)* code.

Early e-mail access was typically provided by government agencies and universities to employees and special groups of people who needed to communicate with one another quickly and directly. Researchers and scientists were among the first consistent users of e-mail.

E-mail addresses are now available for a fee through commercial Internet Service Providers (ISPs)* to anyone who has a home computer and a phone line or other means of Internet access. Users who do not care to contract with an ISP can acquire e-mail addresses through a variety of Internet Web sites; well-known examples of free e-mail providers include Gmail.com, Hotmail.com, and Yahoo.com. Although there is

Women check e-mail at an Internet café in Tehran, Iran. © *AP Images/Vahid Salemi.*

no direct cost to the user for these addresses, the services come with a non-monetary price. Sites providing such e-mail accounts usually are supported by advertising, and the e-mail accounts are often targets of that advertising.

E-mail vs. Snail Mail

E-mail provides a format for written communication that is different from the traditional postal service in number of ways. Messages can be delivered more rapidly through electronic means than on paper through what has been nicknamed "snail-mail." E-mail is generally less formal than postal mail. Messages are often written quickly and respondents can weave their responses into the original message, replying point-by-point to the writer's questions or comments.

Among the advantages of e-mail are speed and convenience. One advantage to using e-mail is the ability to send the same information to a number of recipients easily and simultaneously, complete with electronic attachments. Sending a copy of a message to interested parties at the same time as the intended recipient can save time by ensuring that everyone knows the details and has a chance to respond as needed.

Electronic mail offers new forms of communication that cross barriers of time and geography. Groups of people with similar interests can join together to share and discuss ideas via e-mail discussion groups. Each group can generate hundreds of messages from hundreds or thousands of users within a day. In some cases, discussion groups are moderated, with all incoming messages going to a single person to be screened before they are posted. This protects the entire list of message recipients from receiving messages that are not relevant to the group's discussions.

Other lists are not moderated, allowing any list member to send any message to the entire group.

E-mail vs. Voice Communication

E-mail and telephone contact offer similar benefits in speed of contact. Answering machines and voice mail services provide options for asynchronous communication, similar to e-mail, where the recipient is able to receive messages on a time-delayed basis. With a sophisticated voice mail system, one message can be delivered simultaneously to a number of recipients on the same system, paralleling the ability of e-mail to communicate simultaneous messages and attachments to multiple recipients. This type of telephone delivery system is generally available only in business settings. One advantage of e-mail, however, is that it provides the option of communicating the same message to a number of people while also providing a text version of the message, instead of simply a voice message.

On the other hand, the voice message, whether live or recorded, offers certain advantages, as well. Listening to a voice message can give valuable information as to the emotional state of the speaker. Emotions conveyed through voice contact can clarify the meaning of a message that may be misinterpreted in e-mail format.

In an attempt to provide some emotional content to text-only messages, "emoticons" have been created; many are now widely recognizable. Emoticons consist of several keystrokes used together in a sequence to represent a facial expression. The most common are the use of a colon followed by a right or left parenthesis mark, representing a smiling face, or a frowning one, as in:) or:(respectively. Emoticons have become so popular that some word processing packages include smiling or frowning faces to replace typed in emoticons automatically.

Emoticons can be used to convey certain personal characteristics of a message's author as well. Emoticons can portray glasses, using the numeral 8 followed by a parenthesis mark, or a beard and a wink, made up of a semicolon, a parenthesis mark, and a right-facing angle bracket mark, as in 8) or;)> respectively.

E-mail for Business Use

E-mail has become quite popular for many business uses beyond communication within or between companies. As mentioned earlier, some Internet sites offer free e-mail accounts to attract users to the sites. Many of these are supported by advertising that is targeted toward specific consumer profiles. E-mail lists are also a valuable advertising commodity. They are used much like mailing lists for postal mail, or telephone lists for telemarketing.

For e-mail users who find advertiser-provided information valuable, or at least interesting, these e-mail marketing techniques are not a problem. There are some less scrupulous advertisers who send unsolicited and frequently unwanted messages to large numbers of e-mail accounts. This is a process known as "spamming." E-mail spam is often sent to discussion groups' e-mail lists, especially those that are not moderated. Various ISPs, such as Mindspring/Earthlink, offer their customers spam-filters such as the "Spaminator."

Although e-mail has been fully adopted by business, government, industry, education, and the private sector, concerns about security and privacy still exist. E-mail software and ISPs offer varying levels of security in the e-mail packages they provide. While most providers offer a security level that most personal users find fairly reasonable, there are questions of security in business settings that must be addressed, not only to avoid spam, but to avoid unauthorized access to e-mail messages and accounts. People with basic computer skills can circumvent security systems and illegally access e-mail accounts. In 2008, the potential simplicity of illegally breaking into another person's email account was highlighted nationally when Alaska Governor and Vice Presidential candidate Sarah Palin's email account was hacked. A college student named David Kernell (1988–) guessed the answers to Palin's security questions using publically known information and reset her password to a password of his choosing. He then accessed her email and posted several messages on the internet. Kernell later was arrested and convicted of hacking and sentenced to a year in prison. There are constant improvements made to security for all types of computer networks, including e-mail, but there will always be hackers who respond to every advance in security with new efforts to break through security measures.

E-mail privacy is not only at risk through illegal activity. In most business settings, there are regulations about who has legal access to e-mail sent or received via company-provided accounts. It may be true that e-mail sent with a company-provided account is not accessible to anyone from outside the company, but each e-mail message may be considered company property and can legally be accessed by the appropriate department within the company. On occasion, corporate employees have been fired for using their company e-mail accounts in ways deemed inappropriate by their employers. Such objectionable use of company e-mail has included illegal betting, sending off-color jokes, forwarding chain letters, and sending pornographic photos.

E-mail accounts and messages may also be vulnerable to legal investigations. In the late 1990s and subsequent years, questions arose concerning e-mail contacts that U.S. President Bill Clinton made during ongoing legal investigations. Those e-mail messages were evaluated based on their content and their relevance to the investigations. Internet service providers were asked to provide information about account holders, who were then placed under investigation themselves.

E-mail provides a rapid and comprehensive method of communicating with others. Its low cost and widespread availability makes it a valuable tool for business and personal use. Advances in software and hardware are expected to help alleviate the privacy and security concerns that limit its use for highly confidential correspondence.

E-Mail and Bioterrorism

E-mail's popularity received a boost with the appearance of anthrax-tainted postal mail during 2001. During a period of several weeks that year, large government and industry mailrooms were closed and traditional mail was undeliverable to elected officials and employees of numerous large media outlets. The volume of e-mail sent to these individuals and companies increased noticeably during these periods, because e-mail was the easiest and safest form of written communication that could be delivered to recipients working in affected buildings. However, on the downside, e-mail is often used to spread troublesome computer viruses and worms via infected attachments.

See also **Internet • Intranet • World Wide Web**

Resources

Web Sites

CNN.com and Lateef Mungin. "Prison or Halfway House for Palin e-mail Hacker." http://edition.cnn.com/2010/CRIME/11/12/ tennessee.palin.hacking.case/ (accessed October 24, 2012).

Ergonomics

Ergonomics is the science of designing machines and environments that are well suited to the people working with them. Ergonomics, or human factors, considers the design of machines, workspaces, jobs, health issues, and the human-machine interfaces. There are three different types of ergonomics: physical, cognitive, and organizational. Physical ergonomics refers to anatomical, biomechanical, and physiological characteristics of humans in relation to their physical activities. The effect of mental processes, such as memory, perception, motor response, and reasoning on interactions among humans and other elements of a system (such as a computer) is represented by cognitive ergonomics. Organizational ergonomics is concerned with the optimal methods of development and management of processes, structures, and policies of sociotechnical systems. For example, an ergonomic design of an automobile's dashboard means that the controls can be reached easily and that all displays are visible for a range of drivers, whether they are six foot (1.83 meter) tall men or five foot (1.52 meter) tall women. Since the last decade of the twentieth century, ergonomics has become an important issue in the use of computer technology.

Before the start of World War II, emphasis was placed on conditioning people to fit the machines in their lives. Machines were created, then human beings were trained to operate them according to the machine's requirements; an example of this is training pilots to fly complex airplanes. During World War II, experimental psychologists researching aircraft design found that the machine systems were poorly designed and confusing, even for trained personnel. This led to the redesign of existing systems such as the altimeters on airplanes. Scientists also started looking at how best to distribute tasks, according to what people do best and what machines do best. Eventually, they realized that instead of changing systems after problems were found, they should use their knowledge about how humans process information to design more user-friendly systems from the start.

Many scientists have studied the problem of how to allocate separate pieces of a task to humans and to machines, respectively. Ernest J.

McCormick (1911–1990), in *Human Factors in Engineering and Design* (1976), presented lists of what humans do well and what computers do well. In general, he wrote, humans can respond to perceptual changes in the environment. That is, humans can quickly sense low-level changes in sounds, images, smell, or touch. They can store large amounts of information over long periods of time and retrieve pertinent information. When it is necessary, humans can go beyond the information given to react to unlikely events and create entirely new solutions. Thus, human performance can be described as *flexible*. Although this flexibility is good, it can also cause problems since humans do not exhibit the same response to the same circumstances in every instance. People's responses can vary from one time to the next and can include errors.

By contrast, McCormick's list of machine strengths noted that such devices are good at sensing stimuli outside of the human's normal range of sensitivity (e.g., x-rays, ultraviolet light, and radar wavelengths). Machines can store and retrieve large amounts of information rapidly and respond consistently to signals. They perform repetitive actions reliably such as putting caps on bottles of soda pop and do not get tired or bored, as a human might under similar circumstances. McCormick believed that an understanding of the relative strengths and weaknesses of people and machines would help designers create more effective systems.

Ergonomics and Computers

For people who use computer systems daily, ergonomic design is crucial. Early computer systems of the 1950s and 1960s were extremely difficult to understand and operate. People had to devote much effort to learning how to manage the technology.

As computer technology became more common, it was important to make the technology easier to use by a wide range of people. In the late 1970s, computers evolved to include microcomputers that could be operated by a single person. The first microcomputers were built by their users from components. Users had to write their own programs to make the computer do anything, even play a game. Once the business and education potential for microcomputers was recognized, ease of use for people with varying physical and technological capabilities became very important.

In the early twenty-first century, industrial designers of information technology must address a wide range of ergonomic considerations, from smartphones comfortably fitting in hands and pockets to integrating multi-finger touch and swipe gestures to touchscreens and trackpads to reduce user fatigue.

Designers must ensure that the technology is designed with sensitivity to human capacities and needs and that the resulting work environment is safe and comfortable. Ergonomic design considers the physical, psychological, cognitive, and social aspects of the interaction between the human and the machine. Use of computer technology has been associated with several health issues including eye strain, migraine headaches, muscle and body pain (especially backs and shoulders), repetitive stress injuries (e.g., carpal tunnel syndrome), and mental stress. For example, repetitive stress injuries can be caused by awkward positioning of wrists and hands, extended periods of rapid repetitive motion, and staying in one position for a long time. This can cause inflammation of the tendons in the wrists and hands and in severe cases can continue to cause pain long after the repetitive motion stops.

Following ergonomic workplace guidelines can help minimize injury. Suggestions by experts include:

- Positioning the screen at or below eye level to avoid muscle strain;
- Reducing glare with glare deflectors and careful positioning of computer and tablet screens;
- Changing lighting to eliminate glare or eye strain;
- Positioning the keyboards low enough to avoid arm and wrist fatigue;
- Using an adjustable desk so that the user's feet are firmly on the floor;
- Positioning the seat back of the chair to support the lower back;
- Taking frequent breaks to stretch shoulders, neck, and wrists;
- Training people to use and understand both hardware and software to reduce stress and fear.

The ergonomic principle of flexibility is important to the design of computer technology. People of different sizes, physical characteristics, and varying preferences need equipment that they can adjust. Companies implementing ergonomics programs find they can obtain a significant reduction in productivity losses due to work-related injuries.

Ergonomics also plays a role in software design, although typically termed human-computer interaction when viewed in this manner. Software, which presents an interface to the user, directly impacts the user's efficiency by how its interface is laid out. The field of human-computer interaction has generated numerous guidelines from years of research about what design principles should and should not be followed. For example, research has shown that buttons placed on opposite sides of an interface lead to a higher rate of missed clicks than buttons, which are positioned next to each other. Many software designers can create a graphical user interface (GUI), but fewer are able to distill the needs of their users into a design, which allows the user to flow from one task to another without interruption.

 See also **Keyboard • Microcomputers**

Resources

Books

Bridger, R. S. *Introduction to Ergonomics.* 3rd ed. Boca Raton, FL: CRC Press, 2009.

Salvendy, Gavriel. *Handbook of Human Factors and Ergonomics.* 4th ed. Hoboken, NJ: Wiley, 2012.

G

Games

The video game entertainment industry is a multi-billion dollar international enterprise that has seen many technological advancements since its inception in the early 1960s. From primitive home entertainment systems wired by simple integrated circuitry to the digitally advanced games of the twenty-first century, the industry has been the proving grounds for some very influential scientific minds. The evolution of games technology has resulted in improvements in the quality of computer graphics for business and educational application as well, and aided design efforts in virtual reality (VR)* software and the construction of artificial intelligence (AI)* systems.

Earliest Games

German-American inventor Ralph Baer (1922–), also known as the "Thomas Edison" of the video game, created the first video game console in 1966. While working for a company called Sanders Associates, he was commissioned to design a portable game for military training exercises based on strategy and reflcx skills. Much of the early investment capital for projects at Sanders and in the collegiate think tanks came from the Pentagon. Baer believed the applications he was pursuing for the military would eventually have value in home entertainment.

Even earlier, MIT student Steve Russell brought widespread attention to the ability of computers to play games with his "SpaceWar," which was first played in the labs at Massachusetts Institute of Technology (MIT) on a mainframe computer*. The 1960 game was a precursor to the much later "Asteroids" that captured the hearts and imaginations of many gaming enthusiasts. "SpaceWar" was later adapted from a game to a stand-alone console, under the name of "Computer Space," but the game met with little commercial success. Other MIT techies invented the first joysticks* to replace the original games' simple control knobs.

Video Games Go Public

The 1970s saw the most significant developments in bringing video games into the attention and the homes of the American public. Nolan Bushnell, a former employee of Ampeg of Sunnyvale, California, teamed up with design engineer Al Alcom to found the company Atari. Bushnell and Alcom designed the first "Pong" game, which was a form of computerized table tennis, and introduced it to Andy Capp's bar in Sunnyvale.

* **virtual reality (VR)** the use of elaborate input/output devices to create the illusion that the user is in a different environment

* **artificial intelligence (AI)** a branch of computer science dealing with creating computer hardware and software to mimic the way people think and perform practical tasks

* **mainframe computer** large computer used by businesses and government agencies to process massive amounts of data; generally faster and more powerful than desktop computers but usually requiring specialized software

* **joysticks** the main controlling levers of small aircraft; models of these can be connected to computers to facilitate playing interactive games

The Nintendo Wii experience. © *Jamie McCarthy/WireImage/Getty Images.*

* **analog** a quantity (often an electrical signal) that is continuous in time and amplitude

After the first night of public use, people lined up at ten the next morning to play this novel bar game. The video game craze was about to grip the public's attention.

Further popularizing the game craze in the eyes of Americans was the 1972 release of Magnavox's "Odyssey" that was introduced during a television broadcast hosted by the "Chairman of the Board," Frank Sinatra. These first games were quite simple compared to later technologies. Early games were based on analog* systems using large-scale integrated (LSI) circuits. These game designs offered two-dimensional graphics with a restricted range of motion for participants and often-predictable responses from the computer.

The mid-1970s saw significant improvement in games and especially graphics technology with the introduction of customized microchips. Midway's 1975 game "Gunfight" was the first to utilize a microprocessor. Using an 8080 CPU (central processing unit), the game featured graphic and audio effects that had not been possible before. The simultaneous demand for higher resolution screens and increased depth of field was met by companies like Activision, using the new F8 microchips that were supplied by Fairchild Camera and Instrument.

Violence and Video Games

In 1976 Exidy's "Death Race" video game entered the market. Fashioned after a popular movie at the time, it was one of the games that first sparked public controversy aimed at violent video games. Considering the history of military involvement in early research funding, it is not unusual that the focus of video game design teams resulted in games with highly competitive strategies, a strong emphasis on physical conflict, and action and adventure settings. Many movies of the time period also reflected scenarios depicting violence and adventure: *Jaws* haunted the imaginations of beach-loving moviegoers, while *Star Wars* refreshed popular interest in the exploration and domination of outer space.

Video game violence has not been restricted by public moral outpourings. Games like "Mortal Kombat" continue to win audiences of all ages. Some observers argue that the ability to vent potentially violent aggressions in an electronic setting relieves the pressure to commit public demonstrations of violence. Other critics argue that these games provide a training ground for potentially violent youthful offenders. The 1999 Columbine School massacre in Littleton, Colorado, and other gun-related incidents in public schools throughout the United States are cited as occurrences where the perpetrators had demonstrated a history of fascination with violent games.

Many companies now offer Internet gaming services, which allow up to a few people to thousands of players to play a game simultaneously. Among the most popular applications for these multi-player games are interactive games in which a group of characters, activated by users who may be located geographically anywhere in the world, explore a virtual world to collaborate or kill one another. Regardless of the controversies, graphically sophisticated action video games of all kinds continue to be popular.

Japanese Contributions

The Japanese video game market has been vital to the development, advancement, and growth in popularity of video games around the world, from the 1980s into the twenty-first century. The year 1980 saw the introduction of the "Pac-Man" game, which was invented by Toru Iwatami and associates for Namco, Ltd. Iwatami, who had tired of much of the violence depicted in video games, decided to develop a comical game that he felt everyone could enjoy.

"Pac-Man" became one of the largest selling arcade games ever, with more than 100,000 units sold in the United States alone, surpassing the then-monumental 70,000 unit record of "Asteroids" and the extremely popular "Space Invaders." Heavy use of the coin-operated "Pac-Man" was blamed for a severe coin shortage in the Japanese economy. The merchandising of "Pac-Man" T-shirts, posters, toys, and spin-off games ("Ms. Pac-Man" and others) would start another trend in home entertainment sales.

* **anti-aliasing** introducing shades of gray or other intermediate shades around an image to make the edge appear to be smoother

* **1200-baud** a measure of data transmission; in this case the rate of 1200 symbols (usually bits) per second

While "Pac-Man" and other arcade games grew in popularity during the early 1980s, there was a marked decrease in the sales of video games for home use. Most theories point to Atari's near dominance of the market with its 4-bit VCS console and what the public saw as limited graphical variation in game software available for home units. Nintendo's 1985 introduction of the 8-bit microprocessor dramatically changed the home video game market forever. The Japanese company became the dominant force in gaming technology with its proprietary console, the Nintendo Entertainment System (NES), and such popular games as "Donkey Kong", "The Legend of Zelda" and "Super Mario Bros." The advent of 16-bit technology, most successfully marketed in Sega's "Genesis" console, allowed for a much more sophisticated graphics processing system with as many as 63 times more onscreen colors and the use of anti-aliasing* and screen flipping techniques. This also brought competition to Nintendo's market dominance.

Advanced systems design furthered the competition between Nintendo and Sega and improved the market for video game sales across the globe. The 1990s saw the advent of 32-bit systems such as Sony's Playstation and the Nintendo 64 with turbo 3-D graphics, as well as popular hand-held video game units like Nintendo's "GameBoy." Strong competition from Microsoft's and its Xbox console series and the Sony PlayStation have chipped away at Nintendo's former market position as the leader of the home video game market, but the Japanese influence on the industry remains considerable. The current generation of home video game consoles consists of Microsoft's Xbox 360, Sony's Playstation 3, and Nintendo's Wii. The Xbox 360 and PS3 introduced Hi-definition gaming, while the Wii popularized motion-sensing controller technology. Nintendo's next console, the Wii U, was released in November 2012.

From Video Games to Corporate Giants

The video game industry has nurtured designers and entrepreneurs who have gone on to make major contributions to the computer industry as a whole. Steven Jobs and Steve Wozniak were employees of Atari before leaving to start a small company that grew into a huge corporation—Apple Computer, Inc. While at Atari, Jobs and Wozniak created a game called "Blockbuster." Their game design knowledge and experience would prove influential in their personal computer designs.

Another major player in today's computer marketplace had its roots in video game technology. In 1979 a company called Control Video Corp. offered a service called "Gameline" via the telephone network. Consumers accessed their service using a 1200-baud* modem to receive features including e-mail, news, banking, and financial management information. CVC became Quantum Computer Services in 1985 and in 1989, the company changed its name to America Online.

Simulation Game Technology

One of the most profoundly powerful gaming metaphors to emerge in the 1990s was the use of simulation technology that allows gamers to explore "what if" scenarios. The field was kicked off by Maxis with the game "SimCity," and was refined with various classics such as Microprose's "Transport Tycoon" and Art Dink's "A-Train."

This technology helps people understand and work within complex systems. Although many enjoy the products as entertainment, simulation games are used for education in schools and corporations. Maxis launched a spin-off to apply this technology to business systems. Chevron created "SimRefinery" to simulate the management of a large refinery operation. Another game called "SimHealth," which was commissioned by the Markle foundation, demonstrates some of the tradeoffs of different health care policies.

A number of war games have also been built around this kind of simulation technology. Some of the earliest hits were "Warcraft" and "Command and Conquer," which both allow multiple players to create and control production facilities and armies of soldiers that can be directed in real time. These games introduce an element of non-linearity in which players must be able to focus on multiple things simultaneously.

Gaming technology such as this has deep implications for the way decisions are made in our modern society. We can expect to see electronic information systems monitoring the flow of goods and services in the global economy as well as potentially determining strategies that humans will adapt for their environment.

▶ *See also* **Artificial Intelligence • Game Controllers • Internet • Simulation • Telecommunications**

Resources

Books

Burnham, Van. *Supercade: A Visual History of the Video Game Age, 1971–1984.* Cambridge, MA: MIT Press, 2001.

Kent, Steve L. *The Ultimate History of Video Games: From Pong to Pokemon and Beyond—The Story behind the Craze That Touched Our Lives and Changed Our World.* Roseville, CA: Prima, 2001.

Web Sites

CNet and Scott Stein. "Evolution of the console:Xbox 360, PS3, and Wii" http://reviews.cnet.com/8301-21539_7-20068071-10391702.html (accessed October 25, 2012).

Kotaku. "The Weird, Wonderful History of Nintendo" http://kotaku.com/5925652/the-weird—wonderful-history-of-nintendo (accessed October 25, 2012).

Pong Rocks!

The staff at Andy Capp's bar thought the new Pong machine was defective and asked Atari to remove it. In reality, so many people had played the game, it was filled with quarters and had shorted out.

Computer Chess

Video game technology has contributed to such monumental events as the Deep Blue Chess Competition. In 1997 IBM challenged then-current world chess champion Garry Kasparov to a match against the company's deep parallel supercomputer Deep Blue, to test the abilities of modern artificial intelligence. The entire match and a subsequent rematch were played online in real time.

Deep Blue won game six of the second match and defeated Kasparov before a hugely impressed global community. This pitting of man against a machine with a massive parallel search system matched a human being who makes perhaps two chess moves each second against an opponent who makes a quarter billion chess position decisions every second.

Gates, William Henry (Bill)
American Software Developer, Philanthropist
1953–

Bill Gates. © *George Frey/Bloomberg via Getty Images.*

* **operating system** The supporting software that allows a computer to execute basic functions.

* **graphical interface** a program installed on personal computers that enables users to interact with the computer through icons and menus instead of code commands.

* **personal computer** a computer designed to be used at home or in an office by an individual user, running commercial software.

An internationally renowned computer programming pioneer and businessman, Bill Gates has won fame and fortune as a brilliant software developer, entrepreneur, and philanthropist. Gates co-founded Microsoft Corporation with Paul Allen (1953–) in 1974, and subsequently developed the widely popular MS-DOS operating system* and Windows graphical interface*. As chairman and CEO of Microsoft, Gates is one of the most influential and wealthy leaders of the computer industry. He also has won recognition as a noted philanthropist.

William Henry Gates, III, was born on October 28, 1955, in Seattle, Washington. He was raised with his two sisters in an affluent family. His father, William H. Gates, II, was a prominent attorney, and his mother, Mary, a schoolteacher. His parents nicknamed the younger William "Trey," referring to the III after his full name.

Gates struggled in public elementary school, so his parents enrolled him at private Lakeside School. There, he was first introduced to computers, and at the early age of thirteen wrote a program to play tic-tac-toe.

In 1973 Gates moved across the country to attend Harvard University. While at Harvard, he developed the programming language BASIC for the world's first personal computer* (PC), the MITS Altair. Two years later, at age nineteen, he launched the Microsoft Corporation with childhood friend Paul Allen (1953–), motivated by the belief that every business and household should have a computer. In his junior year, Gates dropped out of Harvard to devote his energies to his new company. Little did he know it would become one of the most successful companies in the world.

In the early 1980s, Gates led Microsoft's evolution from a programming developer to a diversified software company producing operating systems and applications software. In 1981, under Gates's direction, Microsoft introduced MS-DOS, the operating system for the new personal computer produced by International Business Machines Corporation (IBM). MS-DOS became the standard operating system for the majority of personal computers throughout the world.

On March 13, 1986, Microsoft went public on the Stock Exchange. The initial offering for a share of Microsoft stock was $21. At age thirty-one, Gates instantly became the richest man in the United States. His personal stock holdings exceeded $2.8 billion. In 1999 he was reported to be the richest private individual in the world, with a net worth of over $50 billion.

In the mid–1990s Gates dramatically changed the direction of his entire company and began focusing on the rapidly evolving Internet. Although some of his early efforts fizzled, the company hit a milestone with its popular Internet Explorer Web browser, giving the existing Netscape browser some heated competition. By spring of 1998 Microsoft had revenues of $14.4 billion for the fiscal year and employed more than 27,000 people in sixty countries.

In May of that year, Microsoft became the subject of federal antitrust* litigation. The suit, brought by the United States Department of Justice, accused Microsoft of inhibiting competition from rival software companies, such as Netscape, by linking its own Internet Explorer browser with its Windows operating system, used by some 80 percent of desktop computers worldwide. A lower court concluded that the company had violated antitrust laws, and this decision was upheld by the U.S Court of Appeals for the District of Columbia in 2001.

Meanwhile, Gates handed over the position of CEO of Microsoft to Steve Ballmer (1956–), the company's president. Gates remained as chair of the company as well as its chief software architect. He also began stepping up his philanthropic activities, perhaps in response to the negative publicity the anti-trust litigation had stirred up. By 2001, Gates and his wife, former Microsoft executive Melinda French Gates (1964–), had given more than $21 billion to various causes, mostly in education and health. They continued to give through the early 2000s. In January of 2004, Gates was named for honorary knighthood for his philanthropic contributions in the United Kingdom. In 2005, Gates, along with his wife and the singer Bono, were named *Time*'s Persons of the Year for their charitable work.

In June of 2006, Gates announced that he would begin to reduce his role in the day-to-day running of Microsoft. He stepped down as the company's chief software architect, effective immediately, and announced that he would give up all of his managerial positions at the company in July of 2008. After that point Gates would continue to be Microsoft's chairman and a part-time technical adviser to the company, but he would devote most of his time to directing the activities of the Bill and Melinda Gates Foundation. At the same time, billionaire businessman Warren Buffett (1930–) pledged to make an annual gift of stock to the Bill and Melinda Gates Foundation as long as either Bill or Melinda remain involved in directing the foundation's activities. Buffett also announced that he was re-writing his will so that the stock donations would continue after his death. The first year's gift, 500,000 shares, was estimated to be worth more than $1.5 billion.

The main areas of focus for the foundation are finding ways to reduce the effects and spread of malaria, polio, HIV/AIDS, tuberculosis, diarrhea, and pneumonia, with emphasis on the administration of vaccines. The Foundation's primary goal is in developing technologies to fight disease and poverty. Thanks to efforts by the Foundation, as of 2010, vaccines had been administered to more than 250 million children, preventing an estimated five million deaths. The Foundation is continuing research on a malaria vaccine. Although in 2012 initial results for one of the vaccines that it funded resulted in a lower efficacy rate than predicted, the Foundation intends to initiate the next set of trials in 2014. In 2011 the Foundation created a campaign to re-invent the toilet in order to fight

* **antitrust** laws and legislation that protect against business practices that inhibit competition.

Computer Sciences, 2ⁿᵈ Edition

vacuum tube an electronic device constructed of a sealed glass tube containing metal elements in a vacuum; used to control electrical signals

poor sanitation, which often leads to severe diarrhea, killing up to 1.5 million children annually. The Foundation provided funding to several universities to develop a low-cost and water efficient toilet that could be used in poor countries to replace latrines and open sewer systems that often breed fatal disease.

In June of 2008, ready to devote his full-time energy to matters of philanthropy and manage the foundation, Gates stepped down as a full-time employee of Microsoft. He remained as Microsoft's non-executive chair, and he also worked part-time on special projects for the company, but he focused on the foundation's work in the areas of education and health. He and Melinda make trips to project sites around the world.

Resources

Periodicals

Beckett, Andy. "Inside the Bill and Melinda Gates Foundation." *Guardian*, July 12, 2010.

Web Sites

The Bill and Melinda Gates Foundation "Reinvent the Toilet" http://www.gatesfoundation.org/infographics/Pages/reinvent-the-toilet-info.aspx (accessed November 11, 2012).

Generations, Computers

The first computers and the models and innovations that followed typically are grouped into five "generations." Each generation is marked by improvements in basic technology. These improvements in technology have been extraordinary and each advance has resulted in computers of lower cost, higher speed, greater memory capacity, and smaller size.

This grouping into generations is not clear-cut nor is it without debate. Many of the inventions and discoveries that contributed to the modern computer era do not neatly fit into these strict categories. The reader should not interpret these dates as strict historical boundaries.

First Generation (1945–1959)

The vacuum tube* was invented in 1906 by an electrical engineer named Lee De Forest (1873–1961). During the first half of the twentieth century, it was the fundamental technology that was used to construct radios, televisions, radar, x-ray machines, and a wide variety of other electronic devices. It is also the primary technology associated with the first generation of computing machines.

The first operational electronic general-purpose computer, named the Electronic Numerical Integrator and Computer (ENIAC), was built in 1943 and used 18,000 vacuum tubes. It was constructed with government funding at the University of Pennsylvania's Moore School of Engineering, and its chief designers were J. Presper Eckert, Jr. (1919–1995) and John W. Mauchly (1907–1980). It was almost 30.5 meters (100 feet) long and had twenty 10-digit registers for temporary calculations. It used punched cards* for input and output and was programmed with plug board wiring. The ENIAC was able to compute at the rate of 1,900 additions per second. It was used primarily for war-related computations such as the construction of ballistics* firing tables and calculations to aid in the building of the atomic bomb.

The Colossus was another machine that was built during these years to help fight World War II. A British machine, it was used to help decode secret enemy messages. Using 1,500 vacuum tubes, the machine, like the ENIAC, was programmed using plug board wiring.

These early machines were typically controlled by plug board wiring or by a series of directions encoded on paper tape. Certain computations would require one wiring arrangement, while other computations would require a different arrangement. So, while these machines were clearly programmable, their programs were not stored internally; instead, the instructional program that directed the computer's operations was present in the external plug board wiring arrangement. This would change with the development of the stored program computer.

The team working on the ENIAC was probably the first to recognize the importance of the stored program concept. Some of the people involved in the early developments of this concept were J. Presper Eckert Jr. (1919–1955) and John W. Mauchly (1907–1980), and John von Neumann (1903–1957). During the summer of 1946, a seminar was held at the Moore School that focused great attention on the design of a stored program computer. About thirty scientists from both sides of the Atlantic Ocean attended these discussions and several stored programmed machines were soon built.

One of the attendees at the Moore School seminar, Maurice Wilkes (1913–), led a British team that built the Electronic Delay Storage Automatic Calculator (EDSAC) at Cambridge in 1949. On the American side, Richard Snyder led the team that completed the Electronic Discrete Variable Automatic Computer (EDVAC) at the Moore School. Von Neumann helped design the Institute for Advanced Study (IAS) machine that was built at Princeton University in 1952. These machines, while still using vacuum tubes, were all built so that their programs could be stored internally.

Another important stored program machine of this generation was the UNIVersal Automatic Computer (UNIVAC). It was the first successful, commercially-available electronic computer. The UNIVAC was designed by Eckert and Mauchly. It used more than 5,000 vacuum tubes

* **punched card** a paper card with punched holes which give instructions to a computer in order to encode program instructions and data

* **ballistics** the science and engineering of the motion of projectiles of various types, including bullets, bombs, and rockets

Stevenson vs. Eisenhower

Despite commentators's predictions that Adlai Stevenson would beat Dwight Eisenhower in the 1952 presidential election, the UNIVAC correctly determined that Eisenhower would win.

magnetic tape a way of storing programs and data from computers; tapes are generally slow and prone to deterioration over time but are inexpensive

* **transistor** a contraction of TRANSfer resISTOR; a semiconductor device, invented by John Bardeen, Walter Brattain, and William Shockley, which has three terminals; can be used for switching and amplifying electrical signals

* **integrated circuit** a circuit with the transistors, resistors, and other circuit elements etched into the surface of a single chip of semiconducting material, usually silicon

* **silicon** a chemical element with symbol Si; the most abundant element in the Earth's crust and the most commonly used semiconductor material

Did You Know...

Jack Kilby and Robert Noyce were the founders of the integrated circuit. However, they worked independently of each other for different companies.

and employed magnetic tape* for bulk storage. The machine was used for tasks such as accounting, actuarial table computation, and election prediction. Forty-six of these machines were eventually installed.

The UNIVAC, which ran its first program in 1949, was able to execute ten times as many additions per second as the ENIAC. In modern dollars, the UNIVAC was priced at about $5 million. Also, during this period, the first IBM computer was shipped. It was called the IBM 701 and nineteen of these machines were sold.

Second Generation (1960–1964)

As commercial interest in computer technology intensified during the late 1950s and 1960s, the second generation of computer technology was introduced—based not on vacuum tubes but on transistors*.

John Bardeen (1908–1991), William B. Shockley (1910–1989), and Walter H. Brattain (1902–1987) invented the transistor at Bell Telephone Laboratories in the mid-1940s. By 1948 it was obvious to many that the transistor would probably replace the vacuum tube in devices such as radios, television sets, and computers.

One of the first computing machines based on the transistor was the Philco Corporation's Transac S-2000 in 1958. IBM soon followed with the transistor-based IBM 7090. These second generation machines were programmed in languages such as Common Business Oriented Language (COBOL) and Formula Translator (FORTRAN) and were used for a wide variety of business and scientific tasks. Magnetic disks and tape were often used for data storage.

Third Generation (1964–1970)

The third generation of computer technology was based on integrated circuit* technology and extended from approximately 1964 to 1970. Jack Kilby (1923–) of Texas Instruments and Robert Noyce (1927–1990) of Fairchild Semiconductor were the first to develop the idea of the in 1959. The integrated circuit is a single device that contains many transistors.

Arguably the most important machine built during this period was the IBM System/360. Some say that this machine single handedly introduced the third generation. It was not simply a new computer but a new approach to computer design. It introduced a single computer architecture over a range or family of devices. In other words, a program designed to run on one machine in the family could also run on all of the others. IBM spent approximately $5 billion to develop the System/360.

One member of the family, the IBM System/360 Model 50, was able to execute 500,000 additions per second at a price in today's dollars of around 4.2 million. This computer was about 263 times as fast as the ENIAC.

During the third generation of computers, the central processor was constructed by using many integrated circuits. It was not until the fourth generation that an entire processor would be placed on a single silicon* chip—smaller than a postage stamp.

Fourth Generation (1970–)

The fourth generation of computer technology is based on the microprocessor. Microprocessors employ Large Scale Integration (LSI) and Very Large Scale Integration (VLSI) techniques to pack thousands or millions of transistors on a single chip.

The Intel 4004 was the first processor to be built on a single silicon chip. It contained 2,300 transistors. Built in 1971, it marked the beginning of a generation of computers whose lineage would stretch to the current day.

In 1981 IBM selected the Intel Corporation as the builder of the microprocessor (the Intel 8086) for its new machine, the IBM-PC. This new computer was able to execute 240,000 additions per second. The computer was an excellent deal for the average consumer. Although much slower than the computers in the IBM 360 family, this computer would cost only about $4,000 in 2012 dollars. This price/performance ratio caused a boom in the personal computer market.

In 1996, the Intel Corporation's Pentium Pro PC was able to execute 400,000,000 additions per second. This was about 210,000 times as fast as the ENIAC–the workhorse of World War II. The machine cost about $4,500 in inflation-adjusted dollars.

Microprocessor technology is now found in all modern computers. The chips themselves can be made inexpensively and in large quantities. Processor chips are used as central processors and memory chips are used for dynamic random access memory (RAM)*. Both types of chips make use of the millions of transistors etched on their silicon surface. The future could bring chips that combine the processor and the memory on a single silicon die.

During the late 1980s and into the 1990s cached, pipelined, and superscaler microprocessors became commonplace. Because many transistors could be concentrated in a very small space, scientists were able to design these single chip processors with on-board memory (called a cache*) and were able to exploit instruction level parallelism by using instruction pipelines along with designs that permitted more than one instruction to be executed at a time (called superscaler). The Intel Pentium Pro PC was a cached, superscaler, pipelined microprocessor.

Also, during this period, an increase in the use of parallel processors occurred. These machines combine many processors, linked in various ways, to compute results in parallel. They have been used for scientific computations and are now being used for database and file servers as well. They are not as ubiquitous* as uniprocessors because, after many years of research, they are still somewhat difficult to program and many problems may not lend themselves to a parallel solution.

The early developments in computer technology were based on revolutionary advances in technology. Inventions and new technology were the driving force. The more recent developments are probably best viewed as evolutionary rather than revolutionary.

According to the market research firm Computer Industry Analysts, the number of personal computers (PCs) in use worldwide by the end of 2007 reached 1 billion, while in 2008 there were some 1.5 billion Internet users globally. The same firm has predicted that 2 billion PCs will be in use

* **random access memory (RAM)** a type of memory device that supports the nonpermanent storage of programs and data; so called because various locations can be accessed in any order (as if at random), rather than in a sequence (like a tape memory device)

* **cache** a small sample of a larger set of objects, stored in a way that makes them accessible

* **ubiquitous** to be commonly available everywhere

around the world by the mid-2010s. Even more astounding is the fact that PCs make up only a very small percentage of all functioning computers at any given time, since many more computers (in the form of microprocessors) are embedded in machines such as aircraft, cars, and industrial robots.

Fifth Generation

It is generally held that the fifth generation of computer technology centers upon the wide-spread use of sophisticated artificial intelligence (AI) technologies. In the early 2010s, the enormous potential of AI systems was yet to be realized on a societal level. Certain applications, such as speech recognition, did take advantage of the capabilities inherent in AI. But the goal of ubiquitous devices in society that are capable of accepting, processing, and responding appropriately to human language, as well as being able to learn from their environment, is still a work in progress. Other important computer technologies that are currently hot topics of research include optical computing, advances in parallel processing, quantum computing, and the application of nanotechnology to computers. These, and other, technologies may dramatically alter the capabilities of computers in the coming decade. Like previous computer generations, however, it may be somewhat difficult to conclude when the fourth generation of computing ended, and the fifth generation commenced.

It is important to note that the term "Fifth Generation" was also used by a consortia of Japanese companies and government to identify a major computer project of the 1980s. That government/industry project—more formally known as the "Fifth Generation Computer Systems (FGCS) project"—should not be confused with the term "Fifth Generation" as used in this article concerning the next phase in computer evolution. Incidentally, the Japanese FGCS project fell short of at least some of its original aims, probably due in large part to the incorrect projection that parallel processing (using many microprocessors to share computational processing) would be of decisive importance to computing in the decades to come (meaning, at that time, the 1990s and 2000s). Advances in microprocessing capabilities throughout the 1980s, 1990s, and 2000s, meant that the Japanese project was eclipsed by the unanticipated improvements in the processing speed and power of single microprocessors.

▶ *See also* **Apple Computer, Inc** • **Artificial Intelligence** • **Bell Labs** • **Eckert, J Presper, Jr and Mauchly, John W** • **Integrated Circuits** • **Intel Corporation** • **Microsoft Corporation** • **Xerox Corporation**

Resources

Books

Patterson, David A., and John Hennessy. *Computer Organization and Design*. 4th ed. San Francisco: Morgan Kaufmann Publishers, 2000.

Periodical

Rockett, Frank H. "The Transistor." *Scientific American* 179, no. 3 (December 1948): 53–54.

Generations, Languages

Programming languages are the primary tools for creating software. As of 2012, hundreds exist, some more used than others, and each claiming to be the best. In contrast, in the days when computers were being developed there was just one language—machine language.

The concept of language generations, sometimes called levels, is closely connected to the advances in technology that brought about computer generations. The four generations of languages are machine language, assembly language, high-level language, and very high-level language.

First Generation: Machine Language

Programming of the first stored-program computer systems was performed in machine language. This is the lowest level of programming language. All the commands and data values are given in ones and zeros, corresponding to the on and off electrical states in a computer.

In the 1950s, each computer had its own native language, and programmers had primitive systems for combining numbers to represent instructions such as *add* and *compare*. Similarities exist between different brands of machine language. For example, they all have instructions for the four basic arithmetic operations, for comparing pairs of numbers, and for repeating instructions. Different brands of machine language are different languages, however, and a computer cannot understand programs written in another machine language.

In machine language, all instructions, memory locations, numbers, and characters are represented in strings of zeros and ones. Although machine-language programs are typically displayed with the binary* numbers translated into octal (base-8*) or hexadecimal (base-16*) these programs are not easy for humans to read, write, or debug.

The programming process became easier with the development of assembly language, a language that is logically equivalent to machine language but is easier for people to read, write, and understand.

Second Generation: Assembly Language

Assembly languages are symbolic programming languages that use symbolic notation to represent machine-language instructions. Symbolic programming languages are strongly connected to machine language and the internal architecture of the computer system on which they are used. They are called low-level languages because they are so closely related to the machines. Nearly all computer systems have an assembly language available for use.

Assembly language was developed in the mid-1950s and was considered a great leap forward because it uses mnemonic* codes, or easy-to-remember abbreviations, rather than numbers. Examples of these codes include A for add, CMP for compare, MP for multiply, and STO for storing information into memory. Like programs written in other

* **binary** existing in only two states, such as on or off, one or zero

* **base-8** a number system in which each place represents a power of 8 larger than the place to its right (octal)

* **base-16** a number system in which each place represents a power of 16 larger than the place to its right (hexadecimal)

* **mnemonic** a device or process that aids one's memory

* **operands** when a computer is executing instructions in a program, the elements on which it performs the instructions are known as the operands

* **bit** a single binary digit, 1 or 0—a contraction of Binary digIT; the smallest unit for storing data in a computer

* **byte** a group of eight binary digits; represents a single character of text

* **mainframe** large computer used by businesses and government agencies to process massive amounts of data; generally faster and more powerful than desktop computers but usually requiring specialized software

programming languages, assembly language programs consist of a series of individual statements or instructions that tell the computer what to do.

Normally an assembly language statement consists of a label, an operation code, and one or more operands*. Labels are used to identify and reference instructions in the program. The operation code is a symbolic notation that specifies the particular operation to be performed, such as *move, add, subtract,* or *compare.* The operand represents the register or the location in main memory where the data to be processed is located. However, the format of the statement and the exact instructions available will vary from machine to machine because the language is directly related to the internal architecture of the computer and is not designed to be machine-independent. Machine dependence is a significant disadvantage of assembly language. A program coded in assembly language for one machine will not run on machines from a different or sometimes even the same manufacturer.

The principal advantage of assembly language is that programs can be very efficient in terms of execution time and main memory usage. Nearly every instruction is written on a one-for-one basis with machine language. Since all the instructions of a computer are available to the assembly language programmer, the programmer can readily manipulate individual records, fields within records, characters within fields, and even bits* within bytes*.

Programs written in assembly language require a translator to convert them into machine language. An assembly language instruction for multiply, *MP,* has no meaning to the computer because it only understands commands in the form of *11010110.* Therefore, a program called an assembler is needed to translate each assembly language instruction into a machine-language instruction.

Although assembly languages are an improvement over machine language, they still require that the programmer think on the machine's level. Because the level of detail required to write assembly programs is very high, it is easy to make mistakes. Although some programmers still use assembly language to write parts of applications where speed of execution is critical, such as video games, most programmers today think and write in very high-level or fourth-generation languages.

Third Generation: High-Level Language

Third-generation languages spurred the great increase in data processing that occurred in the 1960s and 1970s. During that time, the number of mainframes* in use increased from hundreds to tens of thousands. The impact of third-generation languages on society has been huge.

A programming language in which the program statements are not closely related to the internal characteristics of the computer is called a high-level language. As a general rule, one statement in a high-level programming language will expand into several machine language instructions. This is in contrast to assembly languages, where one statement normally generates one machine language instruction. High-level programming languages were developed to make programming easier and less error-prone.

High-level languages fall somewhere between natural languages and machine languages, and were developed to make the programming process more efficient. Languages like FORTRAN (FORmula TRANslator) and COBOL (COmmon Business Oriented Language) made it possible for scientists and business people to write programs using familiar terms instead of obscure machine instructions. Programmers can now pick from hundreds of high-level languages.

The first widespread use of high-level languages in the early 1960s changed programming into something quite different from what it had been. Programs were written in an English-like manner, making them more convenient to use and giving the programmer more time to address a client's problems.

Although high-level languages relieve the programmer of demanding details, they do not provide the flexibility available in low-level languages. A few high-level languages like C and FORTH combine some of the flexibility of assembly language with the power of high-level languages, but these languages are not well suited to the beginning programmer.

Some third-generation languages were created to serve a specific purpose, such as controlling industrial robots or creating graphics. Others are extraordinarily flexible and are considered general-purpose. In the past, the majority of programming applications were written in BASIC (Beginners' All-purpose Symbolic Instruction Code), FORTRAN, or COBOL—all considered to be general-purpose languages. Some other popular high-level languages today are Pascal, C, and their derivatives.

Again, a translator is needed to translate the symbolic statements of a high-level language into computer-executable machine language. The programs that translate high-level programs into machine language are called interpreters and compilers. Regardless of which translator is used, one high-level program statement changes into several machine-language statements. Each language has many compilers, and there is one for each type of computer. The machine language generated by one computer's COBOL compiler, for example, is not the same as the machine language of some other computer. Therefore, it is necessary to have a COBOL compiler for each type of computer on which COBOL programs are to be run.

Using a high-level language makes it easier to write and debug a program and gives the programmer more time to think about its overall logic. In addition, high-level programs have the advantage of being portable between machines. For example, a program written in standard C can be compiled and run on any computer with a standard C compiler. Since C compilers are available for all types of computers, this program can run as written just about anywhere. However, porting a program to a new machine is not always easy, and many high-level programs need to be partially rewritten to adjust to differences between user interfaces, hardware, compilers, and operating systems.

Computer Sciences, 2nd Edition

* **syntax** a set of rules that a computing language incorporates regarding structure, punctuation, and formatting

* **logic** a branch of philosophy and mathematics that uses provable rules to apply deductive reasoning

Fourth Generation: Very High-Level Languages

With each generation, programming languages have become easier to use and more like natural languages. However, fourth-generation languages (4GLs) seem to sever connections with the prior generation because they are basically nonprocedural. Procedural languages tell the computer how a task is done: add this, compare that, do this if something is true, and so on, in a very specific step-by-step manner. In a nonprocedural language, users define only what they want the computer to do, without supplying all the details of how something is to be done.

Although there is no agreement on what really constitutes a fourth-generation language, several characteristics are usually mentioned:

■ the instructions are written in English-like sentences;

■ they are nonprocedural, so users can concentrate on the "what" instead of the "how";

■ they increase productivity because programmers type fewer lines of code to get something done.

An example of a 4GL is the query language that allows a user to request information from a database with precisely worded English-like sentences. A query language is used as a database user interface and hides the specific details of the database from the user. For example, Structured Query Language (SQL) requires that the user learn a few rules of syntax* and logic*, but it is easier to learn than COBOL or C. It is believed that one can be ten times more productive in a fourth-generation language than in a third-generation language.

Consider a request to produce a report showing the total number of students enrolled in each class, by teacher, in each semester and year, and with a subtotal for each teacher. In addition, each new teacher must start on a new page. Using a 4GL, the request would look similar to this:

```
TABLE FILE ENROLLMENT
SUM STUDENTS BY SEMESTER BY TEACHER BY CLASS
ON TEACHER SUBTOTAL PAGE BREAK
END
```

Although some training is required to do even this much, one can see that it is fairly simple. Conversely, a third-generation language like COBOL would typically require a few hundred lines of code to fulfill the same request.

4GLs are still evolving, which makes it difficult to define or standardize them. A common perception of 4GLs is that they do not make efficient use of machine resources. The benefits of getting a program finished more quickly, however, can far outweigh the extra costs of running it.

Object-Oriented Languages

Smalltalk, developed in the 1970s by American computer scientist Alan Kay (1940–) at Xerox's Palo Alto Research Center, was the first object-oriented programming language. In object-oriented programming, a program is no longer a series of instructions, but a collection of objects.

These objects contain both data and instructions, are assigned to classes, and can perform specific tasks. With this approach, programmers can build programs from pre-existing objects and can use features from one program in another. This results in faster development time, reduced maintenance costs, and improved flexibility for future revisions. Some examples of object-oriented languages are: C++, Java, and Ada (the language developed by the U.S. Department of Defense).

What will be the next step in the development of programming languages? Future languages will probably have little in common with earlier ones. They will likely be much closer to natural languages.

 See also **Algol-60 Report • Algorithms**

Resources

Books

Beekman, George. *Computer Currents. Navigating Tomorrow's Technology.* Redwood City, CA: Benjamin/Cummings Publishing Co., 1994.

Blissmer, Robert H. *Introducing Computers: Concepts, Systems and Applications.* New York: John Wiley & Sons, Inc., 1994.

Brightman, Richard W., and Jeffrey M. Dimsdale. *Using Computers in an Information Age.* Albany, NY: Delmar Publishers Inc., 1986.

Savitch, Walter. *Absolute C++.* 5th ed. Boston: Addison-Wesley, 2013.

Sipser, Michael. *Introduction to the Theory of Computation.* 3rd ed. Boston: Cengage Learning, 2013.

Web Sites

About.com, and Mary Bellis. "Fortran: The First Successful High Level Programming Language." http://www.swansontec.com/sprogram. html (accessed October 3, 2012).

Swanson Technologies. "Introduction to Assembly Language." http:// www.swansontec.com/sprogram.html (accessed October 3, 2012).

The Dynabook

Alan Kay designed the first object-oriented programming language in the 1970s. Called Smalltalk, the programs were the basis for what is now known as windows technology—the ability to open more than one program at a time on a personal computer. However, when he first developed the idea, personal computers were only a concept. In fact, the idea of personal computers and laptops also belongs to Kay. He envisioned the Dynabook—a notebook-sized computer, with a keyboard on the bottom and a high-resolution screen at the top.

Government Funding, Research

Government funding of scientific research has a long and fruitful history. The computer revolution was built by the combined efforts of industry, universities, and governments. One of history's first government research and development grants, excluding support for geographic exploration, was given to Charles Babbage (1791–1871), the father of modern computing, in England, in 1823. Babbage was granted an initial sum of 1,500 pounds by the British government to fund the development of his Difference Engine and later given additional monies.

Computer Sciences, 2ⁿᵈ Edition

* **algorithm** a rule or procedure used to solve a mathematical problem—most often described as a sequence of steps

* **punched card** a paper card with punched holes which give instructions to a computer in order to encode program instructions and data

* **vacuum tube** an electronic device constructed of a sealed glass tube containing metal elements in a vacuum; used to control electrical signals

* **graphical user interfaces (GUIs)** interfaces that allow computers to be operated through pictures (icons) and mouse-clicks, rather than through text and typing

Some ten years later, Babbage turned his attention to designing a new machine, which he called the Analytical Engine. The Analytical Engine had some innovative features including stored memory, algorithms*, and the use of punched cards*. Babbage had some help in describing the machine and in writing programs for it from Ada Byron King, the Countess of Lovelace (1815–1852). Many people consider her the first computer programmer. Although Babbage did not obtain additional funding from the British government to support his work on the Analytical Engine, and the machine itself was a conceptual design rather than a commercial product, the funding of developmental computer research by governmental agencies had begun.

Just before the start of World War II, Alan Turing (1912–1954) in Cambridge, England, defined the basic theoretical underpinnings of a universal computer. The British defense industry supported his efforts to construct vacuum tube* computers able to break military codes from the Germans.

After the war, much of what had been learned in government laboratories, industry, and universities was publicized and used by U.S. companies to build an industrial base for computing. New demands for data and data processing were created by the growing consumer economy. Technological advances made since the end of World War II, including many made possible through the financial support of national governments and military agencies, exponentially increased the power of computer technology between 1945 and 1995.

Since the mid-twentieth century, the United States has become a leader in computing and related communications technology. Tabulating machines, graphical user interfaces (GUIs)*, real-time, online operating systems, the mouse, the ARPANET, the Internet, and microprocessors have been developed through the interaction of government, universities, and industry. For example, the U.S. Census Bureau was one of the first organizations to use both Herman Hollerith's tabulating machines and punched cards and the first viable electronic computer (UNIVAC I).

Research is a vital part of new advances in computer technology. However, computer manufacturers spend an average of only twenty percent of their research and development budgets on research. Research activities carried out in industrial or university laboratories such as IBM's J. T. Watson Research Center, AT&T's Bell Laboratories, and the Xerox Palo Alto Research Center (PARC) are often funded jointly by industry and government resources.

A recent report by the National Research Council states that in 1996, $1.7 billion was invested in research by computer manufacturers, most of which was carried out in their own facilities. In contrast, federal expenditures for computer research reached almost $960 billion in 1995. Approximately $350 million supported university research; the remainder was distributed to industrial and government laboratories. A 2012 report by the National Science Foundation stated that in 2012 the United States government had spent $148,962,000 on all facets of research and development, with $10,509,000 dedicated to general science and basic research.

The U.S. government provides support for research funding, human resources, and physical facilities (e.g., computers, offices, and equipment). This support for the research infrastructure is intended to create a pool of resources that can benefit a variety of users in both the private and public sectors. For example, when universities receive government support, they can train students, conduct research, and build research facilities.

Federal funding is provided for both basic research and applied research. Federal funding comes from several sources, including the Department of Defense (DoD), which is the largest sponsor of computing and communications research with a particular military emphasis. The DoD's Defense Advanced Research Projects Agency (DARPA) provides more support for computer science research than all other federal agencies combined. By the 1970s, the National Science Foundation (NSF) was the second largest supporter of research in computers and communications. The NSF funds basic and university research, providing between forty and forty-five percent of all basic research funding in computer science.

Many concepts developed by industry and designed into products received their initial funding from government-sponsored research and large-scale government development programs. Some examples include computer core memories, computer time-sharing, the mouse, network packet switching, computer graphics, virtual reality (VR)*, speech recognition* software, and relational databases. The federal government is the primary source of funding for university research in computer science and electrical engineering as well as for research equipment. It is also the primary support for graduate students who study and conduct research in these fields. This support complements industry's efforts to build the technological infrastructure needed to make the United States a leader in computer technology.

▶ *See also* **Babbage, Charles** • **Hollerith, Herman** • **King, Ada Byron** • **Tabulating Machines**

Resources

Books

National Research Council (U.S), Committees on Innovations in Computing and Communications. *Funding a Revolution: Government Support for Computing Research.* Washington, DC: National Academy Press, 1999.

Shurkin, Joel. *Engines of the Mind: The Evolution of the Computer from Mainframes to Microprocessors.* New York: W. W. Norton & Company, 1996.

Web Sites

The National Science Foundation. "Federal R&D Funding by Budget Function: Fiscal Years 2010–12" http://www.nsf.gov/statistics/ nsf12322/pdf/nsf12322.pdf (accessed November 4, 2012).

* **virtual reality (VR)** the use of elaborate input/output devices to create the illusion that the user is in a different environment

* **speech recognition** the science and engineering of decoding and interpreting audible speech, usually using a computer system

H

Hollerith, Herman
American Inventor and Engineer
1860–1929

Born on February 29, 1860, in Buffalo, New York, Herman H. Hollerith was a prolific inventor and a pioneer in data processing. His punched-card tabulating machines, although primitive by modern standards, provided the first viable method of processing vast amounts of information in a timely and cost-effective way. When he died on November 17, 1929, he left behind a technology that, with continued improvement, would eventually lead to the development of the modern computer.

Hollerith was the son of German immigrants and one of five children. His father died in an accident when Hollerith was only seven, and to support the family, his mother kept a millinery shop, making one-of-a-kind hats for ladies of fashion. At barely nineteen, Hollerith graduated with distinction from Columbia University's School of Mines. One of his professors, who was also a consultant for the U.S. Bureau of the Census, introduced Hollerith to Dr. John Shaw Billings, head of Vital Statistics, who hired the young engineer to assist in the statistical analysis of the 1880 census. Over dinner one evening, Billings discussed the tabulating process and wondered whether it could be mechanized, a question that fired Hollerith's imagination and transformed his life.

Although Hollerith left Washington, D.C., in 1882 to become an instructor of mechanical engineering at Massachusetts Institute of Technology (MIT), he never abandoned the concept of automated tabulation. At MIT, he developed the basic ideas for his machine and the flair for invention that would ultimately result in thirty-one patents.

In 1883 Hollerith received an appointment as an assistant examiner in the U.S. Patent Office and returned to Washington, D.C. As an engineer and statistician, he knew little, if anything, about patent law, but as a fledgling inventor he understood its importance. Eager to learn, he used his three years at the Patent Office to develop a real expertise.

On September 23, 1884, Hollerith filed the first patent application for his tabulating machine. His initial design approach used rolls of perforated paper tape, but these were soon replaced by punched cards*. Years before, he had watched a train conductor punch tickets that contained brief descriptions of each passenger, including hair and eye color. On the basis of this recollection, he adopted the as a standardized unit for recording and processing information.

▲

Herman Hollerith. © *SSPL via Getty Images.*

* **punched card** a paper card with punched holes which give instructions to a computer in order to encode program instructions and data

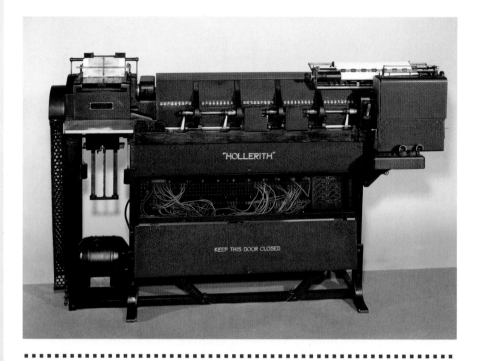

Punched cards had been introduced in the textile industry more than a century earlier by Joseph-Marie Jacquard (1752–1834), who had designed a mechanical loom. In Jacquard's loom, the hooks lifting the warp threads were controlled by cards perforated to the desired pattern. Hollerith's system used a similar approach but added a new ingredient—electricity. Information was recorded by punching holes on a card with twenty-four vertical columns and twelve punching places in each one. The cards were punched, sorted, and fed by hand into a machine, where electrical contacts were made through the holes as the cards passed through. Selected data were counted on electromechanical tabulators.

Hollerith's card processing system was first used in 1886 to tabulate census returns in Baltimore, Maryland, and subsequently in New Jersey and New York City. In 1889, when automated data tabulation systems were evaluated for the 1890 census, the Hollerith Electrical Tabulating Machine won the assignment. Consequently, the 1890 census was counted twice as fast as the previous one, and more than a billion holes were punched to record information from 63 million people.

For independent studies in developing Hollerith's tabulating system, the Columbia School of Mines waived its usual requirements and awarded Hollerith a doctor of philosophy degree in 1890. On September 15 of that year, he married Lucia Talcott, the daughter of a noted civil engineer. The couple had six children: Lucia; Herman, Jr.; Charles; Nan; Richard; and Virginia.

During the decades that followed, Hollerith continued to modify and improve his machines, which were used again in the 1900 census. By that time, they were used in Europe as well. To maximize commercial opportunities, he formed the Tabulating Machine Company in 1896 and successfully promoted his machines to insurance companies, department stores, and railroads.

In 1911 the Tabulating Machine Company became part of the Computing-Tabulating-Recording Company, a small conglomerate that was renamed the International Business Machines (IBM) Corporation in 1924. Hollerith continued as a consultant and director until 1914, when he retired to a farm in Virginia's Tidewater country. On November 17, 1929 he died of a heart attack at the age of sixty-nine, but his concept, although improved over the years, remained the basis of the information processing industry well into the 1940s.

▶ *See also* **Generations, Computers** • **IBM Corporation** • **Mainframes** • **Tabulating Machines** • **Watson, Thomas J., Sr**

Resources

Books

Austrian, Geoffrey D. *Herman Hollerith: Forgotten Giant of Information Processing.* New York: Columbia University Press, 1982.

Bernstein, Jeremy. *The Analytical Engine: Computers—Past, Present, and Future*, revised ed. New York: Random House, 1981.

Goldstine, Herman H. *The Computer from Pascal to von Neumann.* Princeton, NJ: Princeton University Press, 1970, reprint. 1993.

Luebbert, William F. "Hollerith, Herman." In *Encyclopedia of Computer Science and Engineering,* eds. Anthony Ralston and Edwin D. Reilly, Jr. New York: Van Nostrand Reinhold Co., 1983.

Morison, Elting E. *From Know-How to Nowhere: The Development of American Technology.* New York: Basic Books, 1974.

Hopper, Grace
American Mathematician
1906–1992

A mathematician and computer programmer, Grace Murphy Hopper worked extensively with computers—including the Mark I, II, and III— throughout her career. She joined the U.S. Naval Reserves, distinguishing herself by working with computer languages as well as by becoming one of the first female rear admirals in history. Remembered for her work with Common Business Oriented Language (COBOL), she is also credited with coining the term "computer bug."

Born in New York City on December 9, 1906, Hopper was the eldest of three children. Early in life, she expressed an interest in how devices work and began taking apart various alarm clocks. Hopper's parents believed that girls should be encouraged to learn and should have the same educational opportunities as boys, a unusual position to take in the

Census 2000

In 2000 the U.S. Census Bureau reported the American population at 281,421,906. To calculate the population, the Census Bureau uses survey forms that are processed through tabulating machines. The Census Bureau first began using tabulation machines in 1890 that were designed by Herman Hollerith. At that time, the American population was nearly 63 million.

Grace Hopper. © *AP Images.*

* **arc tangent** the circular trigonometric function that is the inverse of the tangent function; values range from -π/2 to π/2

* **punched card** a paper card with punched holes which give instructions to a computer in order to encode program instructions and data

early 1900s. Her father instilled the belief that Hopper could do anything she determined to do, regardless of her gender. This belief, coupled with her natural inquisitiveness, especially in how gadgets worked, and her innate determination, informed her approach to problem solving.

When she was sixteen, Hopper applied to Vassar College but had to wait a year before she could attend as she had failed the Latin exam. She spent that year at Hartridge School in New Jersey. The following year, Vassar accepted her; four years later, in 1928, she graduated Phi Beta Kappa with a B.A. in mathematics and physics.

Upon graduation Hopper became a mathematics graduate student at Yale. After receiving her master's degree, Hopper returned to Vassar as an instructor while continuing her graduate studies. In 1934 she became the first woman to earn a doctorate in mathematics from Yale. Hopper remained at Vassar until 1943 when, during World War II, she took a leave of absence to join the U.S. Navy. Her age, gender, and low body weight all worked against her enlisting in the military. It took a waiver of the weight requirement and special government permission for Hopper to join the WAVES (Women Accepted for Volunteer Emergency Service) as part of the U.S. Naval Reserves.

After graduating first in her class from the Midshipman's School for Women, Hopper was assigned to the Bureau of Ordnance Computation at Harvard University. Her first assignment was to program the Mark I computer to calculate the coefficients of the arc tangent* series. The Mark I was another gadget for Hopper to explore and understand. Hopper put together a manual of operations that included an outline of the fundamental operating principles of computers.

At the end of the war in 1945, Hopper was working on the Mark II. It was during this time that she was credited for coining the term "bug." The story is that a moth flew in through a window and became trapped in the computer relays, causing a shutdown. The moth, after being extracted from the computer, was placed in the log book and labeled "computer bug."

In 1946 Hopper was released from active military duty. Rather than return to Vassar, she accepted an appointment at Harvard as a research fellow. The position allowed her to continue working on the Mark II and the Mark III until 1949. At that time she accepted a position as senior mathematician at Eckert-Mauchly Corporation, which introduced the BINAC (Binary Automatic Computer). This computer was programmed using C-10 code instead of the punched cards* used by the Mark series of machines. With the development of a new computer, UNIVAC (Universal Automatic Calculator) I, Hopper worked on developing a compiler, the A-0, for translating symbolic mathematical notations into binary, machine language. After two more generations of the compiler, Hopper proposed developing a compiler that would recognize English commands. Hopper succeeded by developing the B-0 compiler, which became known as Flow-Matic. Using Flow-Matic, the UNIVAC could be used for business applications such as payroll calculations and to automate billing functions. The Flow-Matic served as the foundation for COBOL, which debuted in 1959.

Hopper continued working on related problems such as setting standards for compilers and programming language. In 1966 she retired from the U.S. Navy with the rank of commander. About seven months into retirement, she was called back to help standardize high-level naval computer languages. The reappointment was initially for six months but was later extended indefinitely. In 1973 Hopper was promoted to captain and in 1977 became special adviser to the commander, Naval Data Automation Command (NAVDAC). Hopper remained in this position until she retired. She was promoted to the rank of commodore by presidential appointment and elevated to the rank of rear admiral. Hopper retired after forty-three years of service in 1986. She was eighty years old, the oldest active duty officer and one of the first women to achieve the rank of rear admiral. After retirement, Hopper served as a senior consultant to Digital Equipment Corporation (DEC).

While in the U.S. Navy, Hopper taught as a guest lecturer at various colleges and universities. She received many awards and honors. In 1969 Hopper was named the first computer science "Man of the Year" by the Data Processing Management Association, and in 1991, President George H. Bush awarded her the National Medal of Technology. Rear Admiral Grace Hopper died on January 1, 1992 and was buried with military honors in Arlington National Cemetery in Virginia. The U.S.S. *Grace Hopper* was named in her honor.

 See also **Telecommunications**

Resources

Web Sites

"Grace Hopper." Women's International Center. http://www.wic.org/bio/ghopper.htm (accessed November 2, 2012).

"Rear Admiral Grace Hopper, USN." Naval History & Heritage. http://www.history.navy.mil/bios/hopper_grace.htm (accessed November 2, 2012).

Hypertext

Hypertext is normally defined as accessing information in a non-linear fashion. Predating the emergence of computers by a few years, it was first suggested in 1945 by inventor, scientist, and teacher Vannevar Bush (1890–1974).

Bush was science adviser to President Franklin Delano Roosevelt during World War II—an era full of scientific advances, including nuclear capabilities. But he is best remembered for his idea to create an interactive, cross-referenced system of scientific research, and is

Honorary Titles

Grace Hopper was well respected for her contributions to computer sciences. In fact, she earned the nicknames "Grand Old Lady of Software" and "Amazing Grace."

Individiuals in Rio de Janeiro, Brazil, viewing a multimedia installation about forest fires during the Green Nation Fest, a sensory and interactive festival. © *Buda Mendes/Latin Content/Getty Images.*

considered by some as the grandfather of hypertext. Bush developed plans to build a system, called Memory Extender (Memex), because he was worried about the sudden increase of scientific information, which made it difficult for specialists to follow developments in their disciplines. Bush explored different ways to allow people to find information faster and easier.

Memex was supposed to be a machine that would hold thousands of volumes in a very small space and would allow users to retrieve any requested information just by touching a few buttons. Although the Memex was never implemented, computer scientists like Douglas Engelbart and Theodor (Ted) Nelson were inspired by Bush's ideas and became pioneers in the development of interactive systems.

The hypertext field remained dormant until Engelbart started work in 1962 on one of the first major projects related to office automation and text processing. This project was conducted at the Stanford Research Institute (SRI) and was demonstrated in 1968 at a special session of the Fall Joint Computer Conference. This first public presentation of many of the basic ideas in interactive computing was risky, but it changed the way people thought about computers.

Many miles from the conference site, Engelbart and a co-worker controlled a stream of computer graphics and text and video images that were displayed on a large screen. This system, called Augment, was years ahead of its time because it introduced the mouse and video display editing. It allowed mixing text and graphics, and implemented windows. It also demonstrated video conferencing and hypermedia. Engelbart introduced what is now known as an interactive multimedia workstation.

Nelson coined the word "hypertext" in 1965 while working on a computer system, Xanadu, that was to serve as storage for everything that anybody had ever written. Plans allowed access to those documents from anywhere in the world. Because it demanded a certain degree of computing power, storage, graphics, user interface, and networking sophistication, hypertext did not gain widespread public attention until Apple Computer, Inc. introduced HyperCard in 1987.

Hypertext was important because it presented two fundamental changes in the storage and retrieval of data. The first was the capability to move rapidly from one part of a document to another by means of an associative link. The sequential pattern of reading so familiar from the print world was replaced by a truly interactive format. The second change was the capability of sharing information across different machines and systems. Hypertext built upon the advances made in networking to provide transparent access to data regardless of where it was located. In short, hypertext is about connectivity within and across databases.

 See also **Apple Computer, Inc • Hypermedia and Multimedia • World Wide Web**

Resources

Books

Beekman, George. *Tomorrow's Technology*, 8th ed. Upper Saddle River, NJ: Pearson Prentice Hall, 2008.

Landow, George P. *Hypertext 3.0: Critical Theory and New Media in an Era of Globalization.* 3rd ed. Baltimore, MD: The Johns Hopkins University Press, 2006.

Douglas Engelbart

Douglas Engelbart is known as one of the creators of hypertext linking. But that is not all he is known for doing. Engelbart is reputed to be the inventor of the pointing cursor, shared-screen teleconferencing, e-mail, and the mouse. For his lifelong achievements in the field of technology, he was awarded the U.S. National Medal of Technology in 2000.

I

IBM Corporation

The IBM Corporation plays a significant role in the development of commercial applications for emerging computer technology. Although IBM did not invent the computer, it holds many patents in computer-related technology. For decades it was the world's leading computer manufacturer, and its innovations were vital to the technological world.

IBM's Beginnings

The history of the IBM Corporation can be traced to the year 1890, when a new process to record census information was developed by German immigrant Herman Hollerith (1860–1929). He developed an encoding that could instruct someone on how to punch holes in cardboard cards to represent data. These holes could then be sensed electrically by his punched card tabulating machine to sort or total the data represented by the punched cards*. Hollerith's code was adopted by the U.S. Census Bureau and was still widely used into the 1960s. In 1896 Hollerith created the Tabulating Machine Company to market his product. Eventually, data encoded on s was used to represent instructions to a computer and served the purpose of loading a program onto a computer. Punched cards were used extensively by corporations and the U.S. government until the 1960s.

Hollerith's company merged with the Computing Scale Company of America and the International Time Recording Company in 1911 to form the Computing-Tabulating-Recording Company or C-T-R. In addition to Hollerith's tabulating machine, the new company also made time clocks, meat and cheese slicers, and a unique new calculating scale.

The Early Watson Years

In 1914 American businessman Thomas J. Watson (1874–1956) was hired from the National Cash Register (NCR) Company as the firm's general manager. Watson was an effective leader—stern but compassionate, motivated yet ethical. He dramatically grew the company's revenues, consolidated its products, and expanded its operations internationally. In 1924 he formally changed C-T-R's name to International Business Machines Corporation (IBM). Watson's success was based on two key beliefs: that employees are truly a valuable asset and should be treated as such, and that his customers' success would be his number one goal.

Due to the high initial costs of his product, Watson leased his equipment to customers. This enabled IBM to enjoy a regular stream of income

*__punched card__ a paper card with punched holes which give instructions to a computer in order to encode program instructions and data

throughout the economic pitfalls of the Great Depression of the 1930s. While other companies were laying off employees and declaring bankruptcy, Watson was building a large inventory of data processing equipment based on Hollerith's system. This helped IBM land the massive data processing contract for the new Social Security Administration in 1935. Continuing production through the Depression was a big gamble, but it worked.

In 1937 Watson hired his son Thomas J. Watson Jr. (1914–1993) as a salesman, and the next leader of IBM began his training. He would eventually become chief executive officer in 1956, the year his father died. T.J. Jr. later served as American Ambassador to the Soviet Union.

Early in his career, T. J. Jr. became enamored with the idea of electronic calculation as opposed to the mechanical approach. His dreams became reality in 1944 with the Mark I, a large-scale electronic calculating computer developed at Harvard with IBM support. This computer was followed by the 701 in 1952 and the RAMAC 305 in 1956. These early machines were experimental, rather than commercially viable units. They were built using vacuum tubes and relays, and were so expensive that only a few of the largest companies and the federal government could afford them.

Creating an Industry Standard

In the 1960s the computer industry centered on the development of the mainframe computer. IBM was the best-known name in the commercialization of the mainframe computer for business use, but it was not the only company developing computer technology. Other players in the mainframe computer industry in the early 1960s included RCA, Sperry Rand, Burroughs, and NCR.

No standardization existed for computer design and programming, so computers from each of these companies were incompatible with each other in both hardware and software. Often, even new computers released by a given manufacturer were not compatible with their predecessors. In this atmosphere of industry fragmentation, T. J. Jr. took a gamble as significant as the one his father made during the Great Depression. Betting on a technological evolution generically termed the microchip*, IBM developed Solid Logic Technology (SLT) and designed a bold, new commercial computer system, the System/360, around it.

Computers of the early 1960s were based on the transistor*, which had been invented by Bell Labs. While the transistor was a major improvement over the vacuum tube, it still was a discrete component. Only a limited number of discrete components could be connected together to make a bigger computer that would still be reliable and as fast as its predecessors. In comparison, SLT chips could hold hundreds of transistors on a single 0.64-centimeter (0.25-inch) square silicon wafer, thus breaking through the discrete component limitation.

Although SLT was a significant hardware advance, the software was even bigger. OS/360 was developed as the standard operating system. It would remain constant through the evolution of the 360, 370, and 390 and would always be compatible with the versions before it.

The enormity of the 360 project taxed IBM to the breaking point. At times, the junior Watson's dream took on nightmarish proportions. He had literally bet the company on the success of the 360. Eventually, his staunch belief in his father's business approach prevailed over the technical problems. The IBM System/360 was announced in 1964 and IBM became the predominant—and, at times the only—mainframe computer manufacturer.

Eventually, the S/360 evolved into the S/390. The standard of the mainframe industry, S/390 turned out to be one of IBM's most enduring and valuable products. There were only two major competitors, Hitachi and Fujitsu, both of which made clone computers which emulated the instructions of the S/390. These machines used the IBM OS/390 operating system, which provided IBM with large amounts of ongoing revenue. IBM has since released the zSeries of mainframes, which continue the legacy of backwards compatibility with older mainframes, even back to the original S/360.

IBM's strategies proved so powerful that its competition gradually disappeared. As IBM grew in size and became the dominant force in the industry, it achieved monopoly status and the government took action to rein in the giant. Three separate and enormously draining anti-trust suits were filed between 1932 and the 1980s. The U.S. Justice Department finally prevailed in undoing IBM's dominance. Although the final suit was settled as being without merit, IBM had become a victim of its own success.

Starting in 1914, the Watsons had built a vast, highly respected, and profitable company known for its ethics and honest concern for customers

* **microchip** a common term for a semiconductor integrated circuit device

* **transistor** a contraction of TRANSfer resISTOR; a semiconductor device, invented by John Bardeen, Walter Brattain, and William Shockley, which has three terminals; can be used for switching and amplifying electrical signals

and employees. T. J. Jr.'s retirement in 1971 marked the start of a succession of CEOs and, some say, a general decline at IBM.

Birth of the IBM-PC

By the late 1970s, it was possible to make a functional computer that would fit on an individual's desktop. Great debates took place at IBM over the development of such a unit. The main detractors were the executives in charge of the mainframe program, who considered the development of individual computers a threat to the demand for mainframe computers.

In 1981 American businessman John R. Opel (1925–) was named CEO. He ordered the creation of the personal computer. Internal opposition to this decision was so strong that Opel set up a separate lab in Boca Raton, Florida, to create and manufacture the device. This was geographically as far away from the mainframe and storage advocates as he could place it. American computer scientist Phil Estridge (1937–1985), the leader of the PC project, was given a great deal of autonomy to make decisions necessary to carry out his mission.

Although IBM had a huge internal staff of programmers and processor designers, they were all too busy and their departments were too bureaucratic to help with the PC project. Estridge turned instead to two new startup companies for help: Intel and Microsoft. Intel would design and manufacture the microprocessors and Microsoft would develop the operating system based on DOS (Disk Operating System). In an attempt to foster acceptance of the IBM-PC, Estridge decided the architecture would be "open," thus fostering the development of complementary attachments. This was in stark contrast to the strategy of competitors Apple and PET. The result was that the IBM-PC was the most successful architecture of all the PC approaches.

Unfortunately for IBM, the company does not own any of it. Estridge failed to obtain the ongoing rights to the intellectual property IBM was paying Microsoft and supporting Intel to develop.

In 1992, during American businessman John Akers (1934–) administration, IBM finally crashed. It had amassed many more employees than it really needed. Facing losses for the first time in decades, IBM divested itself of more than 100 thousand employees, mostly through generous early retirement programs.

Akers left IBM in 1993 as the stock price hit an all-time low. The board hired Louis V. Gerstner Jr. (1942–), the former CEO of RJR Nabisco, Inc. and American Express. He immediately started to attack the entrenched bureaucracy and redefine the company. Gerstner inherited many problems stemming from decisions made by his predecessors; for example, in 1998, IBM's PC division lost more than $900 million dollars. However, Gerstner worked to resolve the profitability problem and restore the stock price. He reversed the strategy of the previous CEO, and began to reconsolidate many of IBM's business units into one cohesive company. At the time business units had been isolated from each other in order to reduce their expenses and allow them to quickly respond to growing competition in a variety of computer-related fields. By reintegrating the units, Gerstner was able to pursue a strategy of focusing on consulting services to other businesses first, and providing hardware and software second. This allowed high revenue opportunities without requiring a lot of capital invested in new manufacturing or long development periods before product launch. By the time he retired in 2002, Gerstner succeeded in transforming IBM into a global power in business consulting and restored the prestige to IBM's reputation. Since then, IBM has also focused on expanding its intellectual property portfolio, and aggressively pursued patents on new technology. Licensing its intellectual property has produced over one billion dollars in revenue for IBM.

Since the early 1990s, IBM researchers have worked on artificial intelligence. In 1996, Deep Blue, an IBM computer designed to play chess, competed against reigning world champion Garry Kasparov (1963–). Kasparaov defeated Deep Blue in a six-game series by a score of 4–2. In a 1997 rematch, an improved Deep Blue defeated Kasparov by a score of 3.5–2.5. Following the rematch, Kasparov stated that some of Deep Blue's moves exhibited creativity and intelligence, which he attributed to unauthorized intervention by human competitors.

In 2011, IBM's Watson, an artificial intelligence computer system, competed on *Jeopardy!*, a U.S. quiz show. Watson had to analyze natural language clues before searching its databases and formulating a natural language response. The computer used thousands of language analysis algorithms to analyze key words from each clue and search for related terms to devise answers. Watson competed against, and defeated, former *Jeopardy!* champions during the week-long competition.

 See also **Hollerith, Herman • Intel Corporation • Mainframes • Watson, Thomas J., Sr.**

Resources

Books

Copeland, B. Jack, ed. *The Essential Turing: Seminal Writings in Computing, Logic, Philosophy, Artificial Intelligence, and Artificial Life Plus the Secrets of Enigma.* Oxford, UK, and New York: Clarendon Press; New York: Oxford University Press, 2005.

Hoskins, Jim. *IBM on Demand Technology for the Growing Business: Building a Flexible Infrastructure for Today and Tomorrow.* Gulf Breeze, FL: Maximum Press, 2005.

International Business Machines Corporation, and IBM Global Services. *The Enterprise of the Future: Global CEO Study.* Somers, NY: IBM Global Business Services, 2008.

THINK About It

"THINK" became the daily directive for IBM and was printed on signs throughout the company. IBM's focus was on quality and customer service.

IBMers made sure their equipment worked to the benefit of the customer. In the complex and precarious world of data processing, the statement "No one ever got fired for buying IBM" became an industry adage.

Olsen, Dan R. *Building Interactive Systems: Principles for Human-Computer Interaction.* Boston: Course Technology, 2010.

Reilly, Edwin D. *Milestones in Computer Science and Information Technology.* Westport, CT: Greenwood Press, 2003.

Sudkamp, Thomas A. *Languages and Machines: An Introduction to the Theory of Computer Science.* 3rd ed. Indianapolis, IN: Addison Wesley, 2005.

Te'eni, Dov, Jane M. Carey, and Ping Zhang. *Human Computer Interaction: Developing Effective Organizational Information Systems.* Hoboken, NJ: John Wiley & Sons, 2007.

Watson, Thomas J. *A Business and Its Beliefs.* New York: McGraw-Hill, 1963; reprint. 2003.

Web Sites

IBM Corporation. "IBM's History of Progress." http://www-03.ibm.com/ibm/history/ (accessed October 19, 2012).

U.S. Government; science.gov. "Computer Hardware." http://www.science.gov/browse/w_117A1.htm (accessed October 19, 2012).

United States Environmental Protection Agency (EPA). "Electronics and Computer Industry." http://www.epa.gov/compliance/resources/publications/assistance/sectors/notebooks/elecmpsn.pdf (accessed October 19, 2012).

Information Retrieval

Information retrieval, commonly referred to as IR, is the process by which a collection of information is represented, stored, and searched in order to extract items that match the specific parameters of a user's request—or query—for information. Though information retrieval can be a manual process, as in using an index to find certain information within a book, the term is usually applied when the collection of information is in electronic form, and a computer carries out the process of matching query and document. The collection usually consists of text documents (either bibliographic information such as title, citation and abstract, or the complete text of documents such as journal articles, magazines, newspapers, or encyclopedias). Collections of multimedia documents such as images, video clips, music, and sound are also becoming common, and information retrieval methods are being developed to search these types of collections as well.

The information retrieval process begins with an information need—someone (referred to as the user) requires certain information to answer a question or carry out a task. To retrieve the information, the user develops a query, which is the expression of the information need in concrete terms ("I need information on whitewater rafting in the Grand Canyon").

The query is then translated into the specific search strategy best suited to the document collection and search engine to be searched (for example, *whitewater ADJ rafting AND grand ADJ canyon* where ADJ means adjacent and AND means and). The search engine matches the terms of the search query against terms in documents in the collection, and it retrieves the items that match the user's request, based on the matching criteria used by that search engine. The retrieved documents can be viewed by the user, who decides whether they are relevant; that is, whether they meet the original information need.

Information retrieval is a complex process because there is no infallible way to provide a direct connection between a user's query for information and documents that contain the desired information. Information retrieval is based on a match between the words used to formulate the query and the words used to express concepts or ideas in a document. A search may fail because the user does not correctly guess the words that a useful document would contain, so important material is missed. Or, the user's search terms may appear in retrieved documents that pertain to a subject other than the one intended by the user, so material is retrieved which is not useful. Research in information retrieval has aimed at developing systems which minimize these two types of failures.

History of Information Retrieval

Almost as soon as computers were developed, information scientists suggested that the new machines had the potential to perform text processing as well as arithmetical operations. By representing text as ASCII* characters, queries formulated as character strings could be matched against the character strings in documents. The first computer-based IR systems, which appeared in the 1950s, were based on punched cards*. These were followed in the 1960s by systems based on storage of the database on magnetic tape*.

These first systems were hampered by the limited processing power of early computers, and the limited capacity for and high cost of storage. They operated offline*, in a batch processing* mode. It was not until the 1970s that IR systems made it possible for users to submit their queries and obtain an immediate response, allowing them to view the results and modify their queries as needed. The development of magnetic disk storage and improvements in telecommunications networks at this time made it possible to provide access to IR systems nationwide.

At first very little textual information was available in electronic form, though printed indexing and abstracting services for manual searching had been available for many years. Over time, however, a significant back file of a number of databases was created, making it realistic to do a retrospective search for literature on a given topic.

* **ASCII** an acronym that stands for American Standard Code for Information Interchange; assigns a unique 8-bit binary number to every letter of the alphabet, the digits (0 to 9), and most keyboard symbols

* **punched card** a paper card with punched holes which give instructions to a computer in order to encode program instructions and data

* **magnetic tape** a way of storing programs and data from computers; tapes are generally slow and prone to deterioration over time but are inexpensive

* **offline** the mode of operation of a computer that applies when it is completely disconnected from other computers and peripherals (like printers)

* **batch processing** an approach to computer utilization that queues noninteractive programs and runs them one after another

One of the best known commercial information systems is DIALOG (also sometimes denoted as Dialog; an online information service owned by ProQuest as of 2012), which currently has hundreds of databases containing many types of information—newspapers, encyclopedias, statistical profiles, directories, and full-text and bibliographic databases in the sciences, humanities, and business. Another well-known commercial system is LEXIS-NEXIS (owned by the LexisNexis Group), which is widely used for its full-text collection in business and particularly law, since it provides computer searching of statutes and case law.

Much early work in information retrieval was conducted at U.S. government institutions such as the National Aeronautics and Space Administration (NASA) and the National Library of Medicine (NLM), and included the forerunners of today's systems. NASA and the Atomic Energy Commission first operated versions of the DIALOG system; it later became a commercial system. The MEDLINE system (short for Medical Literature Analysis and Retrieval System Online, or MEDLARS Online) currently operated by NLM originated in an experimental system for searching the company's medical database, MEDLARS (an abbreviation for Medical Literature Analysis and Retrieval System).

Boolean Information Retrieval

For many years, the standard method of retrieval from commercially available databases was Boolean retrieval. In Boolean retrieval, queries are constructed by combining search terms with the Boolean operators *AND*, *OR*, and *NOT*. The system returns those documents that exactly match the search terms and the logical constraints.

In addition to the basic AND, OR, NOT operators, most operational Boolean systems offer proximity operators so that searchers can specify that terms must be adjacent or within a fixed distance of one another. This allows the specification of a phrase as a search term, for example *grand ADJ canyon*, meaning grand must be adjacent to canyon in retrieved documents. Many other functions are commonly available, such as the ability to search specific parts of a document, to search many databases simultaneously, or to remove duplicates. However the basic functionality in commercial systems remains the standard Boolean search.

Problems with Boolean Retrieval

Boolean searching has been criticized because it requires searchers to understand and apply basic Boolean logic in constructing their search strategies, rather than posing their queries in natural language. Another criticism is that Boolean searching requires that terms in the retrieved document exactly match the query terms, so potentially useful information may be missed because a document does not contain the specific term the searcher thought to use. A Boolean search essentially divides a database into two parts: documents that match and those that do not match the query. The number of documents retrieved may be zero, if

* **cosine** a trigonometric function of an angle, defined as the ratio of the length of the adjacent side of a right-angled triangle divided by the length of its hypotenuse

the query was very specific, or it could be tens of thousands if very common terms were used. All documents retrieved are treated equally so the system cannot make recommendations about the order in which they should be viewed. Because of its complexity, Boolean searching has often been carried out by information professionals such as librarians who act as research intermediaries for their patrons.

Boolean retrieval has also been criticized on the basis of performance. The standard measures of performance for IR systems are precision and recall. Precision is a measure of the ability of a system to retrieve *only* relevant documents (those that match the subject of the user's query). Recall is a measure of the ability of the system to retrieve *all* the relevant documents in the system. Using these measures, the performance of Boolean systems has been criticized as inadequate, leading to the continuing search for other ways to retrieve information electronically.

Alternatives to Boolean Retrieval

Since the 1960s and 1970s, IR researchers explored ways to improve the performance of information retrieval systems. Gerard Salton (1927–1995), a professor at Cornell University, was a key figure in this research. For more than thirty years, he and his students worked on the *SMART* system (the acronym for the System for the Mechanical Analysis and Retrieval of Text), a research environment that allowed them to explore the impact of varying parameters in the retrieval system. Using measures such as precision and recall, he and other researchers found that performance improvements can be made by implementing systems with features such as term weighting, ranked output based on the calculation of query-document similarity, and relevance feedback.

In these systems, documents are represented by the terms they contain. The list of terms is often referred to as a document vector and is used to position the document in N-dimensional space (where N is the number of unique terms in the entire collection of documents). This approach to IR is referred to as the vector space model.

For each term, a weight is calculated using the statistics of term frequency, which represents the importance of the term in the document. A common method is to calculate the *tfxidf* value (term frequency x inverse document frequency). In this model, the weight of a term in a document is proportional to the frequency of occurrence of the term in the document, and inversely proportional to the frequency with which the term occurs in the entire document collection. In other words, a good index term is one that occurs frequently in a particular document but infrequently in the database as a whole.

The query is also considered as a vector in N-dimensional space, and the distance between a document and a query is an indication of the similarity, or degree of match, between them. This distance is quantified by using a distance measure, commonly a similarity function such as the cosine* measure. The results are sorted by similarity value and displayed in order, best match first.

* **algorithm** a rule or procedure used to solve a mathematical problem—most often described as a sequence of steps

* **hyperlinks** connections between electronic documents that permit automatic browsing transfer at the point of the link

* **proprietary** a process or technology developed and owned by an individual or company, and not published openly

* **artificial intelligence (AI)** a branch of computer science dealing with creating computer hardware and software to mimic the way people think and perform practical tasks

* **expert system** a computer system that uses a collection of rules to exhibit behavior which mimics the behavior of a human expert in some area

A Boolean Search Example

A Boolean search for *winter AND Yosemite AND camping* would only retrieve documents that contained all three words winter, Yosemite, and camping since the AND operator requires that a term be present. The OR operator allows one of the terms to be present, and the NOT operator rejects documents if a term is present. A more complex search, *winter AND (Yosemite OR Yellowstone) AND skiing NOT downhill* would retrieve all documents that referred to skiing in either Yosemite or Yellowstone in winter, unless there was a specific reference to downhill. Of course, the documents would have to match the search terms exactly, so a document discussing skiing in Yosemite in January would not be retrieved unless it specifically mentioned the word *winter*.

The relevance feedback feature allows the user to examine documents and make some judgments about their relevance. This information is used to recalculate the weights and rerank the documents, improving the usefulness of the document display.

These systems allow the user to state an information need in natural language, rather than constructing a formal query as required by Boolean systems. The ranked output also imposes an order on the documents retrieved, so that the first documents to be viewed are most likely to be relevant. The search is modified automatically based on the user's feedback to the system.

More recently, information retrieval systems have been developed to search the World Wide Web (commonly shortened to, the Web). These search engines use software programs called crawlers that locate pages on the Web that are indexed on a centralized server. The index is used to answer queries submitted to the Web search engine. The matching algorithms* used to match queries with Web pages are based on the Boolean or vector space model.

Individual search engines vary in terms of the information on the Web page that they index, the factors used in assigning term weights, and the ranking algorithm used. Some search engines index information extracted from hyperlinks* as well as from the text itself. Because information on the search engine is usually proprietary*, details of the algorithms are not readily available. Comparisons of retrieval performance are also difficult because the systems index different parts of the web and because they undergo constant change. Recall is impossible to measure because the potential number of pages relevant to a query is so large.

The Future of Information Retrieval

Researchers continue to improve the performance of information retrieval systems. An ongoing series of experiments called TREC (Text Retrieval Evaluation Conference) is conducted annually by the National Institute of Standards and Technology (NIST) to encourage research in information retrieval and its use in real-world systems.

One long-term goal is to develop systems that do more than simply identify useful documents. By considering a database as a knowledge base rather than simply a collection of documents, it may be possible to design retrieval systems that can interpret documents and use the knowledge they contain to answer questions. This will require developments in artificial intelligence (AI)*, natural language processing, expert systems*, and related fields. Research so far has concentrated primarily on relatively narrow subject areas, but the goal is to create systems that can understand and respond to questions in broad subject areas.

 See also **Boolean Algebra • E-Commerce • Search Engines • World Wide Web**

Resources

Books

Baeza-Yates, Ricardo, and Berthier Ribeiro-Neto. *Modern Information Retrieval: The Concepts and Technology behind Search.* 2nd ed. New York: Addison Wesley, 2011.

Bates, Marcia J. ed. *Understanding Information Retrieval Systems: Management, Types, and Standards.* Boca Raton, FL: CRC Press, Taylor & Francis Group, 2012.

Chowdhury, G. G. *Introduction to Modern Information Retrieval.* 3rd ed. New York: Neal-Schuman, 2010.

Jouis, Christophe, ed. *Next Generation Search Engines: Advanced Models for Information Retrieval.* Hershey, PA: Information Science Reference, 2012.

Manning, Christopher D., Prabhaker Raghavan, and Hinrich Schütze. *Introduction to Information Retrieval.* New York: Cambridge University Press, 2008.

Meadow, Charles T., Bert R. Boyce, and Donald H. Kraft. *Text Information Retrieval Systems.* 3rd ed. Amsterdam and London: Academic, 2007.

Web Sites

The College of New Jersey, and Eric Thul. "The SMART Retrieval System." http://www.tcnj.edu/~mmmartin/EThul/SMART/smart-pres.pdf (accessed October 4, 2012).

National Institute of Standards and Technology. "Text Retrieval Conference (TREC)." http://trec.nist.gov/ (accessed October 4, 2012).

Information Technology Standards

Standards are quantifiable metrics to which parties adhere for purposes of allowing some common ground for interchange. Some view monetary systems developed for the exchange of goods as the earliest standards. A language is a standard for communication. The alphabet is a base standard for the exchange of information. For example, all English speakers agree that the letters "d," "o," and "g" in this order stand for the word "dog," which in turn stands for a four-legged furry animal that can be trained to fetch a ball or newspaper. What most people think of as the classic standards include a variety of different measurement standards—the rod, cubit, pint, quart, foot, yard; and the meter, liter, and gram. The U.S. Congress, in accord with Section 8 of the U.S. Constitution, has the power to "coin money, regulate the value thereof, and of foreign coin, and fix the standard of weights and measures." Most national governments assign similar responsibilities to provide standards to promote commerce. International treaties and organizations facilitate trade by defining standards across borders.

Standards may be broken down into a variety of categories. One simple classification breaks them down into three groups: measurement, minimum attribute, and compatibility. A measurement standard is the one that most people associate with the word "standard." Examples would include an inch, a volt, a kilogram. A minimum attribute standard provides a measurement in context—the quality of certain grades of motor oil (SAE 10-30), or the voltage that may safely be carried by a given gauge of wire, for example. Finally, compatibility standards, which constitute the majority of the standards in the realm of information technology, specify the nature of the agreement that will allow two things to interact.

For thousands of years, standards were primarily a matter of currency and standard weights and measures. An explosion in standards came about with the industrial revolution. The growth in standardization in the manufacturing arena was caused by both mass production and the development of railroads as a means of transportation. Railroads themselves required standardization on many fronts, from track gauge to time. The current system of standardized time zones is an outgrowth of the need to be able to publish schedules for train stops. Through the 1830s, the time was set in each geographic area by a local observatory. When it was 9 P.M. in Washington, D.C., it might be 9:12 P.M. in Philadelphia. By 1850, the Harvard Observatory was telegraphing a form of standard time to various railroad hubs. In 1879, the United States had about seventy-five standard times! The lack of standard time created problems for railroads. How could they tell someone when a train would arrive or depart if everyone's watches used a different time? After a series of negotiations, it was agreed in 1885 that there would be four basic time zones in the United States. Interestingly, it was not until 1918 that the general population agreed to use these four standard time zones.

The railroads had the capability to move mass-produced goods great distances creating a need for standardized parts that could be obtained from local sources. A stove manufactured in New Haven, Connecticut, could be repaired in Denver, Colorado, if the parts used in manufacture were standardized. From guns to watches to washing machines, the growth of mass production and the growth of catalog sales by companies such as Sears created a need for manufacturing standards and standard parts. The development of new methods of heating homes and buildings involved the development of boilers as heat exchangers. Boiler explosions led to a call for standards for testing boilers and the development of modern safety standards.

One of the key events in the development of standards in the United States occurred as a result of a major fire in Baltimore. Many of the fire companies from other cities that responded to the call for help could not connect their hoses and pumpers to the Baltimore fire hydrants because of different pipe diameters and thread sizes. This led the U.S. Congress, with its constitutional mandate to set standards, to establish the National Bureau of Standards (now the National Institute for Standards and Technology). To this day, one of the nine standards laboratories is concerned with standards for fire fighting and fire prevention.

Among the first information technology standards were those in the telecommunications arena. Standards have played an important role in telecommunications. Any landline phone manufactured for use in the United States could be connected to any phone outlet. Thousands of manufacturers and network owners agreed to the same power and signaling conventions. However, cellular networks in the United States traditionally maintained different communications standards. Some carried established Code Division Multiple Access (CDMA) networks while others used the more globally prevalent Global System for Mobile (GSM) standard. Although users inside the United States may not notice a difference, those on GSM networks can use their phones in many other countries because GSM was adopted by several international standards organizations (including in the European Union).

Manufacturers of information processing equipment, particularly telecommunications equipment, have developed standards for hardware and software to cover areas such as data packet construction, power specifications, and connection types. The number of standards for software design and information formatting is growing.

Standards Organizations

Standards originate from a variety of sources and processes. Industries set shared standards to allow them to interoperate. These range from standard parts such as bolts and pipe sizes to standards for Electronic Data Interchange (EDI). De facto* standards emerge from the adoption of a common way of doing something. De jure* standards emerge from the legislative and judicial branches of government. These include standards set by the Occupational Health and Safety Administration (OSHA) and environmental standards set by the Environmental Protection Agency (EPA).

Standards are also set by organizations that seek to achieve a voluntary consensus as to what the standard should be. Three main organizations operate internationally to assist in the development of voluntary standards—the International Organization for Standardization (ISO), the International ElectroMechanical Commission (IEC), and the Telecommunication Standardization Sector of the International Telecommunications Union (ITU-T). The ITU-T is a multilateral treaty organization concerned with all aspects of international telephony. The United States is represented in the ITU-T by representatives of the various U.S. organizations concerned with telephone

* **de facto** as is

* **de jure** strictly according to the law

service. A trade organization, the Alliance for Telecommunications Industry Solutions (ATIS), serves as the host for the U.S. standards committee, T1.

The IEC has a number of technical committees concerned with electrical, electromechanical, and electronic standards. ISO is the largest of the international standards organizations and has technical committees covering all aspects of standards from fasteners to pressure vessels to wood products. All three of these organizations have committees to develop information technology standards. The most notable of these is ISO Joint Technical Committee 1, which serves as the liaison to the other organizations.

Input to these international standards committees comes from national-level standards organizations. These include the British Standards Institute (BSI), the Deutsch Institute fur Normung (DIN), and the Association Francais de Normalization (AFNOR). In the United States, the American National Standards Institute (ANSI) serves as the conduit for contributions from a federation of more than 100 American standards organizations.

In the information technology arena, several organizations based in the United States contribute time and expertise through individual and corporate contributions. These organizations include the National Committee for Information Technology Standards (NCITS), the Engineering Industries Association (EIA), the National Information Standards Organization (NISO), the Institute of Electrical and Electronics Engineers (IEEE), the Internet Engineering Task Force (IETF), and the World Wide Web Consortium (W3C). Their work is coordinated through ANSI.

Information Technology Standards

As the use and importance of computers and computer networks have grown, standards in this area have become increasingly important. Individual and organizational consumers of information processing equipment and software demand that the services and equipment they purchase comply with selected standards. Standardization efforts in the information technology arena have produced more pages of standards than all other standardization efforts combined.

Information technology standards include both hardware and software standards. Software and information formatting standards are increasingly important. Standards exist for operating systems, programming languages, communications protocols, and human computer interaction. For example, the global exchange of electronic mail messages requires standards for addressing, formatting, and transmission.

For one word processor to be able to read another word processor's output requires standards for organization of the information within the file. From an information encoding point of view, the most basic standard is how to represent a character. Because computers exchange information as numbers, there must be agreement as to what the numbers mean. For decades, this standard was the American Standard Code for Information Interchange (ASCII) and later related permutations of ASCII that could represent specialty characters for languages other than English. It was agreed that computers would exchange information as sequences of bytes—packages of numbers represented as a sequence of ones and zeros. A byte is defined as eight binary digits—for example, the binary number 00000001 is the same as the decimal number one and the binary number 10000000 is equivalent to the decimal number 128. It is possible to represent 256 different decimal numbers using eight binary digits.

ASCII defines the association between these numbers and characters. The number 65 is A and the number 66 is B, for example. At the end of the 1990s, ASCII began to be replaced by a more comprehensive standard that uses sixteen bits that can represent more than 65,000 different characters. This standard, known as UNICODE, has made it possible to exchange information not only in English but also in Arabic, Chinese, Japanese, and other languages. Information formatting and processing standards are growing to include more and more kinds of information in increasingly complex aggregate forms. There are now several standards for digital documents (PDF), images (JPEG), audio files (MP3, MPEG-4, AAC), and movies (MPEG).

A growing array of standards allows the World Wide Web to operate, including the standards for the basic protocol, the hypertext transfer protocol (HTTP), the standard for the messages (HTML), and standards to describe more general documents (the eXtended Markup Language or XML), links (the XML Linking Language or XLL), and appearance (CSS, XSL).

Standards Issues

Standards have come to play an increasingly prominent role in the restriction or promotion of trade. In very simple terms, a standard may be used by a nation to constrain the products that may be sold within its boundaries. Similarly, getting a nation to adopt a standard can cause a whole new market to be opened to business. Thus, engineers and scientists who have historically engaged in standardization as a technical process now find themselves engaged in the process with an eye to how it impacts an organization's ability to promote and market its products.

 See also **Association of Computing Machinery • Government Funding, Research • Institute of Electrical and Electronics Engineers (IEEE)**

Resources

Web Sites

American National Standards Institute. "About ANSI." http://www. ansi.org/about_ansi/overview/overview.aspx?menuid=1#. UJckCUJhVMI (accessed November 2, 2012).

International Organization for Standardization. http://www.iso.org/iso/ home.html (accessed November 2, 2012).

International Organization for Standardization (ISO)

The International Organization for Standardization was founded in 1947 to promote the exchange of goods and services throughout the world. Comprised of member organizations from 140 nations, the international group sets standards for everything, from the size of credit cards, to the representation of country names. The organization is also known as the ISO, which is a play on words. It is not the acronym for the group; it is based on the Greek word *isos,* meaning "equal."

Institute of Electrical and Electronics Engineers (IEEE)

The Institute of Electrical and Electronics Engineers, Inc. (IEEE) is the world's largest technical professional association with more than 400 thousand members in 160 countries. It is a non-profit organization that is dedicated to advancing the theory and application of electrical and electronics engineering and computer science. Through its members, the IEEE is a leading authority on areas ranging from aerospace, computers, and telecommunications to biomedicine, electric power, and consumer electronics. According to its Web site, the IEEE is "dedicated to advancing technological innovation and excellence for the benefit of humanity."

The IEEE (pronounced Eye-triple-E), has served electrical and electronics engineers and scientists since 1884, when a group of inventors and entrepreneurs including American inventor Thomas Edison (1847–1931) and Scottish-born American inventor Alexander Graham Bell (1847–1922) founded the American Institute of Electrical Engineers (AIEE). In 1912, radio technology practitioners formed a separate international society, the Institute of Radio Engineers (IRE). In 1963, the AIEE and IRE merged to form the IEEE.

In the 2010s, the IEEE produces about 30 percent of the world's literature in the electrical, electronics, and computer engineering fields, and sponsors or cosponsors more than 900 technical conferences each year. It also has produced 900 active industry standards, more than one third of which influence the information technology and computer industries.

The IEEE consists of about 1,860 local sections and almost eighteen hundred student chapters as well as forty-five Societies and technical Councils that cover a wide range of technical interest areas. The largest of the institute's societies is the IEEE Computer Society. In addition, ten geographic regions for the IEEE are found around the world. In addition, the IEEE has 130 journals, transactions, and magazines, and coordinates about 300 conferences annually.

Dr. James "Jim" Prendergast heads the IEEE as its executive director. Prendergast is the leader of the IEEE's Management Council, which consists of himself along with eleven senior executives who manage IEEE operations. The Management Council coordinates the work of about 1,100 full-time, part-time, and temporary IEEE employees. Prendergast took on the responsibilities of executive director in April 2009. IEEE offices are located in the United States, along with China, India, Japan, and Singapore. Its main corporate office is in New York City and its U.S. office is in Washington, D.C.

The IEEE Computer Society

Tracing its origins back to 1946, the Computer Society is the leading provider of technical information and services to the world's computing professionals. The society's mission is to advance computer and information processing science and technology; promote professional interaction; and keep members up-to-date on the latest developments.

The growth of the IEEE Computer Society mirrors the growth of the computing profession. In 2012, the Computer Society has over 375 chapters, national and international, professional and student; with more than 200 of them being professional. Society membership has expanded from less than ten thousand in the 1950s to more than 375,000. About 60 percent of these members work in industry, with the rest in government and academia. They include computer scientists, computer engineers, electrical engineers, information scientists, software engineers, information technology managers, and practitioners in emerging classifications. Students comprise about 21 percent of the membership. With 45 percent of its constituents living outside of the United States, the society is truly a global organization.

To serve the profession, the Computer Society supports a variety of activities. It publishes a wide array of magazines and archival transactions and delivers more than 15,000 editorial pages in twenty titles every year. The society also is a leading publisher of conference proceedings, which contain peer-reviewed papers containing the latest technical information. These proceedings stem from the many technical workshops, symposia, and conferences the society sponsors or cosponsors each year. Additionally, more than thirty technical committees in specialty areas organize meetings, produce newsletters, and provide networking opportunities for Computer Society members.

In addition to its headquarters in Washington, D.C., the IEEE Computer Society has other main offices in California and Japan. John W. Walz is the current president of the Computer Society.

Society Functions

The society is a leader in developing standards for the computing industry, supporting more than 200 standards development groups in twelve major technical areas. Among these standards are wireless networking, Web page engineering, and software engineering. IEEE standards are widely adopted by industry to assure consistent operability and functionality. One example is the IEEE 1012 Software Verification and Validation standard, which, among other uses, helps to ensure airplane and nuclear power plant safety and provide consistent performance of cell phones, beepers, and video games.

In addition to these activities, the society develops curriculum recommendations for programs in computer science and engineering and related disciplines. The society supports the Computer Sciences Accreditation Board (CSAB), a member society of the leading accreditation board in the United States, and has participated in international accreditation efforts.

Undergraduate and graduate students play an important role in the Computer Society's conferences, technical activities, and student chapter activities. Students receive significantly discounted rates for publications and conference fees, and several conferences offer student travel grants

Computer Sciences, 2nd Edition

or opportunities to attend for free by volunteering to work at the conferences. Many conferences encourage student paper submissions and award a best student paper certificate.

Students create and support chapters of their own at academic institutions worldwide. The society currently has about 85,000 student members. Student chapters sponsor a newsletter written by and for students which is distributed three to four times yearly with the society's flagship magazine, *Computer*. Student activities are highlighted on the IEEE's Web site at http://www.computer.org/portal/web/studentactivities/home.

The society sponsors a program of student awards and scholarships. The IEEE Computer Society International Design Competition (CSIDC) is a computer science and engineering system design competition open to undergraduate teams around the world. The Richard E. Merwin Scholarship awards up to four annual scholarships for exemplary undergraduate or graduate Computer Society student chapter volunteers. The Lance Stafford Larson Outstanding Student Scholarship is given to a student submitting the best student paper on a computer-related subject. The Upsilon Pi Epsilon/ Computer Society Award was created to encourage academic excellence and offers up to four awards annually. Upsilon Pi Epsilon is the International Honor Society for the Computing Sciences.

Standards

The IEEE is one of the world's leading standards producing organizations, developing standards in a wide variety of fields. Around 900 standards and 400 projects are under development at the IEEE, as of 2012. The IEEE Standards Association (IEEE-SA) leads the coordination of standards for the IEEE. The role of standards in computers is often overlooked but critical to the development of the modern computer industry. Standards ensure that devices manufactured by separate entities will be able to interface with each other. An IEEE standard for a communications standard will typically include information about what messages are valid to send, what the size and layout of data within a message should be, and what to do when an error occurs. Examples of these types of standards are portions of IEEE 802.11, Wireless Networking or WiFi, and IEEE 1149.1, JTAG. Other IEEE standards describe programming languages and physical layout of peripheral equipment.

 See also **Association of Computing Machinery • Computer Professional**

Resources

Web Sites

IEEE Computer Society. "About Us." http://www.computer.org/portal/web/about (accessed October 8, 2012).

IEEE Computer Society. "Student Activities." http://www.computer.org/portal/web/studentactivities/home (accessed October 8, 2012).

Institute of Electrical and Electronics Engineers. "About IEEE." http://www.ieee.org/about/index.html (accessed October 8, 2012).

Institute of Electrical and Electronics Engineers. "History of IEEE." http://www.ieee.org/about/ieee_history.html (accessed October 8, 2012).

Integrated Circuits

Integrated circuits are electronic devices that contain many transistors*, resistors*, capacitors*, and connecting wires in one package. Integrated circuits, also called ICs or chips, were invented in 1959 and have become critical components in virtually all electronic devices, including computers, radios, televisions, and cell phones. The microprocessor is the most complex integrated circuit, and also the most complex single device of any kind, ever produced.

Integrated circuits are produced on a piece of semiconductor crystal. As its name implies, a semiconductor is a material that conducts electricity better than an insulator, but not as well as a conductor. The conductivity can be adjusted by introducing other elements into the crystal during manufacture. Conductivity is also changed by applying an electric field to the crystal.

Elements Used as Semiconductors

Silicon* is the most commonly used semiconductor. It is the second most common element in earth's crust, after oxygen. To be used in an integrated circuit, silicon must be processed to extreme purity. The silicon is heated until it melts, and is allowed to cool very slowly. If cooled too quickly, silicon has a tendency to crack, which would render it unusable for use in an integrated circuit. Once cooled, the ingot* is sliced into thin sheets. Many identical integrated circuits are formed simultaneously on each sheet.

In the periodic table of the elements, silicon is one of the group IV elements. This means each atom has four electrons in its outer shell available for combination with other atoms. It also means each atom would like to have four more electrons from adjacent atoms to fill up the outer shell. These characteristics cause pure silicon to form a crystalline structure. Germanium*, the second most popular semiconductor material, is also in group IV, directly below silicon in the periodic table.

For a semiconductor to be useful, trace amounts of other elements must be carefully added to the crystal. This process is called doping*. Phosphorous and boron are common elements. Phosphorous is a group V element that has five electrons in its outer shell. The extra electrons from

transistor a contraction of TRANSfer resISTOR; a semiconductor device, invented by American physicists John Bardeen (1908–1991), Walter Brattain (1902–1987), and William Shockley (1910–1989), which has three terminals; can be used for switching and amplifying electrical signals

resistors electrical components that slow the flow of current

capacitor a fundamental electrical component used for storing an electrical charge

silicon a chemical element with symbol Si; the second most abundant element in earth's crust and the most commonly used semiconductor material

ingot a formed block of metal (often cast) used to facilitate bulk handling and transportation

germanium a chemical often used as a high performance semiconductor material; chemical symbol Ge

doping a step used in the production of semiconductor materials where charged particles are embedded into the device to tailor its operational characteristics

the phosphorous atoms, each with a negative charge, are available to conduct electricity. Silicon doped with phosphorous is called N-type (for negative) silicon.

In a similar way, boron, a group III element, is used to produce P-type (P for positive) silicon. Other elements from groups III and V may be used as well. N-type (N for negative) and P-type silicon together can form transistors, the most important elements in an integrated circuit.

Transistors in Integrated Circuits

The transistor was invented at Bell Labs in 1947 by American physicists Walter Brattain (1902–1987), John Bardeen (1908–1991), and William Shockley (1910–1989). They were interested in developing a solid state amplifier that would replace the vacuum tube*. Vacuum tubes are large, consume a lot of power to heat the filament, and are subject to filament burnout.

Transistors are much smaller, less costly, and more efficient than vacuum tubes. The transistor is a three-terminal, solid-state electronic device. The terminals are called the collector, the emitter, and the base. Electricity is conducted between the collector and emitter to a greater or lesser extent depending on the current of the base. This allows a small base current to control a much larger current in the collector.

As transistors came into widespread use, circuit designs using large numbers of them were limited by a problem: connecting them together. The solution to this problem occurred independently to Jack Kilby (1923–) at Texas Instruments and Robert Noyce (1927–1990) at Fairchild Semiconductor in 1959. Many transistors could be produced on one semiconductor base simultaneously. Noyce also determined how to produce resistors, diodes, capacitors, and connecting wires on the silicon chip. The integrated circuit was born.

Types of Integrated Circuits

A transistor can be operated either as an amplifier or as a switch. When used as an amplifier, the transistor collector current replicates the base current but at a much larger scale. This amplification enables a small signal, such as that produced by a microphone, to be reproduced with enough power to drive a large device, such as loud speakers. A transistor used as an amplifier is said to be operating in its linear range, neither all the way on nor all the way off. Linear integrated circuits are used in signal processing analog signals, such as in radios and communications systems and also in analog computers.

In digital integrated circuits, transistors are used as switches. The transistor is not operating in its linear range; there is no attempt to make the output replicate the input. Instead, it is either fully on or fully off, representing either a logic one or zero. Digital integrated circuits are the heart and brains of digital computers.

The first digital integrated circuits implemented logic gates and simple memories using flip-flops. A gate is a logic device with no memory; the output at any time is determined by the inputs at that time. The simplest gate is a one input device called a *not* gate. The output is simply the opposite of the input. In a two-input *and* gate, the output is one (true) if both inputs are one, and zero otherwise. In a two-input *or* gate, the output is one (true) if either input is one, and zero otherwise. Other gates include *nand* (an *and* gate followed by a *not* gate), and *nor* gates. A flip-flop is a one-bit memory. It can be made by interconnecting the inputs and outputs of two *nand* gates. A flip-flop can be flipped to a one state or flopped to a zero state. It remains in a state until switched to the other. Gates and flip-flops are the most basic computer building blocks.

Smaller and More Powerful

Over time, the complexity of integrated circuits has increased, while the size of features continues to shrink. The feature size of an integrated circuit is indicated by the width of a wire, measured in microns (one micron is one millionth of a meter), also called a micrometer. Around the turn of the century (2000) the wire sizes within advanced integrated circuits, like those used in microprocessors, had shrunk to fractions of a micron; dimension sizes began to be referred to in nanometers (nm). A nanometer is one billionth of a meter, and one thousandth of a micron.

In 1971, Intel produced the first microprocessor, designated 4004. It contained 2,300 transistors, used 10-micron technology, and powered an electronic calculator. The original International Business Machines personal computer (IBM-PC) was based on the Intel 8088 processor, which was first produced in 1979 and contained 29,000 transistors (3-micron technology). In 1989, Intel introduced the 80486 processor, containing 1.2 million transistors (0.8-micron technology). In 1999, the company began production of the Pentium III Xeon processor, with 28 million transistors on a silicon chip (0.18-micron technology). A year later, it debuted its Pentium IV processor, which featured 42 million transistors on a silicon chip (0.13-micron technology). By 2006, Intel had introduced a microprocessor with more than a billion transistors, and in 2008, a microprocessor with more than 2 billion transistors. In 2010, Intel's Core i7 was produced using 32-nm technology. As of 2012, a typical chip has about 9 million transistors per square millimeter, with an average chip area from a few square millimeters to more than 400 square millimeters. These chips with more than one million transistors are described as ultra-large-scale integration, which reflects their increasingly complex nature. The same trend toward smaller and more powerful devices is evident in memory chips, and in microprocessors from other manufacturers, such as Texas Instruments, Motorola, Advanced Micro Devices, and International Business Machines.

With the complexity of integrated circuits growing faster each year, several terms have been introduced in the twenty-first century. For example, a system-on-a-chip, what is commonly abbreviated SoC, is an integrated circuit where all its components exist on one chip. Sometimes such

After the Transistor

American physicists Walter Brattain (1902–1987), John Bardeen (1908–1991), and William Shockley (1910–1989) were awarded the 1956 Nobel Prize in Physics for the invention of the transistor. After inventing the transistor, Brattain and Bardeen continued in basic research, Bardeen concentrating on the area of superconductivity, which is the complete absence of resistance to electric current in some materials at low temperatures. In 1972, Bardeen was awarded a second Nobel Prize in Physics for his work in superconductivity, the first person ever to receive two Nobel Physics prizes. Shockley left Bell and founded Shockley Semiconductor near Palo Alto, California, the first semiconductor firm in the area that eventually became known as Silicon Valley.

Race for a Patent

Jack Kilby (1923–2005) and Robert Noyce (1927–1990) individually filed patent applications at nearly the same time. Noyce received the first patent award, probably because his application was more narrowly worded. Eventually Kilby was awarded a patent also, and a bitter legal dispute ensued. It was resolved in 1966 when Fairchild and Texas Instruments agreed to cross-license their patent rights to each other. Noyce, who originally worked at Shockley Semiconductor, later left Fairchild and founded the Intel Corporation, which became the most successful manufacturer of microprocessors in the world.

* **integrated circuit** a circuit with the transistors, resistors, and other circuit elements etched into the surface of a single chip of semiconducting material, usually silicon

integrated circuits are not possible. In those instances, a system in package (SiP) method is used, which consists of several chips in a single unit. Further, a three-dimensional integrated circuit (3D-IC) is the term for an integrated circuit that contains two or more vertical and horizontal layers of electronic components. As of the early 2010s, 3D-IC technology is not yet widely used commercially. Lastly, a wafer-scale integration (WSI) system is one in which gigantic integrated circuits eventually could be assembled in the near-future using a single silicon wafer, resulting in an appropriately named super-chip.

▶ *See also* **Generations, Computers • Microcomputers • Minicomputers • Transistors**

Resources

Books

DeMassa, Thomas A., and Zack Ciccone. *Digital Integrated Circuits.* Hoboken, NJ: John Wiley & Sons, 1996.

Fitzgerald, Benjamin M., ed. *Transistors: Types, Materials, and Applications.* Hauppauge, NY: Nova Science, 2010.

Riordan, Michael, and Lillian Hoddeson. *Crystal Fire: The Birth of the Information Age.* New York: W. W. Norton, 1997.

Saxema, Arjun N. *Invention of Integrated Circuits: Untold Important Facts.* Hackensack, NJ: World Scientific, 2009.

Web Sites

IEEE Global History Network. "The History of the Integrated Circuit." http://www.nobelprize.org/educational/physics/integrated_circuit/history/ (accessed October 8, 2012).

PBS. "Integrated Circuits." http://www.ieeeghn.org/wiki/index.php/Integrated_Circuits (accessed October 8, 2012).

Intel Corporation

The Intel Corporation of Santa Clara, California, was founded in 1968 by American physicist Robert Noyce (1927–1990), co-inventor of the integrated circuit*, and his colleague American chemist Gordon Moore (1929–), the originator of Moore's law. The name Intel was a shortened form of Integrated Electronics. Noyce and Moore were joined by Hungarian-American businessman Andy Grove (1936–) and the three, all formerly from Fairchild Semiconductor, led the firm on its initial mission to produce the world's first semiconductor-based memory chips. The

* **silicon** a chemical element with symbol Si; the most abundant element in the Earth's crust and the most commonly used semiconductor material

company went on to commercialize the microprocessor, the product that Intel is best known for today.

In 1969 the Japanese manufacturer Busicom commissioned Intel engineers to design a set of a dozen custom chips for its new family of scientific calculators. At the time, all logic chips were custom-designed for each customer's product. Logic chips perform calculations and execute programs, unlike memory chips, which store instructions and data.

Intel engineer American electrical engineer Marcian (Ted) Hoff (1937–) improved on Busicom's idea. Instead of designing twelve custom chips, he recommended a set of only four chips for logic and memory, which featured a central processing unit. Although Busicom was satisfied with this alternative approach, Hoff realized its full potential—the design team had created the first general-purpose microprocessor chip, though the term microprocessor would not appear for many years.

But there was a problem: Intel did not own the rights to the new technology, Busicom did. Hoff urged company officials to buy the design from its former client. But others in the company claimed that Intel's future lay in fast and inexpensive memory chips, not in logic chips. Eventually, Hoff's side won by arguing that the success of the new logic chips would enhance the market for memory chips.

Busicom, strapped for cash, agreed to sell the rights for the four-chip set for $60,000. Intel used that agreement as the basis for its microprocessor business, eventually becoming a powerful global corporation. Sales in 2000 reached $33.7 billion.

In 1971, armed with its new technology, Intel engineers introduced the model 4004 microprocessor, which sold for $200 and could perform 60,000 operations per second. It was the size of a thumbnail, featured 2,300 transistors on a sliver of silicon* (Si), and could deliver the same amount of computing power as the first electronic computer, ENIAC. In

1972 the model 8008 microprocessor featured 3,500 transistors. Although that was powerful at the time, it was primitive compared to the Core 2 Duo processor offered in 2006, which had almost 300 million transistors.

A series of chips followed, each more powerful than the previous one. By 1981 Intel's 16-bit 8086 and 8-bit 8088 processors took the design world by storm, winning an unprecedented 2,500 design awards in a single year. That year, IBM selected the Intel 8088 microprocessor to run its first desktop personal computer, the IBM-PC.

The significance of the IBM alliance was not evident immediately. An Intel sales engineer who worked on the IBM project said, "At the time, a great account was one that generated ten thousand units a year. Nobody comprehended the scale of the PC business would grow to tens of millions of units every year." The success of the IBM-PC helped change the company's direction. In 1986 Intel left the memory-chip market to focus on microprocessors and, under the leadership of Andy Grove who succeeded Moore as CEO in 1987, the company became the world's dominant supplier of microprocessors.

Intel followed up the 8088 with the 80286 in 1982, the 80386 in 1986, and the 486 processor in 1989. After the 486 was released, Intel started designing two new processors simultaneously, codenamed P5 and P6 respectively. The P5 became known as the Pentium processor, and the P6 became the Pentium Pro and later the basis of the Pentium II. The Pentium III and Pentium IV completed the original Pentium line, although the brand name has been reintroduced for a line of unrelated processors. The Pentium IV was not as highly regarded as its predecessors in the Pentium line, and its performance was matched or exceeded by offerings from Intel's competitor AMD. Intel followed the Pentium IV with the introduction of its Core series processor. The Core series began with Intel enhancing the P6 architecture to improve the performance in mobile computing environments, sacrificing raw speed for lower power consumptions and cooler operation. The new architecture also was able to address some architecture decisions, which hampered the Pentium IV. The original Core processor was followed by the Core Duo, Intel's first dual core processor targeted for mobile computers. The Core 2 series of processors followed shortly after, and have re-entrenched Intel as the leader in microprocessor performance. Intel's newest architecture is the Nehalam architecture with the Core i7 being the first widely available processor of this line.

Moore's law, which predicts ever-more complex circuits, drives Intel's designers. By constantly reducing the size of transistors within chips, Intel has reduced their cost. Smaller chips are cheaper because more of them can be made from a single expensive silicon wafer. There are additional benefits. Smaller chips work faster, system reliability is increased, and power requirements are reduced.

To make these tiny chips successfully, Intel's manufacturing technology has had to improve constantly. The earliest chips were made by workers wearing smocks. In the twenty-first century microprocessors are created in a sterile environment, termed cleanrooms, which are thousands of times cleaner than those of the 1970s. Robots move the silicon wafers from process to process. Operators working in these cleanrooms wear non-linting, anti-static fabric, termed bunny suits, with face masks, safety glasses, gloves, shoe coverings, and even special breathing equipment. The bunny suits were immortalized in a series of Intel commercials in the late 1990s.

Time magazine named Intel CEO Andy Grove, a Hungarian immigrant born Adras Gróf, as its 1997 Man of the Year as "the person most responsible for the amazing growth in the power and innovative potential of microchips."

As Intel grew to become the world's largest chipmaker, its dominant market share did not go unnoticed by competitors and the federal government. In 1998 the Federal Trade Commission (FTC) announced an investigation into allegations of anti-competitive business practices. The company cooperated fully during the nine-month inquiry. The case was settled before it went to court.

Intel continues to explore possible barriers to microprocessor design. In 2007, company engineers demonstrated a forty-five nanometer process technology using an ultra tiny transistor gate and the thinnest of thin films. In time, this advance will allow the company to manufacture chips with transistors that are approximately 1/2000th the width of a human hair. In 2011, Intel completed its acquisition of the security company McAfee. This partnership aimed at creating new security pathways for devices ill-prepared for security breaches. These include wireless and mobile devices, cars, TVs, ATMs, and more. In 2012, Intel unveiled a new chip in the Clover Trail product line. This chip was built specifically for the tablet market as a rival of Apple. They run on the 1.8Ghz dual-core Atom Z2760.

 See also **Apple Computer, Inc.** • **Bell Labs** • **Integrated Circuits** • **Microchip** • **Microcomputers** • **Microsoft Corporation**

Resources

Books

Colwell, Robert P. *The Pentium Chronicles: The People, Passion, and Politics behind Intel's Landmark Chips.* Hoboken, NJ: Wiley, 2006.

Kelly, Brian W. *Chip Wars: Intel V. AMD ; Intel V. IBM.* Scranton, PA: Lets Go Publish!, 2005.

Tedlow, Richard S. *Andy Grove: The Life and Times of an American.* New York: Portfolio, 2006.

Web Sites

Intel Corporation. "Company Overview." http://www.intel.com/content/www/us/en/company-overview/company-overview.html?iid=HPAGE%20Header_About (accessed November 3, 2012).

Moore's Law

In 1965, Gordon Moore observed that the number of transistors on a microprocessor doubles every eighteen to twenty-four months. He concluded that the trend would cause computing power to rise exponentially over time. His prediction—Moore's law—has held true, though some industry experts believe the physical limitations of silicon will cause it to fail eventually. Of late, the predictions of the failure of Moore's law have been met with ingenious solutions, which continue its remarkable run. The recent trend to include multiple processor cores in one package effectively doubles the number of transistors on a chip. Techniques like this do not increase raw clockspeed, the traditional measure of how computing power increases, but increase system computing power by enabling more instructions to be processed at once. Even those who predict the continued accuracy of Moore's law expect future gains in performance to occur via holistic methods such as these.

The resulting trend toward ever-smaller chip design explains the falling prices of microprocessors. As Moore noted, "If the auto industry advanced as rapidly as the semiconductor industry, a Rolls Royce would get a half a million miles per gallon, and it would be cheaper to throw it away than to park it."

Intel Corporation. "Intel Completes Acquisition of McAfee" http://newsroom.intel.com/community/intel_newsroom/blog/2011/02/28/intel-completes-acquisition-of-mcafee (accessed September 29, 2012).

PCWorld. "Clover Trail Tablets Pitched as Workplace-friendly" http://www.pcworld.com/article/2010798/clover-trail-tablets-pitched-as-workplacefriendly.html (accessed September 29, 2012).

Interactive Systems

Interactive systems are computer systems characterized by significant amounts of interaction between humans and the computer. Most users have grown up using Macintosh or Windows computer operating systems, which are prime examples of graphical interactive systems. Editors, CAD-CAM (Computer Aided Design-Computer Aided Manufacture) systems, and data entry systems are all computer systems involving a high degree of human-computer interaction. Games and simulations are interactive systems. Web browsers and Integrated Development Environments (IDEs) are also examples of very complex interactive systems.

Some estimates suggest that as much as 90 percent of computer technology development effort is now devoted to enhancements and innovations in interface and interaction. To improve efficiency and effectiveness of computer software, programmers and designers not only need a good knowledge of programming languages, but a better understanding of human information processing capabilities as well. They need to know how people perceive screen colors, why and how to construct unambiguous icons, what common patterns or errors occur on the part of users, and how user effectiveness is related to the various mental models of systems people possess.

Types of Interactive Systems

The earliest interactive systems were command line systems, which tightly controlled the interaction between the human and the computer. The user was required to know the commands that might be issued and how the arguments were to be ordered. Both the Unix (trademarked as UNIX) operating system and DOS (Disk Operating System) are classic examples. Users were required to enter data in a particular sequence. The options for the output of data were also tightly controlled, and generally limited. Such systems generally put a high demand on the user to remember commands and the syntax for issuing these commands.

Command line systems gradually gave way to a second generation of menu-, form-, and dialog-based systems that eased some of the demands on memory. Automatic Teller Machines (ATMs), or Automated Teller

Machines, which are seen at banks and other convenient locations, represent a good example of a form-based program where users are given a tightly controlled set of possible actions. Data entry systems are frequently form-or dialog-oriented systems offering the user a limited set of choices but greatly relieving the memory demands of the earlier command line systems.

A third generation of interactive computing was introduced by Xerox Corporation in 1980. The Xerox Star was the result of a half dozen years of research and development during which the mouse, icons, the desktop metaphor, windows, and bit-mapped displays were all brought together and made to function. The Xerox Star was replicated in the Lisa and Macintosh first offered by Apple Computer Inc. in the mid-1980s. The windows, icon, menu, and pointer (or WIMP) approach was made universal by Microsoft in the Windows family of operating systems introduced in the 1990s. With the maturation of WIMP interfaces, also known as graphical user interfaces* (or GUIs—pronounced *gooey*), interaction moved from command-based to direct manipulation.

In command-based systems, the user specifies an action and then an object on which that action is to be performed. In a direct manipulation system, an object is selected, and then the user specifies the action to be performed on that object. The most recent developments in interactive systems have focused on virtualization*, and agents. The following sections describe in more detail the nature of the current generation of direct manipulation systems and the coming generation of agents and virtual systems.

The Importance of Understanding Human Capabilities

It is important that users be able to understand how to use a highly interactive computer system. American cognitive science professor Donald A. Norman (1935–) describes the human-computer interaction in terms of the "gulfs of execution and evaluation." Basically this means that the user has a goal in mind and must reformulate that goal in terms of a plan that ultimately involves the execution of a series of actions on the system. These actions result in changes in the state of the system, which must be perceived, interpreted, and evaluated by the user. Computer system developers need to understand how human beings perceive, interpret, evaluate, and respond to these computer actions.

Although even a cursory review of the literature on human perception, human information processing, and human motor skills is far beyond this brief overview, it may be useful to consider a very select set of principles developed from that literature. Hundreds of research studies have been done on the limits of short-term memory. These include research on how information is *chunked*, on how many chunks can be kept in memory at one time, and at how the number of chunks varies when the information is sensory or symbolic. Similarly, there are hundreds of research studies on how to best access information in long-term memory. For example, by

* **graphical user interfaces** interfaces that allow computers to be operated through pictures (icons) and mouse-clicks, rather than through text and typing

* **virtualization** as if it were real; making something seem real; e.g., a virtual environment

priming, a subject with some fact that requires access to long term memory, the access time for closely related concepts can be improved. Finally, there are thousands of studies on the acuity* of and variation in human sensory and motor capabilities. All of these studies have led to principles for:

■ menu construction, related to the limits of short term memory;

■ system design based on metaphors that activate areas of long term memory;

■ the target size of buttons and icons, based on studies of motor skills;

■ the use of visual and auditory cues, based on human sensory capabilities and limits.

Although these references are only the tip of a vast and growing field of research in human perception and use of data provided by computers, they represent the kinds of developments that are moving interactive system design from an art to an engineering science.

Direct Manipulation Systems

As noted earlier, a direct manipulation system is one in which the user is able to select an object and then specify which actions are to be taken. This is in opposition to command line systems where the user would normally specify an action and then select an object upon which the action was to be performed. This fundamental paradigm* shift caused a number of changes in how these systems were designed and implemented in code.

The basic programming paradigm had to change from the process-driven approach to an event-driven perspective. In earlier systems, the program's main process would control what the user could do. Now, it was possible for the user to initiate a broad series of actions by selecting an object—a window, an icon, or a text box, for example. This required some method for collecting events and handling them. The X Window System on Unix was one of the early popular systems for doing this. Each graphical component of the interface was capable of producing one or more events. For example, a window might be opened or closed generating an event. Similarly, a button might be pressed, or the text in a text box might be changed. There are mouse events as well—such as when a mouse enters a window or moves over a button. These events are dispatched to a window manager. For Apple systems and all the Windows systems since Windows 95, which was released on August 24, 1995, this functionality is built into the operating system.

The programmer's task is to display a coordinated set of components that can generate events. The programmer is also required to write code that will initiate some action when an event occurs. These code fragments are called event-handling functions. Once the programmer has defined the objects that might generate events and the code to respond to those events, the final programming task is to register the event handlers as having an interest in certain classes of events produced by certain objects. When those events occur, the window manager dispatches them to the appropriate event handler. In object-based and object-oriented programming environments, this task of handling events is made easier through object classes that associate default event-handling methods with specific classes of objects. For example, the code for how the appearance of a button is changed when it is pressed may be provided as a default method of the button objects. Similarly, the class may provide default button release code. The programmer simply needs to add additional code that performs some application-specific action when the button is released.

Visualization, Virtualization, and Agents/Embedded Systems

Throughout the 1980s and 1990s, there were numerous efforts to take advantage of the human ability to process information visually. At the simplest level, consider that a human looking at an image on a television screen has no problem in discerning a pattern that consists of millions of individual pixels* per second, changing in both time and space. Or consider the example provided in Figure A. Ask yourself what pattern is represented by the following set of numbers: a set of X,Y pairs with the X value being the upper value in each column and the Y value being the lower value?

Even knowing they are pairs of X,Y coordinates, most people have trouble seeing a pattern in this numerical example. If however, these points are plotted, or visualized, a pattern emerges rather quickly as shown in Figure B. Visualization systems manipulate information at high levels of aggregation, making the information more accessible to users. The aggregates may be records, documents, or any other entity defined as an object. Working with large numbers of objects that have multiple attributes, users can map these attributes to the interface in such a way as to visualize the data or simulate some process. The visualization of abstract data to sensory interfaces is central to software including geographic information systems and data mining* applications, among others.

In the 1990s, researchers began to experiment with extending interactive systems from symbolic interaction—icons, mice, and pointers—to virtual systems. In these systems, every effort was made to allow the user to explore a virtual world with little or no translation to symbolic form. Thus, with visualization techniques and new forms of input devices, such as data gloves, hand movements could be used to manipulate virtual objects represented graphically in a virtual world. This virtual environment was presented to the user via two display screens, each of which provided a slightly different perspective, giving the user a stereoscopic view of a virtual space that appeared to have depth. Work on virtual and

* **pixel** a single picture element on a video screen; one of the individual dots making up a picture on a video screen or digital image

* **data mining** a technique of automatically obtaining information from databases that is normally hidden or not obvious

| 47 | 42 | 93 | 122 | 63 | 85 | 105 | 133 | 137 |
| 58 | 100 | 35 | 46 | 126 | 133 | 131 | 108 | 68 |

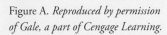

Figure A. *Reproduced by permission of Gale, a part of Cengage Learning.*

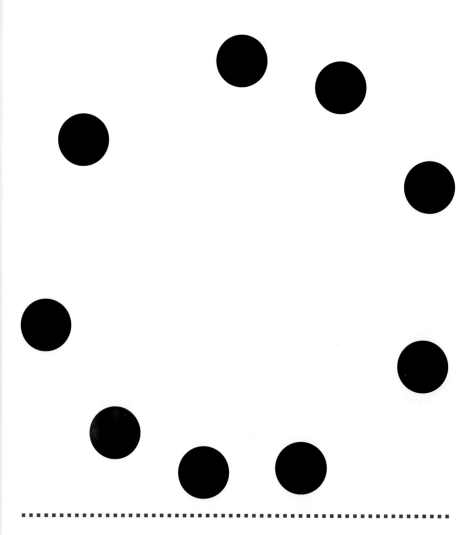

Figure B. *Reproduced by permission of Gale, a part of Cengage Learning.*

* **telemedicine** the technology that permits remote diagnosis and treatment of patients by a medical practitioner; usually interactive bi-directional audio and video signals

* **agents** systems (software programs and/or computing machines) that can act on behalf of another, or on behalf of a human

* **embedded systems** another term for "embedded computers"; computers that do not have human user orientated input/ output devices; they are directly contained within other machines

artificial reality continues on a number of specialized fronts, including a field known as telemedicine*.

The next generation of interactive systems, represented by agents in embedded systems, will again change how humans and computers interact. Direct manipulation environments will still be around for many years to come. Both agents* and embedded systems* are beginning to make their appearance. Embedded systems can be as simple as the analog sensor systems that open a department store door, or turn on lights when someone enters a room. At a more complex level, most cars being built today include air bag deployment systems and antilock brakes that operate invisibly by gathering data from the environment and inserting computer control between our actions and the environment. As air bag deployment systems become more complex, they react based not simply on acceleration data, but also based on the weight of the individuals occupying the seat and their relative position (leaning forward or back) on the seat.

As the information processing of sensory inputs becomes more complex, these embedded systems begin to act like agents. For example, programs that monitor typing activity and automatically correct spelling errors are beginning to mature. Although early versions frustrated sophisticated users, more advanced versions are demonstrating their ability to learn user preferences and new forms of errors to correct. The perceptive user will note that the most recent applications remember lots of things about user activity—which Web sites they frequent, for example, or where they hold meetings and with whom they meet. In the next generation, programs will use these data stores to communicate on the user's behalf with agents of other users.

In summary, new systems are emerging where the interface between the human and the computer system is becoming invisible. When the programs are very complex and act on behalf of the user, they are called agents. These agents make use of increasingly sophisticated methods of data acquisition. Agents are evolving from using stores of data acquired from user activity to acquiring real-time data based on new information including facial and gesture pattern recognition* and speech recognition*. Increasingly, these agents will perform tasks such as storing and retrieving files for the user and undertaking simple actions such as making or confirming appointments. The help feature in Microsoft's *Office* software is an example of an active agent that observes user activity and offers help based on actions that suggest it may be needed, from formatting documents to correcting common spelling and grammatical errors.

 See also **Game Controllers • Games • Hypermedia and Multimedia • Mouse**

Resources

Books

Gokcay, Didem, and Gulsen Yildirim, eds. *Affective Computing and Interaction: Psychological, Cognitive, and Neuroscientific Perspectives.* Hershey, PA: Information Science Reference, 2011.

Karapanos, Evangelos. *Modeling Users' Experiences with Interactive Systems.* Berlin: Springer, 2013.

Shneiderman, Ben, and Catherine Plaisant. *Designing the User Interface: Strategies for Effective Human-Computer Interaction.* 5th ed. Boston: Addison-Wesley, 2010.

Tsihrintzis, George A., and Lakhmi C. Jain, eds. *Multimedia Services in Intelligent Environments: Integrated Systems.* Berlin: Springer, 2010.

Web Sites

The Open Group. "UNIX Past." http://www.unix.org/what_is_unix/ history_timeline.html (accessed October 9, 2012).

The Xerox 8010 Star

Office professionals of today arrive at their cubicles, log onto their computers, and enter the company's network where they have access to shared files, programs, and printers. All of the tools needed to prepare and distribute correspondence, documentation, and presentations are located right on their desktops—their desktop computers, that is. However, that was not always the case. The Xerox Corporation pioneered the concept of an automated office system when it introduced the Xerox 8010 Star in 1981. Complete with recycling bins and file cabinets, the Xerox 8010 Star was the forerunner of the modern desktop computer.

* **pattern recognition** a process used by some artificial-intelligence systems to identify a variety of patterns, including visual patterns, information patterns buried in a noisy signal, and word patterns imbedded in text

* **speech recognition** the science and engineering of decoding and interpreting audible speech, usually using a computer system

Internet

The Internet is a computer network that was designed to interconnect other computer networks. Its origins lie in the ARPANET, an experimental network designed for the U.S. Department of Defense Advanced Research Projects Agency (DARPA) in 1969. The original ARPANET had some features that were unique in its day.

The first unique feature was that it supported peer to peer networking. In this system, each computer has the same rights and abilities as any other computer on the network. The commercial computer networks at that time were hierarchical, where some devices performed special control functions, and other devices had to wait for permission to transmit from the controller.

Another unique feature of ARPANET was that it was not designed with a particular application or set of applications in mind. The designers created a network whose uses were not fully specified. As a result, ARPANET was designed to be transparent to applications. This allowed new Internet applications to be developed by placing the necessary functions (usually computer software) in end user devices rather than in the network. Thus, new applications did not require changes to the network.

Yet another unique feature of ARPANET was that it enabled organizations to have operational control of their local networks while still allowing them to be interconnected.

In the 1980s, ARPANET split into a military component and a civilian section. The civilian part became known as NSFnet, in acknowledgement of support from the National Science Foundation. Other developments in this decade included the development of local area networks (LANs)*, which pushed peer to peer networking closer to many end users, and the

* **local area networks (LANs)** high-speed computer networks that are designed for users who are located near each other

British computer scientist Tim Berners-Lee. © *PHILIPPE DESMAZES/AFP/ Getty Images.*

microcomputer, or personal computer, which made it possible for many people to have dedicated computer access. NSFnet was limited by its charter to educational and not-for-profit organizations. Although commercial firms began to see the advantages of NSFnet, they were not able to participate fully in this new age of communications until NSFnet was privatized* in 1993.

The Internet has grown in leaps and bounds since privatization, fueled by the emergence of the World Wide Web. Individuals now access the Internet through a variety of increasingly portable devices, including computers, laptops, tablets, portable music players, and cell phones.

The Internet has become a change agent in many areas of the economy. Few industries have not been touched in a significant way by the Internet. Many industries have reorganized themselves as a direct result of the economic changes brought about by Internet-based applications and sales. Most companies have Web sites and social media pages, and engage in Internet-based marketing.

For the most part, computers on the Internet communicate via two communications protocols: the Transmission Control Protocol (TCP) and the Internet Protocol (IP). The role of finding a path through a complex network is left to IP. This is a "best effort" protocol, in that it does the best it can to deliver a packet to the desired destination, but makes no promises. Thus, if a portion of the network failed, IP would attempt to reroute around the failure if it could, but would not guarantee that all packets would survive intact. Many applications require stronger assurances than this, and that is the role of TCP. The TCP is a communications protocol that operates between two end devices, ensuring that the complete information that was transmitted arrives safely at the destination. If some of the information is lost by IP, TCP retransmits it until it is received correctly. Thus, the two protocols operate in tandem to provide a complete, reliable service to end users.

The Internet differs from telephone networks in that information is broken into packets, each of which is treated separately, much like a letter. The Internet allocates its resources to individual packets as needed. By contrast, the telephone network treats a telephone call as a stream of information, and allocates resources to that call (or stream of information) regardless of whether the users are speaking or are silent. In a packet network, resources are allocated only when there is information to transmit. This packet switching feature is commonly found in computer networks.

Physically, the Internet consists of special purpose computers called routers* that are interconnected with each other. Routers are equivalent to switches in the telephone network, in that they decide what to do with a packet when it arrives from a neighboring router. This decision is aided by a routing table, which is used by the router to determine where the packet should be sent next. The routing tables are constructed by the themselves, which communicate with each other so that efficient paths

* **privatized** to convert a service traditionally offered by a government or public agency into a service provided by a private corporation or other private entity

* **routers** network devices that direct packets to the next network device or to the final destination

International Internet-Free Day

On Sunday, January 27, 2002, a British organization called for an International Internet-Free Day. As announced on the nonprofit DoBe.org Web site, hosted by the Institute for Social Inventions in the United Kingdom, the event was held in an effort to motivate people to turn off their computers for a day, chat in person with family and friends, and go out and participate in activities such as listening to concerts and poetry readings, taking a walk, visiting a museum or art gallery, or just getting outdoors. Event organizers encouraged people to spend time participating in group activities to counter the social isolation they sometimes experience by communicating so often via the Web.

through the network can be found for packets traveling between any pair of destinations, and so that congested or failed can be avoided.

Today, many users access the Internet through Internet Service Providers (ISPs)*. For a monthly fee, an ISP enables users to access the Internet, and provides other features such as an e-mail address and mailbox, Web site hosting, electronic or cloud storage space, and voice over Internet Protocol (VoIP) phone connections. These retail ISPs often interconnect with large, high-capacity backbone ISPs, which provide the transport functions so that a packet from one user can reach any other user.

The Internet is a constantly changing resource. It has had a deep impact on industries and on the lives of many Americans.

Additional Information

Although the Internet has changed economic and social patterns in much of the world, access to the Internet remains limited throughout developing regions. For example, in 2011, 74 percent of all Europeans used and had daily access to the Internet whereas Africa's daily Internet access reached only 13 percent.

Computer scientists such as Tim Berners-Lee (1955–), inventor of the World Wide Web, warn that the nature of the Internet is being threatened by censorship and the desire of Internet service providers to begin favoring some types of content over others, especially those from higher-paying customers. Since its beginnings in the 1970s, the Internet had been characterized by "net neutrality"—that is, all users had equal access to long-distance transmission equipment. Favoring certain corporate or higher-paying customers over others results in slower access for non-favored clients, eliminating net neutrality, which Berners-Lee and others claim is essential to the Internet's continued growth and vitality.

 See also **E-Commercelers • Government Funding, Research • Internet: Applications • Internet: Backbone • Internet: History • Intranet • Networks • Routing • Telecommunications • World Wide Web**

Resources

Books

Blum, Andrew. *Tubes: A Journey to the Center of the Internet.* New York: Ecco, 2012.

Curran, Keven, ed. *Understanding the Internet: A Glimpse into the Building Blocks, Applications, Security and Hidden Secrets of the Web.* Oxford, UK: Chandos Publishing, 2009.

Gralla, Preston. *How the Internet Works.* 8th ed. Indianapolis: Que Publishing, 2007.

JKL

Jacquard's Loom

Although the automated assembly line and computers in the workplace might seem to be modern creations, data has been used to aid manufacturing since the early nineteenth century. It was then that Joseph-Marie Jacquard (1752–1834) invented a system of punch cards that contained data that provided instructions to weavers and were used to automate the weaving industry in France.

Jacquard was born on July 7, 1752, in a small village near Lyon. Both his parents worked in the weaving trade. At the age of ten, he went to work as a drawboy with his father. Drawboys had the tedious job of maneuvering by hand the weighted cords that controlled the pattern in the weaving of silk fabrics. Jacquard later invented a mechanical device to replace the drawboys. He started working on it in 1790, but his efforts were interrupted by the French Revolution. He finally succeeded in presenting a new silk drawloom at the Paris Exhibition in 1801. He completed an automated loom with punched cards controlling the weaving of very complicated patterns in 1805.

To use this new invention, the weaver weaves threads into the cloth. Some, the warp, run lengthwise; others, the woof, run crosswise. In the loom, each thread of the warp can be lifted by a hook connected to a rod. At each weaving step, a thread of the woof is carried crosswise. A pattern in the fabric is created by lifting the warp threads, changing the choice of threads to lift from step to step. The choice, originally made by hand, is obtained by touching the tips of all the rods to a card in which holes have been previously punched according to a program. If a rod finds a hole, the thread is lifted. At the next step in the weaving process, the card is changed. The holes may or may not be in the same order as before. If not, the weaving occurs in a different way. Jacquard butted the cards one after the other in a very long loop and put the loop on a drum rotating in tempo with the advance of the fabric, so that the preprogrammed pattern could be repeated at every cycle of the loop.

Jacquard's loom was not welcomed by the silk weavers, who were afraid of being replaced by this new machine. The weavers of Lyon expressed their anger by burning the new looms and even attacking Jacquard. Ultimately, the loom proved its usefulness and became generally accepted. By 1812 there were 11,000 in use in France.

The Jacquard loom was a technological breakthrough that earned its inventor a pension from French Emperor Napoleon Bonaparte as well as a gold medal and the Cross of the Legion of Honour. By 1834 there

The Jacquard loom, developed by the Frenchman Joseph Marie Jacquard (1752-1834) in 1804. © *SSPL via Getty Images.*

Punched Card Piracy

Jacquard's loom revolutionized the weaving industry in France during the nineteenth century. Master weavers and skilled trades people spent long hours creating elaborate patterns and designs for silk cloth, which could then be transferred to the looms' punched cards. Because of the effort involved, the cards themselves became a highly-prized commodity. Reports of theft at textile mills increased, as the cards were stolen by competing mills. These thefts represented the first known cases of data piracy.

were 30,000 looms in use in Lyon alone, and they were widely used throughout Europe and England. Jacquard died on August 7, 1834, at the age of 82.

▶ *See also* **Babbage, Charles** • **Hollerith, Herman**

Resources

Books

Essinger, James. *Jacquard's Web: How a Hand-Loom Led to the Birth of the Information Age.* Oxford and New York: Oxford University Press, 2007.

Web Sites

Columbia University. "The Jacquard Loom." http://www.columbia.edu/cu/computinghistory/jacquard.html (accessed November 3, 2012).

Jobs, Steve

American Software Developer
1955–2011

Steve Jobs helped revolutionize the personal computer industry, creating the innovative Macintosh computer and developing Apple Computer, Inc., into a multibillion dollar company.

Beginnings

Born in 1955, Steve Jobs was orphaned as an infant. He was adopted by Paul and Clara Jobs, and grew up in the California suburbs of Mountain View and Los Altos, which would later become the heart of Silicon Valley. While in high school, Jobs was hired as a summer employee at the Hewlett-Packard electronics firm in Palo Alto. There he met Stephen Wozniak (1950–), an engineering whiz kid. Wozniak was in the process of developing his "blue box," an illegal device that allowed a user to make free long-distance calls. Jobs helped Wozniak sell his device, forging a partnership that would, several years later, change the face of the home-computer industry.

In 1972 Jobs entered Reed College in Portland, Oregon, but his college career was short-lived: After one semester, he dropped out to become involved with the counterculture of the 1970s. In early 1974 he signed on as a video game designer with Atari, Inc., which in the early 1980s would become famous for its Pac-Man and Space Invaders arcade games.

After only a few months at Atari, Jobs had saved up enough money to travel to India on a search for spiritual enlightenment. When he returned in the fall of 1974, Jobs again caught up with Wozniak, who was then

holding regular meetings of his "Homebrew Computer Club." Unlike Wozniak, Jobs was not interested in building computers; he wanted to market them. Jobs convinced Wozniak to help him create their own personal computer, one that was smaller, cheaper, and easier to use than what was currently available to consumers. In Jobs's bedroom and garage they designed and built their prototype. With $1,300 (earned from selling Jobs's Volkswagen microbus and Wozniak's scientific calculator), they started their own company. Wozniak quit his job at Hewlett-Packard to become vice president in charge of research and development. Jobs came up with the name Apple, in honor of the summer he worked in an Oregon orchard.

The Age of Apple

The first computer the pair designed and marketed, the Apple I, sold for $666 in 1976. It was the first single-board computer with built-in circuitry allowing for direct video interface, along with a central ROM, which enabled it to load programs from an external source. The Apple I earned Jobs and Wozniak $774,000. A year later, the Apple II was launched with a simple, compact design like the Apple I, plus a color monitor. Within three years, the Apple II's sales had grown by 700 percent, to $139 million.

In 1980 Apple made its move on Wall Street, its stock rising to $29 on the first day of trading, bringing the company's value to $1.2 billion. Business was good for the two Apple founders, but the fledgling computer company was not without competition. The corporate might of IBM, with its two-year-old personal computer (PC), was beginning to get

* **microprocessor** an integrated circuit containing all of a computer's central processing functions

* **computer-generated imagery** making moving images with use of computers

the edge with consumers. Jobs realized that to compete against this industry Goliath, Apple would have to make its operating system compatible with that of IBM.

Enter the Macintosh, a powerful new computer with 128K of memory—twice that of the PC. The Mac, as it became known, had a 32-bit microprocessor*, which outperformed the PC's 16-bit version. Not only was it faster, it was more versatile and easier to use than the PC, offering—as its print campaign suggested-—a computer "for the rest of us." The Macintosh was introduced to the world on Super Bowl Sunday 1984 in an Orwellian-themed commercial that promised a revolutionary new wave in personal computing. The world was watching, and the Macintosh caught on like wildfire.

But just as sales of the Macintosh were taking off, president John Sculley (1939–) persuaded Apple's board of directors that Jobs's emphasis on technical performance over consumer needs was hurting the company, and Jobs was sent off to a remote office that he termed "Siberia"—far from the inner workings of the company he had created. In September of 1985 Jobs resigned as chairman of Apple. In 1989 he formed a new computer company called NextStep, which he believed would compete with Apple in the personal-computer market. Eight years and $250 million later, NextStep was forced to close its hardware division. Ironically, Apple went on to acquire NextStep several years later.

By the late 1990s Jobs had moved on to a new venture as chairman and CEO of Pixar, the Academy Award-winning computer animation computer-generated imagery* (CGI) studio he founded in 1986. Prior to Pixar there had been no market for CGI films, but Pixar's first feature film, "Toy Story" changed that. It was released by Walt Disney Pictures in 1995 and became the third-highest-grossing animated film up to that time, paving the way for a new form of filmmaking. When Pixar began offering stock on the stock market, it made Jobs a billionaire.

Thinking differently

Jobs rejoined Apple in 1996 and immediately helped rejuvenate the company. He took over immense amounts of creative control, requiring the final say in product design. In 1998, along with the slogan "Think Different" the iMac was revealed to the public. The computer boasted a sleek design that coupled a powerful computer housed in a colorful case. Jobs presented Apple's iBook, another Apple entry into the portable computer market, at the Mac World convention in July 1999. The iBook was a clam-shaped laptop that was available in bright colors and included Apple's AirPort technology. AirPort was a computer version of the cordless phone that enabled the user to surf the Web wirelessly. On July 24, 2000, Jobs presented the Power Mac G4 Cube, an eight inch-cube suspended in a clear plastic shell. The G4 Cube came with features that included an optical mouse and crystal-ball-like speakers. Following his success with the stand-alone version of the iBook, the iMac, and the G3 and G4 PowerMacs, which addressed the needs of the publishing and multimedia markets long dominated by the Macintosh, Jobs then brought out a movie-making application, iMovie, that enabled non-experts to make their own home videos.

Next came the iPod, which revolutionized both the computer and music industries. Introduced in 2001, the iPod was a small digital music player that was able to hold at least 1,000 songs. Other personal computer makers soon tried to imitate the iPod's success, though the Apple product dominated the industry early on. In 2003, iTunes was put on the market. Using iTunes, customers could buy songs that could be downloaded onto an iPod or personal computer. It also allowed novices to burn their own CDs. Another offering was an application that enabled users to make their own DVD discs at home.

In April 2005, Jobs was named to the *Time* 100, the magazine's list of the world's 100 most influential people. In early 2006, he announced his intention to sell Pixar to Disney, its distribution partner, for about $7 billion. Meanwhile, though Apple held only a small percentage of the personal computer market, it was retaining its lead as an innovator in software and digital media. Its annual fall product unveilings had become great dramatic events that thrilled tech fans and terrified the competition. In 2005, Jobs announced the debut of video iPods and a new line of thin computers with video cameras built in. In 2006, he announced that entire films would soon become available for downloading on iTunes, and that in 2007 Apple would release a new device, first called iTV but quickly renamed Apple TV, which would stream video files from iTunes to TV sets via a wireless connection, so that viewers could watch iTunes files the same way they watch DVDs. The innovations had the potential of changing the way people buy films, much as iTunes had already changed the way people buy music.

In January of 2007, at the Macworld Conference and Expo in San Francisco, Jobs announced that Apple would debut the iPhone, a high-tech cell phone that could also access the Internet and play songs downloaded from iTunes, that June. Jobs also announced that Apple Computer Inc. was shortening its name to Apple Inc., presumably to signify that inventions such as iTunes and the iPhone, rather than Macs, had become its signature products. The iPhone generated huge early buzz, though some industry observers argued that it faced hurdles because of its high cost ($499 to $599), and because it would be available only through Cingular Wireless.

Meanwhile, the same week, Jobs faced increased scrutiny in a growing scandal about Apple's backdating of stock options. Like many companies, Apple had given out stock options with effective dates chosen in retrospect because the stock had a low value on those dates, making the stock more valuable once it was sold. The company argued that Jobs had never benefited from two stock option grants he received, but some analysts disputed this. Executives at other companies had been forced to resign because of backdating scandals, but observers suggested that Apple would not force out Jobs because he was too important to the company's success.

The scandal eventually passed and Jobs's belief in the iPhone was confirmed when the device sold an estimated 500,000 to 700,000 in the first weekend alone. Reviews were similarly positive. By September 2007, sales of the iPhone increased when Apple reduced the price from $599 to $399, a move meant to help reach Job's goal of selling 10 million iPhones by the end of 2008. In September 2007, Apple also introduced the newly redesigned line of iPods to similar acclaim. While also well received, the iPods were overshadowed by the hype over the iPhones. In 2008, Jobs and Apple introduced a faster cheaper iPhone, the iPhone 3G, which sold for only $199.

The continuing success of Apple was overshadowed, however, by Jobs's health problems. When he introduced new Apple products in the fall of 2008, he was quite gaunt and many were worried about the state of his health and its effect on his company. In January 2009, Job announced that he had a treatable hormone imbalance. Although he vowed to run Apple while receiving treatment, a few weeks later he stated that he was going to take a six-month medical leave of absence from his company because his health problems were more complex than originally believed. Chief operating officer Timothy D. Cook (1960–) took over Apple during this time period. By early June 2009, Jobs was sending some emails to Apple employees and it was revealed that he had undergone a liver transplant in April. His prognosis was considered excellent and Jobs returned to part-time work at Apple by July 2009. Still, many investors and observers were concerned that Jobs's health eventually would force him to leave Apple, creating many questions about the company's future without him.

Under the direction of Jobs, by 2011 Apple's string of successful multi-touch-interface products—including the iPod, iPhone, and iPad—continued to set industry standards. The iPad introduced the tablet computer, a sleek magazine-sized mobile device that performs many functions of a computer, to the market. When queried as to whether any market research went into the very strange iPad, Jobs answered that there had not, because "it's not the consumers' job to know what they want." Next, the MacBook Air line of hard-disk free computers became iconic standard in laptop technology.

In 2011 Jobs once again took medical leave, returning to debut the iPad2. Just weeks before his death in 2011, Jobs resigned as CEO of Apple. Tim Cook, Job's hand-picked successor, took over as CEO in August 2011.

Jobs's death caused immediate outpouring from around the world. Billionaire Warren Buffet (1930–), Walt Disney Company, and some-time-competitor Google released their official condolences. Celebrities and the public took to Twitter and other forms of social media to express their final respects. His death also brought out detractors, saying the way he treated his employees and competitors could be harsh. Yet, many chose to remember him by advice which he gave students at a Stanford University commencement speech in 2005 "Stay Hungry. Stay Foolish."

Jobs' constant innovations led *Business 2.0* to name him the fifth most important leader in business in 2006. It called him "easily the greatest marketer since P.T. Barnum" and a muse for innovators. "Is there anyone in American business today," the magazine asked, "whose style, creativity, and pugnacious genius are more celebrated?" Although market challenges mounted to existing multi-touch-interface products, Apple's profits soared as it became one of the world's highest valuation companies. In 2011, Apple vied with Exxon Mobile as America's highest valuation company. Jobs' personal wealth consistently placed him in the ranks of the world's wealthiest individuals.

Resources

Periodicals

Kane, Yukari Iwatani and Fowler, Geoffrey A. "Steven Paul Jobs, 1955-2011" *The Wall Street Journal*, October 5, 2011.

Markoff, John. "Apple's Visionary Redefined Digital Age." *The New York Times*, October 5, 2011.

Web Sites

The New York Times Blog. "Reaction to Steve Jobs' Death." http://bits.blogs.nytimes.com/2011/10/05/live-updates-on-reaction-to-steve-jobss-death/ (accessed November 12, 2012).

Keyboard

The keyboard is the most commonly used computer input device. It translates each key pressed by the typist into a signal that the computer can understand. Keyboards can be wireless or connected to the computer by a cable.

How It Works

A keyboard consists of two parts: a set of keys that are pushed in sequence by the typist (or keyer) and an encoder that identifies each pressed key and generates a code that uniquely identifies that key. The key set includes the standard alphanumeric keys found on old typewriters and additional keys, such as cursor keys, navigation and function keys, Apple or Windows keys, and a numeric keypad. Keyboards for laptop computers have the minimum number of keys.

The encoder is a microprocessor located in the keyboard that detects each key as it is pressed and released. To do so, the encoder maintains a set of signals in a grid of intersecting rows and columns. When the typist presses a key, a connection is made on the grid. If, for

A standard keyboard for a desktop computer. © *Kiyoshi Ota/Bloomberg via Getty Images.*

▶

* **binary** existing in only two states, such as on or off, one or zero

example, the connection is in the first row and the third column, the encoder immediately identifies the pressed key and sends a special signal, called a scanning code, to the computer. The computer translates the scanning code into the appropriate binary* code and displays the character on the monitor so that the typist can verify that the correct key was pushed.

The lights on the keyboard (for Caps Lock, Num Lock, Scroll Lock, and so on) are controlled by the computer, not the keyboard. For example, when the typist presses the Caps Lock key, the keyboard encoder sends the code for the Caps Lock key to the computer, and the computer turns on the keyboard's Caps Lock light.

Key Arrangement

The computer keyboard is based on the layout of early typewriters. Until the late nineteenth century, typewriter keys were arranged in alphabetical order. In 1872, American inventor Christopher Latham Sholes (1819–1890) developed the first typewriter, which featured the QWERTY keyboard (pronounced "kwer-tee"), so named because the first six letters near the top left of the keyboard are Q-W-E-R-T-Y. The new layout was designed to slow down fast typists and place the keys most likely to be hit in rapid succession on opposite sides of the typewriter. This was done so that the machine would be less likely to jam.

The arrangement resolved the jamming problem, but it created two others. First, many common letters are not located on the center row, also called the home row. Second, some of the most common letters are concentrated on the left side, favoring left-handed typists. For example, the most common letter, E, is a stretch for the left middle finger, and the second most common letter, A, is typed with the left hand's weakest finger.

The QWERTY keyboard continues to be featured on the vast majority of computer keyboards in English-speaking countries even though the reason for its creation, to minimize typewriter jamming, ceased to be relevant with the invention of electric typewriters and computers.

Dvorak Keyboard

American psychologist August Dvorak (1894–1975) patented an alternative English-language layout in 1936. The top row has p, y, f, g, c, r, and l. The middle row has a, o, e, u, i, d, h, t, n, and s. The bottom row has q, j, k, x, b, m, w, v, and z. Dvorak, a professor at the University of Washington (Seattle), claimed that his layout could speed typing by approximately 35 percent. The Dvorak keyboard is considered by some to be a more efficient design because it concentrates the most-used keys on the center row of the keyboard. Advocates claim that Dvorak's layout allows 70 percent of the keystrokes to take place on the center row, compared to 35 percent with the standard QWERTY layout.

Although QWERTY is by far the most widely used layout, some popular operating systems (such as those by Microsoft and Apple) have a built-in option to accommodate Dvorak as well as QWERTY keyboards. In addition, one-handed Dvorak layouts are available for typists using only the right or the left hand.

Multilingual Keyboards

Many operating systems include support for keyboard layouts for non-U.S. typists. For example, Microsoft Windows operating systems support dozens of locales—a locale determines how the computer accommodates regional language and conventions such as keyboard layout, sort order, currency format, and date, time, and number format.

Some non-U.S. language keyboards are electronically identical to those produced for U.S. customers, but they have special key caps and a special software program, called a driver*, to translate each keystroke into the appropriate symbol for that language. For example, a Thai-language keyboard would need a Thai driver to translate keystrokes into the correct Thai characters.

Ergonomic Keyboards

Ergonomic keyboards were developed to address hand, wrist, and arm ailments common among typists. Awkward wrist positions can lead to muscle, tendon, and nerve damage in the wrists (carpal tunnel syndrome*) and forearms because of diminished blood supply or compression caused by inflamed tendons.

Ergonomic keyboards claim to reduce the incidence of repetitive stress injury, including carpal tunnel syndrome, by positioning the keys for each hand in a more natural position for the typist's arms, wrists, and hands. Ergonomic keyboards include wavy keyboards, split keyboards, and separate keypads.

The First Typewriter

The computer keyboard is based on the typewriter invented by Christopher Latham Sholes in Milwaukee, Wisconsin. Sholes's first typewriters, patented in 1868 by Sholes, Carlos Glidden, and Samuel W. Soulé, featured a keyboard with keys arranged in alphabetical order. The machine lacked a shift key and typed only in capital letters. Although typists found the alphabetical arrangement advantageous for finding the correct keys, it had two primary disadvantages. First, the letters used most often were not easily reached. Second, when typists hit a series of neighboring keys in rapid succession, such as R-S-T, the typewriter bars would jam, requiring the typist to stop and untangle them. Sholes developed the QWERTY keyboard in 1872 to resolve both problems. It is still the standard layout because millions of typists are trained in its use.

* **driver** a special program that manages the sequential execution of several other programs; a part of an operating system that handles input/output devices

* **carpal tunnel syndrome** a repetitive stress injury that can lead to pain, numbness, tingling, and loss of muscle control in the hands and wrists

Keyboard operators should pay special attention to ergonomic factors in their work environment. The chair and keyboard should be positioned so that the typist can sit up straight with feet flat on the floor and both arms able to move freely without hitting the armrests or becoming fatigued.

Special Needs Keyboards

Computer keyboards are also available for people with special needs. Keyboards with large keys (Large Key keyboards) and large print characters and symbols (Large Print keyboards) can be purchased at most retail establishments. People with limited eyesight or motor skills will find these keyboards easier to use. Other special needs keyboards include Braille labels for the blind and color-coordinated keyboards for children who are learning how to type.

 See also **Ergonomics**

Resources

Books

Clements, Alan. *Principles of Computer Hardware.* 4th ed. New York: Oxford University Press, 2007.

Lindsell-Roberts, Sheryl. *Mastering Computer Typing*, rev. ed. Boston: Houghton Mifflin Harcourt, 2010.

Marmel, Elaine. *PCs Simplified.* Indianapolis, IN: Wiley, 2011.

Web Sites

DisabledOnline.com. "Large Key/Large Print Keyboards." http://www.disabledonline.com/disabled-online-store/keyboards-and-mice/large-keylarge-print-keyboards/ (accessed October 9, 2012).

HowStuffWorks.com. "Why Are the Keys Arranged the Way They Are on a QWERTY Keyboard?" http://computer.howstuffworks.com/question458.htm (accessed October 9, 2012).

King, Ada Byron
English Mathematician and Scientist
1815–1852

Augusta Ada Byron King, Countess of Lovelace, is considered to be the first computer programmer even though she was born before computers existed, and the program she wrote was for a machine that was never built. Lovelace (King) was born on December 10, 1815, in London, England, to Annabella Milbanke and one of England's most famous poets, George Gordon, better known as Lord Byron.

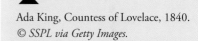

The Byrons' marriage did not last long. A month after Lovelace was born, Lady Byron took the child and left the house, never to return. Lord Byron left England shortly after the separation and had no direct contact with his daughter ever again. Although Lady Byron assumed sole control of Lovelace's upbringing, Lord Byron worried about his child from the time of his separation until his death in 1824 and asked about her constantly. Many of Lovelace's childhood letters bear the signature AAda, but her first name, Augusta, for Lord Byron's half-sister Augusta Leigh, was not used after 1816 when rumors arose of scandalous behavior between the half-siblings.

Nineteenth-century society did not encourage women to use their minds, but Lady Byron was interested in developing her child's intellect and hired the best tutors for Lovelace. With the help of William Frend, her old mathematics tutor, she was able to provide science and mathematical studies to help control Lovelace's overactive imagination. By age six, according to the journal of one governess, Lovelace's morning schedule was divided into fifteen-minute lessons of arithmetic, grammar, spelling, reading, and music, while in the afternoon she studied geography, drawing, French, music, and reading.

At the age of thirteen, she corresponded with Frend, who influenced her studies in astronomy and algebra. But before long, Lovelace was studying mathematics that went beyond Frend's understanding. By the time she was thirty, Lovelace had written accurate descriptions of a new machine—the first digital computer—designed by British mathematician Charles Babbage (1791–1871). Even Babbage was astonished at the depth of her perception.

Lovelace had met Babbage at the age of seventeen when she attended a party at his house and he demonstrated the Difference Engine*. It captured her imagination and she spent time studying its gears, rods, and wheels until she understood how the machine worked. However, their friendship did not blossom until much later.

In 1835 Lovelace married William King, who became the first Earl of Lovelace in 1838. During this time, Charles Babbage invented the Analytical Engine*. By the time Lovelace wrote "Notes" on the Analytical Engine, she had been married eight years and had three children. Some of Lovelace's letters to her mother make clear her love for her children, while others show her being frustrated about the lack of time available to pursue her intellectual interests. Her desire to return to the study of mathematics was so intense that both her mother and husband sought ways to give her time to pursue her studies.

In 1840 Lovelace began to study mathematics with Augustus De Morgan, a famous British logician and mathematician. He was an exceptional teacher who was impressed with Lovelace's ability to learn and considered her a promising young beginner. He believed, however, that her intense study of mathematics would aggravate her health and lead to a nervous breakdown.

Ada King, Countess of Lovelace, 1840. © *SSPL via Getty Images.*

* **Difference Engine** a mechanical calculator designed by Charles Babbage that automated the production of mathematical tables by using the method of differences

* **Analytical Engine** Charles Babbage's vision of a programmable mechanical computer

punched card a paper card with punched holes which give instructions to a computer in order to encode program instructions and data

Bernoulli numbers the sums of powers of consecutive integers; named after Swiss mathematician Jacques Bernoulli (1654-1705)

During the same year, Babbage attended a meeting of scientists in Turin, Italy, to explain the features of the Analytical Engine. He hoped that an eminent scientist would write an official report about his invention. He felt that this would impress the British government, which might then provide more funding for his project. Instead, a young Italian captain named Luigi Federico Menabrea, who later became prime minister of Italy, became the author.

In his paper, written in French, Menabrea described how the machine worked. This was a difficult task because the actual machine did not exist, and he had to work from Babbage's drawings, which used Babbage's own system of engineering notation. The article appeared in 1842 in the *Bibliotheque Universelle de Geneve*. A few months later, Charles Wheatstone, developer of the electric telegraph and a family friend, contacted Lovelace about translating it for the British journal *Taylor's Scientific Memoirs*.

When Babbage found out about this request, he tried to persuade Lovelace to write an entirely new article. She rejected the offer but proposed to add notes to bring Menabrea's text up to date. Lovelace was under a great deal of physical and mental stress during the time that she wrote the "Notes." She had moments of great anxiety, and although her doctors prescribed potentially dangerous remedies, her concentration did not weaken. The dual purpose of the notes, numbered A through G, was to clarify and elaborate on specific points about the machine and to gain support for it from the British government. They were not part of the original document, but were added to the end.

The first set of notes, A through D, explains the differences between the Difference and Analytical Engines, and the use of punched cards* that controlled the actions of the machine and allowed it to divide a complex problem into a series of smaller steps. They also compare the Analytical Engine to Jacquard's Loom and emphasize that the Analytical Engine uses fewer cards because the cards can return to their original position in a process called backing, which today's programmers know as a loop.

Note E gives a complicated example of how the machine can work through a problem. Lovelace described properties that are present in modern computers, such as loops within loops and if-then statements. Note F suggests that the Analytical Engine would be capable of solving problems that had not been solved before, such as astronomical tables. Note G summarizes the functions of the machine and stresses that it can follow instructions but is not capable of generating any original work. In this note Lovelace detailed how the machine could be programmed to compute the calculation of Bernoulli numbers*. She used the information and formulas supplied by Babbage and determined where the calculations would go into the machine and where the answers would be displayed. Since Lovelace had no machine on which to test the program, printed editions of her "Notes" available today contain some errors. The "Notes" were published in 1843. Following the Victorian norm, they did not carry her full name, but only her initials, A.A.L.

Lovelace liked the outdoors and loved horses and riding, a passion that her husband shared. During her work on the "Notes," she often went riding to clear her head. Later in life, her love of horses caused her to fall heavily in debt. The full extent of her racetrack gambling is unknown because the record of such transactions is no longer available. But by the spring of 1851, she had accumulated a debt of more than 3,200 pounds, which was a substantial sum in those days. At the same time her health deteriorated and she was diagnosed with cancer. The doctors prescribed opium and morphine to relieve the pain. Lovelace died in November 1852, and was buried beside her father. Her most important accomplishment was that she envisioned multiple uses for a machine she never saw.

In the early 1970s the U.S. Department of Defense commissioned the development of a programming language that could perform concurrent processing. In 1980 the Ada Joint Program Office was created to launch and maintain the Ada computer language, named in Lovelace's honor. Its documentation became a national standard and is stored in document number MIL-STD-1815 to honor the year of her birth.

 See also **Analytical Engine • Babbage, Charles**

Resources

Books

Baum, Joan. *The Calculating Passion of Ada Byron.* Hamden, CT: Archon Books, 1986.

Stein, Dorothy. *Ada: A Life and Legacy.* Cambridge, MA: MIT Press, 1985.

Wade, Mary Dodson. *Ada Byron Lovelace: The Lady and the Computer.* New York: Dillon Press, 1994.

Famous Father

George Gordon, the sixth Baron Byron of Rochdale, and father of Ada Byron King, the Countess of Lovelace, is considered by scholars to be one of England's most famous romantic poets. He wrote numerous plays and books, as well as tomes of poetry, including *Don Juan, The Curse of Minerva,* and *The Corsair.*

M

Mainframes

Prior to the advent of the personal computer (PC), the minicomputer, and the microcomputer, the term computer simply referred to mainframes. What differentiates the modern mainframe from these other classes of computers is the scope of the processing taking place. The typical mainframe today serves tens of thousands of users processing thousands of transactions every second while maintaining centralized terabyte*-size, or petabyte-size databases (a petabyte—abbreviated PB—is equal to one quadrillion bytes, i.e., 10^{15} bytes; equivalent to 1,000 terabytes). Even the mighty supercomputer, although unquestionably faster doing one thing at a time, is not up to this task.

Surprisingly, the processors used in these machines are not much faster than those found in PCs. The architecture of the mainframe, however, provides that the processors can work together in parallel and focus primarily on the actual processing of data and instructions. They are relieved of the time-consuming duties of controlling input and output. Mundane tasks such as reading data from disk, handling transmissions to user terminals, and even reading and writing into main memory, are handled by sub-systems that may well be as powerful as the main processor.

Although a PC is designed to provide very fast processing to a single user, the mainframe must be able to control many tasks being run by many users simultaneously. Thus, the mainframe is differentiated from other computing systems in the areas of data bandwidth*, organization, reliability, and control.

Evolution of Mainframes

In the early 1960s, companies such as Burroughs, International Business Machines Corporation (IBM), Radio Corporation of America (RCA), National Cash Register Corporation (now known as NCR Corporation), and Sperry Rand manufactured mainframes. Since the 1970s, the only mainframes in use are the System/390, made by IBM, or clones made by Hitachi and Fujitsu. This provides a high degree of hardware compatibility both within and across manufacturer lines. The System/390 evolved from the System/360, which was initially introduced by IBM in 1965. In 2000, the System/390 was renamed IBM eServer zSeries; then in 2006, another change occurred to IBM System z; for instance, the IBM System z9 and z10 mainframe models were eventually introduced. In July 2010, IBM introduced the first of its zEnterprise System mainframe computers. The ZEnterprise mainframes consist of three components: the zEnterprise 196

* **terabyte** one million million (one trillion, or 10^{12}) bytes

* **bandwidth** a measure of the frequency component of a signal or the capacity of a communication channel to carry signals

An IBM trade fair host explains a high-performance mainframe to participants. © *Sean Gallup/Getty Images.*

(z196) enterprise-class server (introduced in July 2010), the zEnterprise 114 (z114) business-class server (July 2011), and the zEnterprise EC12 enterprise-class server (August 28, 2012).

Over time, the physical size and cost of mainframes have been reduced dramatically. What once cost millions and filled a large data center can now literally fit in a single 48.7-centimeter (19-inch) wide cabinet for a few hundred thousand dollars. Power consumption and heat dissipation have also been reduced. In the 1970s and 1980s, mainframes gave off so much heat they had to be cooled with chilled water.

The fifth generation machines on the market now use Complementary Metal Oxide Semiconductor, or CMOS, technology and require no special cooling. They can provide up to 12 parallel 650 megahertz (MHz) processors, terabyte-range memory, and hundreds or thousands of terabytes of data storage. Compare that to a typical PC with a one or two processors, a few gigabytes (GB) of memory, and a terabyte (TB) of disk storage!

Mainframe vs. Personal Computer

Another contrast to the PC is the type of jobs the mainframes run. Transaction processing jobs run constantly in real-time and must be available more than 99.99 percent of the time. The reboots and lock-ups common with PCs are simply not acceptable. Thousands of individual users can log in simultaneously from a variety of sources such as computer terminals, automatic teller machines (ATMs), or Internet Web sites, and complete a single transaction.

Time-sharing jobs can be started when needed from a computer terminal by authorized users who then use the mainframe as their own big PC. Finally, batch jobs are started automatically by the system at regular times according to a strict predetermined schedule. Batch jobs are used to do the periodic processing required on the data being received from transaction and time-sharing jobs. Closing the accounting books at month-end or copying disk files to tape for backup are examples of batch type processing.

Mainframe Components

Unlike the single box used by the PC, the mainframe has many components. Typically, they include the following.

Operating System Although many would argue that the operating system (OS) is software and therefore not a component, it is in fact the most important and complex component of the mainframe. The OS used in the largest of mainframes, including clones, is IBM's OS/390, running Multiple Virtual Systems (MVS). The OS/390 also runs Virtual Memory (VM), VSE, and Unix. MVS has proven itself to be the only OS capable of handling the multiple processing requirements of today's largest businesses.

A key feature of MVS is Job Control Language (JCL), which enables the operators to automate all jobs, scheduling their running times, and handling exceptions that occur. Within MVS, a software sub-system called Customer Information Control System (CICS) enables the concurrent processing of transactions by thousands of users. There are many other subsystems such as IMS (Information Management System) and DB/2 (Database 2) for database, Time-Sharing Option (TSO) for user jobs, VTAM (Virtual Telecommunications Access Method) for telecommunications, and RACF (Resource Access Control Facility) for security. The OS runs the overall system and provides the environment in which application programs can do the actual jobs users want to accomplish. The vast majority of mainframe application programs are written in Common Business Oriented Language (COBOL).

Central Processing Unit Similar to the processor in a PC, the central processing unit (CPU) decodes instructions, performs calculations, and issues instructions to other components. Unlike the PC, however, the mainframe will typically have many CPUs connected in parallel. It is the job of the OS to dispatch jobs to parallel processors in an efficient manner. To date, this has proven to be a formidable task. Although once a separate component of the mainframe, main storage—also known as high speed memory or random access memory (RAM)*—is now typically packaged within the CPU. This is done to increase the speed of data transfer.

Channels The job of the channel is to connect the CPU and main storage to other components of the mainframe configuration. The channel ensures that data are moved in an orderly fashion and verifies the integrity of the data. The cables used for these channels once consisted of dozens of small coaxial cables that created quite a congested area under the computer room floor. Fiber optic* cable has resolved this problem while dramatically increasing data transfer speeds.

* **random access memory (RAM)** a type of memory device that supports the nonpermanent storage of programs and data; so called because various locations can be accessed in any order (as if at random), rather than in a sequence (like a tape memory device)

* **fiber optic** transmission technology using long, thin strands of glass fiber; internal reflections in the fiber assure that light entering one end is transmitted to the other end with only small losses in intensity; used widely in transmitting digital information

* **parity** a method of introducing error checking on binary data by adding a redundant bit and using that to enable consistency checks

* **dumb terminal** a keyboard and screen connected to a distant computer without any processing capability

* **local area network (LAN)** a high-speed computer network that is designed for users who are located near each other

* **wide area network (WAN)** an interconnected network of computers that spans upward from several buildings to whole cities or entire countries and across countries

Disk Storage Subsystems

Disk storage subsystems provide for the long term storage and quick retrieval of large amounts of data. They use a magnetically coated disk spinning at high speed. The latest in this technology incorporates redundant array of inexpensive disks (RAID) technology, which is basically an array of inexpensive disks. RAID spreads data across many small disk drives similar to those used in a PC, and uses a method called parity* to recreate data should one drive fail. The bad drive can then be replaced without turning off the system or losing any data.

Mass Storage Devices Over the years, many schemes have been developed to increase the capacity of data storage. Recent advances in disk storage technology have rendered obsolete many of these devices, such as magnetic strip and optical disk storage. One device that remains in common use is the tape drive. Tape is used today primarily as a means to back up data. These tapes can then be stored somewhere else to be used if a major disaster destroys the data center. In situations where truly massive amounts of data must be archived for occasional use, tapes are organized into libraries and accessed using automated equipment to find and load the tape.

Communications Controllers To gain access to a mainframe computer, a user will typically use a dumb terminal* or a PC programmed to act as such. The job of keeping track of which user is at which terminal and transferring data is performed by the communications controllers. The connection may be established over a local direct connection, a local area network (LAN)*, or a wide area network (WAN)*.

Line Printers Although many commentators have said that computers will bring about a paperless society, there is still a tremendous amount of data output in printed form. Printers are normally attached via a print controller, although the largest and fastest can connect directly to the channel. There are various types of printers available, but the two types most associated with mainframe computer output have been impact printers and laser printers. Impact printers are used for multiple carbon copies; however, impact printers are largely on their way to becoming obsolete, due to the inherent noise generated during operation and their comparatively slow speed, as well as other drawbacks. By contrast, laser printers are the workhorse of the industry and produce the majority of output from mainframes. They not only print text, but also graphics and forms at the same time.

Conclusion

The role of the mainframe has changed gradually from that of a data processor to that of a server, with the processing being done on the user's PC. It has also been modified to interface to the Internet through the addition of transmission control protocol/Internet protocols (TCP/IPs), Unix, and Java programming, to enable businesses to connect to their customers over that network. Once the only form of business computer available, the mainframe has survived the PC revolution and maintained an important function in commercial computing. However, with this added competition from other computer sources, the mainframe, though still important, is not as essential as it once was. For instance, NASA recently eliminated its last mainframe computer, the IBM Z9, at its Marshall Space Flight Center, in Huntsville, Alabama. The February 11, 2012, NASA article *The End of the Mainframe Era at NASA* ends with: "But all things must change. Today, they are the size of a refrigerator but in the old days, they were the size of a Cape Cod. Even though NASA has shut down its last one, there is still a requirement for mainframe capability in many other organizations. The end-user interfaces are clunky and somewhat inflexible, but the need remains for extremely reliable, secure transaction oriented business applications."

▶ *See also* **Central Processing Unit • Generations, Computers • Generations, Languages • Memory • Operating Systems**

Resources

Books

Ebbers, Mike, et al. *Introduction to the New Mainframe: z/OS Basics.* 2nd ed. IBM: International Technical Support Organization, 2009.

Stephens Williams, David. *What on Earth Is a Mainframe?: An Introduction to IBM zSeries Mainframes and z/OS Operating System for Total Beginners.* Raleigh, NC: Lulu Press, 2008.

Web Sites

International Business Machines Corporation. "1.3 Introducing the zEnterprise System." http://www.redbooks.ibm.com/redbooks/SG247832/wwhelp/wwhimpl/common/html/wwhelp.htm?context=SG247832&file=1-3.htm (accessed October 9, 2012).

National Aeronautics and Space Administration. "The End of the Mainframe Era at NASA." http://blogs.nasa.gov/cm/blog/NASA-CIO-Blog/posts/post_1329017818806.html (accessed October 9, 2012).

Memory

In computer science, the term memory is used to describe any device that stores information, including data and program instructions. Memory can be thought of as the computer's workspace; it determines the size and number of programs that can be run at the same time, as well as the amount of data that can be processed. Memory is sometimes referred to as primary storage, primary memory, main storage, main memory, internal storage, or random access memory (RAM). There are four major types of

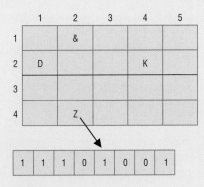

Figure 1. Cell (4,2) contains eight bits representing the letter "Z" (as it would be coded in Extended Binary Coded Decimal Interchange Code [EBCDIC]). *Reproduced by permission of Gale, a part of Cengage Learning.*

* **volatile** subject to rapid change; describes the character of data when current no longer flows to a device (that is, electrical power is switched off)

* **capacitor** a fundamental electrical component used for storing an electrical charge

computer memory: random access memory, read only memory, CMOS memory, and virtual memory.

Random Access Memory (RAM)

When most people think of computer memory, random access memory (RAM) is what they mean. RAM is composed of chips. These chips can hold:

1. data for processing;
2. instructions, or programs, for processing the data;
3. data that has been processed and is waiting to be sent to an output, secondary storage, or communications device;
4. operating system instructions that control the basic functions of the computer system.

All data and instructions held in RAM are temporary. The contents can and do change as data are processed, programs are run, and instructions are carried out by the computer. RAM is a reusable computer resource.

Most RAM is said to be volatile*. This means that when the power to the computer is turned off, or the power goes out, all contents of RAM instantaneously disappear and are permanently lost. Because RAM is temporary and, other forms of more permanent storage were developed. Secondary storage is long term, non-volatile storage of data or programs outside the central processing unit (CPU) and RAM. Some of the more common types of secondary storage include magnetic tape, magnetic disk, and optical disk.

The storage capacity of RAM varies in different types of computers. Capacity is important because it determines how much data can be processed at once and how large and complex a program may be. The computer's operating system manages RAM so that programs run properly. To understand the capacity of RAM, the following terms are used:

■ Bit—a binary digit representing the smallest unit of data in the computer system. A bit can be only a 1 or a 0. In the computer, a 0 means that an electronic or magnetic signal is absent, while a 1 signifies its presence;

■ Byte—a group of eight bits. A byte represents one character, one digit, or one value. The capacity of the computer's memory, RAM, is expressed in bytes or in multiples of bytes.

Data, instructions, and programs stored in RAM are really stored as bits that represent those data, instructions, and programs. These bits are stored in microscopic electronic parts called capacitors.*

Read Only Memory

Read Only Memory (ROM) is a set of chips that contain portions of the operating system that are needed to start the computer. ROM is also known as firmware. ROM cannot be written to or altered by a user. It is nonvolatile memory. ROM chips come from the manufacturer with programs or instructions already stored and the only way to change their contents is to remove them from the computer and replace them with another set. ROM chips can contain frequently used programs, such as computing routines for calculating the square root of numbers.

The most common use for ROM chips is the storage of manufacturer-specific programming such as the Basic Input Output System (BIOS). The BIOS is a critical part of the operating system that tells the computer how to access the disk drives. When the computer is started, RAM is empty and the instructions in the ROM BIOS are used by the CPU to search the disk drives for the main operating system files. The computer then loads these files into RAM and uses them.

There arc three variations of ROM:

1. PROM, or programmable read only memory. PROM chips are blank chips on which programs can be written using special equipment. PROM chips can be programmed once and are usually used by manufacturers as control devices in their products.

2. EPROM, or erasable programmable read only memory. EPROM is similar to PROM, but the program can be erased and a new program written by using special equipment that uses ultraviolet light. EPROM is used for controlling devices such as robots.

3. EEPROM, electronic erasable programmable read only memory. EEPROM chips can be reprogrammed using special electric impulses. They do not need to be removed to be changed.

CMOS

CMOS (pronounced SEE MOSS) stands for complementary metal oxide semiconductor. It is a specialized memory that contains semi-permanent vital data about the computer system's configuration. Without this data, the computer would not be able to start. CMOS is more permanent than RAM and less permanent than ROM. CMOS requires very little power to retain its contents; the chip is powered by a battery. When a change is needed in the computer system's configuration (i.e., a new hard drive is installed, more RAM is added, or the number of disk drives is changed), CMOS can be updated by running a special utility program available through the operating system.

Virtual Memory

Virtual memory is a storage method where portions of a program or data are stored on magnetic disk rather than in RAM until needed, giving the illusion that main memory is unlimited. Virtual memory simulates RAM. It allows the computer to run more than one program at a time, manipulate large data files, and run large programs without having sufficient RAM. Virtual storage is slower than RAM, and is nonvolatile.

How Data and Programs are Stored in Memory

Computer main memory can be thought of as a two-dimensional table where each cell has a unique address. Each cell can store one byte of data by using eight capacitors to represent the eight bits in a byte.

Multiples of Bytes

A kilobyte, abbreviated K or KB, equals 1,024 bytes, but is commonly rounded to 1,000. A megabyte, which is abbreviated M or MB, equals one million bytes (actually 1,048,576 bytes). Gigabyte, abbreviated G or GB, represents about 1 billion bytes (actually 1,073,741,824 bytes). Terabyte, abbreviated T or TB, equals about 1 trillion bytes (actually 1,009,511,627,776 bytes). A petabyte equals about 1 million gigabytes.

Related Information

In April 2008, American experimental physicist and researcher Stuart Stephen Papworth Parkin (as of October 2012, an International Business Machines Corporation [IBM] manager of the Magnetoelectronics group at the Almaden Research Center in San Jose, California) announced a demonstration of a new memory technology, namely a working 3-bit register (unit of digital memory) built using racetrack memory. Racetrack memory, or sometimes also called Domain Wall Memory (DWM), stores information as domains of magnetization in a microscopic metal wire. It is called racetrack memory because data moves (races) around a wire (track). Short lengths of a wire are magnetized one way to represent a 0 and the other to represent a 1. To read or write data, a whole string of domains is pushed back and forth at high speed by running a current through the wire. When the magnetized data races through nanowires, a spin is imparted to the electrons (what is called electron spin). By controlling the angular momentum of these electrons, the spin can be interpreted by the computer to represent binary data, either off (0) or on (1). This technology is generally called spintronics.

Racetrack memory chips could keep their data even with the power off. Flash memory chips can do this, but store data slowly and wear out after a limited number of reads and writes. A racetrack memory chip could in theory store as much data as a hard drive, be as fast as or faster than a random-access memory chip (which cannot keep its data without power), have no moving parts, and endure an unlimited number of reads and writes. Parkin, already famous for applying the phenomenon known as giant magnetoresistance to hardware, making today's high-density computer hard drives possible, said that racetrack memory chips might be ready for market in ten years or less. Many details of device design and manufacturing would have to be resolved before this could happen. Racetrack memory is being developed and tested to provide the high reliability and performance of flash memory and the high capacity and low cost of hard disks. As of 2012, this technology was still not ready for the commercial market.

 See also **Binary Number System** • **Integrated Circuits** • **Microchip** • **Transistors** • **Vacuum Tubes**

Resources

Books

Clements, Alan. *Principles of Computer Hardware.* 4th ed. Oxford and New York: Oxford University Press, 2007.

Laudon, Kenneth C., and Jane Price Laudon. *Essentials of Management Information Systems.* 9th ed. Upper Saddle River, NJ: Pearson Prentice Hall, 2011.

test2

* **semiconductor** solid material that possesses electrical conductivity characteristics that are similar to those of metals under certain conditions, but can also exhibit insulating qualities under other conditions

Parsons, June Jamrich, and Dan Oja. *New Perspectives on Computer Concepts.* 11th ed. Boston: Thomson/Course Technology, 2009.

Zelkowitz, Marvin V. *Advances in Computers, Volume 78: Improving the Web.* Amsterdam: Elsevier, 2010.

Web Sites

The Register. "'Spintronics' Brings IBM's Racetrack Memory Closer to Reality." http://www.theregister.co.uk/2012/07/26/spintronics_advances_racetrack_memory/ (accessed October 10, 2012).

Microchip

Although semiconductors* and microchips are essential components of modern computers, many people do not realize that computing machinery does not really need to be constructed with components that are normally associated with electronic equipment. In fact, some of the earliest computers were purely mechanical machines—they did not rely on electrical technology at all. For example, English mathematician and engineer Charles Babbage's (1791–1871) Analytical Engine, designed in 1834 at a time when the use of electricity was in its infancy, was a purely mechanical machine. Had Babbage actually been able to build it, his Analytical Engine would have been a bona fide computing machine.

Similarly, many of the early computers and calculators were mostly mechanical, using carefully constructed linkages, levers, and cogs. It is important to note that the technology used to implement computers

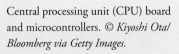

Central processing unit (CPU) board and microcontrollers. © *Kiyoshi Ota/Bloomberg via Getty Images.*

does not define them. Instead, machines are termed computers if they are programmable—regardless of the form the programming takes. Therefore, once mechanical computers and calculators had proven themselves somewhat cumbersome and inefficient, designers looked toward the then newly emerging electro-technologies (those using the application of electricity) as a means for implementing computers and calculators.

Around the mid-twentieth century, the analog computer was becoming an increasingly popular tool for solving differential equations. Valve and triode devices used in analog amplification equipment were being mass-produced for the radio and wireless sets that were consumer items of the day. They were also suitable building blocks for the implementation of analog computers. Yet, while analog computers were predecessors of modern digital computers, they did not bear much resemblance to current digital computers.

To explain the development of these technologies, it is helpful to analyze their development history. Scientists and mathematicians have known since the eighteenth century that differential and integral calculus can be used to model problems in the physical sciences. Also, while solutions to differential equations can be developed manually, this process tends to be tedious. Analog computers offered a way of automating the process of generating solutions to differential and integral equations. Building blocks made from valves and triodes* were constructed to perform specific operations that are common in the solution of differential and integral equations. Blocks that could complete arithmetic operations—such as addition, subtraction, multiplication, and division—could be assembled, along with others that affected operations like integration, differentiation, and other forms of filtering. These building blocks could be assembled and connected using temporary wiring connections—this was actually the programming of these computers.

In the beginning, programming an analog computer was a rather labor-intensive activity and the computers themselves would consume a relatively large amount of electrical power. But, their speed of computation was phenomenal compared to mechanical computers. The valves and triodes that made these machines possible are still occasionally found in esoteric* modern audio amplifier equipment, but have been largely consigned to history. The cause of this was the invention of the semiconductor transistor device in 1948.

American solid-state physicist William B. Shockley (1910–1989) described the operation of the semiconductor transistor in 1950, and its development foreshadowed a revolution in electronics. The fundamental physical difference between a conductor of electricity and an insulator is that conductors permit free flow of electrons, and insulators do not. In other words, if someone takes a piece of conducting material, like a metal, and drops a packet of electrons onto it at one point, they will almost instantaneously redistribute themselves throughout the volume of the metal sample. They will tend to spread out so that their distribution is uniform. A piece of insulating material, like polyvinyl chloride (PVC plastic), would tend to resist the redistribution of a packet of electrons. The PVC would try to prevent the localized collection of electrons from redistributing themselves—instead they would be contained in the one area making that region negatively charged.

Shockley and his contemporaries discovered that there was a certain class of materials that could sometimes be seen as acting like conductors, but with a certain amount of manipulation, the same material could be made to act as an insulator. This property made them somewhat special—they could conduct or insulate under control, making them ideal as switching devices. These materials became known as semiconductors because of their unusual position logically between conductors and insulators. Silicon* and germanium* were identified early as semiconductor materials.

The production process for the creation of a semiconductor is a complex multistage activity, but essentially involves minuscule semiconductor elements being impregnated with charged particles (known as doping) so as to influence their behavior in useful ways. They are bonded to conductors and encased in plastic or ceramic containers ready for use. Since this time, the word silicon in the context of electronics has been used synonymously with terms such as silicon chip, chip, and microchip.

Silicon, germanium, and other semiconductor materials derived from metal oxides have been used ever since, along with metals such as gold, aluminum, and copper to produce semiconductor integrated circuit devices of extraordinary complexity and performance. Their successful miniaturization has meant that a great deal of functionality can be synthesized on a relatively small device. Additionally, these devices consume much less electrical power and operate at vastly greater speeds than the older valve and triode devices. Extra benefits have resulted from the perfection of the manufacturing processes as well, which has in turn lead to these devices becoming inexpensive to purchase and reliable in operation.

An entire industry of massive proportions has been supported by these developments, with its genesis in an area near San Francisco, California, which has since become known as Silicon Valley*. Subsequently, other regions in Europe and Asia—notably Japan and South Korea—have also established credibility in the mass-production of semiconductors.

For some time theorists and visionaries have proposed the idea that semiconductors might eventually be replaced in computers by devices that have the capacity to implement computer circuitry by using optics or quantum physical concepts, but these are yet to be proven beyond the research laboratory. Any replacement technology will need to possess very impressive credentials indeed if it is to be as operationally effective, as economical and efficient as devices implemented from semiconductors.

* **silicon** a chemical element with symbol Si; the most abundant element in earth's crust and the most commonly used semiconductor material

* **germanium** a chemical often used as a high performance semiconductor material; chemical symbol Ge

* **Silicon Valley** an area in California near San Francisco, which has been the home location of many of the most significant information technology orientated companies and universities

Optical Microchip Development

Sierra Monolithics Inc. of California (which was acquired by Semtech in 2009) and International Business Machines Corporation (IBM) have teamed up to work on developing optical microchip devices. From the beginning of 2001, the two companies have spent tens of millions of dollars on the research and development of microchip devices that bridge the gap between conventional semiconductor technologies and optical fiber communication networks. It is anticipated that the optical microchips being developed will be capable of operation in gigabit-sized networks. In 2012, IBM announced the completion of the Holey Optochip. This prototype optical chip is the first parallel optical transceiver (a device able to send and receive data simultaneously) that is able to transfer one trillion bits (or one terabit) of information per second. According to the Gizmag article *IBM Unveils One Trillion Bit-per-second Optical Chip*, the Optochip has the ability to download 500 high-definition (hi-def) movies in one second. Emphasizing the speed of this new optical chip, the article adds, "Stated another way, the Optochip is eight times faster than any other parallel optical components currently available, with a speed that's equivalent to the bandwidth consumed by 100,000 users, if they were using regular 10 Mb/s [megabits per second] high-speed internet."

▶ *See also* **Microcomputers**

Resources

Books

Hilton, Alice Mary. *Logic, Computing Machines, and Automation.* Washington, D.C.: Spartan Books, 1963.

Lécuyer, Christophe, and David C. Brock. *Makers of the Microchip: A Documentary History of Fairchild Semiconductor.* Cambridge, MA: MIT Press, 2010.

Sedra, Adel S., and Kenneth C. Smith. *Microelectronic Circuits.* 6th ed. New York: Oxford University Press, 2010.

Wakerley, John S. *Digital Design Principles and Practices.* 4th ed. Upper Saddle River, NJ: Pearson/Prentice Hall, 2006.

Web Sites

Gizmag.com. "IBM Unveils One Trillion Bit-per-second Optical Chip." http://www.gizmag.com/ibm-holey-optochip/21799/pictures#2 (accessed October 10, 2012).

Microcomputers

Microcomputers, sometimes also called micro computers, are computers consisting of a central processing unit (CPU) that functions as a microprocessor, along with memory and input and output devices. They are physically smaller than minicomputers, which are smaller than mainframes. When a microcomputer is fitted with a keyboard and monitor or screen, it often is labeled as a personal computer.

Before the introduction of the personal computer or microcomputer to the general market in the 1970s, computers were physically large, complex, often unreliable, and expensive pieces of machinery. However, computers then operated in much the same way as they do now, loading programs from secondary storage into memory, accepting input, and executing instructions and generating output. Similarities between those early machines and the types that were to follow ended there however—the early machines were manufactured and sold into a small market, as computers were not yet consumer items. The hardware was expensive as semiconductor devices were only just becoming mainstream, and computers of the time were often accommodated in large purpose-built installations that catered to their temperamental operating requirements. The computing machinery needed air conditioned rooms and was maintained by squads of specialized professionals behind closed doors. As such, computers were out of the realm of the average person's experience.

The types of programs these machines usually ran generally contributed to their esoteric* status. Programs dealing with the management of financial transactions in large batches that took many hours to run did not automatically generate much interest in most people. As a result, computing machinery was a somewhat mysterious phenomenon, and its role was restricted to operations principally involving electronic data processing to support financial management, administrative control in large organizations, and specialized scientific research. However, all this was soon to change.

In 1971 the Intel Corporation of Santa Clara, California (an established manufacturer of semiconductor* devices), responded to a particular design problem in a spectacularly successful way. Another company was considering manufacturing hand-held calculators. These calculators were still somewhat primitive because they were incapable of anything other than simple arithmetic operations and could not be programmed by the user. Nonetheless, they were becoming an important school and work accessory at the time. The standard approach to the construction of calculators was to implement a design of several separate devices. Although this approach was workable, it was somewhat inflexible—if a modification was made to the specification of the calculator, a significant amount of adjustment to the hardware design was required. This generally meant costly re-construction of prototype designs from scratch.

In response to the problem, the engineers at Intel proposed an approach whereby most of the complexity of the design was shifted into one particular device called a 4-bit microprocessor, designated the 4004. On this one occasion, it meant a lot of extra work in order to develop the microprocessor, but once the microprocessor had been completed, its function could be modified by supplying it with a different program to run. Essentially, the calculator had become a restricted type of computer. The microprocessor could accommodate changes in requirements imposed upon it by varying the controlling program it contained, thereby changing its functionality. This avoided the extra delays and re-working that would otherwise be needed if the calculator had been developed using the conventional design approach of fixed-function devices. In addition, the programmability of the microprocessor meant that its use could be extended well beyond the limits of a hand-held calculator.

Within a few years Intel and some other manufacturers had built more powerful microprocessors using 8-bit, and then 16-bit, architectures. This opened the way for small-scale computers to be developed around designs based on mass-produced microprocessors. Within five years there was an array of different small computers available for people to purchase, making computing machinery finally available to consumers. These computers were termed microcomputers to distinguish them from the commercially available, business oriented minicomputers* and mainframe computers*.

* **esoteric** relating to a specialized field of endeavor that is characterized by its restricted size

* **semiconductor** solid material that possesses electrical conductivity characteristics that are similar to those of metals under certain conditions, but can also exhibit insulating qualities under other conditions

* **minicomputers** computers midway in size between a desktop computer and a mainframe computer; most modern desktops are much more powerful than the older minicomputers

* **mainframe computers** large computers used by businesses and government agencies to process massive amounts of data; generally faster and more powerful than desktop computers but usually requiring specialized software

Microcomputers in Space

In March 1999, it was announced that microcomputers would form a part of the computing systems facilities on the International Space Station (ISS). Since then, the European Space Agency (ESA) has used IBM personal microcomputers running the Linux operating system to control the flight of an unmanned servicing space craft called the automated transfer vehicle, or ATV. In the 2010s, microcomputers can be entrusted with important real-time tasks and are no longer viewed as just elaborate typewriters. In fact, in January 2010, the National Aeronautics and Space Administration (NASA) announced that a new system aboard the ISS would allow astronauts the ability to surf the Web for the first time. The capability to privately access the Internet was envisioned as a way of easing the loneliness and isolation that the astronauts might experience aboard the space station.

* **multitasking** the ability of a computer system to execute more than one program at the same time; also known as multiprogramming

Nearly all of the microcomputers were quite primitive though—most had very small memory capacity, limited input and output device support, and could only be programmed in low-level languages. As such, they were mainly curiosities and were targeted by technically minded hobbyists and enthusiasts—mostly people who understood computing technology, but were unable to buy their own minicomputer from those that were commercially available, because they were too expensive. Steadily, as interest grew, more user-friendly machines were produced and interpreted programming languages became available, enabling people to develop and distribute programs more easily. In the early 1980s, these small computers were given the opportunity to become very useful in a practical sense, following the development of the spreadsheet by American businessperson Daniel "Dan" Bricklin (1951–), who is sometimes now called the Father of the Spreadsheet. No longer were microcomputers to remain solely within the realm of the technically inclined; for the first time they offered more general users a means of automating very labor-intensive tasks and were truly becoming a business tool.

The International Business Machines Corporation (IBM) became interested in acquiring a portion of the microcomputer market in the early 1980s. This one step did more to establish credibility in personal computing and microcomputer technology than all previous events. IBM was the epitome of corporate computing; it manufactured large computing systems for industrial and commercial computing environments—for IBM to be involved in the world of microcomputers legitimized the whole concept of the less-expensive, desktop computer. From that moment onward, microcomputers became a part of mainstream civilization.

During the first decade of microcomputer history, the hardware was hampered by operating systems that did not support multitasking* (multiprogramming). This was recognized as something of a drawback, but it was more difficult to counter than was earlier imagined. Multitasking operating systems were steadily developed for microcomputers, but they faced several difficulties including the lack of inter-operability, the requirement of significant amounts of expensive random access memory (RAM), and the need to maintain support for older legacy applications. Eventually, many of these problems were overcome as hardware capabilities for microcomputers were enhanced and standards for networking and communication were adopted.

The sheer size of the microcomputer market has meant that more research and development spending has been directed at perfecting the technology, and now modern microcomputers offer performance levels that were only dreamed of in the earlier years. Features such as voice recognition and integration with the Internet, smart phone and other mobile devices, and television technologies promise more for the future. Microcomputers have become indispensable parts of client/server environments in just about all areas of commercial, industrial, educational, and domestic activity.

See also **Mainframes • Minicomputers • Supercomputers**

Resources

Books

Eckhouse, Richard H. *Minicomputer Systems: Organization and Programming (PDP–11).* 2nd ed. Englewood Cliffs, NJ: Prentice-Hall, 1975.

Hilton, Alice Mary. *Logic, Computing Machines, and Automation.* Washington, DC: Spartan Books, 1963.

Lécuyer, Christophe, and David C. Brock. *Makers of the Microchip: A Documentary History of Fairchild Semiconductor.* Cambridge. MA: MIT Press, 2010.

Poslad, Stefan. *Ubiquitous Computing: Smart Devices, Environments and Interactions.* Chichester, U.K.: Wiley, 2009.

Sedra, Adel S., and Kenneth C. Smith. *Microelectronic Circuits.* 6th ed. Oxford and New York: Oxford University Press, 2011.

Wakerley, John S. *Digital Design Principles and Practices.* 4th ed. Upper Saddle River, NJ: Pearson/Prentice Hall, 2006.

Web Sites

Markesino, Anthony. "The History of Micro Computers." HowStuffWorks.com. http://www.ehow.com/about_5336357_history-micro-computers.html (accessed October 10, 2012).

Mazor, Stanley. "The History of the Microcomputer—Invention and Evolution." Xnumber.com. http://www.xnumber.com/xnumber/Microcomputer_invention.htm (accessed October 10, 2012).

Microsoft Corporation

Microsoft Corporation, a software company, was started by American businessperson and philanthropist William "Bill" Henry Gates III (1955–) and American entrepreneur and philanthropist Paul Gardner Allen (1953–) in 1975 when Micro Instrumentation and Telemetry Systems (MITS) produced the first widely available personal computer in kit form, termed the Altair 8800. This computer came with assembly language, making the computer difficult to use. Gates and Allen wrote a compiler for Beginners' All-purpose Symbolic Instruction Code (BASIC), the first computer language for personal computers, specifically for the Altair, and convinced MITS to distribute this software. This version worked so well that it became the foundation of almost all personal

A new tablet is presented by Microsoft.
© *Kevork Djansezian/Getty Images.*

computers at that time, including Apple products. With this modest start Microsoft paved the way for the development of software for two more languages, Microsoft FORTRAN (FORmula TRANslation) and Microsoft COBOL (COmmon Business Oriented Language), and sales of other successful software programs in the budding personal computer market.

The second generation of personal computing occurred when IBM entered the market in 1980. The International Business Machines Corporation (IBM) asked Microsoft to develop an operating system (OS), the computer's nervous system, for its new personal computer based on an Intel microprocessor (the computer brain). Although Microsoft had focused almost exclusively on application software, it agreed to the deal, then bought the operating system from neighboring Seattle Computer Products and renamed it MS-DOS (for Microsoft Disk Operating System). In 1980, American businessperson Steven Ballmer (1956–) was hired at Microsoft as its first business manager and would later assume the role of chief executive officer (CEO) under Gates as chair of the board of directors in 2000. As of October 2012, Ballmer continues as its CEO.

IBM's popular personal computer, produced with a microprocessor* by Intel and utilizing MS-DOS, inspired the production of IBM clones. This in turn stimulated the creation of software and peripheral products throughout the computer industry. Microsoft and Intel products literally set the standard for the personal computer industry, thus ensuring a strong future for both companies.

Microsoft Word (introduced in 1983), Excel (1987), and PowerPoint (a product of Forethought, Inc., which was acquired in 1987 by Microsoft) were other successful applications. Combining these products into Microsoft Office, along with its operating systems, languages, business software, hardware, and computer how-to books helped Microsoft reach $140 million in sales and 900 employees on its tenth anniversary.

The CD-ROM (compact disc-read only memory), introduced in 1987, offered another opportunity for the company. Microsoft's Bookshelf, a collection of ten general-purpose applications, was the first CD-ROM for personal computers. In 1990, Microsoft became the first personal computer company to reach one billion dollars in sales in a single year.

Introducing Microsoft Windows

Computer speed and memory increased with the advent of internal hard drives in personal computers and expanded capacity of microprocessor chips. This allowed the development of more complex software programs, such as Microsoft Windows.

Introduced in 1985, Windows did not arrive without cost and controversy. First, it functioned in a way so similar to Apple, Inc.'s Macintosh operating system that Apple sued Microsoft for copyright infringement. In addition, IBM considered Windows to be in direct competition with IBM's OS/2, a project IBM was developing with Microsoft. This led to the severing of the IBM-Microsoft partnership.

The early versions of Microsoft Windows, up to version 3.1, were normal programs developed to operate in conjunction with MS-DOS. These programs were designed to make it possible for users to run multiple unrelated software applications at once. Windows evolved from software applications into a series of operating systems termed Windows NT, Windows 95, Windows 98, Windows 2000, Windows ME, Windows XP, Windows Vista, and Windows 7, which was introduced in 2009. Windows 95 was the first Microsoft operating system to support true multitasking. Windows 3.1 allowed multiple programs to be run at once but relied on each program to give up control of the processor in order to share time between all programs. Prior to Windows 2000, Microsoft maintained a line of consumer operating systems (Windows 95, 98, and Me) and business-class operating systems (Windows NT). Windows 2000 marked the unification of the two lines, and continued through Windows XP, Vista, and Windows 7. On October 26, 2012, Microsoft released Windows 8 for consumer sale.

*microprocessor the principle element in a computer; the component that understands how to carry out operations under the direction of the running program (CPU)

From Schoolboy to Software Mogul

Bill Gates discovered the fascination of computers as a twelve-year-old at the private Lakeside School in Seattle, Washington. Four years later, Gates and schoolmate Paul Allen wrote software to measure Seattle's traffic flow, and incorporated their first company, Traf-O-Data.

With two others, they formed the Lakeside Programming Group and wrote complex payroll applications for a local company. When Lakeside School bought a computer, Gates and company got the job of scheduling their own classes.

Gates went to Harvard University and Allen accepted a job in Boston. There the two wrote and marketed BASIC for the Altair, the first home computer kit. When Gates dropped out of Harvard to found and run Microsoft, first in Albuquerque, New Mexico, and then in Seattle, he was on his way to becoming one of the world's richest private citizens.

Gates appointed Steve Ballmer as CEO in 2000 and assumed the role of chair of the board of directors of Microsoft. In 2006, Gates announced that he would begin working full-time for the Bill and Melinda Gates Foundation, a global philanthropic organization focused on improving healthcare and reducing poverty. Gates currently acts as non-executive chairman of Microsoft.

* **Sherman Antitrust Act** the act of the U.S. Congress in 1890 that is the foundation for all American anti-monopoly laws

Microsoft and Apple, Inc.

In addition to its early partnership with IBM, Microsoft also had long-standing ties to Apple, Inc. (formerly Apple Computer, Inc.) An early believer in Apple, Microsoft developed software applications (although not the Apple operating system) for the Apple II and later contributed significantly to software applications developed for the successful Macintosh line. In 1997, Microsoft helped bring a troubled Apple, Inc. back into the market after agreeing to invest in Apple and develop Microsoft Office, Internet Explorer, and other applications specifically for Apple's Macintosh. As part of that deal, Apple agreed to drop the copyright infringement lawsuit that had been proceeding against Microsoft for many years.

Microsoft as a Monopoly

The Windows operating system and Internet Explorer, Microsoft's Web browser, became so widely used that competitors claimed that Microsoft had become a monopoly. The Justice Department of the United States, along with the attorneys general of nineteen states and the District of Columbia, filed a lawsuit against Microsoft in 1998.

In April 2000, a court determined that Microsoft had violated the Sherman Antitrust Act*. In his conclusions, U.S. District Judge Thomas Penfield Jackson (1937–) found that "…Microsoft's share of the worldwide market for Intel-compatible PC operating systems currently exceeds ninety-five percent…" and that "Microsoft enjoyed monopoly power." He stated that Microsoft "used anticompetitive methods to achieve or maintain its position." In addition, Microsoft was found to have attempted to monopolize the Internet browser market through anticompetitive acts, especially by its practice of integrating Internet Explorer with its Windows 95 operating system, thereby discouraging or prohibiting the use of other Web browsers. Jackson ordered that Microsoft be split into two companies.

Although that remedy was reversed by the U.S. Court of Appeals in 2001, the appeals court agreed with both Jackson's monopoly ruling and his findings that Microsoft illegally maintained its monopoly. In October 2001, Microsoft agreed to terms to settle the lawsuit out of court.

As of 2012, Microsoft remains a major provider of operating systems for personal computers, along with its very popular office suite product Microsoft Office 2010. Microsoft also produces many other software products for desktops, mobile devices, and servers, including the Internet search engine Bing and the video game consoles Xbox and Xbox 360. As announced in 2012, Microsoft will begin to offer tablet computers under the name Microsoft Surface. As of 2012, Microsoft, with its headquarters in Redmond, Washington, has an estimated revenue of $73.72 billion, with approximately 94,000 employees. The company's assets are estimated to total $121.2 billion. Further, Gates is estimated to be worth $66 billion. Forbes Magazine lists Gates as the second richest person in the world, and the richest person in the United States.

▶ *See also* **Apple Computer, Inc.** • **Intel Corporation** • **Operating Systems**

Resources

Books

Bill Gates: He, Who Reduced the Globe into a Small Town. India bookvarsity. Delhi: Vijay Goel, 2007.

Foley, Mary Jo. *Microsoft 2.0: How Microsoft Plans to Stay Relevant in the Post-Gates Era.* Indianapolis: John Wiley & Sons, 2008.

Lesinski, Jeanne M. *Bill Gates*, revised ed. Minneapolis, MN: Twenty-First Century Books, 2007.

Lockwood, Brad. *Bill Gates: Profile of a Digital Entrepreneur.* New York: Rosen, 2008.

Musolf, Neil. *The Story of Microsoft.* Mankato, MN: Creative Education, 2009.

Slater, Robert. *Microsoft Rebooted: How Bill Gates and Steve Ballmer Reinvented Their Company.* New York: Portfolio, 2004.

Strother, Ruth. *Bill Gates.* Edina, MN: ABDO, 2008.

Web Sites

Bill and Melinda Gates Foundation. "About the Foundation." http://www.gatesfoundation.org/about/Pages/overview.aspx (accessed October 10, 2012).

Microsoft Corporation. "About Microsoft." http://www.microsoft.com/about/en/us/default.aspx (accessed October 10, 2012).

Minicomputers

Minicomputers (sometimes called *minis*) historically have been described as computers possessing capabilities less than those of the larger and costlier mainframe computers, but possessing more power than the less-expensive microcomputer (sometimes called a personal computer, or PC). In the initial decade of the 2000s, as the computing power and capabilities of the microcomputer continually increased, the decades-old line separating minicomputers and microcomputers was gradually erased. Since the increasingly-powerful microcomputer could perform most of the duties previously performed by the minicomputer, the term has largely fallen out of general, everyday use. However, the need for a computer having processing capabilities less than that of a mainframe or supercomputer, but greater than that of a high-end microcomputer, has remained unchanged. Hence, the terms server and midrange computer are often used in place

IBM Series 1 Minicomputer system
© SSPL via Getty Images.

of minicomputer to identify a multi-user computer that is more capable than a microcomputer or the typical workstation. In this context, server is used to emphasize the server-client relationship in computing, in which the computer serves many users.

A Niche for Minicomputers

Large mainframe systems of the 1970s and 1980s cost from a low of $50,000–$100,000, up to several million dollars. The mini was an economical solution to low-end, smaller computing.

The mini was relatively small, less than 0.6-meters (two-feet) wide, and mounted in a rack. Its advent also spurred the development of peripherals that had to be developed at a price consistent with that of the mini while providing satisfactory performance.

Some applications of the minicomputer were data acquisition, process control, time-sharing, and terminal and peripheral communication control. Process control systems involve data acquisition and feedback to control the process, with or without human intervention. The machine-machine system involves the use of a minicomputer as a front-end communications processor or a peripheral control unit. This offloads the tasks of error checking, polling, hand-shaking, line buffering, or other formatting from the large central processor. Minicomputers were also used in stand-alone or single-user mode to do human research such as reaction time studies. The stand-alone mode was necessary to provide timing independent of other processes.

The minicomputer was capable of performing under normal environmental conditions and did not require the extensive power and air-conditioning of larger but more delicate systems. It could also be made rugged (rugged-ized) to perform in adverse environments such as combat fronts. It was a more durable tool than many larger systems and more easily transportable. It could also be used in factories for process control, inventory and manufacturing control, or as a satellite to a larger computer, feeding data to it or acting as a peripheral device.

The growth of the minicomputer market was relatively rapid. It began in the 1960s and expanded in the early 1970s. The key to its growth was the development of large-scale integrated circuitry. Integrated circuits* (ICs) were developed in the 1960s, initially with a single function on a chip, a logic gate or flip-flop (memory element); then with medium-scale integration (MSI), with a dozen or more functions on a chip; and, finally, large-scale integration (LSI), with more than 100 functions on a chip; and later, with very large-scale integration (VLSI). The availability of large-scale integration lowered the costs of developing a computer and aided in the replicability of the manufacturing process. This enabled batch processing*, as well as modular construction and the interchangeability of parts.

Minicomputer peripherals included cassette tape units, minidisks, cartridge disks, and the cathode ray tube (CRT)*. However, there was initially a discrepancy between the cost of the central processing unit (CPU)* and the cost of the peripherals because of declining costs in the batch processing of CPU and memory microchips.

The minicomputer system was designed to balance the needs of input/output and storage with the computing needs in a cost-effective way. The software for a mini usually consisted of an assembler, editor, several compilers*, and utility programs. The operating systems were of various types, including paging systems. Some minicomputers were application-specific; the hardware and peripherals, as well as the software, or driver program, were tailored to the application. This was especially true of military, airborne, or other special uses of the computer. Minicomputers were used in some of the early American space launches.

Two minicomputers of historic note are the CDC 160 and CDC 160-A from Control Data Corporation (CDC). Designed by American electrical engineer Seymour Cray (1925–1996), they were built from 1960 to 1965. For only $60,000 (in those days), the CDC 160 was a simple minicomputer that was much faster than other computers that CDC offered previously, such as the CDC 1604. It was much less expensive than the CDC 1604, which sold for about $1 million.

It is difficult to compare the minicomputer with the personal computers of today. The personal computer is far larger in terms of memory capacity and peripheral storage capacity, and faster in processing speed. It is also considerably cheaper in absolute cost and in cost

* **integrated circuits** circuits with the transistors, resistors, and other circuit elements etched into the surface of a single chip of semiconducting material, usually silicon

* **batch processing** an approach to computer utilization that queues noninteractive programs and runs them one after another

* **cathode ray tube (CRT)** a glass enclosure that projects images by directing a beam of electrons onto the back of a screen

* **central processing unit (CPU)** the part of a computer that performs computations and controls and coordinates other parts of the computer

* **compilers** programs that translate human-readable high-level computer languages to machine-readable code

* **registers** a set of bits of high-speed memory used to hold data for a particular purpose

* **I/O** the acronym for input/output; used to describe devices that can accept input data to a computer and to other devices that can produce output

relative to performance. However, the minicomputer can be compared to the personal computer as a low-cost alternative to computing with a large system. In certain applications, such as large-scale computing or complex graphical designs, a maxicomputer or large computer—even a supercomputer—is still required.

Some of the compilers available with minicomputers were FORTRAN (FORmula TRANslator) IV, Algol, RPG (Report Program Generator), Basic (interpreter), and, eventually, C and Unix (trademarked as UNIX). C and the associated operating system Unix, and much of the early work at Bell Laboratories on computers and computer software, were done on the PDP-series computers (Digital Equipment's Programmed Data Processor x [PDP-x] family). Other manufacturers were Data General, Varian, Hewlett-Packard, Honeywell, and Texas Instruments.

The number of registers* in a mini was limited. Although the PDP-11 and other members of the family had eight, others had fewer. Some minicomputers were single-address machines, with a single register or accumulator. Others, such as the PDP-11 and Interdata 70, were two-address machines, indicating several —one of which is addressed in the instruction, along with a memory location. The I/O* was sometimes under program control, tying up the CPU or central processor, while others offered direct memory access (DMA), stealing cycles from the CPU, but otherwise operating independently of the CPU, through a separate I/O controller or channel.

Disk operating systems were developed for minicomputers because the amount of main memory was limited. If the operating system took up between 12 kilobytes (kb, sometimes also denoted as simply K) and 20K of memory and only 32K was available, a limited amount was left for user programs. The operating system was divided into resident and non-resident portions, and the non-resident portions of the operating system as well as user programs were rolled, or swapped, in and out as necessary. One machine of the PDP series implemented time-sharing by swapping whole programs in and out of main memory, with one user program resident at a time.

The minicomputer led to an unexpected development. The PDP series of computer was expanded in 1975 to the Virtual Address eXtension (VAX) series of computers. The VAX was a 32-bit machine that was comparable to a mainframe, though not in terms of the large cost of some of the mainframes of the day (several million dollars). Although manufacture of the VAXseries of computers ended in 2005, some models were still in use in universities and elsewhere, which stands as quite an achievement in the quickly-evolving computer market.

The development of the VAX family of computers coincided with the development of the personal computer. The introduction of the IBM personal computer (8086/8088) in 1981 started another revolution that continues to the present day.

See also **Mainframes** • **Microcomputers** • **Supercomputers**

Resources

Books

Eckhouse, Richard H. *Minicomputer Systems: Organization and Programming (PDP–11).* 2nd ed. Prentice-Hall series in automatic computation. Englewood Cliffs, NJ: Prentice-Hall, 1979.

Hilton, Alice Mary. *Logic, Computing Machines, and Automation.* Washington, D.C.: Spartan Books, 1963.

Mermin, N. David. *Quantum Computer Science: An Introduction.* Cambridge, UK, and New York: Cambridge University Press, 2007.

Poslad, Stefan. *Ubiquitous Computing: Smart Devices, Environments and Interactions.* Chichester, U.K: Wiley, 2009.

Yechuri, Sitaramarao S. *Microchips: A Simple Introduction.* Arlington, TX: Yechuri Software, 2004.

Web Sites

Computer History Museum. "The Birth of the Minicomputer?" http://www.computerhistory.org/revolution/minicomputers/11/333 (accessed October 11, 2012).

HowStuffWorks.com, and Alex Cosper. "History of the Minicomputer." http://www.ehow.com/about_5465085_history-minicomputer.html (accessed October 11, 2012).

Minitel

Minitel was an interactive network in France that consisted of millions of residential and business computer terminals that transmitted and received information exclusively through the country's national telephone system. Developed in 1978 and officially launched in 1982, the Minitel network performed many of the functions later available through the Internet. Minitel, however, initiated service than a decade before the Internet became available. Originally the network was intended to give French residents universal access to an electronic telephone directory, to reduce the cost of paper telephone books, and to promote the nation's new telephone system run by the government communications agency France Telecom.

To establish the Minitel network and to encourage families to subscribe to the upgraded telephone system, French households were offered a free terminal. The terminal, called "le Minitel," was a dumb terminal*— it had no processing capabilities but used the telephone connection to

* **dumb terminal** a keyboard and screen connected to a distant computer without any processing capability

dial up a central computer server, retrieve the desired information, and
display it on the user's screen.

The free terminals immediately eliminated France Telecom's annual
fee for producing and distributing costly paper telephone books.
Historically, the delivery of paper telephone books routinely took as
long as eighteen months after publication. Therefore, even when they
were newly delivered to the consumer, the books were out of date and
riddled with errors. In 1979 France Telecom calculated that the cost of
distributing free electronic terminals would, by 1988, be cheaper than
delivering free telephone books, which had required 20,000 metric tons
(44 million pounds) of paper in 1979 and would have used an estimated
100,000 metric tons (220 million pounds) by 1985. The potential sav-
ings moved the project forward.

The population, however, did not immediately warm to the idea. In
1980, as Minitel was being introduced, the public voiced distrust of the
technology because of fear it might be shut down in a wartime situation.
Members of Parliament were wary of a potential monopoly by France
Telecom; they moved to restrict a system that would allow the agency to
become too powerful too quickly. Parliament also addressed fears of electronic competition with the paper industries by guaranteeing cooperation
with newspapers and other media.

Despite early obstacles, Minitel was a success by 1984 and its capabilities were broadened beyond its original charter. In addition to providing
information directories, Minitel became the nation's resource for sending
messages, ordering merchandise, viewing store hours or train timetables,

researching theater ticket prices, and playing games—even interactive games with people in distant locations. Interactive chat rooms featuring pseudonyms and a messaging system similar to e-mail were introduced. For residents without a home phone, Minitel kiosks were installed in public places, such as post offices.

Minitel continued to grow throughout the next fourteen years, and in 1998 France Telecom counted 5.6 million terminals installed, from which 176 billion calls were made to Minitel. Most terminals (64 percent) were located in residences, followed by professional locations (25 percent), businesses (10 percent), and other locations (1 percent).

By 1999, the Minitel telephone directory was receiving 150 million calls per month with an additional 100 million calls to other sites. Non-directory services at that time included travel reservations, sports scores, bank account information, stock prices, administrative file access, weather forecasts, lottery results, TV schedules, classified ads, and mail order sales.

The Minitel terminal evolved from its initial appearance and function. Early models featured a simple black and white screen. Subsequent models offered a sophisticated combination of telephone access and color computer graphics that included a telephone receiver and line. The Webphone, which France Telecom began testing in 1999, offered access to both the Internet and Minitel.

In the mid 1990s, the Minitel system gradually was made accessible from personal computers and the Internet itself. By the end of 1999, some 3 million Minitel emulators were being used on desktop computers. That year, of the 82 percent of Minitel users in France who also used the Internet, 14 percent had never used Minitel before the Internet was available.

One key drawback of Minitel, when compared to the Internet, was that Internet users could visit most sites free of charge; Minitel users, conversely, paid a fee every time they accessed a Minitel site. The entrepreneur or organization that sponsored the Minitel site collected part of the fee, called a payback, from France Telecom. Charges were calculated by the minute and billed directly to the user's telephone bill. Prices varied depending upon the services accessed and ranged from a few cents to more than $1 (U.S. dollar) per minute.

In an effort to address increasing competition from the Internet, Minitel services were enhanced in late 2000 by introducing i-Minitel, which helped PC and Mac users connect more easily to the Minitel network. France Telecom also launched Et hop Minitel that allowed businesses to post their web content via Minitel. In spite of the efforts to enhance Minitel's capabilities, competition from the Internet reduced the number of Minitel users throughout the first decade of the 2000s. France Telecom announced that it would cancel Minitel as of March 2009, but delayed final termination of the service until 2012 when the company found that the system still had more than 1 million directory users.

The Minitel system, though now defunct and considered inferior in many ways to the Internet, nevertheless possessed characteristics that were superior to Internet browsing. Chief among those superior attributes was the security of the Minitel network. Unlike personal computers browsing the Internet, Minitel terminals could not be infected by a computer worm or virus. Moreover, sites that one could visit on the Minitel network were considered more secure than comparable Internet web sites because Minitel was a closed network. Because of their superior security features, as well as the opportunity for payback revenue, many banks and reservation agencies initially preferred to maintain a Minitel site as opposed to opening an Internet web site.

▶ *See also* **Apple Computer, Inc • Bell Labs • Intel Corporation • Internet • Supercomputers • Microsoft Corporation • Xerox Corporation**

Resources

Books

Marchand, Marie. *A French Success Story: The Minitel Saga*, trans. Mark Murphy. Paris: Larousse, 1988.

Mouse

In 1963, Douglas C. Engelbart (1925–), working at the Stanford Research Institute, was investigating different ways for humans to communicate with computers. He thought that a pointing device, something that a computer user could move by hand causing a corresponding movement in an object on the screen, would be easier to use and more

▶

A boxed computer mouse. © *Nelson Ching/Bloomberg via Getty Images.*

intuitive than the existing keyboard. The computer mouse made its debut in 1968 at a computer conference in San Francisco, but it was not used widely until the introduction of personal computers in the 1980s. It became a very popular pointing device for operating environments that provide graphical user interfaces (GUIs)*. The mouse remains a popular choice for use with stationary office or home computer systems, but was eclipsed by the trackpad on laptops. Most tablet and smart-phones use touchscreen interfaces that do not require a pointing device other than the human finger.

The mouse is used in conjunction with the keyboard to perform tasks such as moving and pointing to objects displayed on the screen, selecting commands from menus, and working with drawing and painting pro-grams. A mouse has one, two, or three buttons that can be pressed to send to the computer signals that activate commands. As the mouse is moved around a desktop, the on-screen pointer mimics its motion. This technique provides an extremely fast and smooth way to navigate around the computer screen.

How does a computer mouse work? For the vast majority of com-puter mice, there are just two two distinct user movements that activate the mouse: moving it around a desktop and pressing one of its buttons.

The Electromechanical Mouse

As an electromechanical mouse is moved around a desktop, the track-ing ball—a rubber ball underneath its body—translates the mouse movements into input signals that the computer can understand. Those signals are carried to the computer by the long cable that con-nects the mouse to one of the computer's ports. As the ball spins, it makes contact with and rotates two rollers installed at a 90-degree angle to each other. One of the rollers reacts to back-and-forth move-ments of the mouse, which translate into up-and-down movements of the on-screen pointer. The other roller detects sideways movements, which translate into side-to-side movements for the on-screen pointer. Each roller is joined to a wheel, called an encoder, which has a set of tiny metal bars, called contact points, on its rim. When the rollers go around, the encoders do the same, and their contact points touch two pairs of contact bars that reach out from the mouse's cover, thus gen-erating an electrical signal.

A new signal is sent every time a connection is made between the contact points and the contact bars. The total number of signals shows how far the mouse has moved: a large number of signals means it has moved a long distance. The direction in which the mouse is moving—up-and-down or sideways—is communicated by the direction in which the rollers are turning and the ratio between the number of signals from each of the rollers.

The signals sent to the computer through the mouse's tail are used by the software that empowers the mouse. This software converts the num-ber of signals from the encoders and rollers to determine how far and in

* **light emitting diode (LED)** a discrete electronic component that emits visible light when permitting current to flow in a certain direction; often used as an indicating lamp

which direction the on-screen pointer will move. The frequency of signals indicates the speed needed to move the on-screen pointer.

Each of the buttons on the top of the mouse covers a tiny switch that records when a button is pressed or clicked, and the time interval between clicks. Pressing one of the buttons on the mouse sends a signal to the computer, which again is passed on to the software. Based on how many times a user clicks the button, and where the on-screen pointer is positioned during these clicks, the software will execute the task selected.

Other Types of Computer Mice

There are several other kinds of mice in general use: optical, optomechanical, and laser mice. An optical mouse has no ball or wheels but instead depends upon a light emitting diode (LED)* and a photodetector. As the mouse moves across a surface, the photodetector senses movement by changes in reflected light.

An optomechanical mouse combines characteristics of the optical mouse and the standard electromechanical mouse: it is built with a moving ball and shafts with slits through which light can pass. As the mouse moves, the shafts rotate and light pulses strike the photodetector through the slits. The amount of cursor motion is proportional to the number of light pulses detected. No special mouse pad is required with optomechanical mice, and they are less vulnerable to dust and dirt-related failure than are electromechanical mice.

A laser beam gauges the movements of a laser mouse. The laser beam is emitted from the bottom of the mouse during operation. Whereas both laser mice and optical mice use light as the basic mechanism for tracking movements, the laser mouse is capable of achieving much higher resolution in tracking its movements. For most ordinary tasks performed with a personal computer (such as word processing and web browsing), this difference in precision is unimportant. But some applications, like gaming and computer-aided design (CAD), require the higher precision that the laser mouse can supply. Additionally, a laser mouse can be used on almost any surface; by contrast, mechanical mice often perform best on a specialized mouse pad, and optical mice often return erroneous readings to the computer when used on a black or glossy surface, or on glass.

There are also "3D mice" available. Such mice are designed to be held and moved in three-dimensions; that is, in addition to the familiar back-and-forth and side-to-side movements of most computer mice, these devices can be moved up-and-down as well. 3D mice find use in applications such as computer games.

More Mouse Variations

A trackball is an upside-down mouse. With a trackball, the user spins a ball with his or her fingers to determine the speed and direction of the on-screen pointer.

A wireless mouse, which is a mouse without a cord, uses infrared or radio signals (including Bluetooth technology) to communicate with the computer. This type of mouse is powered by a small replaceable battery.

A touch mouse is a hybrid of a wireless optical mouse and a trackpad. The touch mouse or magic mouse responds to different touch commands to move the cursor and do different activities on screen such as scroll pages. In October 2009 Apple introduced the "Magic Mouse." The company's press release boasted that, in place of conventional buttons, the "entire top of the Magic Mouse is a seamless Multi-Touch surface" so that "users can easily scroll through long documents" or "pan across large images or swipe to move forward or backward through a collection of web pages or photos."

▶ *See also* **Game Controllers • Hypertext • Interactive Systems • Microcomputers • Pointing Devices**

Resources

Books

Morley, Deborah. *Understanding Computers: Today & Tomorrow.* 13th ed. Boston: Course Technology, Cengage Learning, 2011.

White, Ron, and Timothy Edward Downs. *How Computers Work.* 9th ed. Indianapolis: Que Publishing, 2008.

Music

Computers have had an impact on all segments of the music industry. Specialized hardware and software help train performers on instruments, such as piano and guitar, and assist with instruction in music theory, ear training, and general musicianship. Composers use computers to create new compositions and analyze existing ones. Computers can also be used to produce the raw sounds of music through synthesis and sequencing software and hardware.

Since the late 1960s, most composers and publishers have used computer notation and typesetting programs instead of engraving and hand copying to make printed scores and parts. The use of digital technology for music production, including recording and editing, and for playback is almost universal. Music can be heard and exchanged over the Internet, and computer-generated music is heard in film scores, television commercials, popular music, and classical music concerts.

However, the most significant impact of computers may be the increased ease with which people are able to participate in the making of music. Performers can create and "play" their own instruments without years of traditional training, for example, and can generate recordings and distribute them over the Internet outside the traditional studio system.

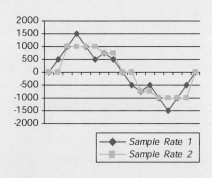

▲

Figure 1.
Reproduced by permission of Gale, a part of Cengage Learning.

---

* **oscillator** an electronic component that produces a precise waveform of a fixed known frequency; this can be used as a time base (clock) signal to other devices

* **analog** a quantity (often an electrical signal) that is continuous in time and amplitude

* **digital** a quantity that can exist only at distinct levels, not having values in between these levels (for example, binary)

* **bit** a single binary digit, 1 or 0—a contraction of Binary digIT; the smallest unit for storing data in a computer

* **byte** a group of eight binary digits; represents a single character of text

* **Analytical Engine** Charles Babbage's vision of a programmable mechanical computer

Sound Synthesis and Recording

The term "electro-acoustic" music is used to describe music in which the sounds are produced, changed, or reproduced by electronic means, or synthesized, rather than being produced by naturally resonating bodies such as the vocal cords. In traditional electronic music, sound is generated by devices such as oscillators* that produce an electrical signal. Processors, such as mixer, filter, and reverberation modules, can then modify the signal.

This process is called analog* synthesis because the electrical signal produced by the synthesizer is a nearly exact representation of the waveshape of the actual sound. In recording, the microphone converts the waveshape of the sound into an electrical signal that is pressed into the groove of a record. As the needle wiggles along this picture of the waveshape, it is converted back into an electrical signal. The representation of sound is on a continuous scale; like the sweep second hand on a watch, it is able to represent any two points and all possible points in between.

Digital* synthesis and recording are based on the idea that it is possible for the continuous waveshape of a sound to be represented by a series of numbers. This process is known as quantization. Computers are ideal machines for generating and storing those numbers. However, special hardware is required: digital to analog converters (DACs) are needed to translate numbers into electrical voltages and analog to converters (ADCs) are used to translate voltages into numbers.

The digital representation of sound is on a discrete scale of steps. The waveshape of a sound is specified, or sampled, at evenly spaced points along the wave. The frequency with which the samples are taken is the sampling rate. The higher the sampling rate, the more exactly the waveshape is represented and the higher the fidelity of the resulting sound. A general principle is that the sampling rate must be at least two times the frequency of the highest sound to avoid distortion.

Figure 1 shows in simple terms how the representation of a waveshape changes if Sample Rate 1 is cut in half.

Another important issue in digital sound representation is the size of the unit used to store samples. Small units, such as eight bits*, can store a limited range of numbers. Many values must be rounded off and information is lost. Achieving high fidelity requires a big memory, however. Representing four seconds of sound in sixteen-bit audio format requires approximately 700,000 bytes*.

Digital synthesis is limited by the time required for the computer to calculate the numbers for each sample. If the time needed is greater than the sampling rate, the sound cannot be produced in real time; the values must be stored in a file that can be played back once all the calculations are complete. This makes experimentation, variation, and modification difficult.

History

As early as 1843, Ada Byron King, Countess of Lovelace, suggested that Charles Babbage's Analytical Engine*, a forerunner of the computer, might be used for music. In 1957 this vision was realized in two very different ways. Lejaren Hiller and Leonard Isaacson wrote a computer program that composed the *Iliac Suite* using the laws of chance and basic rules of music composition. This program generated a score that was played by human musicians.

The pioneering work in computer music was done using software synthesis. This is the most flexible and precise method because synthesis programs can be run on general-purpose computers.

Early music synthesis programs such as MUSIC III (1960) were written using the concept of unit generators, like the modules of analog synthesizers. In the 1960s and 1970s, most computer music was produced at universities and research institutions. Software synthesis became more widespread in the late 1980s with the introduction of low-cost, good quality, digital to analog converters for personal computers and graphical user interfaces (GUI).

By 2000, software synthesis programs included two categories: (1) graphical instrument editors in which the user simulates using an analog synthesizer by clicking on icons on the display screen; and (2) synthesis language programs in which the user specifies sounds by writing text that is interpreted by the program.

Researchers also designed special-purpose hardware for music functions. This path led to commercial digital performing instruments, including the Synclavier (1976) and the Fairlight (1979), which are widely used by performers. However, the flexibility of these machines is limited by the fixed nature of their circuitry, which cannot be modified to perform new functions. Lack of standardization was a problem in the 1970s and early 1980s. Development of the Musical Instrument Digital Interface (MIDI), released in 1983, provided a standard protocol for exchanging musical information among different brands of computers and synthesizers.

By 2012, numerous software synthesizer programs were available for both PC and Mac platforms. With the increase in computing power of smartphones and tablets, several software synthesizer programs also were compatible with mobile operating systems, such as Apple's iOS and Google's Android.

▶ *See also* **Analog Computing** • **Apple Computer, Inc** • **Babbage, Charles** • **Digital Computing** • **King, Ada Byron** • **Microcomputers**

Resources

Books

Holmes, Thom. *Electronic and Experimental Music: Technology, Music, and Culture.* 4th ed. London and New York: Routledge, 2012.

Russ, Martin. *Sound Synthesis and Sampling.* 3rd ed. Amsterdam and Boston: Elsevier/Focal Press, 2009.

Computer Concerts

In 1957 Max Mathews (1926–2011) built the first system for creating computer-generated sound at Bell Laboratories. The first concert of computer-generated music was held in 1958. Among the composers associated with computer music are Iannis Xenakis (1922–2011), Charles Dodge (1942–), and John Chowning (1934–). Recordings of early computer-generated music are available through the Computer Music Series on Wergo Records and the CDCM Computer Music Series on Centaur Records.

N

Napier's Bones

Although John Napier is mainly remembered for the invention of logarithms*, he made other lasting contributions to mathematics as well. Born in the mid–1500s into a wealthy Scottish family, Napier was able to pursue all manner of subjects, ranging from religion to politics to agriculture, during his lifetime.

In 1617, shortly before his death, Napier developed a mechanical method for performing multiplication and division. This method, known as "Napier's bones," was based upon manipulation of rods with printed digits. The rods were made of bone, ivory, wood, or metal. Napier's bones became a very popular device for calculating in England and western Europe, because most people lacked these mathematical skills.

The set is composed of ten bones, nine of which display the multiples of a given number between one and nine. For example the "two" rod contains 02, 04… 18: multiples of two. The tenth bone, known as the index, displays the numerals 1 through 9. To multiply 6 by 58, the index bone is placed beside the 5 and 8 bones. The value for 6×5 from the 58 is read from the sixth location on the five bone, i.e. 30, and it is placed in the hundreds column. Then 6×8 is read from the sixth location on the 8 bone, i.e. 48, and this is placed in the tens column. The columns are added together, resulting in 348.

This same method of adding and subtracting was subsequently applied to logarithmic values, and resulted in the development of the slide rule. As late as the 1960s, English children used Napier's bones to learn multiplication.

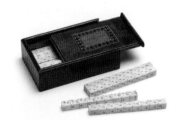

Set of Napier's bones. © *SSPL via Getty Images.*

* **logarithm** the power to which a certain number called the base is to be raised to produce a particular number

▶ See also **Abacus** • **Analog Computing** • **Slide Rule**

Resources

Books

Cooke, Roger. *The History of Mathematics: A Brief Course.* 2nd ed. Hoboken, NJ: Wiley-Interscience, 2005.

Drucker, Thomas. *Perspectives on the History of Mathematical Logic.* Boston: Birkhäuser, 1991; reprint. 2008.

Web Sites

New Mexico Institute of Mining and Technology. "Napier's Bones and the Genaille-Lucas Rulers" http://infohost.nmt.edu/~borchers/napier/napier.html (accessed November 1, 2012).

Cut-the-knot.org. "Napier's Bones in Various Bases" http://www.cut-the-knot.org/blue/Napier.shtml (accessed November 1, 2012).

National Aeronautics and Space Administration (NASA)

NASA's final Space Shuttle flight lifts off from Cape Canaveral. © *Bill Stafford/NASA/Getty Images. News*

▼

The National Aeronautics and Space Administration (NASA) was formed in 1958 from the National Advisory Committee on Aeronautics (NACA) and other agencies in the military and government that might benefit from a centralization of efforts in air and space research. Within a decade, NASA had three piloted and several unpiloted space projects either

* **ubiquitous** to be commonly available everywhere

complete or in the works. In the next few years, NASA introduced digital computers to aeronautics.

During its first fifteen years, NASA experienced its greatest period of influence on computing, both in hardware and software. Since the mid-1970s, NASA has become more of a user than an originator of computing technology, though several research programs still exist. NASA's need for cost-effective and innovative solutions to problems of navigation, safety, and communication has significantly influenced the development of computer technology, particularly in the application of embedded real time systems, redundancy, networks, large systems, and new computing hardware technology.

Embedded Real Time Systems

Canadian software engineer David Parnas (1941–) once said that "all systems are real time systems, it is just that some are faster than others." A real time system has to achieve its results in a time indistinguishable from when they are needed. Non-real time systems periodically check for events in between processing scheduled instructions. There is no guarantee made about the maximum time which can occur between an event being signaled and when the computer will process it. Real time systems can guarantee a maximum time window for processing events. Air traffic control, anti-lock brakes, and microwave ovens are all real time systems according to that definition. When NASA was formed, the technology of the day made real time systems considerably rare. NASA soon determined that one of the great difficulties of travel to the Moon is navigation, and it decided to design the Apollo spacecraft with a real time system for flight control. This is also known as an embedded system because the hardware and its software are an integral part of the entire subsystem, like the computer in an automobile.

The first piloted NASA spacecraft was *Freedom 7* with Project Mercury, which had no computer-controlled guidance on board. The second group of spacecraft was within Project Gemini. NASA chose Gemini to introduce and test the use of on-board computers to provide flight control and navigation, termed fly-by-wire navigation because computers interpret the movement of flight controls (such as the throttle or yoke) and engage or disengage the appropriate subsystem (such as thrusters) to achieve the desired effect. The Gemini and subsequent Project Apollo computers had to be relatively small, about 55 pounds (25 kilograms). They had to operate in real time, since they were used in flight control. Both were a significant change from NASA's room-sized ground-based computers in size and speed, yet both were much less capable than present-day desktop computers and laptops.

For example, although personal computers now have millions of words in memory, the Apollo computer had only 36 thousand. And although the ubiquitous* microprocessors in microwave ovens and automobiles have small memories, they are much faster than the six thousand operations a second that the Gemini computer could manage. A special case of an embedded real time system is airplane flight control systems. NASA put a surplus Apollo digital computer into a Navy F-8 and flew it in 1972. Now, almost all military and commercial aircraft use such fly-by-wire systems. It was NASA's requirement for embedded real time systems on both piloted and unpiloted spacecraft that led to the creation of many of the commercial and consumer systems we take for granted today.

Redundancy

Real time embedded systems in life-critical applications, such as flight control and life support, must not fail. Also, failures during long duration unpiloted missions cannot be repaired. Since NASA frequently conducts both types of flights, reliability has been a continuing concern to the agency. NASA most often ensures reliability through redundancy and backup, as opposed to ground-based systems that can be fixed readily. Perhaps the finest example of a redundant system is the data processing system on the space shuttle orbiter that uses four identical computers in a redundant set and a fifth identical computer running backup software. This concept has been adapted in business and industry to ensure safety and stability in computer-based operations and forms the backbone of the discipline of fault-tolerant computing.

Networks

Computer users today take high speed Internet access for granted, and rue the slowness of a 56K baud modem. Baud means bits per second, a measure of the volume of communication. However, NASA ran the Mercury man-in-space program (1959–1963) with only a 1K baud connection! NASA had radar systems at Cape Canaveral and in Bermuda to track the ascent of Mercury launches. The radar information was received at a computer site near the White House on Pennsylvania Avenue in Washington, D.C., at one thousand bits per second. The computer determined the flight path of the spacecraft and generated displays back in Florida so that the engineers could track the rocket's progress. This is one of the first uses of remote computing, and NASA built many more networks to support all kinds of spacecraft data and communications. Included in these are the complex networks and processors on board each piloted and unpiloted spacecraft.

Large Systems

When NASA was formed, the average computer system filled a room, but was still relatively small in terms of memory that could be accessed quickly. Many computers had a read/write memory of only two thousand to 16 thousand words, compared to machines in the early twenty-first century that have millions of words in storage. Magnetic tapes stored large volumes of data. Apollo and other projects needed fast memories, so the IBM Corporation and other NASA suppliers experimented with large one million word memories and groups of processors. NASA has always shown an interest in big, fast machines, and has sponsored research into parallel processing*, which is now commonplace in the world of information processing and analysis.

New Hardware Technology

Initially, programs like Apollo took a conservative approach to purchasing computer hardware. Piloted space flight programs were risky enough without pushing the leading edge. However, in the case of the Apollo flight computer, the gains from using relatively untried technology outweighed the risks. Also, by the time the actual Moon flights took place, several years had passed, during which newer technology was able to amass a history of reliability. NASA approved the use of integrated circuits* in the Apollo computer design. For a short time in the early 1960s, NASA and the U.S. Air Force (for the Minuteman missile) exhausted the entire production of in the United States.

In unpiloted space probes, NASA could take even more chances. Therefore, the first projects to use CMOS (Complementary Metal Oxide Semiconductor) integrated circuit technology were the Voyager probes to the outer planets. Such low-power chips have found their way onto the upgrades of the space shuttle and are commonplace in modern computers.

Supercomputers

The NASA Advanced Supercomputers (NAS) division houses several supercomputers within its High-End Computing Capability Project. Supercomputers offer the highest capacity and processor speed available. As of June 2012, the HECC has two of the fastest supercomputers in the world, Columbia and Pleiades. Though it is being phased out slowly in favor of new technology, Columbia has been running code for the Finite Volume General Circulation model (fvGCM), which is a global climate and weather prediction model used to produce real-time, high-resolution (approximately 15.5 miles or 25 kilometers) weather forecasting. Pleiades ranks 11th worldwide according to the LINPACK benchmark used by Top500, with a peak performance of more than 1.5 petaflops (1.5×10^{15} floating point operations per second). This enormous amount of computing power comes from the 125,000 processor cores it uses.

Conclusion

Since the 1960s, NASA's need for computer technology has contributed to the development of consumer and business applications of computer knowledge. The real impact of NASA on the computing industry is that it has constantly challenged its contractors to find new solutions to exotic problems, through a blend of trusted technology and cutting-edge computer science. Many parts of those solutions are passed on to consumers in the form of new uses for computers and greater reliability in computer

New Isn't Always Better

Many people think that NASA is such an advanced agency that it has the latest and best computers. This is largely untrue. To achieve the sort of reliability that space flight demands means using computers that are behind the state of the art and have acquired a history of reliability. For instance, the computers running the space shuttle orbiter in the early 2000s represented a forty-year-old architecture. In July 2011, the successful launch and return of the space shuttle *Atlantis* marked the 135th and final flight of the U.S. shuttle program. The international space station (ISS) will be serviced by a combination of launches of Russian-launched Soyuz capsules and private U.S. companies such as Space Exploration Technologies (SpaceX), which have taken over crewed low-orbital service missions. Several of the final shuttle missions involved lifting back-up computing and supporting electronics to the ISS.

* **parallel processing** the presence of more than one central processing unit (CPU) in a computer, which enables the simultaneous execution of more than one program

* **integrated circuits** circuits with the transistors, resistors, and other circuit elements etched into the surface of a single chip of semiconducting material, usually silicon

systems. Innovations designed to help protect the lives of NASA astronauts have become part of everyday life, from time-keeping and food preparation, to computerized automobile navigational systems and airplane flight safety.

▶ *See also* **Apple Computer, Inc.** • **Bell Labs** • **IBM Corporation** • **Intel Corporation** • **Microsoft Corporation** • **Xerox Corporation**

Resources

Books

Chien, Philip. *Columbia, Final Voyage: The Last Flight of NASA's First Space Shuttle.* New York: Copernicus Books, 2006.

Dick, Steven J. *America in Space: NASA's First Fifty Years.* New York: Abrams, 2007.

Parhami, Behrooz. *Computer Architecture: From Microprocessors to Supercomputers.* Oxford series in electrical and computer engineering. New York: Oxford University Press, 2005.

United States Congress, House Committee on Science and Technology. *NASA's Space Shuttle and International Space Station Programs: Status and Issues: Hearing before the Subcommittee on Space and Aeronautics, Committee on Science and Technology, House of Representatives, One Hundred Tenth Congress, First Session, July 24, 2007.* Washington: U.S. G.P.O., 2008.

Web Sites

National Aeronautics and Space Administration (NASA). "Apollo." http://www.nasa.gov/mission_pages/apollo/index.html (accessed August 26, 2011).

National Aeronautics and Space Administration (NASA). "Gemini." http://www.nasa.gov/mission_pages/gemini/index.html (accessed August 26, 2011).

National Aeronautics and Space Administration (NASA). "High-End Computing Capability Computing Environment." NASA Advanced Supercomputing Division (NAS). http://www.nas.nasa.gov/hecc/resources/environment.html (accessed October 27, 2012).

National Aeronautics and Space Administration (NASA). "Mercury." http://www.nasa.gov/mission_pages/mercury/index.html (accessed August 26, 2011).

National Aeronautics and Space Administration (NASA). "Mission to Mars: Mars Pathfinder." Jet Propulsion Laboratory, California Institute of Technology. http://mars.jpl.nasa.gov/missions/past/pathfinder.html (accessed August 26, 2011).

National Aeronautics and Space Administration (NASA). "NASA: Earth Observatory." http://earthobservatory.nasa.gov/ (accessed August 26, 2011).

National Aeronautics and Space Administration (NASA). "Space Shuttle." http://www.nasa.gov/mission_pages/shuttle/main/index. html (accessed August 26, 2011).

Top500. "Top 500 Supercomputer Sites." http://www.top500.org/ (accessed October 27, 2011).

* **topology** a method of describing the structure of a system that emphasizes its logical nature rather than its physical characteristics

Networks

In its simplest form, networking takes place between two devices that are directly connected. However, it is often impractical for devices to be directly connected, such as when devices are far apart or when more than two devices want to communicate. The solution is to attach each device to a communication network. When this happens, each device is said to be networked. Further, communication networks can be categorized on the basis of architecture and techniques to transfer data. Such network categories include:

1. broadcast networks, where a transmission from any device is broadcast and received by all other stations;

2. circuit-switched networks, where a dedicated connection is established between devices on a network across switching nodes within the network;

3. packet-switched networks, where data are sent in smaller units, called packets, from node to node within a network from source to destination.

Basic Configurations

The basic configuration, or topology*, of a network is the geometric representation of all the links and nodes of a network. A link is the physical communication path that transfers data from one device to another. A node is a network-addressable device. There are five basic topologies: mesh, star, tree, bus, and ring. In a mesh topology, every node has a dedicated point-to-point link to every other node, which requires $n(n1)/2$ links to connect n nodes. For example, a network with 5 nodes would need 10 links to connect the nodes. In a star topology, each node has a dedicated point-to-point link to a central hub. If one node wants to send data to another, it sends to the hub, which then relays the data to the destination node. A tree topology occurs when multiple star topologies are connected together such that not every node is directly connected to a central hub. In a bus topology, one long cable connects all nodes in the network; in a ring topology, each node has a dedicated point-to-point connection to

* **byte** a group of eight binary digits; represents a single character of text

the nodes on either side in a physical ring such that a signal from a source travels around the ring to the destination and back to the source.

Network devices use signals in the form of electromagnetic energy to represent data. Electromagnetic energy (sometimes also called radiant energy; defined as the energy of electromagnetic radiation, such as radio waves and visible light), a combination of electrical and magnetic fields vibrating in relation to each other, is emitted by a source into the surrounding environment. Unguided, or wireless, media transport electromagnetic waves do not use a physical conductor to guide the wave. Instead, signals are broadcast through media, such as air or water, and are thus available to any device capable of receiving them. Guided, or wired, communications direct electromagnetic waves within the physical limitations of a conductor, which may be metallic wire, a hollow tube waveguide, or optical fiber. Electrical current is a common example of electromagnetic energy being guided within a conductor.

Optical fiber uses visible light (commonly called light) as a transmission medium. Light is electromagnetic energy at a specific range of frequencies (430 to 750 terahertz) whose speed depends on the density of the medium through which it is traveling. Theoretically, rays of light injected into strands of pure glass at specific angles will experience total internal reflection, meaning that no loss of energy occurs when light travels down the strand. In practice, some attenuation (loss of energy) and dispersion (mixing of frequencies) does occur because of impure glass and injected light signals at multiple frequencies; however, the range of frequencies, and thus data rates, that can be supported is dramatically higher than is possible with copper cables.

Copper cabling that accepts and transports signals in the form of electrical current comes in four different types:

1. unshielded, which is used most commonly in telephone systems;

2. twisted pair, which consists of two copper conductors surrounded by an insulating material and wrapped around each other to reduce significantly the impact of noise;

3. shielded twisted pair, which has a metal foil encasing each twisted pair;

4. coaxial cable, which carries signals of higher-frequency ranges because of its different construction (a central core conductor enclosed in an insulating sheath that is encased in an outer foil, or braid, that is protected by a plastic cover).

Types of Transmission

Asynchronous Transfer Mode (ATM) is a packet-switched technology where all the packets are the same size, referred to as cells. Asynchronous means that the cells are independent of each other with potentially different gaps between them. The fixed cell size of 53 bytes* allows ATM to have traffic characteristics such as increased switching speed and predictably decreased delay/cell loss, which is preferable for the convergence of real-time voice and video with data.

Other important networking techniques include Ethernet and frame relay. Ethernet is a standard for network devices communicating over a bus topology*. Any device wishing to transmit will listen to the bus to determine whether the bus is clear; if the bus is clear, transmission can commence. If a collision between signals from different devices occurs, transmission stops and the process is repeated. Frame relay is a packet-switching protocol with no error correction that is appropriate for fiber optic* links with their corresponding low error rates.

A local area network (LAN)* is usually privately owned and connects nodes within a single office or building designed to share hardware, such as a printer; software, such as an application program; or data. A wide area network (WAN)* provides long-distance transmission over large geographic areas that may constitute a nation, a continent, or even the whole world. A WAN that is wholly owned by a single company is referred to as an enterprise network, but WANs may buy or lease network capacity from other companies. A metropolitan area network (MAN)* is designed to extend over an entire campus or city. A MAN may be a single network, as with cable television, or a series of interconnected LANs.

Two other concepts that are relevant are the Internet and intranets. The Transmission Control Protocol/Internet Protocol (TCP/IP) is a set of protocols (or protocol suite) that defines how all transmissions are exchanged across the Internet. The Internet itself is a network of networks connected with the TCP/IP protocol suite connecting hundreds of million devices and billions of users worldwide in virtually all populated countries. Conversely, an intranet is an organizational network of private addresses not directly accessible from the Internet.

 See also **Internet • Intranet • Telecommunications • World Wide Web**

Resources

Books

Casad, Joe. *Sams Teach Yourself TCP/IP in 24 Hours.* 5th ed. Indianapolis: Sams/Pearson Education, 2012.

Comer, Douglas E. *The Internet Book: Everything You Need to Know about Computer Networking and How the Internet Works.* 4th ed. Upper Saddle River, NJ: Pearson Prentice Hall, 2007.

Estrada, Ernesto. *The Structure of Complex Networks: Theory and Applications.* New York: Oxford University Press, 2012.

Forouzan, Behrouz. *Data Communications and Networking.* 5th ed. New York: McGraw-Hill, 2012.

Computer Sciences, 2ⁿᵈ Edition

* **bus topology** a particular arrangement of buses that constitutes a designed set of pathways for information transfer within a computer

* **fiber optic** transmission technology using long, thin strands of glass fiber; internal reflections in the fiber assure that light entering one end is transmitted to the other end with only small losses in intensity; used widely in transmitting digital information

* **local area network (LAN)** a high-speed computer network that is designed for users who are located near each other

* **wide area network (WAN)** an interconnected network of computers that spans upward from several buildings to whole cities or entire countries and across countries

* **metropolitan area network (MAN)** a high-speed interconnected network of computers spanning entire cities

Stallings, William. *Data and Computer Communications.* 9th ed. Boston and London: Pearson, 2011.

Zalewski, Michal. *The Tangled Web: A Guide to Securing Modern Web Applications.* San Francisco: No Starch Press, 2012.

Web Sites

Microsoft, and Gilbert Held. "Asynchronous Transfer Mode." http://technet.microsoft.com/en-us/library/bb726929.aspx (accessed October 15, 2012).

NetHistory, and Ian Peter. "Early Internet–History of PC Networking." http://www.nethistory.info/History%20of%20the%20Internet/pcnets.html (accessed October 15, 2012).

Office Automation Systems

Office automation systems (OAS) are configurations of networked computer hardware and software. A variety of office automation systems are now applied to business and communication functions that used to be performed manually or in multiple locations of a company, such as preparing written communications and strategic planning. In addition, functions that once required coordinating the expertise of outside specialists in typesetting, printing, or electronic recording can now be integrated into the everyday work of an organization, saving both time and money.

Types of functions integrated by office automation systems include (1) electronic publishing; (2) electronic communication; (3) electronic collaboration; (4) image processing; and (5) office management. At the heart of these systems is often a local area network (LAN)*. The LAN allows users to transmit data, voice, mail, and images across the network to any destination, whether that destination is in the local office on the LAN, or in another country or continent, through a connecting network. An OAS makes office work more efficient and increases productivity.

Electronic Publishing

Electronic publishing systems include word processing and desktop publishing. Word processing software, (e.g., Microsoft Word) allows users to create, edit, revise, store, and print documents such as letters, memos, reports, and manuscripts. Desktop publishing software (e.g., Adobe Pagemaker, Corel VENTURA, Microsoft Publisher) enables users to integrate text, images, photographs, and graphics to produce high-quality printable output. Desktop publishing software is used on a computer with a mouse, scanner, and printer to create professional-looking publications. These may be newsletters, brochures, magazines, books, and others.

Electronic Communication

Electronic communication systems include electronic mail (e-mail), voice mail, facsimile (fax), and desktop videoconferencing.

Electronic Mail (E-mail) E-mail is software that allows users, via their computer keyboards or other devices, to create, send, and receive messages and files to or from anywhere in the world. Most e-mail systems let the user do other sophisticated tasks such as filter, prioritize, or file messages; forward copies of messages to other users; create and save drafts of messages; send carbon copies; and request automatic confirmation of the delivery of a message. E-mail is very popular because it is easy to use,

▲

The Automated Facer Cancelor System (AFCS) is used to identify anthrax in materials processed at a U.S. Postal Services' processing center. © *AP Images/ Tim Larsen.*

* **local area network (LAN)** a high-speed computer network that is designed for users who are located near each other

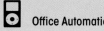

groupware a software technology common in client/server systems whereby many users can access and process data at the same time

offers fast delivery, and is inexpensive. Examples of e-mail software are Qualcom's Eudora, Google's Gmail, and Microsoft's Outlook.

Voice Mail Voice mail is a sophisticated telephone answering machine. It digitizes incoming voice messages and stores them on disk. When the recipient is ready to listen, the message is converted from its digitized version back to audio, or sound. Recipients may save messages for future use, delete them, or forward them to other people.

Facsimile A facsimile (fax) transmission machine scans a document containing text and/or graphics and sends it as electronic signals over an ordinary telephone line to a receiving fax machine. This receiving fax machine recreates the image on paper, what is called the fax, or the printed page from the communication between the source and receiving fax machines. A fax machine can also scan and send a document to a fax modem (circuit board) inside a remote computer. The fax can then be displayed on the computer screen and stored or later printed out by the computer's printer.

Desktop videoconferencing Desktop videoconferencing is one of the fastest growing forms of teleconferencing. It enables groups from multiple locations to communicate by simultaneous video and audio transmissions. Desktop videoconferencing requires a network and a computer with special application software (e.g., CUSeeMe, now called Click To Meet) as well as a small camera installed on top of the monitor or within the screen. Images of a group from one computer are captured and sent across the network to the other computers and users that are participating in the conference. The images from these other participating groups also are sent back to the original computer and to the other computers within the conference. This type of videoconferencing simulates face-to-face meetings of individuals. Skype is an example of a service that provides videoconferencing to its customers. With Voice-over-Internet Protocol (VoIP) service, Skype provides software to its customers that facilitates communications (with other customers) by voice, video, and instant messaging over the Internet.

Electronic Collaboration

Electronic collaboration is made possible through electronic meeting and collaborative work systems and teleconferencing. Electronic meeting and collaborative work systems allow teams of coworkers to use networks of microcomputers to share information, update schedules and plans, and cooperate on projects regardless of geographic distance. Special software called groupware* (sometimes also called collaborative software) is needed to allow two or more people to edit or otherwise work on the same files simultaneously. An example of is Adobe Acrobat, which is used to review portable document format (PDF) files simultaneously.

Teleconferencing is also known as videoconferencing or video teleconferencing. As was mentioned in the discussion of desktop

* **video capture cards** plug-in cards for a computer that accepts video input from devices such as television monitors and video cameras, allowing the user to record video data onto the computer

videoconferencing above, this technology allows people in multiple locations to interact and work collaboratively using real-time sound and images. Full teleconferencing, as compared to the desktop version, requires special-purpose meeting rooms with cameras, video display monitors, and audio microphones and speakers.

Telecommuting and Collaborative Systems Telecommuters perform some or all of their work at home instead of traveling to an office each day, usually with the aid of office automation systems, including those that allow collaborative work or meetings. A microcomputer, a modem, software that allows the sending and receiving of work, and an ordinary telephone line are the tools that make this possible.

Telecommuting is gaining in popularity in part due to the continuing increase in population, which creates traffic congestion, promotes high energy consumption, and causes more air pollution. Telecommuting can help reduce these problems. Telecommuting can also take advantage of the skills of homebound people with physical limitations.

Studies have found that telecommuting programs can boost employee morale and productivity among those who work from home. It is necessary to maintain a collaborative work environment, however, through the use of technology and general employee management practices, so that neither on-site employees nor telecommuters find their productivity is compromised by such arrangements. The technologies used in electronic communication and teleconferencing can be useful in maintaining a successful telecommuting program.

Image Processing

Image processing systems include electronic document management, presentation graphics, and multimedia systems. Imaging systems convert text, drawings, and photographs into digital form that can be stored in a computer system. This digital form can be manipulated, stored, printed, or sent via a modem to another computer. Imaging systems may use scanners, digital cameras, video capture cards*, or advanced graphic computers. Companies use imaging systems for a variety of documents such as insurance forms, medical records, dental records, and mortgage applications.

Presentation graphics software uses graphics and data from other software tools to create and display presentations. The graphics include charts, bullet lists, text, sound, photos, animation, and video clips. Examples of such software are Microsoft's Power Point, International Business Machines Corporation's (IBM's) Lotus Freelance Graphics, and Serif's Harvard Graphics.

Multimedia systems are technologies that integrate two or more types of media such as text, graphic, sound, voice, full-motion video, or animation into a computer-based application. Multimedia is used for electronic books and newspapers, video conferencing, imaging, presentations, and web sites.

Office Management

Office management systems include electronic office accessories, electronic scheduling, and task management. These systems provide an electronic means of organizing people, projects, and data. Business dates, appointments, notes, and client contact information can be created, edited, stored, and retrieved. Additionally, automatic reminders about crucial dates and appointments can be programmed. Projects and tasks can be allocated, subdivided, and planned. All of these actions can either be done individually or for an entire group. Computerized systems that automate these office functions can dramatically increase productivity and improve communication within an organization. Microsoft's Office is one example of office management software.

▶ *See also* **Decision Support Systems • Desktop Publishing • Information Systems • Productivity Software • Social Impact • Word Processors**

Resources

Books

Comer, Douglas E. *The Internet Book: Everything You Need to Know about Computer Networking and How the Internet Works.* 4th ed. Upper Saddle River, NJ: Pearson Prentice Hall, 2007.

Estrada, Ernesto. *The Structure of Complex Networks: Theory and Applications.* New York: Oxford University Press, 2012.

FitzGerald, Jerry, and Alan Dennis. *Business Data Communications and Networking.* 11th ed. Hoboken, NJ: John Wiley & Sons, 2012.

Forouzan, Behrouz A. *Data Communications and Networking.* 5th ed. New York: McGraw-Hill, 2012.

Laudon, Kenneth C., and Jane Price Laudon. *Essentials of Management Information Systems.* 10th ed. Boston: Pearson, 2013.

Stallings, William. *Data and Computer Communications,.* 9th ed. Boston and London: Pearson, 2011.

Zalewski, Michal. *The Tangled Web: A Guide to Securing Modern Web Applications.* San Francisco: No Starch Press, 2012.

Web Sites

eHow.com, and Sharon Mcelwee. "Advantages & Disadvantages of Office Automation." http://www.ehow.com/facts_4842952_ advantages-disadvantages-office-automation.html (accessed October 16, 2012).

Houston Chronicle, and Aurelio Locsin. "Advantages & Disadvantages of Office Automation." http://smallbusiness.chron.com/ advantages-amp-disadvantages-office-automation-41058.html (accessed October 16, 2012).

Optical Technology

Visible light (often simply called light), like radio waves, is electromagnetic radiation, consisting of electromagnetic waves. The major difference between the two is that light waves are much shorter than radio waves. The use of electromagnetic waves for long-distance communications was the beginning of an industry known first as wireless and later as radio. This industry was the foundation for electronics, which brought the world so many fascinating technologies.

When electronic circuits replaced the mechanical components in computers, the electronics were so fast compared to the older mechanical methods that no one ever thought the speed of the calculations would be limited by the speed of electrical signals. When engineers demanded even faster electronic circuits, the very short pulses and the tiny dimensions of their integrated circuits begged for the use of light energy rather than electrical energy. The use of light signals rather than electrical signals allowed for the design of very small and fast systems.

One of the first examples of replacing electrical signals with light was in communications. Special wires called transmission lines distribute

Optical tweezers used in nanolab. © *AP Images/John Ulan.*

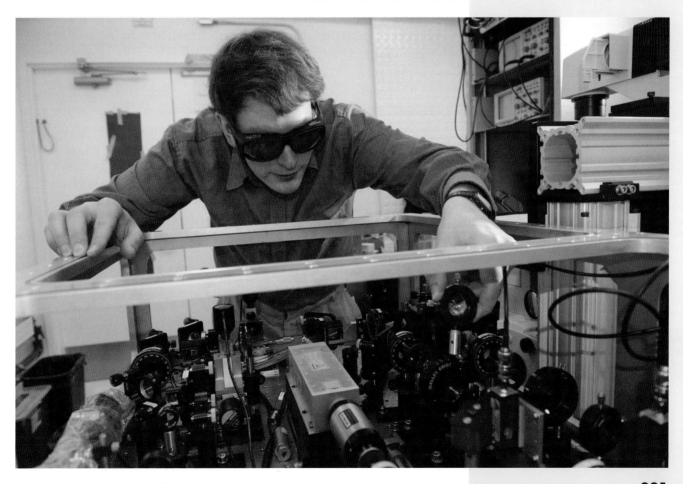

* **bandwidth** a measure of the frequency component of a signal or the capacity of a communication channel to carry signals

* **fiber optics** transmission technology using long, thin strands of glass fiber; internal reflections in the fiber assure that light entering one end is transmitted to the other end with only small losses in intensity; used widely in transmitting digital information

* **diode** a semiconductor device that forces current flow in a conductor to be in one direction only, also known as a rectifier

* **nanometers** one-thousand-millionth (one billionth, or 10^{-9}) of a meter

telegraph, telephone, and television signals. In the mid-nineteenth century, American inventor Samuel Morse's (1791–1872) telegraph was extended from the East to the West Coast of the United States. The fledgling industry painfully discovered how signals transmitted long distances through wires could be degraded. Signals had to be regenerated every 10 to 20 kilometers (6 to 12 miles) depending on the quality of the transmission line. When the telephone industry came along, the situation was even worse. When cable television distributed television signals through transmission lines in the 1960s, amplification was required every few blocks. The problem of signal degradation increases with bandwidth*. Television signals are nearly 2,000 times wider than voice signals.

Light energy can be constrained to a thin glass fiber much as electrical energy can be constrained to a wire. However, unlike wires, glass fibers can be made that generate very little distortion even for signals of extremely wide bandwidth. Therefore, with the use of glass fiber, or fiber optics*, broadband signals can be transmitted for much longer distances without amplifying or repeating. With fiber optics, communications systems with literally hundreds of television channels can be distributed with minimal distortion.

The glass fiber is very thin, extending from about 10 to 125 micrometers (where one micrometer is one millionth of a meter) in diameter. In order for the fiber to contain light energy without loss, the index of refraction of the glass must be less on the surface of the fiber than at its center. The index of refraction is a measure of the speed of light in a medium—in this case, glass. The higher the index of refraction, the slower the light waves propagate.

The slowing of the light energy causes the light path to bend. In the glass fiber, the light energy is bent back toward the center of the fiber. This phenomenon is called total internal reflection. It ensures that very little energy is lost by the fiber.

If the light energy transmitted within a fiber is monochromatic, then it has only one color or wavelength. Although the concepts of the glass fiber and total internal reflection have been known for many years, it was not until the invention of the solid-state laser diode* and the light emitting diode (LED) that glass fibers could be used for communications.

The optimum wavelength for use with a glass fiber depends on the composition of the glass. The most common wavelengths are about 1,300 nanometers*, which is longer than most visible light waves and shorter than infrared waves. Although both the laser and the LED are commonly used, the highest performance systems use laser diodes.

The state of the art in fiber optics is the use of wavelength division multiplexing (WDM), which uses a number of different wavelengths to increase the capacity of the system. The signals of different wavelengths can coexist in the fiber without mutual interference. This is similar to how a number of radio stations can operate on the same FM (short for frequency modulation) broadcast band without interference. The radio receiver is capable of selecting one of the stations while ignoring others.

The advantages of transmitting signals with light energy can be realized not only for long distances but for short distances as well. Even though the dimensions of a computer and the integrated circuits* used to make them are quite small, a certain time is required for the signals to travel around the computer. In the process of computation, signals move from one part of the computer to another before a final answer is reached. If the calculation is complex, the signals may spend considerable time traveling. Because light signals can travel faster than electrical signals, the use of light signals will enhance the computer's performance.

Modern conventional computer circuits can switch electrical signals on and off in less than one nanosecond*. Some specialized logic circuits can switch in a fraction of a nanosecond, but these circuits are not suited for large integrated circuits because they consume large amounts of power and it would be impossible to remove the heat from the chip.

Light energy can be switched in times measured in picoseconds*. If light signals could be switched on and off by other light signals, computer logic elements could subsequently be constructed. Then, by connecting the logic elements together with light signals, an entire computer could be constructed utilizing only light—instead of electrical—signals.

To take advantage of the inherent speed of optical computing, even the computer architecture can be adapted for speed. Most calculations require sequential operations. For example, to find the hypotenuse of a right triangle, the first side is squared and then the second. The two are then added together and the square root is taken of the result. Taking the square root is a sequence of operations. In many cases, the calculations are taken eight bits at a time or even a single bit at a time. A faster way of achieving this would be to square the two sides at the same time or to do the operations in parallel using two computers. It sounds wasteful to employ two computers just to solve a simple triangle problem. But when thousands of numbers are to be squared and added, two computers would make the process go twice as fast; three computers, three times as fast; and so on.

An architecture called massively parallel involves a large number of processors where each processor performs a part of the required calculation. This can involve many thousands of processors. This technique is only useful if the processors can perform fast calculations and can communicate with high speed. Optical computation using massively parallel architecture would result in the fastest computers on earth.

Switching light signals involves esoteric* materials that exhibit what are called non-linear optical properties. One light signal can affect the propagation of another light signal in these materials and can be used to switch another light signal off and on. Switching is the main ingredient for making logic elements.

One important application of optical technology is mass storage. Early computers used crude storage such as paper tape and punched cards*. One of the first computer storage media for random access memory (RAM)*

* **integrated circuits** circuits with the transistors, resistors, and other circuit elements etched into the surface of a single chip of semiconducting material, usually silicon

* **nanosecond** one-thousand-millionth (one billion, or 10^{-9}) of a second

* **picosecond** one-millionth of a millionth of a second (one-trillionth, or 10^{-12})

* **esoteric** relating to a specialized field of endeavor that is characterized by its restricted size

* **punched card** a paper card with punched holes which give instructions to a computer in order to encode program instructions and data

* **random access memory (RAM)** a type of memory device that supports the nonpermanent storage of programs and data; so called because various locations can be accessed in any order (as if at random), rather than in a sequence (like a tape memory device)

used the properties of ferromagnetic materials. Ferromagnetics are materials that are primarily made of iron. Everyone is familiar with magnetized iron and steel and how the north and south poles affect other magnets or pieces of iron or steel. Imagine a simple iron bar that has been magnetized. There are two ways the bar can be magnetized. One orientation could represent a logic zero, and the other—with the north and south poles reversed—a logic one. The first random access memories used small donut-shaped, magnetized cores. These cores would retain their magnetized state when the computer power was removed.

For removable storage, ferromagnetic films are used on tapes, strips, disks (both hard and floppy), and for credit cards, employee badges, and similar items. Magnetic storage is vulnerable because the stored data could be erased if it is subjected to a magnetic field.

The density (bits per unit area) of the ferromagnetic film was good, but the demand for high-density storage was growing stronger. The first use of optics for high-density data storage was not for computers but for recording television signals. However, the optical videodisc failed to gain acceptance in the marketplace. The videocassette recorder (VCR) uses magnetic storage. The main advantage of the VCR was its ability to record. An off-shoot of the videodisc was a smaller version called the compact disc (CD). This device was first used for digital recording of music and later for computer data; a later application was motion picture recording with the more-advanced Digital Video Disc (DVD). By the end of the 2000s, the DVD format was in the process of being superseded by the Blu-ray Disc (BD) technology (the competitor to BD was the HD-DVD format, which was abandoned in 2008 in favor of BD).

Optical disk storage technology relies on recessed pits on a reflecting surface. Light energy reflected from a laser onto the smooth polished surface of the disk would be reflected directly back to the laser. If the surface is not smooth, the energy is scattered, with only a small amount reflected directly back to the laser. As the CD is rotated, a photo detector senses the change as the pits pass by. The disk has a very long track on which the pits are positioned, and the laser light traces out the track. The ones and zeros are encoded by the change of the reflected light intensity. The length of the pit is used to encode a number of digital bits.

Because the wavelength of the light is short, the storage density of optical discs is very high. The spiral track of a CD, if it were unwound, would be more than 5,000 meters (16,400 feet) long. The space between the tracks is 1.6 micrometers and the pits are between 0.833 and 3.05 micrometers long. CDs are very inexpensive to make, are resilient to damage, and are completely immune to magnetic fields. In 2002, a CD could store between 500 and 800 megabytes (MB) of data. When it was introduced in 2006, a single-layer Blu-ray Disc could store 25 gigabytes (GB) of data, whereas a dual-layer could store 50 GB. As of 2012, Blu-ray discs are able to support triple-layer and quad-layer capacities, up to 100 GB and 128 GB of data, respectively, for write-once discs, and

100 GB rewriteable disc for commercial applications through their multi-layer disc BDXL format. These higher-capacity formats are for the secure storage of sensitive data, graphic images, and video that is used regularly in such sectors as broadcasting and medicine.

▶ *See also* **Music** • **Robotics**

Resources

Books

Brady, David J. *Optical Imaging and Spectroscopy.* Hoboken, NJ: Wiley, 2009.

Chen, Chin-Lin. *Foundations for Guided-Wave Optics.* Hoboken, NJ: Wiley-Interscience, 2007.

Fox, Mark. *Quantum Optics: An Introduction.* Oxford and New York: Oxford University Press, 2006.

Ghatak, A. K. *Optics.* Boston: McGraw-Hill Higher Education, 2010.

Hecht, Jeff. *Understanding Fiber Optics.* 5th ed. Upper Saddle River, NJ: Prentice Hall, 2006.

Kirkland, Kyle. *Light and Optics.* New York: Facts on File, 2007.

Lecoy, Pierre. *Fiber-optic Communications.* London: ISTE; Hoboken, NJ: Wiley, 2008.

Pedrotti, Frank, Leno Matthew Pedrotti, and Leno S. Pedrotti. *Introduction to Optics.* 3rd ed. San Francisco: Pearson Prentice Hall, 2007.

Sharma, K. K. *Optics: Principles and Applications.* Amsterdam and Boston: Academic Press, 2006.

Taylor, Jim, Michael Zink, Charles Crawford, and Christen Armbrust. *Blu-ray Disc Demystified.* New York and London: McGraw-Hill, 2008.

Träger, Frank, ed. *Springer Handbook of Lasers and Optics.* 2nd ed. Berlin and New York: Springer, 2012.

Web Sites

Timbercon. "History of Fiber Optics." http://www.timbercon.com/history-of-fiber-optics/ (accessed October 16, 2012).

U.S. Government; science.gov. "Light, Optics, and Photonics." http://www.science.gov/browse/w_129C14.htm (accessed October 16, 2012).

PR

Pascal, Blaise
French Philosopher and Scientist
1623–1662

Blaise Pascal, who was born in 1623 in central France and died in Paris in 1662, made significant contributions to physics, mathematics, and philosophy during his short life. At the time of Pascal's birth, European scientific thought was moving rapidly from deductive reasoning to the experimental method of testing to understand natural phenomena. The established order resisted this new approach. One of the more drastic examples of this resistance was the harsh treatment that Italian astronomer Galileo (1564–1642) suffered at the hands of the Catholic Church's Inquisition in 1633. The church also pressured intellectuals through economic means.

Since the sciences, mathematics, and philosophy had not become separate disciplines, it was common for intellectuals to work in several areas. Societies formed for the presentation and discussion of works in progress in these fields. Pascal's father, a lawyer by profession and a mathematician by avocation, was a member of one such group, the Académie Mersenne, which later grew into the French Academy. Some of the more distinguished Académie participants were Gilles Personier de Roberval (1602–1675), a teacher at the Collége de France; Girard Desargues (1591–1661), an architect; Pierre de Fermat (1601–1665), a lawyer; and René Descartes (1596–1650), a philosopher and mathematician. Through meetings and correspondence with other intellectuals throughout Europe, the members contributed to and learned about advances in mathematics and science. By age fourteen, Pascal had acquired mathematical knowledge and interest that were so advanced that his father introduced him to the Académie. This young man's active and inquiring mind both challenged, and was challenged by, members of the Académie.

Earlier indications of Pascal's intellectual ability were confirmed when he mastered Euclidean geometry* at age twelve without formal instruction. At sixteen Pascal presented a paper to the Académie on the properties of conic sections, based in part on Desargues's treatise on conical sections. This work became known as Pascal's theorem, and it forms the basis for modern projective geometry. Another geometric accomplishment was "Pascal's triangle." In the 1650s, with Fermat as a collaborator, Pascal developed the triangle to calculate possible gambling winnings under various conditions. His triangle is viewed as the preliminary work leading to the binomial theorem*, and the calculus* of probabilities.

Various statistical methods grew out of the solution to the wagering problem. Descartes, Roberval, and Fermat also investigated the arcs that

French mathematician and religious philosopher Blaise Pascal. © *Hulton Archive/Getty Images.*

* **Euclidean geometry** the study of points, lines, angles, polygons, and curves confined to a plane

* **binomial theorem** a theorem giving the procedure by which a binomial expression may be raised to any power without using successive multiplications

* **calculus** a method of dealing mathematically with variables that may be changing continuously with respect to each other

Torricelli and His Hypothesis

Evangelista Torricelli (1608–1647) created the first mercury barometer by filling a 0.9 meter (3 foot) glass tube with mercury and inverting the open end into a dish of mercury. The level of mercury in the tube dropped to 71.8 centimeters (28 inches). He demonstrated that air pressure raises a liquid to a height relative to the weight of the liquid. Torricelli hypothesized that the space above the mercury in the tube was a vacuum.

* **cycloids** pertaining to circles, in either a static way or in a way that involves movement

form in cycloids*. Each found solutions to various aspects of the problem. Pascal succeeded in finding solutions to other aspects using methods similar to integral calculus. These methods were used by German mathematician Gottfried Wilhelm Leibnitz (1646–1716) in his development of calculus. Although his first area of interest was pure mathematics, Pascal often turned his abilities to practical problems.

The most famous Pascal invention is the Pascaline, a mechanical calculating machine. He developed it as an accounting aid for his father, who was the tax collector in Normandy, France. From 1640 to 1642, Pascal built the first model. He continued to perfect the calculator for the next seven years. The calculating mechanism consisted of gears that moved a drum of printed numeric values. Open slots in the housing displayed these values. All calculations were performed through addition. Subtraction was done by adding the complement of the value to be subtracted to the other number. For example, 83 minus 25 adds 75, the complement of 25, to 83. The answer is 58, as there is no carrying of the last value. Multiplication and division were performed through a series of additions. Some 300 years later, the complement method is used by today's computers to perform mathematical functions. A few of Pascal's other practical undertakings included the improvement of the barometer and the syringe.

Pascal's major contribution to the physical sciences was a series of experiments to prove Torricelli's hypothesis about the effect of atmospheric pressure on the equilibrium of fluid. The conclusions that Pascal published stating that vacuums do exist in nature brought him into direct conflict with the traditional Aristotelian assertion that "Nature abhors a vacuum." Noël, the rector of a Jesuit college, attacked Pascal's conclusions by reasserting traditional doctrine. However, Pascal's carefully constructed experiments, which took into account all possible factors that could affect the outcome, and his analysis of the results, proved conclusively that a vacuum does occur naturally. A further result of his experiments was the principle that fluids exert pressure equally in all directions. One form of pressure measurement is known as a Pascal. This work had a direct impact on the development of modern scientific experimental methods.

In later years Pascal concentrated on philosophical and religious questions. His writings, *The Pensés* and *The Provincial Letters*, are still studied by theology and philosophy students.

 See also **Generations, Languages • Programming**

Resources

Books

Hazelton, Roger. *Blaise Pascal: The Genius of His Thought.* Philadelphia: The Westminster Press, 1974.

Krailsheimer, Alban J. *Pascal.* Oxford and New York: Oxford University Press, 1980, reprint. 1986.

Privacy

Concern over personal privacy has risen as a result of two areas of development in computing and related technologies. First, databases used as surveillance tools for gathering, storing, and disseminating personal information have stirred fears that privacy is being eroded. This type of concern for privacy is known as information privacy. Second, vastly expanded communications abilities, including electronic mail and wireless communications networks, have raised questions about the appropriate degree of privacy for these new forms of communications. This type of concern for privacy is known as communications privacy. This article will focus mainly on information privacy.

The practice of collecting, recording, and storing personal data began long before the advent of computers. For example, the Domesday Book was a written record of a census and survey of English landowners and their property made by the order of William the Conqueror in 1085. However, computers greatly expanded the capacity and ease of data collection. This led to further uses of personal information and the need to collect more data. The U.S. government was among the first to take advantage of such technology. A variety of government functions such as taxation, social welfare, crime prevention, national security, and immigration greatly rely on information about citizens. As such, they require efficient communications, exchange, and access to information. Also, the government was a leader in the use of computerized databases because it could afford the computing power, which was initially very expensive and required expert management.

An example of a government computer database is the Federal Bureau of Investigation (FBI) National Crime Information Center (NCIC) database. Established in 1967, NCIC allows law enforcement agencies around the country to enter and share information in order to catch criminals. Although the NCIC has been praised by police officers, it has been criticized by privacy advocates and civil libertarians. They argue that the uncontrolled entry and use of data in the system, and the ease of access by both law enforcement agencies as well as non-criminal justice agencies, provide many opportunities for abuse of police power and privacy, as well as errors in content.

Besides power abuse and privacy invasion, other objections to government databases include: 1) that people whose records are accessed are not informed; 2) that the traditional presumption of innocence is replaced by a presumption of guilt if government agencies can search through huge amounts of information to find people who seem suspicious for any reason; and 3) that the Fourth Amendment, which requires the government to have probable cause or a warrant to search and seize materials from homes and businesses, is being challenged since the government needs neither criteria to search government-created computerized databases.

With the decrease in cost and size of computer equipment, and the increase in the amount of mass-produced consumer software including

* **micromarketing** the targeting of specific products and services to smaller and smaller segments of society

* **encryption** also known as encoding; a mathematical process that disguises the content of messages transmitted

* **cookie** a small text file that a web site can place on a computer's hard drive to collect information about a user's browsing activities or to activate an online shopping cart to keep track of purchases

powerful database programs, a new demand for personal databases emerged from a different sector of society, namely the private sector. In an age where micromarketing* is rapidly becoming the norm, the value of information increases as decision-makers find new ways to use data for strategic advantage. Companies must store and share information about individuals before conducting telemarketing campaigns or selected mailings.

The following are some examples of how the private sector is using consumer data stored in their databases for marketing purposes. American Express mines 500 billion bytes of data on how customers have spent more than $350 billion since 1991. The company then sends discount coupons and special promotions for the specific stores where customers shop. Blockbuster Entertainment Corporation uses video rental histories to generate specialized lists of recommended movies that are mailed to customers. Long-distance telephone companies use lists of subscribers to foreign-language newspapers to find potential customers for special telephone service deals. Once potential customers have been identified, the companies mail advertisements to them in the customer's native language.

One objection concerning the collection and use of such consumer data is that, in many cases, consumers are not aware of this activity. Therefore, the consumer has no opportunity to agree or disagree to the use of this information. The second grievance lies in secondary use—the use of information for a purpose other than originally intended. Most people do not object when businesses use in-house lists to send advertisements or special offers to their own customers. However, many people do mind if information collected by one business or organization is shared with or sold to another without their knowledge or consent.

Social networking giant, Facebook, has come under a particularly significant amount of scrutiny for its privacy practices. The site, which has about 900 million users, uses advertising to make a profit, with ads that are tailored to meet each user's interests. The site has been criticized for not being open about how it gathers and uses information to create these customized commercials.

Computer databases can undoubtedly help both businesses and consumers, but distribution, leakage, and various specific uses of the information by corporations or government agencies can have detrimental effects. The question is, how much risk are we willing to accept in exchange for convenience and the availability of useful information? Also, how can we reduce the risks while still receiving the benefits?

A number of efforts have begun to redress the privacy problem in the United States. First, there is legislation such as the Electronic Communications Privacy Act of 1986, the Computer Security Act of 1987, the Computer-Matching and Privacy Protection Act of 1988, and the Health Insurance Portability and Accountability Act of 1996. Second, industry can voluntarily comply with recommendations such as the posting of privacy policy statements on their web sites. Finally, privacy can be protected through the use of special technologies such as encryption* products like the Anonymizer and Pretty Good Privacy, and by disabling the cookie* on Web browsers.

Other suggested means include establishing a privacy commission to oversee privacy protection at the state and federal levels, such as exists in Canada. Another possibility is to invest individuals with property rights over personal information, thereby shifting the burden from the individual to prove why he or she considers the use of the information undesirable, to the collectors and disseminators, who would need to prove that their actions neither harm nor violate the individual's privacy. These remedies may come about if the public voices its concerns to the authorities. As noted in *The Intruders: The Invasion of Privacy by Government and Industry*, Sen. Edward Long (R-Mississippi) once pointed out: "Privacy is necessary to the development of a free and independent people. To preserve this privacy, our national lethargy and lack of knowledge must be countered." He added: "People must be made to realize that, little by little, they are losing their right to privacy. Once they become aware of this, I think they will shake off their apathy and demand action. Then, and only then, will we get strong legislation to protect a reasonable amount of our right to be left alone."

Communications Privacy Organizations and Publications

The following organizations and publications deal extensively with information and communications privacy.

Organizations:

- American Civil Liberties Union <www.aclu.org>
- Center for Democracy and Technology <www.cdt.org>
- Electronic Frontier Foundation <www.eff.org>
- Electronic Privacy Information Center <www.epic.org>
- Internet Society <www.isoc.org>
- Privacy and American Business <www.pandab.org>
- The Privacy Rights Clearinghouse <www.privacyrights.org>

Publications:

- *Privacy Forum*, a moderated listserv <www.vortex.com/privacy.html>
- *Privacy Journal* <townonline.com/privacyjournal>
- *Privacy Times* <www.privacytimes.com>.

▶ *See also* **Security**

Resources

Books

Baase, Sara. *A Gift of Fire: Social, Legal, and Ethical Issues in Computing.* 3rd ed. Upper Saddle River, NJ: Pearson Prentice Hall, 2008.

Privacy Policy Statements

Title V of the Gramm-Leach-Bliley Act of 1999 addresses financial institution privacy from two different perspectives. Subtitle A requires financial institutions to make certain disclosures regarding their privacy policies and to give certain individuals the opportunity to prevent the institution from releasing information about them to third parties. Subtitle B criminalizes the practice used by certain data collection services and other parties of obtaining personal financial information from financial institutions by misrepresenting their right to such information.

* **autonomy** the capability of acting in a self-governing manner; being able to exist independently or with some degree of independence

Branscomb, Anne Wells. *Who Owns Information? From Privacy to Public Access.* New York: Basic Books, 1994.

Burnham, David. *The Rise of the Computer State.* New York: Random House, 1983.

Cavoukian, Ann, and Don Tapscott. *Who Knows: Safeguarding Your Privacy in a Networked World.* New York: McGraw-Hill, 1997.

Johnson, Deborah G., and Helen Nissenbaum, eds. *Computers, Ethics & Social Values.* Englewood Cliffs, NJ: Prentice Hall, 1995.

Kling, Rob, ed. *Computerization and Controversy: Value Conflicts and Social Choices.* 2nd ed. San Diego, CA: Academic Press, 1996.

Miller, Arthur R. *The Assault on Privacy: Computers, Data Banks, and Dossiers.* Ann Arbor: University of Michigan Press, 1971.

Rosenberg, Richard S. *The Social Impact of Computers.* 3rd ed. Amsterdam and Boston: Academic Press, 2004.

Schoeman, Ferdinand David, ed. *Philosophical Dimensions of Privacy: An Anthology.* Cambridge, UK, and New York: Cambridge University Press, 1984.

Westin, Alan F. *Privacy and Freedom.* New York: Atheneum, 1968.

Web Sites

Fowler, Geoffery A. "Facebook Sells More Access to Members." The Wall Street Journal, October 1, 2012. http://online.wsj.com/article/SB10000872396390443862604578029450918199258.html (accessed November 3, 2012).

Robotics

Robotics is the study of how to design, build, use, and work with robots. Although there is no consensus regarding the definition of the term *robot,* it is commonly defined as a mechanism that can sense its environment, process what it senses, and act upon its environment based on that processing.

Precursors of Robots

Automatons, which are mechanisms that perform predefined tasks with some degree of autonomy*, are the early predecessors of robots and have existed for more than 1,000 years. In the ninth century, the Chinese built a statue of Buddha surrounded by steam-powered servants that would move in a circle around the central figure. In the eighteenth century, the French constructed small mechanical "scribes" that, when powered by hand, could write up to forty pre-set characters using an attached writing

Preparing a robot for competition at an Arts and Technology (ARTEC) festival in France. © *ALAIN JOCARD/ AFP/Getty Images.*

implement. In the nineteenth century, automatons gave way to automation. In 1801 Joseph-Marie Jacquard (1754–1834), a French inventor, designed and built a loom that used a set of punched cards* with which the user could produce complex tapestries simply by pushing a pedal.

Grey Walters, a British scientist, built devices in the 1940s that moved toward lights and retreated from contact. Between 1961 and 1963, Johns Hopkins University staff built the "Hopkins Beast" that wandered the halls, stayed away from walls, and plugged itself in for recharging. All of these mechanisms are considered automatons rather than robots because they responded to stimuli without processing them first.

Early Robots

The devices now called robots developed from the work of scientists in three separate fields of engineering: teleoperation*, manufacturing, and artificial intelligence (AI)*.

American inventor George C. Devol Jr. filed a patent in 1954 for a playback device for controlling machines. Devol's work grew from, among other things, teleoperation, which began in the 1930s to handle nuclear materials. In 1958, Devol and Joseph Engelberger, an American entrepreneur, filed a patent for the first programmable manipulator (robot arm). The Unimation Corporation was formed in 1961 to put such devices into production. Engelberger's vision was to outfit assembly lines, such as those in automobile factories, with robot manipulators to automate the heavy lifting and assembly of large parts. General Motors (GM) installed the first industrial robot, made by Unimation, on a production line in 1962.

Also in the 1960s, scientists at the Stanford Research Institute (SRI) studied artificial intelligence on computers. They wanted to make their

* **punched card** a paper card with punched holes which give instructions to a computer in order to encode program instructions and data

* **teleoperation** any operation that can be carried out remotely by a communications system that enables interactive audio and video signals

* **artificial intelligence (AI)** a branch of computer science dealing with creating computer hardware and software to mimic the way people think and perform practical tasks

work more interesting and applicable to the real world, so the team built Shakey, the first mobile robot, in 1969. Shakey had a camera, a range finder, and bump sensors that allowed it to detect obstacles.

Applications of Robotics

Since the first Unimation robot, the scope and complexity of industrial tasks carried out by robots has steadily increased. Modern automotive factories use robots for assembly, welding, painting, and quality control. Innovation in the Mobile Robotics community has led to the creation of industrial robots that can autonomously harvest grain, mow lawns, and clean spacecraft.

The field of Medical Robotics has adapted and expanded many of the techniques created for robot arms into tools for doctors. A hip replacement, which traditionally requires a 30-centimeter (11.7-inch) incision, can be done with an 8-centimeter (3.1-inch) incision using robotic assistance. These improvements lead to shorter recovery periods for patients and reduce the chance of infection. Robotics allows a doctor to spend less time on standard procedures, and more time on difficult cases and unexpected complications.

Robots are also particularly useful for exploring and working in hazardous environments. Robotic rovers travel to other planets and send back information to scientists. There are robots that clean oil and gasoline tanks, and robots that remove asbestos from underground pipes. The U.S. military is putting a substantial amount of effort into developing robot scouts, advance teams, and tools to save the lives of military personnel in both offensive and defensive situations.

In the transportation field, robots are quickly gaining ground, though the mechanisms are rarely called robots. By 2000, there were automobiles that could autonomously maintain a safe distance behind other cars. Modern airplanes can take off, fly, and land without assistance from the pilot, and are therefore robots by most definitions. The near future will bring cars that do not need drivers, trains that do not need conductors, and planes that do not need pilots. Robotics and robot technologies are also widely used in amusement parks, movies, and toys.

Robotics in Science

Even more varied than the consumer and business applications of robotics are the academic disciplines that have been created to advance the state of the art. Robotics is characterized by a synergy between very practical applications and cutting-edge research. Broadly, while industry focuses on finding robotic ways of doing existing tasks, research focuses on extending the fundamental abilities of robots. However, this division is not a strict rule; many research labs produce usable robots, and industrial development routinely improves basic robotic technology. All areas of robotics are studied, to varying degrees, in academic, governmental, and industrial research laboratories.

In the 1940s, as the mechanisms being controlled in teleoperation became more complex, *telerobotics,* the study of remotely operated robots, was born. As Engelberger created and popularized robots in factories, researchers created the field of *manipulation,* or the study of the physics and control of those machines. *Mobile robotics* studies techniques for enabling robots to move through their environments. There are wheeled robots, legged robots, and treaded robots. There are robots with one, two, four, six, or more legs, and robots with combinations of treads, wheels, and legs. Medical robotics, space robotics, and industrial robotics, among others, are also significant fields of scientific research and study.

Robotics also enhances the work of scientists in other fields. Telerobotics has enabled scientists to study the centers of volcanoes. Mobile robotics has allowed scientists to find meteors in the Antarctic remotely and to explore the surface and atmosphere of Mars.

All fields of robotics are interdependent, as well as dependent on other engineering and science disciplines. Computer vision and sensor technology allow robots to sense their environments. Advances in artificial intelligence have led to robots with greater abilities to understand their environments, while robotics provides artificial intelligence with the physical capacity to interact with the environment. Of course, these relationships are only two examples. Fundamentally, robotics is the science of innovation by integrating and extending other technologies.

Social Implications of Robotics

When Jacquard introduced his mechanized loom, there were rebellions in Paris. Weavers were afraid that they would be run out of business. When robots are installed in automobile factories, managers rejoice, but workers are concerned that they will be replaced by machines and be out of work.

Robots are labor-saving devices, and, by definition, labor-saving devices result in reduced human labor requirements. Although robots cannot replace humans in many ways, there are already hundreds of jobs that have been made easier or eliminated by robots. Throughout history, questions have been raised about the effects of automation on the workforce. There is no consensus on what exactly that effect is. This remains an ongoing debate in the robotic and industrial communities.

One thing that robots will not do any time in the near future is replace humans. Although robots can move and make decisions, and seem to have emotions, robots are not self-aware. That is, they cannot think about their own existence. Scientists and philosophers have also argued that robots do not have a "consciousness" or that they lack a "soul."

Scientists disagree on how long it will be before robots are capable of operating without human assistance or are mistaken for humans. Some scientists, and many philosophers, assert that both tasks are impossible. Other scientists speculate that robots will be able to replace humans by 2030. Most scientists believe that it will take more than a hundred years, perhaps several hundred, before robots even are self-sufficient.

Robots in the Human Image

Many robots are anthropomorphic: they look, act, or seem like humans. Scientists and engineers often design robots to look like humans or other animals. Building machines to operate autonomously is a daunting task, so researchers start with animals and people as models because they are examples of working mechanisms.

The first robot manipulator was built to look and function like an arm. The first mobile robot had a human-like "head." Most legged robots walk with gaits copied from mammals, insects, or lizards. Many sensors are designed to use the same information that humans use: cameras and computer vision allow the robot to "see"; whiskers and contact switches allow the robot to "feel"; and researchers are even working on electronic devices that will enable robots to "smell."

However, robots do not have to be anthropomorphic. Since engineers design robots from scratch, they can be tailored for whatever job they are doing. Thus, a pipe-cleaning robot could have clamps that allow it to crawl along a pipe. Many robots have "range sensors" that permit them to tell the exact distance between it and another object.

"Droids" on Film

Two of the most popular robots ever featured in motion pictures are R2-D2 and C3PO from the *Star Wars* series. Displaying human emotions, including excitement and fear, these "droids" were an instant hit with audiences.

Robotics in Science Fiction

The idea of the robot dates back almost as far as the written word. Homer (9th or 8th century b.c.e.), in the "Iliad," describes Haephestus, the Greek god of the forge, as having golden maid servants that "look like young girls who could speak and walk and were filled with intelligence and wisdom." Early twentieth-century Czech playwright Karel Capek (1890–1938) invented the word robot in his 1921 play, *Rossum's Universal Robots (R.U.R.).* In that work, Rossum's Universal Robots were beings that looked and acted just like human beings and were invented to serve people. Unlike the robots people think of today, these devices were made of biological parts, but like the modern idea of robots, they were built by people to do things for people.

Between 1921 and 1940, robots made many appearances in books, stories, movies, and plays. Although some of the robots in these fictional accounts were designed to help and serve humans, the majority of them were evil, and even the good robots invariably ended up destroying their owner, inventor, or the entire human race. Twentieth-century American science fiction writer Isaac Asimov (1920–1992) invented the word "robotics" in "Runaround." In this 1942 short story, he uses the term to describe the study of robots. Asimov's 1950 novel, *I, Robot,* marked the first piece of writing in which robots were regarded as ultimately non-destructive, and also proposed the "three laws of robotics" that have been used or mentioned in many works of fiction since then.

Robots have made countless appearances in movies, books, stories, and plays since 1942, and they have come to be represented as good as often as they are evil. More importantly, the concepts created by science fiction authors continue to motivate the scientists and engineers who design robots, such as the Personal Satellite Assistant, being built by NASA, that was directly inspired by Luke Skywalker's light saber-training robot in *Star Wars.*

The Future

In the mid-twentieth century, when computers were invented, they were easy to recognize. Computers took up entire rooms and used as much power as an entire building. In the 2010s, computers are everywhere. There is a computer on one's desk, there is a computer in the television, and there is probably a computer in the toaster.

In much the same way, robots started as big machines that were obviously robots. Now, robots have taken on many different forms: automated trams in airports, automatic car washes, and even gas stations that autonomously find a gas tank, open it, and fill it, to name a few. Despite their names and appearances, these mechanisms are, in fact, robots.

Moving to the future, robots will be found everywhere, and robotics will expand to study all of their enabling technologies and their limitless applications.

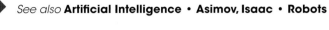

See also **Artificial Intelligence • Asimov, Isaac • Robots**

Resources

Books

Asimov, Isaac, and Karen A. Frenkel. *Robots: Machines in Man's Image.* New York: Harmony Books, 1985.

Kortenkamp, David, R. Peter Bonasso, and Robin Murphy, eds. *Artificial Intelligence and Mobile Robots: Case Studies of Successful Robot Systems.* Cambridge, MA: MIT Press, 1998.

Malone, Robert. *The Robot Book.* New York: Push Pin Press, 1978.

Moravec, Hans P. *Mind Children: The Future of Robot and Human Intelligence.* Cambridge, MA: Harvard University Press, 1988, reprint. 2000.

Reichardt, Jasia. *Robots: Fact, Fiction, and Prediction.* New York: Viking Press, 1978.

S

Security

Computer security has been a consideration of computer designers, software developers, and users for virtually as long as the computer has existed. As any Internet user knows, computer security is a critical factor in the Web-connected electronic-world (e-world). It is also important in business, industry, and government, where internally networked computers create an environment in which confidential or proprietary* data must be protected from unauthorized access.

* **proprietary** a process or technology developed and owned by an individual or company, and not published openly

Computer security measures can be broken into three basic components and functions:

- Identification: "Who are you?"
- Authentication: "OK, I know who you are, but prove it."
- Authorization: "Now that I know you are you, here is what you can do in my system."

Computer security attempts to ensure that the good guys (authorized users) are able to access the systems and data they desire, and that the bad guys (unauthorized users) do not gain access. Although this is a simple idea, the implementation and maintenance of strong computer security is not easy. Multiple vendor equipment, different operating system environments, ease-of-access requirements, and (not the least) difficult users all make for hurdles in the continued operation of effective security measures.

History

The history of computer security starts, of course, with the earliest computers. The UNIVAC (Universal Automatic Computer) and ENIAC (Electronic Numerical Integrator and Computer) were each relatively secure due largely to the fact that the machines were housed in locked buildings or complexes and had few, if any, additional computers connected to them. However, it was not long before the power and capabilities of the computer expanded the number of connected users. As a result, computer designers and programmers had to consider computer security.

The development of computer security has mirrored the evolution of the computer itself and its expanding capabilities. As more and more computer devices—primarily personal computers (PCs)—have been linked together, the need for computer security has grown. Possibly the most significant impact on computer security has been the Internet. With the advent of worldwide connectivity and around-the-clock access to computer systems and data, computer security experts have struggled to keep pace.

Former president Bill Clinton (right) presides over a Web security summit. © *CHRIS KLEPONIS/AFP/Getty Images.*

* **enciphered** encrypted or encoded; a mathematical process that disguises the content of messages transmitted

Timeline

Here is a brief timeline of significant computer security events. Notice that as computer network capabilities have grown, so have the security concerns.

Memory Protection Hardware; Partitioning, Virtual Memory (1960)
Since the late 1950s, most computers contain special registers to define partitions of memory for use by separate programs and ensure that a running program cannot access the partition of another program. Virtual memory extended this by allowing each object to be separately protected as if it were in its own partition. Partitioning and virtual memory capabilities provided one of the first security protection measures in early multi-user environments.

File Access Controls (1962)
Beginning in the early 1960s, time sharing systems provided files for individual users to store personal or private information. The systems were secured using file access controls to allow the owners to specify who else, if anyone, could access their files and under what circumstances. The Massachusetts Institute of Technology (MIT) Compatible Time Sharing System and the University of Cambridge's Multiple Access System were the first examples of this kind of security.

One-way Functions to Protect Passwords (1967)
Password protection was the first user-centered security feature. The authentication system used during login stores enciphered* images of user passwords but not the actual passwords. This protects passwords from being divulged if an attacker happens to read the file.

* **configuration files** special disk files containing information that can be used to tell running programs about system settings

* **cryptosystem** a system or mechanism that is used to automate the processes of encryption and decryption

Multics Security Kernel (1968) The Multics system at MIT made security and privacy one of its central design principles. The designers paid very careful attention to identifying a small kernel of system operations, which, if correct, would guarantee that all security policies of the system would be followed. This design signified the importance of security to the computer's basic programming.

Arpanet (1969) and Internet (1977) The ARPANET (Advanced Research Projects Agency Network) was the first wide-area computer network. It started in 1969 with four nodes and became the model for today's Internet. This inter-connectedness increased the risk of unauthorized user access from outsiders and raised awareness of security issues to network administrators and owners.

Unix-Unix System Mail (UUCP); Mail Trap Doors (1975) Unix-Unix System Mail (UUCP) allowed users on one UNIX machine to execute commands on a second UNIX system. This enabled electronic mail and files to be transferred automatically between systems. It also enabled attackers to erase or overwrite configuration files* if the software programs were not correctly configured. Since there was no central administration of UUCP networks, the ARPANET command-and-control approach to controlling security problems did not apply here. By 2000, the Internet had many of the same characteristics.

Public Key Cryptography and Digital Signatures (1976) Cryptography is the ability to scramble messages based on a secret, prearranged code. Public-key cryptography enables two people to communicate confidentially, or to authenticate each other, without a prearranged exchange of shared cryptographic keys. Although cryptography had been around for many years, this was the point at which it was integrated into the development of computer security.

First Vulnerability Study of Passwords (Morris and Thompson, 1978) This study demonstrated that password guessing is far more effective than deciphering password images. It found that a very high percentage of passwords could be guessed from user names, addresses, social security numbers, phones, and other information stored in the user identification files. Password guessing remains a major threat in the early twenty-first century.

RSA Public-key Cryptosystem (1978) The RSA public-key cryptosystem* is the oldest unbroken one of its kind that provides both confidentiality and authentication. (RSA is the acronym for the first letters of the last names of Ron Rivest, Adi Shamir, and Leonard Adleman, who first publicly described the system in 1977.) It is based on the difficulty of determining the prime factors of a very large number as used in the secret code. RSA provided a quasi-standard in the emerging field of computer cryptography.

Electronic Cash (1978)   As businesses moved onto the Internet, the means to pay for services or goods did as well. Electronic cash is one way to accomplish this. It cannot be easily created, it is anonymous, and it cannot be duplicated without detection. The protection and security of electronic cash, or e-cash, became yet another concern of security professionals; it continues to be a major issue.

Domain Naming System of the Internet (1983)   As the ARPANET grew, the number of computer devices became large enough to make maintaining and distributing a file of their addresses unwieldy, and the network maintainers developed a system to enable quick, simple name lookups. The Directory Name Server (DNS) dynamically updated its database of name and address associations, and became yet another target for hackers* and spoofers*.

Computer Viruses Acknowledged as a Problem (1984)   Computer viruses are deceptive software programs that can cause damage to a computer device, most notably an individual PC. The challenges of such malicious code were first formally recognized in a study published in 1984. Coupled with growing network capabilities, viruses became a serious threat to computer security practitioners and individual users.

Novel Password Schemes (1985)   By the mid-1980s, many alternatives to reusable user passwords were being explored in order to circumvent the weakness of easily guessed configurations. Callback modems* relied on the authentic user being at a fixed location. Challenge-response systems allowed the authentic user to generate personalized responses to challenges issued by the system. Password tokens are smart cards* that generate a new password with each use. Each of these alternatives attempted to strengthen the basic password scheme.

Distributed Authentication (1988)   Authentication servers are computer devices that allow users and system processes to authenticate themselves on any system using one set of data. The data can be updated globally, and the server can pass proof of identity back to the user or process. This proof can be passed to other servers and clients and used as a basis for access control or authorization. Given the advance in distributing computing power both geographically and across platforms (servers), this advancement allowed security to keep pace with these new configurations.

Internet Worm (1988)   The Internet worm was the first large-scale attack against computers connected to the Internet. Unlike a virus, it transmitted itself actively through Internet connections. Within hours, it invaded between 3,000 and 6,000 hosts, between 5 percent and 10 percent of the Internet at the time, taking them out of service for several days. It caused much consternation and anger, and highlighted a vulnerability of large networks.

PGP (1989); PEM (1989)   Electronic mail lacks protection against forgery, alteration, and interception. Privacy-enhanced Electronic Mail (PEM) and Pretty Good Privacy (PGP) provide all these services. As the Internet grew, so did the demand for these security services to help ensure user authentication and protection.

Anonymous Reposting Servers (1990)   These computer servers obscure the identity of the poster or sender by substituting a random string for the sender's name. Some retain the association between sender and random string internally to facilitate reply messages. These services make tracing the original user nearly impossible.

Wily Hacker Attack (1986) and Book (1992)   An attacker (hacker) intruded into computers at Lawrence Berkeley National Laboratory (at the University of California, Berkeley), apparently looking for secret information. Clifford "Cliff" Stoll, an American astronomer turned system administrator, detected the attacker from a seventy-five cent accounting discrepancy. Using a variety of techniques, Stoll helped authorities arrest the attacker, who was being paid by a foreign government. This event helped highlight the vulnerability of all systems and the need for widespread computer security. Stoll described the events of his investigation in the book *The Cuckoo's Egg: Tracking a Spy through the Maze of Computer Espionage* and the paper "Stalking the Wily Hacker."

Network Sniffing; Packet Spoofing; Firewalls (1993)   Internet protocols were designed on the assumption that no one could access the actual wires and listen to the packets of data. In recent years, attackers have hooked up computers to do just that. These methods of sniffing have been used to detect passwords. The attackers also engage in spoofing, or using the same computers to transmit their own packets, with false identification fields, as a way of gaining access to systems. Firewalls are routers that attempt to filter out these spoofed packets. Sniffing and spoofing became key security concerns as the Internet grew.

Java Security Problems (1996)   Java is a language for writing small applications, called applets, that can be downloaded from an Internet server and executed locally by a Java interpreter attached to the Web browser. The design goal is that the interpreter be highly confined so that Trojan horses* and viruses cannot be transmitted; that goal has yet to be met. Java has had several security problems related to malicious applet designers reading, altering, and deleting information supposedly outside the constrained environment.

I Love You or Lovebug virus (2000)   In May, the I Love You, or Lovebug, virus created major problems for business and government systems worldwide. A computer science student in the Philippines created the virus; however, the Philippine government had no laws at the time to prosecute the student. Because of the incident, the world's first international treaty on cybercrime was enacted. The Convention on Cybercrime, held in Budapest, Hungary, helps to unify the world's cybercrime laws and to improve cooperation and investigation across international borders.

White House Cybersecurity Adviser (2001)

In October, U.S. president George W. Bush (1946–) established the President's Critical Infrastructure Protection Board, which was tasked to develop a national cybersecurity strategy. Richard Clarke was named the first White House cybersecurity adviser.

Cybersecurity Research and Development Act (2002)

President Bush signed the Cybersecurity Research and Development Act into law. Nine hundred million dollars was allotted for security education and research over a five-year period.

Cybersecurity Attacks on United States and Estonia (2007)

A series of cyberattacks were made on various U.S. government agencies and departments. In all, approximately 10 to 20 terabytes of data is lost. In addition, numerous banks, ministries, and news media in Estonia, along with its Parliament, were deluged with distributed denial of service (DDoS) traffic, which caused the sites to go down. Later in the year, employees at the Oak Ridge National Laboratory, part of the U.S. Department of Energy, were sent attachments within e-mails that allow unauthorized access to the organization's non-classified databases.

Computer Security Compromised in the United States and Georgia (2008)

In August, hackers accessed the Foreign Ministry Web site in Georgia with pictures of German Nazi leader Adolf Hitler (1889–1945), while other of its government Web sites are disabled with DDoS traffic. Military conflicts between Georgia and Russia at the time are seen to be at the core of these attacks. During the U.S. presidential campaigns between Barack Obama (1961–) and John McCain (1936–), hackers accessed e-mails and computer files at both candidates' headquarters. China was thought to have been behind the intrusions. At the end of the year, the U.S. Central Command, in Tampa, Florida, was infected with malicious software (malware). Unauthorized thumb drives were thought to have been the source of the infection.

GhostNet (2009)

Researchers at the University of Toronto (Canada) uncover a large cybernetwork. Named GhostNet, over one thousand computers around the world were infected. The perpetrator of the GhostNet was not verified, but experts point the finger in the direction of China. Later in the year, numerous U.S. companies, such as Google, were attacked through the Internet, resulting in the loss of large amounts of technological data.

Stuxnet (2010)

In October, malware called Stuxnet was discovered in Iran, along with other international locations, which caused damage to the Iranian nuclear program; specifically causing problems with the Siemens industrial control systems within the Iranian complexes.

Major Cyberintrusion Attack in Canada (2012)   In January, the Canadian research agency, Defense Research and Development Canada (National Defense Finance and the Treasury Board), was subjected to a major cyberintrusion attack that caused the agency to go offline from the Internet.

Conclusion

Concerns about computer security will grow as computer system capabilities increase. Hackers eager to beat a new security challenge, as well as unauthorized users intent on accessing data for criminal or malicious purposes, will continue trying to circumvent security protocols designed to protect data, equipment, and users from their efforts.

▶ *See also* **Association For Computing Machinery • Ethics • Privacy**

Resources

Books

Andreasson, Kim J. *Cybersecurity: Public Sector Threats and Responses.* Boca Raton, FL: CRC Press, 2012.

Bosworth, Seymour, Michel E. Kabay, and Eric Whyne, eds. *Computer Security Handbook.* 5th ed. New York: Wiley & Sons, 2009.

Lehtinen, Rick, Deborah Russell, and G. T. Gangemi Sr. *Computer Security Basics.* 2nd ed. Sebastopol, CA: O'Reilly & Associates, 2006.

Moeller, Robert. *IT Audit, Control, and Security.* 2nd ed. Hoboken, NJ: Wiley, 2010.

Stoll, Clifford. *The Cuckoo's Egg: Tracking a Spy through the Maze of Computer Espionage.* New York: Doubleday, 1989.

Zubairi, Junaid Ahmed, and Athar Mahboob. *Cyber Security Standards, Practices and Industrial Applications: Systems and Methodologies.* Hershey, PA: Information Science Reference, 2012.

Web Sites

BankInfoSecurity.com. "Time Line of Major Global Cyber Incidents 2010-2011." http://www.bankinfosecurity.com/time-line-major-global-cyber-incidents-2010-2011-a-3440 (accessed November 5, 2012).

Computer Security Resource Center, National Institute of Standards and Technology. "Early Computer Security Papers, Part I." http://csrc.nist.gov/publications/history/ (accessed October 22, 2012).

Ecommerce, Net Industries. "Computer Security — History of Computer Security Problems, Types of Computer Security Problems, Computer Security Programs." http://ecommerce.hostip.info/pages/252/Computer-Security.html (accessed October 22, 2012).

NPR. "Timeline: Major Cybersecurity Incidents Since 2007." http://www.npr.org/templates/story/story.php?storyId=125518567 (accessed November 5, 2012).

Washington Post. "Timeline: The U.S. Government and Cybersecurity." http://www.washingtonpost.com/ac2/wp-dyn?pagename=article&node=&contentId=A50606-2002Jun26&notFound=true (accessed November 5, 2012).

Simulation

Simulation, from the Latin *simulare,* means to "fake" or to "replicate." The *Concise Oxford Dictionary of Current English* defines simulation as a "means to imitate conditions of (situation etc.) with a model, for convenience or training." Sheldon Ross of the University of California, Berkeley, states less formally that "computer simulations let us analyze complicated systems that can't be analyzed mathematically. With an accurate computer model, we can make changes and see how they affect a system." Simulation involves designing and building a model of a system and carrying out experiments to determine how the real system works, how the system can be improved, and how future changes will affect the system (called "what if" scenarios). Computer simulations of systems are effective when performing actual experimentation is expensive, dangerous, or impossible.

One of the principal benefits of using simulation to model a real-world system is that someone can begin with a simple approximation of the process and gradually refine it as his or her understanding of the system improves. This stepwise refinement enables good approximations of complex systems relatively quickly. Also, as refinements are added, the simulation results become more accurate.

The oldest form of simulation is the physical modeling of smaller, larger, or exact-scale replicas. Scaled-down (smaller) replicas include simulations of chemical plants and river–estuary systems. Scaled-up (larger) replicas include systems such as crystal and gene structures. Exact-scale replicas include an aircraft cockpit used for pilot training or a space shuttle simulator to train astronauts.

Simulation is central to the rise of digital computers, and the story starts, strangely enough, with the pipe organ. American inventor Edwin Link (1904–1981) received his inspiration for the first pilot training simulator while working for his father's piano and organ company in the 1930s.

Link developed mechanical "trainers" that used a pneumatic* system to simulate the movement of aircraft. During World War II (1939–1945), the Link Trainer proved the training value of flight simulation and convinced the U.S. Navy to ask that the Massachusetts Institute of Technology (MIT) develop a computer that would power a general-purpose flight simulator. This endeavor became Project Whirlwind and "evolved into the first real-time, general purpose digital computer… [which] made several important contributions in areas as diverse as computer graphics, time-sharing, digital communications, and ferrite-core memories," according to Thomas Hughes in his book *Funding a Revolution.*

In a society of limited resources and rapid technological change, training challenges are increasingly being addressed by the use of simulation-based training devices. Economic analysis supports the use of simulators as a sound investment, a flexible resource that provides a return for many years. Since the early 1960s, simulation has been one of many methods used to aid strategic decision-making in business and industry. As computer technology progresses and the cost of simulation for realistic training continues to decline, it is becoming increasingly possible to train simultaneously at different geographic locations and where training cannot be carried out in real life, as in shutting down a nuclear power plant after an earthquake.

Simulations can be classified as being discrete or analog. Discrete event simulation builds a software model to observe the time-based behavior of a system at discrete time intervals or after discrete events in time. For example, customers arrive at a bank at discrete intervals. Between two consecutive time intervals or events, nothing can occur. When the number of time intervals or events is finite, that simulation is called a "discrete event." The discrete event simulation software can be a high-level general-purpose programming language (C or C++) or a specialized event/data driven application (a simulator).

However, in the real world, events can occur at any time, not just at discrete intervals. For example, the water level in a reservoir with given inflow and outflow may change all the time, and the level may be specified to an infinite number of decimal places. In such cases, continuous, or analog, simulation is more appropriate, although discrete event simulation could be used as an approximation. Some systems are neither completely discrete nor completely analog, resulting in the need for combined discrete–analog simulation.

A common way to simulate the random occurrence of events is to use Monte Carlo simulation. It is named for Monte Carlo, Monaco, where the primary attractions are casinos containing games of chance exhibiting random behavior, such as roulette wheels, dice, and slot machines. The random behavior in such games of chance is similar to how Monte Carlo simulation selects variable values at random to simulate a model. For example, when someone rolls a die, she knows that a 1, 2, 3, 4, 5, or 6 will come up, but she does not know which number will occur for any particular roll. This is the same as the variables used in computer simulations; these variables have a known range of values but an uncertain value for any particular time or event. A Monte Carlo simulation of a specific model randomly generates values for uncertain input variables over and over again (called "trials") in order to produce output results with statistical certainty, that is, providing a percentage chance that an actual output from the physical system will fall within the predicted range with virtual certainty.

Modeling is both an art and a science. It is an art to decide which features of the physical object need to be included in an abstract mathematical model. Any model must capture what is important and discard interesting features (uninteresting and irrelevant features are easy to discard). Complexity and processing performance also guide the art of deciding on a minimal set of features to be modeled from the physical object.

The science of simulation is the quantitative description of the relationship between features being modeled. These relationships dictate a model's transformation from one state to another state over time. Often when a mathematical model is eventually derived in a solvable form (closed form), it may or may not accurately represent the physical system. Computer simulation is preferable when the physical system cannot be mathematically modeled because of the complexity of variables and interacting components. Well-known examples of simulation are flight simulators and business games. However, there are a large number of potential areas for simulation, including service industries, transportation, environmental forecasting, entertainment, and manufacturing factories. For example, if a company wishes to build a new production line, the line can first be simulated to assess feasibility and efficiency.

Simulation and Computers

Although discrete event simulation can be carried out manually, it can be computationally intensive, lending itself to the use of computers and software. Simulation became widespread after computers became popular tools in scientific and business environments.

At this point, it may be helpful to define the relationship of computer simulation to the related fields of computer graphics, animation, and virtual reality (VR)*. Computer graphics is the computational study of light and its effect on geometric* objects, with the focus on graphics to produce meaningful rendered images of real-world or hypothetical objects. Animation is the use of computer graphics to generate a sequence of frames that, when passed before one's eyes very quickly, produce the illusion of continuous motion. Virtual reality is focused on immersive* human–computer interaction, as found in devices such as head-mounted displays, position sensors, and the data gloves. Simulation is the infrastructure* on which these other fields are built; a simulation model must be created and executed and the output analyzed. Simulation is thus the underlying engine that drives the graphics, animation, and virtual reality technologies.

Visual interactive simulation has been available since the late 1970s. Before this, simulation models were simply "black boxes," with data going in and results coming out, and the output requiring extensive statistical processing. Using on-screen animations in a simulation model enables the status of a model to be viewed as it progresses; for example, a machine that breaks down may change color to red. This enables visual cues to be passed back to the user instantaneously so that action can be taken.

Although the simulation examples outlined here thus far have been physical systems, social situations can also be simulated in the electronic equivalent of role-playing or gaming. Both simulation and gaming can be defined as a series of activities in a sequence in which players participate, operating under overt constraints (agreed-on rules), and that usually involve competition toward an objective. The classic examples of simulation games are board games, such as chess and Monopoly. Simulation games vary widely and have advanced along with time and technology, making them more interesting, enjoyable, realistic, and challenging.

According to the Interactive Digital Software Association (IDSA), the sale of interactive game simulation software for computers, video consoles, and the Internet generated revenues of $5.5 billion in 1998 for companies such as Nintendo and Sony, second only to the motion

* **virtual reality (VR)** the use of elaborate input/output devices to create the illusion that the user is in a different environment

* **geometric** relating to the principles of geometry, a branch of mathematics related to the properties and relationships of points, lines, angles, surfaces, planes, and solids

* **immersive** involved in something totally

* **infrastructure** the foundation or permanent installation necessary for a structure or system to operate

picture industry, which generated revenues of $6.9 billion in 1998. In fact, computer companies, including Intel, Apple, and AMD (Advanced Micro Devices), are increasingly designing their central processing units for gaming entertainment performance and not for office applications.

▶ *See also* **Analog Computing • Digital Computing**

Resources

Books

Banks, Jerry, John S. Carson II, and Barry L. Nelson. *Discrete-Event Simulation.* 2nd ed. Englewood Cliffs, NJ: Prentice Hall, 1999.

Khoshnevis, Behrokh. *Discrete Systems Simulation.* New York: McGraw-Hill, 1994.

Law, Averill M., and W. David Kelton. *Simulation Modeling and Analysis.* 4th ed. New York: McGraw-Hill, 2007.

Periodicals

Killgore, J. I. "The Planes That Never Leave the Ground." *American Heritage of Invention Technology* 4, no. 3 (Fall 1989): 56–63.

Macedonia, Michael. "Why Digital Entertainment Drives the Need for Speed." *IEEE Computer* 33, no. 2 (February 2000): 124–127.

Slide Rule

The slide rule is an analog device for performing mathematical computations. The first slide rule was created around 1630 by British mathematician William Oughtred (1574–1660). His device was based on the logarithmic scale created by British astronomer Edmund Gunter (1581–1626) in 1620. Gunter's work, in turn, was based on the principle of logarithm* set forth by Scottish mathematician John Napier (1550–1617) in 1614. What is known as the modern slide rule took shape during the first half of the 1800s.

The slide rule was used by scientists and engineers from 1640 through the 1960s and 1970s. The most familiar modern slide rule is basically a ruler with a sliding piece. Both parts of the device are marked with a scale of digits. The number of significant digits that a slide rule can contain is limited by the size of the rule. Circular and cylindrical slide rules were created to provide more significant digits. Circular slide rules operate on a set of concentric circles*, while cylindrical slide rules use scales that can be manipulated by spinning them around a central rod. Today, slide rules are primarily a collector's item, having been replaced by computers and hand-held electronic calculators.

Logarithms and Slide Rules

In the 1600s, John Napier determined that any real number can be expressed as a power (log) of another number and these values could be published as logarithmic tables. He discovered that adding and subtracting logs is the same as multiplying and dividing real numbers.

The common logarithmic tables express real numbers as powers of ten. For example, 2 is $10^{0.3}$ and 2's log is 0.3 (both to one decimal place). Also, $2 \times 2 \times 2 = 8$; whereas $0.3 + 0.3 + 0.3 = 0.9$, the log of 8 (also to one decimal place). Edmund Gunter's logarithm scale arranged numbers from 1 to 10, spacing the numbers in proportion to their logs. Number 2 was spaced 0.3 from 1; 4 was 0.6 from 1, and so forth. Based on this scale, William Oughtred created the slide rule as an instrument for multiplying and dividing, based on logs. As mathematicians discovered new ways to use the slide rule, more scales were added to determine squares, roots, common logarithms, and trigonometric functions.

 See also **Analog Computing • Digital Computing • Napier's Bones**

Resources

Books

Cajori, Florian. *William Oughtred—Teacher of Mathematics.* Merchant Books, 2008.

Slide Rule's Inventor

English mathematician William Oughtred (1574–1660) is credited with developing the first slide rule around 1630. About the same time, he assembled a book on mathematics called *Clavis Mathematicae.* In addition to his mathematical pursuits, Oughtred was an Episcopal minister.

Thompson, James E. *The Standard Manual of the Slide Rule.* 2nd ed., Princeton, NJ: D. Van Nostrand Co., Inc., 1952.

Young, Neville W. *A Complete Slide Rule Manual.* New York: Drake Publishers, 1973.

Web Sites

The Department of Mathematics, The University of Utah. "What Can You Do With A Slide Rule?" http://www.math.utah.edu/-pa/slidcrules/ (accessed October 23, 2012).

The Museum of HP Calculators. "Slide Rules." http://www.hpmuseum.org/sliderul.htm (accessed October 23, 2012).

Supercomputers

Supercomputers are the world's largest and fastest computers. These high-speed computers, with the highest processing speeds yet developed by humans, are used primarily for solving complex scientific calculations, problems, and simulations. The parts of a supercomputer are comparable to those of a desktop computer: they both contain hard drives, memory, and processors (circuits that process instructions within a computer program).

Although both desktop computers and supercomputers are equipped with similar processors, their speed and memory sizes are significantly different. For instance, a desktop computer built in the year 2012 typically possesses a hard disk data capacity of between 500 gigabytes (GB,

Fujitsu Ltd. K supercomputers stand at Riken Kobe Institute in Kobe City, Japan. © *Tetsuya Yamada/Bloomberg via Getty Images.*

or 0.5 terabyte [TB]) and 4,000 GB (4 TB) and one or two processors with 4 to 16 gigabytes of random access memory (RAM)—enough to perform tasks such as Web browsing and video gaming. Meanwhile, a supercomputer of the same time period has hundreds of thousands of processors, hundreds of terabytes of RAM, and data storage space consisting of many exabytes (quintillions of bytes, where 1 quintillion is equal to 10^{18} bytes).

The supercomputer's large number of processors, enormous data storage, and substantial memory greatly increase the power and speed of the machine. Although desktop computers can perform millions of floating-point operations per second (megaflops), or billions of floating-point operations per second (gigaflops), supercomputers in the early 2010s can perform at speeds of quadrillions of floating point operations per second (the prefix for a quadrillion is peta; and the performance of a single numerical operation per second is termed a FLOPS (or Flops), short for floating point operation per second, so such processing speeds are referred to as petaflops, also referred to as PFLOPS, or PFlops).

Evolution of Supercomputers

Most current desktop computers are actually faster than the first supercomputer, the Cray-1, which was developed by Cray Research in the mid–1970s. The Cray-1 was capable of computing at 167 megaflops by using a form of supercomputing called vector processing*, which consists of rapid execution of instructions in a pipelined fashion. Contemporary supercomputers are much faster than the Cray-1, but an ultimately faster method of supercomputing was introduced in the mid–1980s: parallel processing*. Applications that use parallel processing are able to solve computational problems by simultaneously using multiple processors.

Using the following scenario as a comparative example, it is easy to see why parallel processing is becoming the preferred supercomputing method. If you were preparing ice cream sundaes for yourself and nine friends, you would need ten bowls, ten scoops of ice cream, ten drizzles of chocolate syrup, and ten cherries. Working alone, you would take ten bowls from the cupboard and line them up on the counter. Then, you would place one scoop of ice cream in each bowl, drizzle syrup on each scoop, and place a cherry on top of each dessert. This method of preparing sundaes would be comparable to vector processing. To get the job done more quickly, you could have some friends help you in a parallel processing method. If two people prepared the sundaes, the process would be twice as fast; with five it would be five times as fast; and so on.

Conversely, assume that five people will not fit in your small kitchen, therefore it would be easier to use vector processing and prepare all ten sundaes yourself. This same analogy holds true with supercomputing. Some researchers prefer vector computing because their calculations cannot be

* **vector processing** an approach to computing machine architecture that involves the manipulation of vectors (sequences of numbers) in single steps, rather than one number at a time

* **parallel processing** the presence of more than one central processing unit (CPU) in a computer, which enables the true execution of more than one program

Computer Sciences, 2nd Edition

readily distributed among the many processors on parallel supercomputers. But, if a researcher needs a supercomputer that calculates quadrillions of operations per second, parallel processors are preferred—even though programming for the parallel supercomputer is usually more complex.

Applications of Supercomputers

Supercomputers are so powerful that they can provide researchers with insight into phenomena that are too small, too big, too fast, or too slow to observe in laboratories. For example, astrophysicists use supercomputers as time machines to explore the past and the future of the universe. A supercomputer simulation was created in 2000 that depicted the impending collision of two galaxies: Earth's own Milky Way and Andromeda. Although this collision is not expected to happen for another three billion years, the simulation enabled scientists to run the experiment and see the results now. This particular simulation was performed on Blue Horizon, a parallel supercomputer at the San Diego Supercomputer Center. Using 256 of Blue Horizon's 1,152 processors, the simulation demonstrated what will happen to millions of stars when these two galaxies collide. This would have been impossible to do in a laboratory.

Another example of supercomputers at work is molecular dynamics (the way molecules interact with each other). Supercomputer simulations allow scientists to dock two molecules together to study their interaction. Researchers can determine the shape of a molecule's surface and generate an atom-by-atom picture of the molecular geometry. Molecular characterization at this level is extremely difficult, if not impossible, to perform in a laboratory environment. However, supercomputers allow scientists to simulate such behavior easily.

Supercomputers of the Future

Research centers are constantly delving into new applications like data mining to explore additional uses of supercomputing. Data mining is a class of applications that look for hidden patterns in a group of data, allowing scientists to discover previously unknown relationships among the data. For instance, the Protein Data Bank (PDB) at the San Diego (California) Supercomputer Center is a collection of scientific data that provides scientists around the world with a greater understanding of biological systems. Over the years, the Protein Data Bank has developed into a Web-based international repository for three-dimensional molecular structure data that contains detailed information on the atomic structure of complex molecules. The three-dimensional structures of proteins and other molecules contained in the Protein Data Bank and supercomputer analyses of the data provide researchers with new insights on the causes, effects, and treatment of many diseases.

Other modern supercomputing applications involve the advancement of brain research. Researchers are beginning to use supercomputers to provide them with a better understanding of the relationship between the structure and function of the brain, and how the brain itself works.

Specifically, neuroscientists use supercomputers to look at the dynamic and physiological structures of the brain. Scientists are also working toward development of three-dimensional simulation programs that will allow them to conduct research on areas such as memory processing and cognitive recognition.

In addition to new applications, the future of supercomputing includes the assembly of the next generation of computational research infrastructure and the introduction of new supercomputing architectures. Parallel supercomputers have many processors, distributed and shared memory, and many communications parts; we have yet to explore all of the ways in which they can be assembled. Supercomputing applications and capabilities will continue to develop as institutions around the world share their discoveries and researchers become more proficient at parallel processing.

Related Information

In June 2008, scientists at the Los Alamos National Laboratory, a facility in New Mexico operated by the U.S. government, announced that they had built a new supercomputer named Roadrunner that performed over 1 quadrillion (1×10^{15}) numerical operations per second (1 petaflop). Like many other recent supercomputers, Roadrunner was built using off-the-shelf technology, in this case 12,960 IBM microprocessors similar to those found in the Playstation 3 video game. To achieve high computation speeds using these unremarkable chips, Roadrunner's designers used a parallel computing architecture. In late 2009, a Cray XT5 supercomputer dubbed Jaguar installed at Oak Ridge National Laboratory (ORNL) in Oak Ridge, Tennessee, surpassed Roadrunner with a performance capability of 1.75 petaflops. Jaguar achieved the new speed after an upgrade to nearly a quarter million processor cores.

 See also **Animation • Parallel Processing • Simulation**

Resources

Books

Dubitzky, Werner, Krzysztof Kurowski, and Bernhard Schott, eds. *Large-scale Computing.* Hoboken, NJ: Wiley, 2012.

Hager, Georg, and Gerhard Wellein. *Introduction to High Performance Computing for Scientists and Engineers.* Boca Raton, FL: CRC Press, 2011.

Web Sites

Que Publishing, and Ed Tittel. "Is 8–12 GB the "New Normal" for RAM Size, or Should You Go Bigger?" http://www.quepublishing.com/articles/article.aspx?p=1941419 (accessed October 24, 2012).

Top500.org. "Top 500 Supercomputer Sites." http://www.top500.org/ (accessed October 24, 2012).

Faster and Faster

In June 2012, IBM unveiled a supercomputer named Sequoia for use at Lawrence Livermore National Laboratory (LLNL) in Livermore, California. Sequoia has a performance of more than sixteen petaflops, making it the fastest computer in the world. Some industry experts expect that supercomputers will attain processing speeds of one exaflops—equal to 10^{18}, or one quintillion FLOPS—before the year 2020.

T

Telecommunications

Telecommunications is acknowledged by many observers to be the hottest industry segment in the early twenty-first century. The word telecommunications comes from *tele*, which means *distant*, and *communication*, which means *to make common*. Thus, telecommunications is about sharing (or making common) information over distance.

The telecommunications industry consists of several distinct components, including telephony, the broadcast of audio and visual signals via cable and radio frequencies, and computer communications. Telegraphy was the earliest form of telecommunications, but this technology has all but disappeared from commercial use.

Birth of Telecommunications

Telecommunications began as a one-to-one form of communicating over geographic distances. The telegraph*, which came into commercial operation in the late 1840s, was the first modern-day example of this form of communications. Because the required trained personnel at both ends of the line, all communication between individuals had to be processed through operators. The invention of the telephone in the mid-1870s eventually supplanted telegraphy, allowing users to communicate directly with one another.

The telephone was the first technology to allow a human voice to be transmitted over significant geographic distances. Until the late 1890s, telephone callers were limited to a relatively small geographic area. The growth of telephone networks required many supplementary inventions, notably the ability to switch calls. Although it was initially limited to short distances, telephone technology evolved to allow coast-to-coast calls across the United States by 1915. In parallel with this, automatic switching exchanges began to supplant human operators as early as 1900, although manual exchanges persisted in the United States for many decades to come.

Digital Telephony

In the 1960s, digital transmission technologies were introduced into the long distance telephone network. These were followed in short order by digital switches. These technologies allowed for improved telephone transmission quality. Today, all domestic long distance calls and many local calls are carried digitally over fiber optic* networks. Internationally, some calls are carried by satellite-based communications systems while others are transmitted via undersea cables.

* **telegraph** a communication channel that uses cables to convey encoded low bandwidth electrical signals

* **fiber optic** transmission technology using long, thin strands of glass fiber; internal reflections in the fiber assure that light entering one end is transmitted to the other end with only small losses in intensity; used widely in transmitting digital information

Other developments in telephony include the introduction of wireless communications for the purpose of mobility. Although these systems had been available for a very limited number of users as early as the 1950s, the development of cellular communications systems in the 1970s and 1980s enabled many more users to obtain the benefits of mobile telephone systems. By the 1990s, these systems had become available worldwide. However, large imbalances existed in the global distribution of wireless cellular technology throughout the 1990s, and into the 2000s—whereas cell phone technology was widely available in the developed nations, many underdeveloped countries were severely underrepresented in cell phone availability and usage. But, the situation changed dramatically over the course of the 2000s. According to a 2008 announcement from the United Nations, worldwide cell phone usage was just 12 percent in 2002; by 2008, however, worldwide cell phone penetration had increased to 60 percent. According to the International Telecommunication Union, mobile phone usage reached, as of the end of 2011, 87 percent of the world's population, with 79 percent penetration into all of the developing countries. Eighty-seven percent represents more than 5.9 billion people out of a total of about 7 billion.

Broadcast Telecommunications

The broadcasting industry began in the 1920s as the ability to transmit speech via wireless radio became economically feasible. Prior to this, communications technology was limited to one-to-one communications—that is, one person communicating with exactly one other person. The transmission of speech over wireless systems made it possible for one sender to communicate with many receivers. Thus, one of the distinguishing features of broadcasting is that it is a one-to-many form of communication.

Until the 1950s, broadcasting and wireless communications were synonymous. All programming signals were transmitted to individual antennas that were either built in to televisions and radios or added to buildings to enhance signal reception. Around that time, communities in rural and mountainous areas, where it was difficult to receive over-the-air broadcast signals, began installing Community Antenna Television (CATV) systems. In these systems, a community would pool their resources to invest in an expensive antenna that was designed and placed for good signal reception. These superior signals were then distributed throughout the community via cables. Operators of cable systems gradually expanded their infrastructure and began to offer a rich variety of programming on these cable-based systems, making them attractive to viewers beyond their original service markets. Today, the majority of American communities are wired to provide television programming via cable systems.

Computer-Based Telecommunications

The computer networks of today had their genesis in the dedicated teleprocessing systems of the 1960s. These early computer networks were designed to support terminals communicating with a central mainframe* computer. In the late 1960s, researchers began experimenting with different types of networks; ones that allowed any device on the network to communicate with any other device. Networks of this kind are called peer-to-peer networks, as each computer has the same operational privileges as any other computer.

As minicomputers* became popular in the 1970s, networks of this kind expanded to meet new business needs and applications. Peer-to-peer networking accelerated with the development of local area networks (LANs)* and microcomputers, better known as personal computers (PCs), in the 1980s. Concurrent with these developments in local network technologies, work continued on new systems such as wide area networks (WANs) that would be capable of interconnecting these LANs. The most ubiquitous* and successful of these networks is the Internet.

The Internet is a network of networks designed to interconnect general purpose computers. The Internet was designed to be application-transparent, so users could develop any kind of networked application without having to make changes to the network. Thus, when the World Wide Web (or simply the Web) was developed in the late 1980s, the network could easily accommodate it. All that was needed were application programs in computers, called Web browsers, and hardware systems containing information, called servers, to be attached to the network. Despite many advances in technology and exponential growth in the number of computers on the network, the basic structure of the Internet remains intact.

Telecommunications Industry Challenges

The telecommunications industry is facing new technological pressures from the phenomenon of convergence. Since all major forms of communication are now transmitted primarily with digital technology, it is a relatively small

* **mainframe** large computer used by businesses and government agencies to process massive amounts of data; generally faster and more powerful than desktop computers but usually requiring specialized software

* **minicomputers** computers midway in size between a desktop computer and a mainframe computer; most modern desktops are much more powerful than the older minicomputers

* **local area networks (LANs)** high-speed computer networks that are designed for users who are located near each other

* **ubiquitous** to be commonly available everywhere

"Hoy! Hoy!"

Telephone inventor Alexander Graham Bell (1847–1922) and his former assistant Thomas A. Watson (1854–1934) tested out the new transcontinental telephone system in early 1915. Bell was in New York City and Watson was in San Francisco, California. So, what did they talk about? The conversation went like this: Bell: "Hoy! Hoy! Mr. Watson? Are you there? Do you hear me?" Watson: "Yes, Dr. Bell, I hear you perfectly. Do you hear me well?" Bell: "Yes, your voice is perfectly distinct. It is as clear as if you were here in New York."

matter for any of the network types—CATV, telephone, or computer—to carry any type of information. So, for example, although CATV systems were originally designed for broadcast television service, technologies have converged such that cable systems carry not just television programming, but also high speed data for computer use and voice data for telephony.

One of the more recent developments, at least from a historical perspective, is the availability of many forms of communication to portable devices. The vast majority of laptop PCs, tablet PCs, and smartphones are now produced with built-in capabilities for wireless communications. Most smartphones, for instance, not only allow the user the cell phone and texting capabilities present in basic cell phones, but high-speed Internet access as well. Cellular wireless technology, initially developed with just cell phones in mind, has undergone several major upgrades over the past several decades. Those upgrades in service quality and capability have been identified by generation. The first generation, or 1G, of cellular wireless technology appeared in the early 1980s and was analog in nature. The 2G phase was characterized by digital transmissions starting around the early 1990s. With significantly higher transmission rates, the third generation, or 3G, was first introduced commercially in the early 2000s. The next generation of cellular technology, namely 4G, became available in the United States in late 2010 and early 2011, with its Long Term Evolution (LTE) technology. 4G technology contains much higher data transmission rates—in the gigabit per second (Gbps) range—than 3G achieved. The Samsung Galaxy Craft, sold by MetroPCS beginning on November 4, 2010, was the first commercially sold LTE smartphone. The HTC Thunderbolt, provided by Verizon Wireless starting on March 17, 2011, was the second LTE smartphone to be made commercially available.

The evolution of telecommunications has changed more than the physical aspects of the telecommunications networks. Along with the technological changes described earlier, dramatic changes have occurred in the way telecommunications companies do business in this industry, as well as in the way governments regulate the various networks. The changes in telecommunications over the past 170-plus years—from the advent of the telegraph, to the latest Internet-capable smartphones—has been quite astonishing. One thing is almost certain: advances in technology, coupled with evolving user expectations, will continue to drive progress in the telecommunications industry.

 See also **Apple Computer, Inc. • Bell Labs • Intel Corporation • Microsoft Corporation • Xerox Corporation**

Resources

Books

Bates, Regis, and Donald Gregory. *Voice & Data Communications Handbook.* 5th ed. New York: McGraw-Hill Osborne Media, 2006.

Dodd, Annabel Z. *The Essential Guide to Telecommunications.* 5th ed. Upper Saddle River, NJ: Prentice Hall, 2012.

Iannone, Eugenio. *Telecommunication Networks.* Boca Raton, FL: CRC Press, 2012.

Mulligan, Catherine. *The Communications Industries in the Era of Convergence.* Abingdon, Oxon, UK, and New York: Routledge, 2012.

Rutenbeck, Jeffrey B. *Tech Terms: What Every Telecommunications and Digital Media Person Should Know.* Amsterdam and Boston: Elsevier Focal Press, 2006.

Valdar, A. R. *Understanding Telecommunications Networks.* London: Institution of Engineering and Technology, 2006.

Web Sites

CNET, and Lance Whitney. "2011 Ends with Almost 6 Billion Mobile Phone Subscriptions." http://news.cnet.com/8301-1023_3-57352095-93/2011-ends-with-almost-6-billion-mobile-phone-subscriptions/ (accessed October 25, 2012).

International Telecommunication Union. "Overview." http://www.itu.int/en/about/Pages/default.aspx (accessed October 29, 2012).

TechnoFunc. "History of Telecommunications Industry." http://www.technofunc.com/index.php/domain-knowledge/telecom-industry/item/history-of-telecommunications-industry (accessed October 25, 2012).

Transistors

A transistor is an electrically controlled resistor that has three terminals: two for the end-to-end flow of electrical current and one for the electrical signal that controls its end-to-end resistance. They are used in almost every electronic device now made. John Bardeen (1908–1991), Walter H. Brattain (1902–1987), and William B. Shockley (1910–1989) invented the transistor in 1947. Billions of transistors have been made since then, many of them located inside the integrated circuits* that make up the processors and memory modules of modern computers. The transistor is such an important device, and its invention was such a scientific breakthrough, that its three inventors were awarded the Nobel Prize in 1956.

Impact of the Transistor

Since early in the twentieth century, vacuum tubes* had been used in electronic circuits, such as amplifiers, to make electronic equipment, such as radios. Even the first computer, built before the invention of the

* **integrated circuits** circuits with the transistors, resistors, and other circuit elements etched into the surface of a single chip of semiconducting material, usually silicon

* **vacuum tube** an electronic device constructed of a sealed glass tube containing metal elements in a vacuum; used to control electrical signals

Power transistors. © *Guenter Schiffmann/ Bloomberg via Getty Images.*

▶

transistor, was made with vacuum tubes. But vacuum tubes were large, they consumed and dissipated a lot of energy, and they had a short lifetime before they burned out.

In the 1950s, only shortly after the transistor's invention, battery-powered portable radios were introduced. They were called transistor radios, or simply "transistors," and were extremely popular. By the end of the 1950s, transistors were used regularly in digital circuits. Then it became possible to put entire circuits on a single chip, making what are called integrated circuits. Digital electronics subsequently became significantly faster and cheaper, leading to the advent of personal calculators and computers.

Hand-held calculators appeared in the late 1960s. The market competition on price and functionality was so fierce that consumers were almost afraid to buy one, worried that their purchase would become obsolete quickly. Personal computers (PCs) were introduced in the late 1970s, and there was a similar explosion of low price and higher functionality in the PC market.

Integration of circuits also made electronics lighter, so complex electronics could fit inside satellites. As crystal growing and photolithography* improved during the last decades of the twentieth century and in the twenty-first century it has become easier to increase the number of transistors on a single chip, so they have become cheaper to produce and can be made much faster.

Transistor Basics

Transistors are made from crystals of semiconductor* material, typically silicon*. With +4 valence*, silicon lies near the center of the periodic table of the chemical elements. The elements on its left, the metals with valence

+1 and +2, are good conductors (low resistors) of electricity and those on its right, the non-metals with valences 0 through –2, are poor conductors (high resistors). The elements in the center can be good or poor conductors, depending on their chemical composition and physical structure; so they are called s.

When silicon forms a crystal, each atom's four outer electrons are tied to surrounding atoms in covalent bonds. Since these electrons are not very free to move, the crystal is a poor conductor. However, if the crystal is not pure, and some of the atoms in the crystal, called impurities, have valence +5 or +3, then any extra electron or any hole, where an electron could fit in the crystal, can conduct electricity.

Impurities with +5 valence are called donors because they donate an extra electron to the crystal. Impurities with +3 valence are called acceptors because they contribute a hole in which an extra electron could be accepted into the crystal. A crystal with a majority of donor impurities is called an N-type semiconductor because electricity conducts by negative electrons. A crystal with a majority of acceptor impurities is called a P-type semiconductor because electricity conducts by positive holes (actually, electrons hop from hole to hole in the opposite direction).

The effect of donor impurities (extra electrons) is canceled by the effect of acceptor impurities (holes where electrons could go). So, a silicon crystal's ability to conduct electricity can be controlled by varying the type and density of impurities when making the crystal—or by electrically controlling the impurities' effect, as in a silicon transistor.

How Are Transistors Made?

Although a single transistor resides on a tiny chip of crystalline silicon, transistors are manufactured in batches. The process begins with a thin circular wafer, about the size and shape of a CD-ROM (compact disc-read only memory), that is sliced off a large cylinder of pure crystalline silicon. Imagine inscribing an imaginary square inside the circle on the surface of the wafer and partitioning the square into an N-by-N array containing N^2 imaginary cells, where N is any positive integer. A process called photolithography allows the creation of N^2 transistors, one inside each cell, simultaneously.

The wafer is coated with a substance, called photo-resist, and then exposed to a black-and-white pattern as if the pattern were being photographed and the coated wafer were the film in the camera. The white areas of the pattern correspond to the upper surfaces of the end regions (called the emitter and collector) of all N^2 transistors. Light hits the wafer in these white areas of the pattern and chemically alters the photo-resist there. The wafer is dipped in a solvent that dissolves away the chemically altered photo-resist, where the pattern had been white, but not the unaltered parts, where the pattern had been black.

The wafer is then heated in an air-tight oven, filled with a gas of donor impurities. Although the wafer is not heated enough to melt the silicon, it is hot enough that some of the gas atoms diffuse from the surface into the body of the material. Donor impurities fix themselves into the crystal structure, but only under the open places in the photo-resist. The wafer is cooled and removed from the oven. The emitter and collector regions of N^2 separate transistors have been embedded in the wafer.

The patterned photo-resist is washed away and the wafer is given a second fresh coat of photo-resist. Again, the wafer is exposed to a black-and-white pattern, but this time the white areas of the pattern correspond to the upper surfaces of the control regions (called the base) of all N^2 transistors. After similar chemical processing, the wafer is heated again in an air-tight oven, filled this time with a gas of acceptor impurities. They fix themselves into the crystal structure, but again only under the open places in the photo-resist. The wafer is cooled and removed from the oven. The base regions of N^2 separate transistors have been embedded in the wafer, in between and touching the respective emitter and collector regions previously made. The N^2 complete transistors are all disconnected from each other, but they are also disconnected from any wires. So, photolithography is performed a third time on the wafer.

The patterned photo-resist is washed away again and the wafer is given a third fresh coat of photo-resist. This time, the wafer is exposed to a black-and-white pattern, where the white areas of the pattern correspond to small openings on the upper surfaces of all three regions of all N^2 transistors. After similar chemical processing, the wafer is sputtered (like being spray-painted) with a metal. The metal forms a small blob that adheres to the wafer's surface, but only in the open places in the photo-resist. When the photo-resist is washed off, the metal on top of the photo-resist washes away with it, leaving the small blobs. These blobs are the electrical contacts on the three regions of each transistor.

The wafer is then sliced and diced into its N^2 chips. For each chip, wires are attached to the transistor's three metal blobs and the chip is encapsulated, with only the three wires sticking out. Transistors can be made extremely small, or many transistors can be constructed on the same chip. Transistors on the same chip can even be connected together, by thin P-type or N-type regions, in complex integrated circuits, like amplifiers, digital circuits, or memories.

How Does a Transistor Work?

Suppose a silicon chip has an N-type region on one side, a P-type region on the other side, and a distinct junction in the middle where the two regions touch each other. Any loose charges—electrons on the N-side and holes on the P-side—naturally wander around a little; this is called diffusion. Any electrons from the N-side that cross the junction into the P-side, combine with holes there, and any holes from the P-side that cross the junction into the N-side, combine with electrons there.

There are two effects. First, the region around the junction becomes depleted of any free carriers of charge. Second, the negative charge accumulating on the P side of the junction and the positive charge accumulating on the N-side of the junction act to repel further diffusion.

Now, suppose a battery is connected to this chip. Connecting the battery's positive terminal to the N-side and its negative terminal to the P-side, called a reverse bias, attracts the carriers in each side away from the junction, reinforcing the depletion region near the junction. So, very little current flows.

Connecting the battery's positive terminal to the P-side and its negative terminal to the N-side, called a forward bias, overcomes the charge barrier at the junction and pushes the appropriate carriers toward the junction. Since this action forces continuing electron-hole combinations, the chip is a good conductor (low resistor) in this direction. An electronic device, like this PN semiconductor chip, that allows current to flow in one direction but not the other, is called a diode.

There are several kinds of transistors; the two most popular are the Field Effect Transistor (FET) and the Bipolar Junction Transistor (BJT). This article describes only the BJT.

The BJT

A BJT has three regions in series: the emitter, the base, and the collector. Each region has a connecting wire. The two outer regions, the emitter and collector, have the same kind of impurity and the base in the middle has the opposite kind of impurity. A PNP transistor has P-type silicon in its emitter and collector and N-type silicon in its base region. An NPN transistor is the opposite.

A BJT consists of two back-to-back diodes. If the collector-base diode is reverse-biased, one expects little current to flow through the device, from emitter to collector. If the emitter-base diode is forward-biased, carriers move through the base region to its connecting wire. But, if the base region is made extremely thin, then perhaps only 5 percent of the carriers in the base reach the wire and 95 percent reach the collector, even through the reverse-biased diode. One sees that the emitter-to-collector current is 19 times greater (0.95/0.05 = 19) than the emitter-to-base current and thus one can control the end-to-end emitter-to-collector flow by controlling a smaller flow in the emitter-to-base. The FET is a little different, but it has the same effect.

A transistor can increase the intensity of, or the amplification of, an electrical signal. The electrical signal received from a microphone has insufficient intensity to make an audible sound in a speaker. The electrical signal received from the head of a CD-ROM drive has insufficient intensity to be processed by digital electronics. However, a series of transistors can amplify an electrical signal so that the output signal from the last stage of a multistage is sufficient to create the desired effect.

The basic building blocks of digital design can be implemented as simple transistor circuits. Since circuits like these can be integrated, making it possible to fit many of them on a single chip, one begins to appreciate how this technology has had such a huge impact on computing.

No Royalties for Bell

The inventors of the transistor worked at Bell Labs, the research and development branch of what was then the Bell System. In 1956, as part of settling a ten-year federal anti-trust suit, the Bell System agreed to waive royalties on all its patents, retroactive to 1946. So the Bell System never collected a cent of royalty on its patent for the transistor, which was invented in 1947.

Smaller and Smaller

In 2001, another team from Bell Labs made transistor history when they produced an organic transistor from a single molecule. The tiny transistor and about 10 million others could all fit together on the head of a pin. This fast-evolving science led to significant advances in flexible electronics.

Conclusion

The ease with which transistors regenerate digital signals is probably the single most important factor that underlies the success of today's digital electronics, digital transmission, and digital computing. Computers were once large and expensive machines that only large corporations, universities, and government agencies could own. This is, of course, no longer the case. More than any other technology, the transistor is responsible for making computers so small and fast and inexpensive that they are now relatively common household appliances used by people of all ages for work, education, entertainment, and communication.

In the 2010s, scientists are developing a new type of transistor that has a three dimensional structure instead of the flat (two-dimensional) structures that have been used traditionally. However, in order to accomplish this feat, scientists will need to replace silicon with more suitable semiconducting materials, such as indium-gallium-arsenide. These improved transistors will provide even smaller and more efficient integrated circuits for electronic devices. Scientists also are working on an enhanced two-dimensional approach that they hope will overcome the difficulties seen in such older planar transistors. This approach uses an extremely thin channel of pure, what is called fully depleted, silicon that is located on a layer of insulation. Known by the term fully-depleted silicon-on-insulator (FD-SOI), this approach also could increase the efficiency and reduce the size of integrated circuits.

 See also **Generations, Computers • Integrated Circuits • Vacuum Tubes**

Resources

Books

Fitzgerald, Benjamin M., ed. *Transistors: Types, Materials, and Applications.* Hauppauge, NY: Nova Science, 2010.

Riordan, Michael, and Lilliam Hoddeson. *Crystal Fire: The Invention of the Transistor and the Birth of the Information Age.* New York: W. W. Norton, 1997.

Saxema, Arjun N. *Invention of Integrated Circuits: Untold Important Facts.* Hackensack, NJ: World Scientific, 2009.

Sedra, Adel S., and Kenneth C. Smith. *Microelectronic Circuits.* 6th ed. Oxford and New York: Oxford University Press, 2011.

Shur, Michael S., and Paul Maki, eds. *Advanced High Speed Devices.* Singapore: World Scientific Publishing, 2010.

Shurkin, Joel N. *Broken Genius: The Rise and Fall of William Shockley, Creator of the Electronic Age.* London and New York: Macmillan, 2006.

Sze, S. M., and M. K. Lee. *Semiconductor Devices, Physics and Technology.* 3rd ed. Hoboken, NJ: Wiley, 2012.

Web Sites

EE Times, and Brian Bailey. "Fully Depleted Silicon on Insulator devices." http://www.eetimes.com/electronics-blogs/eda-designline-blog/4375676/Fully-Depleted-Silicon-on-Insulator-devices (accessed October 26, 2012).

NobelPrize.org. "The Transistor." http://www.nobelprize.org/educational/physics/transistor/ (accessed October 26, 2012).

PBS. "Transisterized! The History of the Invention of the Transister." http://www.pbs.org/transistor/ (accessed October 26, 2012).

Phys.org. "New 3-D Transistors Promising Future Chips, Lighter Laptops." http://phys.org/news/2011-12-d-transistors-future-chips-lighter.html (accessed October 26, 2012).

Turing, Alan M.
British Mathematician and Cryptographer
1912–1954

Alan Mathison Turing was one of the leading theoreticians in computer science. Turing was something of a visionary in that his hypothetical "Turing Machine" set the standard for the description of computation and its relation to human computing.

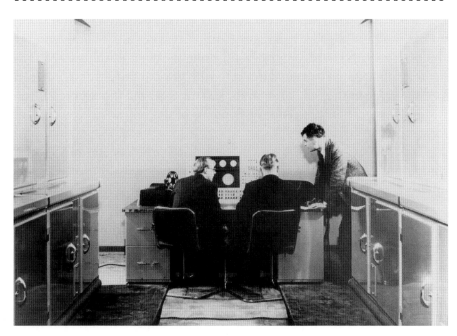

Alan M. Turing and colleagues working on the Ferranti Mark I Computer, 1951. © *SSPL via Getty Images.*

Education

Turing was born on June 23, 1912, to upper-middle-class parents in London, England. He was educated in traditional British schools including St. Michael's, a day school, where he learned Latin; Hazelhurst, a preparatory boarding school, where he studied to pass Great Britain's Common Entrance exam; Sherbourne, a high-school-level boarding institution, where he prepared for university admission; and finally, King's College, Cambridge, for university.

Upon graduation from the university, he won a research scholarship of 200 British pounds per year, which enabled him to stay on another year and try for a King's fellowship. This required a dissertation, which he wrote on the Gaussian error function, the Central Limit Theorem in statistics. In 1935 he was one of forty-five students who won the King's fellowship. This enabled him to attend Princeton University in the United States.

At Princeton he had contact with John von Neumann (1903–1957), who is widely credited as the inventor of the "stored program" computer, although this concept pre-dated him through the work of Charles Babbage (1791–1871). Turing also worked with Alonzo Church (1903–1995), one of the leading logicians of the day during his time at Princeton. He eventually earned his Ph.D. from Princeton in 1938. His dissertation, "Systems of Logic Based on Ordinals," was on the axioms of mathematics.

The Turing Machine

In 1936 Turing wrote an article describing a general machine for computation. It is taken as a description of a hypothetical computing machine, although Turing had in mind the human computer performing a typical calculation or computation. He suggested that the machine would need a tape of indefinite length to serve as a data storage device; a set of instructions; the ability to read, write, and manipulate cells on the tape; and the ability to move forward and backward along the tape. With this system, a single symbol would be stored in a cell, with the computing device able to read the value in the cell, write to the cell, or erase the value stored there. It would take action based on the contents of the cell, write, erase, move forward or backward.

The Turing Machine is widely regarded as the general model of a computing device, and its basic premise is sometimes still used to determine whether a computation or other problem can be solved by a general purpose computer. If it can be solved using the Turing Machine principles and methods, it can be done with a general-purpose computer.

Although the concept of the Turing Machine was not immediately accepted, nor even widely known in its day, it has come to be the standard in computing theory. As a result, the Association of Computing Machinery (ACM) has instituted an award in Turing's name which is given to the most accomplished practitioners and theoreticians of its field.

Turing's Career

Turing worked with or was friends with many of the leading scientists of his day including Donald Michie (1923–), who became famous for his work in machine learning; Claude Shannon (1916–2001), the developer of mathematical communication theory; E.C. Titchmarsh (1899–1963), an Oxford mathematician; and M.V. Wilkes (1913–), among others. He met Shannon at Bell Laboratories, where he worked for a time with the speech encryption unit during World War II.

As a war-time cryptographer, Turing worked for the British government, deciphering codes for Allied military operations. This occurred at Bletchley Park, for the Government Code and Cypher School. He also worked for the government secret service, in speech encryption, and was an envoy to Washington, D.C., as a liaison for the encryption and decryption effort.

After the war, Turing went to work at the National Physical Laboratory, and then, in 1948, at the University of Manchester, where he worked with one of the early computers. Although he developed a plan for an early computer, the ACE, or Automatic Computing Engine, it was never implemented.

Turing also devised "a Turing test" that is still used to determine humanlike behavior in the development of artificial intelligence, albeit imperfectly. He indicated that a computer and a person (or a male and a female) could be isolated in a separate room and interrogated by an "observer." If the observer, asking whatever questions he or she wanted, could not tell the difference between the answers given by the two, then there was no difference in their behavior. This is, of course, not entirely certain, but it gives an operational definition of "humanlike" behavior, in determining if indeed a computer "can think."

Turing was appointed to the Order of the British Empire, and, in 1951, elected a fellow of the Royal Society. Although he was considered a slow student during his early schooling, Turing was later acknowledged as one of the innovative thinkers of his time. He received a number of honors during his lifetime, but he has received greater acclaim in the decades since his death.

Personal Life

Turing was avidly interested in solitary pursuits such as bicycling, running, and general exploration of the countryside. He was said to have been a playful sort, once he trusted a person's friendship, although it is also reported that this was not always an easy accomplishment.

At one point, Turing was engaged to be married to Joan Clark, a colleague at Bletchley Park, although this never materialized. He was also befriended by and was a friend to Lyn Newman, the wife of Max Newman, a professor of mathematics at Cambridge.

Turing's professional life was complicated by the fact that he was an avowed homosexual in an era when this was not publicly accepted. In

"Can a Machine Think?"

"Can a machine think?" has become a rallying cry of the artificial intelligence community and other computer scientists investigating human behavior. It is one that interested Turing beginning in the 1930s and before, and one to which he devoted considerable energy.

1952 he was arrested and subsequently required to undergo treatment, which led to a certain amount of embarassment, though he tried to minimize this. He continued to work at Manchester on several projects: the computer, mathematics, and his interest in human cognition and the development of living things. However, this period was to be shortlived. Turing died a short time later, on June 7, 1954.

The circumstances of Turing's death are unresolved. He died of cyanide poisoning; a partially eaten apple was found nearby his body, but it was never examined. Although Turing's mother attributed the death to a tragic accident, the coroner's office ruled it a suicide.

▶ *See also* **Artificial Intelligence • Codes • Mathematics • Turing Machine**

Resources

Books

Hodges, Andrew. *Alan Turing: The Enigma.* New York: Simon and Schuster, 1983.

Web Sites

The Alan Turing Homepage. http://www.turing.org.uk/turing/ (accessed November 2, 2012).

Turing Machine

British mathematician Alan Turing (1912–1954) described what became known as the "Turing Machine" in his 1936 paper, "On Computable Numbers, with an application to the *Entscheidungsproblem*," which was published in the *Proceedings of the London Mathematical Society* in early 1937. The machine was actually a concept, not a piece of equipment, but its principles set the stage for the development of digital computers later in the twentieth century.

The machine can be described as a finite state control device (meaning that it has a finite number of states that control its operations), with a tape of unlimited length, divided into squares, upon which symbols may be written or stored. A sequence of actions can take place when a symbol is scanned by a read/write head and the machine is in a certain state. The sequence of actions is the "program."

At any point in time, the finite state control will be in one state and the tape head will be scanning a single symbol, or square, on the tape. On the basis of this symbol and the current state, it will write a symbol on the square, or choose to leave the symbol alone, move the tape one square to the left or the right, and change to a "new" (possibly the same) state. All this constitutes a "move" of the basic machine.

The purpose of the machine was to provide a method for deciding mathematical questions. Turing had become interested in the foundations of logic, and one of the unsolved or open questions was the "decideability" problem. The problem, posed in 1928 by German mathematician David Hilbert (1862–1943), was: "could there exist, at least in principle, a definite method or procedure by which all mathematical questions could be decided?"

The key to answering the question lay in the provision of a method, and this is what Turing's machine was to provide. The machine would be given a set of instructions to carry out some process or procedure, and the procedure would be carried out in order to answer a particular question. A different procedure would be provided for each problem. However, one could imagine a procedure for each particular problem being written on a single Turing Machine that would interpret the instructions to mimic or emulate other machines. This would be a Universal Turing Machine, capable of carrying out any problem or program supplied to it.

The Turing Machine was intended to reproduce the actions or the activities of a human carrying out a computation. In this sense, it introduced a definition of computing that was "mechanical," i.e., it could be carried out by following a set of instructions. Thus, the Turing Machine can be considered as a device or a set of devices for carrying out an algorithm*.

An algorithm is a procedure that comes to a halt after a finite number of steps, no matter what the values given for the variables. A mathematical procedure is one that can be performed mechanically, without risk of unexpected situations, once the value of the variables has been provided. A decision algorithm is one that gives a "yes" or "no" answer to a particular problem in a finite number of steps. A problem is said to be "algorithmically decideable" if a decision algorithm exists for it.

The *Entscheidungsproblem*, proposed by Hilbert in 1928 and written about by Turing in 1936, was the problem of decideability. Ultimately, Turing analyzed the formulas or functions of the predicate calculus or predicate logic and concluded that it was not possible, for a Turing Machine or other logical method, to answer all mathematical questions. This same conclusion was reached independently by Alonzo Church (1903–1995), an American logician, shortly before. Turing and Church later worked together at Princeton University, where Turing was a graduate student and Church was a faculty member.

Turing developed this idea for a mathematical machine in 1936. He did so to answer a specific question. The Turing Machine's value extends beyond its inventor's original purpose, however. It provided an abstract model of computation, a conceptual device that could compute any effective procedure, i.e., one that comes to a halt after a finite number of steps. Although Turing's machine was never implemented, its conceptualization served as a model in the development of the digital computer, a machine that could be programmed to perform any computable task. The conceptual Turing Machine is still studied by computer scientists, logicians, and philosophers.

Computer Sciences, 2nd Edition

Turing's Mentor

Alonzo Church (1903–1995) was one of Alan Turing's instructors at Princeton. He is remembered for his belief that recursiveness (or repetitiveness) plays a key role in solving logical problems. In 1944, he issued the book *Introduction to Mathematical Logic*.

The Turing Award

The Association for Computing Machinery (ACM) presents an annual award named in honor of Alan Turing. The award is given to one or more recipients for "contributions of a technical nature made to the computing community" that are "of lasting and major technical importance to the computer field." As of 2012, the award was accompanied by a cash prize of $250,000 (US dollars). The 2009 recipient was Charles P. Thacker (1943–) who, in addition to his many other contributions to computing, was recognized for his instrumental development of the *Alto* (developed at Xerox's Palo Alto Research Center [PARC] in 1972 and released in 1973), which is considered by many to have been the first modern personal computer.

* **algorithm** a rule or procedure used to solve a problem, most often described as a sequence of steps

See also **Turing, Alan M**

Resources

Books

Petzold, Charles. *The Annotated Turing: A Guided Tour through Alan Turing's Historic Paper on Computability and the Turing Machine.* Indianapolis, IN: Wiley, 2008.

Web Sites

Association for Computing Machinery. "A. M. Turing Award." http://amturing.acm.org/ (accessed November 3, 2012).

Sedgewick, Robert, and Kevin Wayne. "Turing Machines." Introduction to Programming in Java, Department of Computer Science, Princeton University http://introcs.cs.princeton.edu/java/74turing/ (accessed November 3, 2012).

V

Vacuum Tubes

A vacuum tube is an electronic device used for the processing of electrical signals. It consists of two or more electrodes inside a metal or glass tube which has been evacuated, hence the name.

In the mid–1800s Sir William Crookes (1832–1919) performed early experiments with passing electric current through an evacuated glass tube. In 1883 Thomas Edison (1847–1931) noticed that current would flow between two electrodes inside a light bulb if the negative electrode was heated. John Ambrose Fleming (1849–1945) constructed the first practical diode tube*, containing two electrodes. When the heated electrode, called the cathode, was at a negative voltage compared to the other electrode, called the anode or plate, electrons flowed from the cathode to the anode. When the voltages were reversed, electron flow was prevented.

This type of action is called *rectification*; it is used to change alternating current into direct current. This is a basic operation needed in radio receivers to demodulate a radio frequency signal into audio.

Later, Lee De Forest (1873–1961) developed a tube with three electrodes, called a triode. The third electrode was called a grid. It was a fine mesh placed between the cathode and the anode. De Forest discovered that a small change in voltage on the grid produced a large change in current flow between the cathode and anode. A positive voltage attracts the electrons from the cathode toward the anode and produces a larger current. A negative voltage repels the electrons and produces less current. Thus, the current flow is proportional to the voltage of the grid. Called *amplification*, this discovery was central to the growth of the electronics industry.

Further developments in vacuum tube technology led to the development of the tetrode, which contained four electrodes; the pentode with five electrodes; and others. The additional electrodes are used to enhance the amplification action of the basic triode: extending power, availability, frequency, efficiency, or fidelity.

The cathode of all vacuum tubes must be heated. The heat is supplied by passing a high direct current through the cathode or, more commonly, by providing another element, called a filament, near the cathode and passing high current through it. The filament is not considered an electrode since it is electrically isolated from the other elements and its sole purpose is to heat the cathode. It is the filament that produces the characteristic glow of the vacuum tube.

The filament represents many of the disadvantages of the vacuum tube. It requires a lot of power, which is essentially wasted energy since

* **diode tube** an obsolete form of diode that was made of metal elements in a sealed and evacuated glass tube

ENIAC Anniversary

In 1996, in commemoration of the fiftieth anniversary of ENIAC, the Moore School of Electrical Engineering, University of Pennsylvania, designed and built "ENIAC-on-a-chip." The chip is about 7.44 millimeters by 5.29 millimeters and contains about 175,000 transistors. It has the same functional architecture as the original ENIAC, however the programming cables have been replaced by a transistorized switching network. It is programmed and displays its results via a personal computer.

* **ballistics** the science and engineering of the motion of projectiles of various types, including bullets, bombs, and rockets

* **supercomputer** a very high performance computer, usually comprising many processors and used for modeling and simulation of complex phenomena, like meteorology

it does not add to the output power of the device. In a large device, a cooling system is needed to remove the heat generated by this process. Also, filament burn-out is the most common failure mechanism of most vacuum tubes.

Vacuum Tubes in Computers

The first general-purpose, electronic digital computer was the Electronic Numerical Integrator and Computer (ENIAC), built in 1946 at the University of Pennsylvania's Moore School of Electrical Engineering. It weighed 30 short tons (60,000 pounds; or about 27 metric tons), contained 18,000 vacuum tubes, and consumed 150,000 watts of electricity. It was originally designed to compute artillery ballistics* tables for the U.S. Ballistics Research Lab. However, it was a general purpose computer that could be programmed by reconfiguring the machine's modules with electrical cables.

Prior to ENIAC, mathematicians computed ballistics tables with mechanical adding machines, a process that took up to twenty hours for each table. Because ENIAC was electronic—rather than mechanical—and programmable, it was able to perform about 5,000 integer additions per second, reducing the time required to generate a ballistics table to about thirty seconds. By comparison, Oak Ridge National Laboratory (ORNL) in Oak Ridge, Tennessee, reported in late 2009 that its Cray XT5 Jaguar supercomputer* could perform calculations at nearly 2 petaflops—or nearly 2 quadrillion (10^{15}) floating point operations per second.

Of course, the reliability of ENIAC was a real concern. As noted earlier, a vacuum tube filament is susceptible to burn out. Some felt that a device with so many tubes would never work long enough to produce useful results. By de-rating the tubes (running them with less than full rated

Workers produce solar vacuum tubes in a factory in China. © *Nelson Ching/Bloomberg via Getty Images.*

voltage and current), the ENIAC team managed to keep the system running for several days without failure. This was a significant accomplishment.

Still, reliability was a continual problem for ENIAC and other vacuum tube-based computers. Another significant cause of failure with these early computers was large insects that crawled between vacuum tube electrodes and caused short circuits. The process of finding and fixing these short circuits was called *debugging*. The term has endured; it is used today to refer to the process of finding and fixing errors in the computer's program, or software.

Vacuum Tubes Today

Although they have been replaced with transistors* and other integrated circuits* in many low-power applications, vacuum tubes are still used in many high-power applications, including specialized sensors and television and computer display devices.

The only type of vacuum tube used in modern computer systems is the cathode ray tube (CRT)*, which for many decades was the main component in a computer display monitor. However, the advent of other display technologies onto the consumer electronics marketplace in the 1990s—technologies such as liquid crystal display (LCD) and plasma displays—meant that the larger and heavier CRT design faced increasing competition for market share, especially as the price of the newer competing technologies fell.

The cathode assembly in a cathode ray tube is called an electron gun. Located in the narrow tube neck, it generates a very narrow beam of electrons that are accelerated at high speed toward the anode. The anode is a large rectangular screen coated with phosphors* that glow when struck by the beam. The electron beam is guided by a strong magnetic field induced by deflection coils around the tube neck. The electron beam traces a raster scan pattern* that covers the entire surface of the screen at a speed higher than the human eye can detect. The intensity of the beam determines the brightness of the spot.

Colors seen on a CRT computer screen are produced by different phosphors that glow red, green, or blue. A color tube has three electron guns, one for each color. Each gun can only "see" spots on the tube corresponding to its color. Other colors are made by combinations of varying intensities of the three primary colors. The cathode ray tube became so common in computer display devices that the acronym *CRT* came to be synonymous with the entire display unit.

 See also **Early Computers • Generations, Computers • Integrated Circuits • Transistors**

Resources

Books

Eichmeier, Joseph A. and Manfred Thumm. *Vacuum Electronics: Components and Devices*, New York: Springer, 2008.

End of the Line?

In 2003 sales of LCD computer monitors caught up to those of CRTs. And in late 2007, sales of LCD televisions surpassed CRT TVs for the first time. Compared to the older CRT technology, LCDs of comparable screen size take up less space, are much lighter, and use considerably less power to operate. In 2007, the CRT market share fell 46 percent, with CRT monitors representing just 10.2 percent of monitor sales. In 2009, the EPA estimated that CRTs accounted for 47 percent of electronics ready for "end-of-life management," and were the most likely electronic items to be put away in storage by end-users.

* **transistor** a contraction of TRANSfer resISTOR; a semiconductor device, invented by John Bardeen, Walter Brattain, and William Shockley, which has three terminals; can be used for switching and amplifying electrical signals

* **integrated circuits** circuits with the transistors, resistors, and other circuit elements etched into the surface of a single chip of semiconducting material, usually silicon

* **cathode ray tube (CRT)** a glass enclosure that projects images by directing a beam of electrons onto the back of a screen

* **phosphor** a coating applied to the back of a glass screen on a cathode ray tube (CRT) that emits light when a beam of electrons strikes its surface

* **raster scan pattern** a sequence of raster lines drawn on a cathode ray tube such that an image or text can be made to appear

* **ImmersaDesks** large screens that allow for stereoscopic visualization; the three dimensional (3D) computer graphics create the illusion of a virtual environment

Web Sites

PC Magazine. "CRT Monitors Dying Off as LG, Samsung Mill Exit" http://www.pcmag.com/article2/0,2817,2181457,00.asp (accessed October 8, 2012).

Environmental Protection Agency. "Statistics on the Management of Used and End-of-Life Electronics" http://www.epa.gov/osw/conserve/materials/ecycling/manage.htm (accessed October 8, 2012).

Virtual Reality in Education

Flying over the Mississippi River from Canada to the Gulf of Mexico and continuing on to South America, learning about the migratory habits of swans; walking across a busy intersection; or becoming a hydrogen molecule as one bonds with a second hydrogen molecule and an oxygen molecule to form a drop of water—these are just a few examples of the experiences offered by virtual reality technology today. And now, climbing the Eiffel Tower, fishing in the Chesapeake Bay, and investigating the far regions of the world are closer to becoming virtually possible in the very near future because of recent advances in computer technology.

Scientists and educators are working together throughout the United States to introduce virtual reality to teachers and students via Cave Automated Virtual Environments (CAVEs), ImmersaDesks*,

Students learning how to use editing software. © *AP Images/Brad Puckett.*

Students learn to mine through simulaton. © *AP Images/The Appalachian-News-Express, Leigh Ann Wells.*

ImmersaWalls*, and head-mounted displays (HMD)*. The CAVE is a standard ten foot by ten foot by ten foot (3.05 meter by 3.05 meter by 3.05 meter) space, with three walls, a ceiling, and a floor. The student typically wears a pair of stereographic glasses that enhances images and carries the standard CAVE wand that is used to help the student as bird/pedestrian/molecule navigate the virtual environment. Researchers at the Electronic Visualization Laboratory (the University of Illinois at Chicago) originally developed the CAVE. The CAVElib software provides the foundation for creating CAVE applications, though multiple alternatives exist which seek to simplify the process. The ImmersaDesks, ImmersaWalls, and HMDs that are now available are less costly alternatives to the CAVE, and are alternatives that are also portable.

The emergence of virtual reality as an instructional aid in the classroom is just beginning. Although there are numerous examples of educational applications in use throughout the United States today, the growth of virtual reality has not reached anywhere near its potential in the classroom and beyond. This article explores several examples of how scientists and educators are collaborating to develop new ways of learning, including considering the student's ability to learn by being totally immersed in that learning environment.

At George Mason University, in Fairfax County, Virginia, for example, American educator Chris Dede, a professor at the Graduate School of Education, Harvard University, as of 2012, and his colleagues developed a SpaceScience World that consists of three applications, referred to as NewtonWorld, MaxwellWorld, and PaulingWorld. In NewtonWorld, students are introduced to the laws of motion from multiple reference

* **ImmersaWalls** large-scale, flat screen visualization environments that include passive and active multi-projector displays of 3D images

* **head-mounted displays (HMD)** helmets worn by a virtual reality (VR) participant that include speakers and screens for each eye, which display three-dimensional images

points, including becoming a ball hovering above the ground, colliding with another ball, and virtually experiencing motion with neither gravity nor friction being a factor. MaxwellWorld allows the student to experience an electrostatic field from multiple reference points that are influenced by force and energy. Finally, PaulingWorld introduces chemical bonding and molecular structures, such as becoming a drop of water through the bonding of hydrogen and oxygen molecules, or even becoming complex proteins as a result of manipulating amino acids. Such activities are described in Dede's book *Learning the Sciences of the 21st Century: Research, Design, and Implementing Advanced Technology Learning Environments.*

At the University of Illinois, research has focused on providing opportunities to learn important safety skills for students of all ages across K–12 (kindergarten to twelfth grade), including those with disabilities. American professor Frank R. Rusch (1949–), at Pennsylvania State University, as of 2012, and his colleagues were motivated to combine the emergence of virtual reality technologies and self-instructional strategies in the promotion of traffic safety among school children, including students with disabilities The CAVE provided multiple opportunities for school children to learn street-crossing skills without having to cross real streets, reducing the time needed for instructional learning to occur and reducing safety-related concerns during training.

In this demonstration, Rusch, Umesh Thakkar, and Laird Heal sought to determine whether students could use a self-instructional sequence in their navigating with a wand as they crossed three different intersections (an intersection with two-way stop signs, an intersection with four-way stop signs, and an intersection with electronic lights); each intersection virtually displayed three levels of difficulty (simple, typical, and complex). Difficulty was directly related to how many cars crossed the intersections, including a Porsche driven by ex-basketball star Dennis Rodman. Utilizing their own verbally generated cues, eighty-one students learned to cross the three intersections, with little or no differences between those students with disabilities versus those without.

Virtual reality is becoming increasingly important as a learning tool in the school as well as in university laboratories where CAVEs are typically located. Recent research has investigated the use of an ImmersaDesk in an effort to teach students to understand better the concepts that do not fit with their pre-existing conceptualizations by guiding them through a series of exercises that confront their pre-existing knowledge with alternative ideas. For example, young students are quick to disbelieve their teachers when they are told that the world is round. For most young students, earth is simply flat, and they do not have the cognitive capacity, nor the conceptual firepower, to make the leap from what they see and experience (a flat earth) to what they do not see (a spherical earth).

The Round Earth Project at the University of Illinois at Chicago, as described in *The Round Earth Project: Deep Learning in a Collaborative Virtual World,* conducted a series of studies to better comprehend the emergence of complex understandings when given the opportunity to become involved in virtual representations of Earth as a globe as seen from a spaceship. Using an ImmersaDesk, Andrew Johnson and his colleagues found that they could teach new concepts like a round earth versus a flat earth. They allowed students to assume the role of astronauts and provided the astronauts with activities that displayed earth as round versus flat.

The U.S. military is making use of virtual reality to reduce the amount of training new soldiers need. Virtualizing combat scenarios enables soldiers to simulate decision-making in combat environments without the cost necessary to recreate an enemy force and without the danger of routine injuries. Virtual reality is also being researched by the military as a method to treat post-traumatic stress disorder (PTSD) by recreating a virtual version of events that caused the trauma and, counterintuitively, allowing the individual to cope by reliving the event.

Virtual reality will continue to make important contributions to education. In the very near future, high schools should be able to utilize ImmersaWalls and ImmersaDesks to learn new concepts, to use HMDs to help students who are easily distracted to learn, and to teach increasingly complex concepts outside of the textbook. Further, imagine taking a virtual trip to Spain to study Spanish with native speakers rather than learning it from a textbook. Likewise, think how much more exciting a history lesson will be when students can interact virtually with historic politicians, scientists, and leaders such as George Washington, Isaac Newton, and Martin Luther King, Jr. As dramatic increases in computer bandwidth, processing power, and image resolution occur in the future, virtual reality indeed will become a reality for students and educators alike.

▶ *See also* **Virtual Reality**

Resources

Books

Cohen, Steve. *Virtual Decisions: Digital Simulations for Teaching Reasoning in the Social Sciences and Humanities.* Mahwah, NJ: L. Erlbaum Associates, 2006.

Gillespie, Helena. *Learning and Teaching with Virtual Learning Environments.* Exeter, UK: Learning Matters, 2007.

Kanna, Elizabeth, Christina Erland Culver, and Lisa Gillis. *Virtual Schooling.* Basingstoke, UK, and New York: Palgrave Macmillan, 2009.

Nelson, Nickola, Katharine G. Butler, Trisha L. Self, and Rosalind R. Scudder, eds. *Virtual Reality: Exploring New Dimensions for Conversation, Language, and Learning.* Hagerstown, MD: Lippincott Williams & Wilkins, 2007.

VR CAVES

CAVE is an acronym for the CAVE Automated Virtual Environment, a room-sized advanced visualization tool that combines high-resolution, stereoscopic projection and three dimensional (3D) computer graphics to create the illusion of complete sense of presence in a virtual environment.

Weiss, Joel, ed. *The International Handbook of Virtual Learning Environments*, 2 vols. Dordrecht, The Netherlands, and New York: Springer, 2006.

Web Sites

Electronic Visualization Laboratory, University of Illinois at Chicago. "The Round Earth Project." http://www.evl.uic.edu/roundearth/ (accessed October 29, 2012).

Laboratory for Scientific Visual Analysis, Virginia Polytechnic Institute and State University. "What Is a CAVE™?" http://www.sv.vt.edu/future/vt-cave/whatis/ (accessed October 29, 2012).

Viruses

Computer-based hardware and applications can be compromised by agents that alter or disable, including computer viruses.

A computer virus is a program or segment of executable computer code that is designed to reproduce itself in computer memory and, sometimes, to damage data. Viruses are generally short programs; they may either stand alone or be embedded in larger bodies of code. The term virus is applied to such code by analogy to biological viruses, microorganisms that force larger cells to manufacture new virus particles by inserting copies of their own genetic code into the larger cell's DNA. Because DNA

Attorney General Peter Verniero speaks at a news conference on e-mail virus, Melissa. © *AP Images/Jeff Zelevansky.*

can be viewed as a data-storage mechanism, the parallel between biological and computer viruses is remarkably exact.

Many viruses exploit computer networks to spread from computer to computer, sending themselves either as e-mail messages over the Internet or directly over high-speed data links. Programs that spread copies of themselves over network connections of any kind are termed worms, to distinguish them from programs that actively copy themselves only within the memory resources of a single computer. So many worm/virus hybrids have appeared that any distinction between them is rapidly disappearing.

A program that appears to perform a legitimate or harmless function, but is in fact designed to propagate a virus is often termed a Trojan Horse, after the hollow, apparently-harmless, giant wooden horse that was supposedly used by the ancient Greeks to sneak in inside the walls of Troy and overthrow the city from within. Chain letters have also been used as carriers for executable viruses, which are attached to the chain letter as a supposedly entertaining or harmless program (e.g., one that will draw a Christmas card on the screen).

The first wild computer viruses, that is, viruses not designed as computer-science experiments but spreading through computers in the real world, appeared in the early 1980s and were designed to afflict Apple II personal computers. In 1984 the science fiction book *Necromancer* by William Gibson appeared; this book romanticized the hacking of giant corporate computers by brilliant freelance rebels, and is thought by some experts to have increased interest among young programmers in writing real-world viruses. The first IBM PC computer viruses appeared in 1986, and by 1988 virus infestations on a global scale had become a regular event. An anti-virus infrastructure began to appear at that time, and anti-virus experts have carried on a sort of running battle with virus writers ever since. As anti-virus software increases in sophistication, however, so do viruses, which thrive on loopholes in software of ever-increasing complexity.

All viruses cause some degree of harm by wasting resources, that is, filling a computer's memory or clogging networks with copies of itself. These effects may cause data to be lost, but some viruses are designed specifically to delete files or issue a physically harmful series of instructions to hard drives. Such viruses are termed *destructive*.

Because even non-malicious or non-destructive viruses may clog networks, shut down businesses or websites, and cause other computational harm (with possible real-world consequences, in some cases), both the private sector and governments are increasingly dedicating resources to the prevention, detection, and defeat of viruses.

The first virus designed to be mass propagated, and perhaps the most famous virus to date, is a virus dubbed Melissa. The virus' creator, David Smith, initially unleashed the virus as part of an attachment in a file posted to a pornographic news group. The popularity of the group ensured a swift spread. For his dubious efforts, Smith was ultimately sentenced to 20 months in federal prison and fined $5,000.

An exhaustive list of current viral threats is essentially impossible. Dozens of new viruses are identified every day. Most viruses are written merely as egotistical pranks, but a successful virus can cause serious losses. Malicious software constitutes a material threat to businesses, government, and home computer users.

Currently, there are three categories of malicious software threats, including viruses, worms, and Trojan horses. All of these threats are built from the same basic instructions and computer logic that make up application programs on one's computer such as word processors, games, or spreadsheets. Like traditional application programs, malicious software is written by people and must be intentionally designed and programmed to self-replicate or cause damage.

While almost all Trojan horses attempt to cause harm to the computer system, more than 70 percent of all computer viruses and worms are designed only to self-replicate. Those viruses, worms, and Trojan horses that do inflict intentional damage to computer systems are said to deliver a "payload." Common payloads include formatting a hard drive, deleting files, or gathering and sending passwords to an attacker. These threats typically have trigger criteria. They wait until the criteria are met before delivering the payload (for example, waiting until a predetermined date to reformat the hard drive).

The typical malicious software author is a male between fourteen and twenty-five years of age. These demographics are expected to change as organized crime, terrorist groups, and rogue organizations begin to target the Internet. In addition, many governments around the world are researching how to use malicious software for both offensive and defensive information warfare.

Viruses

A virus is a computer program that is designed to replicate itself from file to file (or disk to disk) on a single computer. Viruses spread quickly to many files within a computer, but they do not spread between computers unless people exchange infected files over a network or share an infected floppy diskette.

Viruses are classified by the type of file or disk that the virus infects:

- Boot viruses attach themselves to floppy diskettes and hard drives. When a user boots from an infected floppy diskette or hard drive, the virus is activated and the computer becomes infected. The virus spreads to other floppy diskettes as they are used on the system.

- Application viruses spread from one application to another on the computer. Each time an infected application program is run, the virus takes control and spreads to other applications.

- Macro viruses spread through documents, spreadsheets, and other data files that contain computer macros. A macro is a small, self-contained program that is embedded directly within a document or spreadsheet file. Typically, macros are used to automate simple computer tasks such as summing a set of numbers in a spreadsheet. Modern macros are powerful enough to copy themselves between documents or spreadsheets.

■ Script viruses infect other script files on the computer. Script viruses, which are written in high-level script languages such as Perl or Visual Basic, gain control when a user runs an infected script file.

A typical computer virus works in a regular pattern. First, the user runs infected program A. Program A immediately executes its viral logic. The virus locates a new program, B, that it thinks it can infect. The virus checks to see if the program is already infected. If program B is already infected, the virus goes back to locate another program to infect. If it is not already infected, the virus appends a copy of its logic to the end of program B and changes program B such that it, too, will run the malicious logic. The virus then runs program A so the user does not suspect any malicious activities.

Viruses can be written in numerous computer programming languages including assembly language, scripting languages (such as Visual Basic or Perl), C, C++, Java, and macro programming languages (such as Microsoft's VBA).

Worms

A worm is a computer program that exploits a computer network to copy itself from one computer to another. The worm infects as many machines as possible on the network, rather than spreading many copies of itself on a single computer, as a computer virus does. Usually, a worm infects (or causes its code to run on) a target system only once; after the initial infection, the worm attempts to spread to other machines on the network. Because computer worms do not rely on humans to copy them from computer to computer, they can spread much more rapidly than computer viruses.

The first computer worms were written at Xerox Palo Alto Research Center in 1982 to understand how self-replicating logic could be leveraged in a corporation. A bug, however, in the worm's logic caused computers on the Xerox network to crash. Xerox researchers had to build the world's first "antivirus" solution to remove the infections. In 1987 the "CHRISTMA EXEC" worm made millions of copies of itself in the IBM and BITNET e-mail systems. In 1988 the "Internet" worm spread itself to roughly 6,000 machines (10 percent of the Internet at the time).

More recently, viruses have begun to spread through infected internet URLs, sometimes embedding in the code of legitimate websites. Additionally, some virus authors take advantage of social media sites like Facebook and Twitter, infecting shortened URLs, attaching them to a popular topic, and linking them to infected websites. As of August 2012, virus infections of Macintosh computers have been reported. The Apple product had previously been immune from viral attack.

Viral Origins

What was the first mainstream computer virus? It is widely believed that it was the Pakistani Brain boot virus. It first began making the rounds in 1986.

The typical computer worm works as follows: The user unknowingly runs a worm program. The worm accesses a "directory" source, such as an e-mail address list, to obtain a list of target computers on the network. The worm sends itself to each of the target computers. A user on a target computer receives a copy of the worm in e-mail, unknowingly runs the worm e-mail attachment, and starts the process over again.

Some worms automatically connect to target computers and use a "back door" to install and run themselves on the target without human intervention. Like viruses, computer worms can be written in assembly language, scripting languages, macro languages, or in high level languages.

Detection Avoidance

Virus and worm authors have invented a number of techniques to avoid detection by antivirus software. Three of the more interesting techniques are the polymorphic virus, the retrovirus, and the stealth virus.

The term "polymorphic" means many-formed. Polymorphic viruses (or worms) mutate themselves each time they spread to a new file or disk. This behavior eliminates any consistent digital fingerprint and makes virus detection much more difficult. These digital pathogens avoid detection in the same way that HIV (human immunodeficiency virus) and other viruses evade the human immune system.

Computer retroviruses actively seek out and disable antivirus programs. The retrovirus deletes components of the antivirus program as an offensive attack to prevent detection.

Finally, stealth viruses inject themselves into the computer operating system and actively monitor requests to access infected files. The virus automatically disinfects infected files before they are accessed by other software on the computer, then reinfects them at a later time. This technique enables the viruses to sneak past antivirus software because every time the antivirus program attempts to scan an infected file, the virus disinfects the file first.

Weaponization of Computer Viruses

In 2010, the Stuxnet computer worm damaged as many as 1,000 uranium enrichment centrifuges at Iranian nuclear enrichment facilities. Stuxnet specifically targeted certain types of industrial machinery control systems, including those used on centrifuges, causing the centrifuges to spin uncontrollably until they destroyed themselves. Most computer security analysts and several European intelligence agencies believed that either Israel or the United States—or both countries—were involved in creating Stuxnet. In June 2012, following a *New York Times* report on the incident, U.S. officials revealed that Obama secretly ordered the Stuxnet attack to slow Iran's nuclear weapons program. According to anonymous U.S. officials, the United States and Israel collaborated to create the Stuxnet worm, although Israel has denied participating in its development. Some cybersecurity experts assert that the virus, in part or in whole, has resurfaced outside of Iran, possibly indicating that Iran also has attempted to engage in cyberwarfare.

Resources

Books

Aycock, John. *Computer Viruses and Malware.* New York: Springer, 2010.

Bowden, Mark. *Worm: The First Digital World War.* New York: Atlantic Monthly Press, 2011.

Johnston, Jessica. *Technological Turf Wars: A Case Study of the Computer Antivirus Industry.* Philadelphia: Temple University Press, 2008.

Web Sites

Forbes Magazine. "Researchers Say the Web May Be Offering Fewer Footholds to Hackers." http://www.forbes.com/sites/andygreenberg/2012/06/28/researchers-say-the-web-may-be-offering-fewer-footholds-to-hackers/ (accessed October 3, 2012).

Kaspersky. "Shortened URLs Direct Users to Infected Websites." http://www.kaspersky.com/about/news/virus/2011/Shortened_URLs_Direct_Users_to_Infected_Websites/ (accessed October 3, 2012).

ZDNet, Ed Bott. "The Malware Numbers Game: How Many Viruses Are Out There?" http://www.zdnet.com/blog/bott/the-malware-numbers-game-how-many-viruses-are-out-there/4783/ (accessed October 3, 2012)

WX

Watson, Thomas J., Sr.
American Business Executive
1874–1956

Thomas John Watson, born on February 17, 1874, was neither an inventor nor a technician, but his contributions to computer science were substantial nonetheless. During Watson's forty-two years of leadership at IBM Corporation, his marketing and management skills and his emphasis on research and development helped create the Computer Age. He died on June 19, 1956.

The fifth child of an immigrant Scots-Irishman, Watson was born in a four-room cabin in Painted Post, New York. He showed no affinity for the family farm and lumber business and chose to study business and accounting instead. After a year at the Miller School of Commerce in Elmira, New York, he accepted a bookkeeping job at the then relatively high salary of $6 a week. He was seventeen years old.

The job was shortlived, however, as Watson succumbed to the lure of the open road and the life of a traveling salesman, peddling pianos, organs, and sewing machines off the back of a wagon. He soon joined forces with a more established salesman named C. B. Barron, this time selling stock in the Northern New York State Building and Loan Association.

During this period, Watson began honing the selling skills that would someday earn him the nickname of the world's greatest salesman. But first there were a few bumps on the road: Barron absconded with the money they had earned, and Watson was fired. However, fortune smiled on Watson in October 1895, when he took a sales job with the National Cash Register Company (NCR) and was soon outperforming everyone in NCR's Buffalo, New York, office.

By 1912, after a series of rapid promotions, Watson had risen to second-in-command at NCR's corporate headquarters in Dayton, Ohio. At the age of thirty-eight, this tall, strikingly handsome man was one of the town's most eligible bachelors—but not for long. He met Jeannett Kittredge, daughter of a prominent businessman, at a country club dinner, and a year later they were married. The couple eventually had four children: Thomas, Jr.; Jane; Helen; and Arthur.

During the NCR years, to raise the morale of a dispirited sales force, Watson adopted his famous motto "THINK" and placed framed placards with that single word throughout the company's offices. Years later, he would use that same slogan at IBM, a company he was soon to join.

▲

Thomas Watson. © *MPI/Getty Images.*

In His Father's Footsteps

Thomas J. Watson Jr. (1914–1993) took the helm of IBM shortly before his father's death. Leading IBM from 1956 until 1971, he is credited for bringing IBM from the tabulator era into the Computer Age. After his retirement, he spent several years as U.S. Ambassador to the Soviet Union.

Watson's departure from NCR was preceded by two serious impediments to his career path. The first of these was an accusation by the company's main competitor, American Cash Register Company, that Watson and twenty-nine other executives had violated the Sherman Antitrust Act by engaging in unfair business practices, some designed to eliminate the second-hand trade in business machines. Although Watson was sentenced to one year in jail and a $5,000 fine, the verdict was quickly appealed and eventually set aside. Nonetheless, the widely publicized trial did little for his standing at NCR. In addition, there was a public disagreement with NCR President John H. Patterson, and shortly thereafter Watson was dismissed.

Watson was recruited by Charles R. Flint, the founder of what was to become IBM, and on May 1, 1914, he became general manager of the Computing-Tabulating-Recording Company (CTR), a small conglomerate in need of a major turnaround. Watson was intrigued by the product line, particularly the tabulating machine invented by Herman Hollerith (1860–1929) to help tally census results. Believing that automated accounting and record keeping had great commercial potential, Watson focused on the tabulating-machine division. Later that year, as CTR president, he borrowed the funding for research and development and began a transformation of the company. In 1924, at the age of fifty, he became chief executive officer and changed CTR's name to International Business Machines Corporation (IBM), reflecting his vision of the future.

To realize that vision, Watson motivated his employees through slogans and songs, a company newspaper and school, a country club that any employee could join for a dollar a year, and the promise of lifetime employment. One of his slogans was "World peace through world trade." A master of sales promotion, he understood the needs of the customer and met those needs through continuous funding of engineering and research. It was primarily Watson's support that ensured the development of Howard Aiken's Mark I calculator—the first digital computer made in the United States and IBM's first step into the Computer Age. Advancements continued and in 1952 IBM introduced its first production computer, the 701, and the company was firmly established in the computer business.

Watson retired as president of the firm in 1949 to become chairman of the board, and on May 8, 1956, he passed on executive power to his eldest son, Thomas Watson Jr. Six weeks later, he died of a heart attack at the age of eighty-two.

 See also **Hollerith, Herman • IBM Corporation • Mainframes**

Resources

Books

Belden, Thomas, and Marva Belden. *The Lengthening Shadow: The Life of Thomas J. Watson.* Boston: Little, Brown, 1962.

Fishman, Katharine Davis. *The Computer Establishment.* New York: Harper & Row, 1981.

Levinson, Harry, and Stuart Rosenthal. *CEO: Corporate Leadership in Action.* New York: Basic Books, 1984.

Rodgers, William. *THINK: A Biography of the Watsons and IBM.* New York: Stein and Day, 1969.

Slater, Robert. "Thomas J. Watson, Sr.: Founder of IBM." In *Portraits in Silicon.* Cambridge, MA: MIT Press, 1987.

Watson, Thomas J., Jr., and Peter Petre. *Father, Son & Co.: My Life at IBM and Beyond.* New York: Bantam Books, 1990.

Window Interfaces

Window interfaces refers to the commonly used way to organize space on a computer screen for interaction with a human user. Screen space is organized into regions called windows. Each window utilizes some screen space for computer–human interaction. Typically, a computer system

Nvidia Interface for Windows. © *AP Images/PRNewsFoto/NVIDIA Corporation.*

▼

* **dragged** to have been moved by the application of an external pulling force; quite often occurring in graphical user interfaces when objects are moved with a mouse

* **title bar** the top horizontal border of a rectangular region owned by a program running in a graphical user interface (GUI); it usually contains the program name and can be used to move the region around

with window interfaces also supports the mouse and the keyboard as interactive devices for user input.

Two Styles of Window Interfaces

There are various styles of organizing the windows on a screen. One approach is to treat the screen as a desktop and the windows as documents on the desktop. The windows may overlap one another so that some windows partially or completely obscure other windows. Only those windows that stay on top are fully visible. Users can use the mouse to drag the windows around on the screen or to bring a certain window to the top.

Another way to organize windows is by tiling: subdividing screen space so that the windows do not overlap and arranging the windows like tiles to fill the screen space. Tiling attempts to keep all the windows entirely visible at the same time.

General Operations on Windows

Window interfaces allow users to work on multiple tasks at the same time. Windows supports certain standard operations that are both versatile and practical:

1. *Dragging* a window to a different position on the screen;
2. *Resizing* the dimensions of a window;
3. *Iconifying* a window (to suspend the use of a window, the user may hide the window in use, turning it into an icon on the desktop, that is, the screen);
4. *Restoring* a window from an icon (an icon is simply a small window that supports the restore operation);
5. *Closing* a window.

Typically, someone uses the mouse or other pointing device to perform these operations. The mouse moves a corresponding cursor on the screen.

A window has other designated areas, some of which are like buttons. The cursor can be placed over a designated area and then pressed to invoke the desired operation on the window. For example, a window can be dragged* to a new location by placing the cursor over the title bar* of a window and moving the mouse while keeping the button pressed down; when the mouse button is released, the window stays at the new location on the screen. (A mouse with more than one button most often uses the left button to invoke the operation.)

When the cursor is on the Close button, a window can be closed by clicking on the mouse button—that is, pressing the button down and releasing it momentarily. A window can be iconified by clicking over the Iconify button. A window can be restored from an icon by double-clicking over the icon—that is, clicking two times quickly. The border around a window is often the area specifically designated to resize the window.

When the cursor is over the window border, the system may even change the appearance of the cursor, indicating that the user can now resize the window. The mouse button can then be held down and the window border dragged to resize the window to the desired dimensions.

Other Features

Many other functions can be performed in a windows environment. A sampling of these operations follows.

Focus Window—For Keyboard Input   These are the common window operations in application programs using window interfaces. A user may use the window to interact with a program in many other application-specific ways. If a user wants an application program to read keyboard input as it is being typed, the program can display the keys in a window as typing progresses. However, because there are multiple windows, one of the windows needs to be designated the Focus window to receive keyboard input. Usually, a simple mouse click or any operation on the window brings it into focus to receive keyboard input. The Focus window usually will have a slightly different appearance to indicate this distinction.

Menu Bar   Another common application design is to use a menu bar in the window. The menu bar is a designated area strip labeled with menu items. When the mouse cursor is placed over a menu label*, the becomes highlighted. A click on the mouse button will then bring up a drop-down menu*. A user can then move the mouse cursor to any item in the menu to select an operation and then click on a menu item to invoke the operation.

Scroll Bar   Sometimes the screen space in the window is not large enough, and parts of the program output may be obscured. A common practice in program design is to use a scroll bar, which allows the user to move the window within a larger, imaginary screen space for output. Scrolling the window then exposes other parts of program output. Clicking on the direction buttons* scrolls the window in increments along the indicated direction. A user may also scroll the window smoothly with the mouse by placing the cursor over the thumbnail* on the scroll bar, holding down the mouse button, and moving the thumbnail in the desired direction.

Application Wizard   A powerful application of windows is their ability to provide online help information with an application wizard. When a user needs help working with a particular program, the program will, on the user's request, hold the progress of the program at that stage and pop up a separate window to provide helpful information online. The program can provide help that is specific to the task at hand and even guide the user through the rest of the task. This style of intelligent online help is provided by an application wizard. For example, Mabasoft released Application Wizard 3.3.2 in October 2012. It provides easy access to a computer user's applications, documents, and folders. Application Wizard

* **menu label** the text or icon on a menu item in a program with a graphical user interface

* **drop-down menu** a menu on a program with a graphical user interface that produces a vertical list of items when activated

* **direction buttons** buttons on a program with a graphical user interface that provide a way of navigating through information or documents

* **thumbnail** an image that is a scaled down copy of a much larger image; used to assist in the management of a large catalog of images

Shaping a New Idea

Until the late 1980s, windows had been mostly rectangular. At that time, however, Sun Microsystems developed a system called NeWs (for networked windows) for workstations in a local area network. NeWs supported windows of various shapes but was soon discontinued.

is described as a "popular menu-based launcher, quitter, switcher, and navigation tool for Mac OS X."

Customizable Look and Feel   Most any implementation of window interfaces is highly customizable. The look and feel of window interfaces may be quite different, but the fundamental generic operations are not.

Brief History of Window Interfaces

In the mid-1970s, the Xerox Palo Alto Research Center first used the Alto computer to access multiple computers as an intelligent gateway. The Alto computer divided the monitor screen into windows, each of which could run a different program or access a different computer in the network. Later, Xerox, in the Dynabook project, developed a programming language called Smalltalk. Designed into the execution of Smalltalk was the use of multiple overlapping windows on the screen for interaction with the human user.

During the 1980s, while the use of interactive computer graphics was becoming commonplace, window interfaces caught on. The Macintosh computer and the later Sun workstation applied the desktop metaphor to the monitor screen, using overlapping windows on the screen as if they were documents on the desk; each window provided screen real estate for human–computer interaction.

Another system for window interfaces on networked computers, called X-Windows, was developed by an industry consortium led by the Massachusetts Institute of Technology (MIT). Soon this system became the industry standard. Today, many derivative systems of X-Windows are available from various computer vendors for use on the Unix platform, including Linux. Macintosh, from Apple Computer, Inc., continues to carry its own system of window interfaces. Microsoft Corporation rode on the success of marketing DOS (Disk Operating System) on the Intel-based personal computer (PC) developed by the International Business Machines Corporation (IBM), called the IBM-PC during the late 1980s, and imitated the Macintosh window interfaces to develop Windows on DOS. Windows became very popular on its release in the early 1990s, and Microsoft has developed later versions, called Windows 95, Windows 98, and Windows 2000, including Windows NT (which was developed in the early 1990s for networked computers), Windows XP, Windows Vista, Windows 7, and Windows 8. For the most part, all these systems are similar in their user-interface design.

 See also **Apple Computer, Inc. • Microsoft Corporation • Xerox Corporation**

Resources

Books

Goldberg, Adele, and David Robson. *Smalltalk-80: The Language and Its Implementation.* Reading, MA: Addison Wesley, 1983.

Hiltzik, Michael. *Dealers of Lightning: Xerox PARC and the Dawn of the Computer Age.* New York: Harper Business, 2000.

Rathbone, Andy, and Wallace Wang. *Windows 7 & Office 2010 for Dummies.* Indianapolis, IN: Wiley, 2011.

Reiss, Levi, and Joseph Radin. *X-Window Inside & Out.* Berkeley, CA: Osborne/McGraw-Hill, 1992.

Web Sites

About.com. "The Unusual History of Microsoft Windows." http://inventors.about.com/od/mstartinventions/a/Windows.htm (accessed October 29, 2012).

Mabasoft. "Application Wizard 3.3.2." http://www.mabasoft.net/products/applicationWizard/index.html (accessed October 29, 2012).

World Wide Web

To some people, the term "World Wide Web" is synonymous with "Internet," but others define it as a graphical interface for using many parts of the Internet. The World Wide Web has become one of the best known and most used aspects of the Internet.

The Internet itself began as an experiment created by the Advanced Research Projects Agency of the U.S. Department of Defense (DoD) in the 1960s. It was a network called the Advanced Research Projects Agency Network (ARPANET). The first networked computers of ARPANET were connected in 1965; a low-speed telephone line brought together a computer in California and another in Massachusetts. As it grew, ARPANET connected DoD sites with university research facilities worldwide, but not in a linear way. The connections were made so that if several of them were broken, many sites would still be in full contact with one another. The non-linear connections reminded people of a web, and that is where some people believe that the name World Wide Web originated.

In 1972 ARPANET was given its first public demonstration at an International Conference on Computer Communications. It was still primarily an entity within the domain of the DoD and its university research partners. During the next decade, however, the corporate world began to enter the networked computer world. In 1979 CompuServe was the first service to offer electronic mail communication. By 1985, the Internet was used heavily to support communications among researchers and technology developers in a variety of academic and corporate fields.

Once people outside of the original group of users obtained access, this network began linking with other networks and the Internet began its fast growth. Soon software was developed that took advantage of

* **Hypertext Markup Language (HTML)** an encoding scheme for text data that uses special tags in the text to signify properties to the viewing program (browser) like links to other documents or document parts

* **graphical user interface (GUI)** an interface that allows computers to be operated through pictures (icons) and mouse-clicks, rather than through text and typing

"clickable buttons" and non-linear connections. This software was written in code called Hypertext Markup Language (HTML)*. It enabled users to move from place to place on the Web without having to follow a set path, and without having to type in strings of text commands as they previously had to do.

In 1990 Tim Berners-Lee (1955–) wrote the first graphical user interface (GUI)* browser program for the Internet. He called it "WorldWideWeb," although the name was later changed to Nexus, to avoid confusing the program itself with the larger entity that became known as the World Wide Web.

By October 1993, there were at least 200 known HTTP (Hypertext Transfer Protocol) servers on the Web, and the Mosaic browser had been released for all common computer platforms, including PC/Windows and Macintosh computers. America Online, which was first available to Macintosh and Apple II users in 1989, launched a Windows-based online service and reached 500,000 subscribers by the end of 1993.

The next year, Marc Andreessen, who was one of the developers of the Mosaic browser, formed the company that would become known as Netscape, which is also the name of the company's popular Web browser. Also in 1994, Stanford University Ph.D. candidates David Filo (1966–) and Jerry Yang (1968–) began compiling an online guide to interesting sites on the Internet. Once known as *Jerry's Guide to the World Wide Web*, the list was renamed *Yahoo!* What started as a hobby turned into a rapidly growing business by the following year.

The dominant Web browser package in the mid-to-late 1990s was Netscape Navigator. However, Microsoft's entry into the Web browser market—as well as the appearance of "open source" Web browsers—slowly eroded Navigator's large initial lead, until Navigator was virtually eliminated from the marketplace by 2002. The elimination of Navigator occurred in spite of an antitrust lawsuit filed against Microsoft in 1998 by the U.S. Department of Justice and joined by twenty U.S. states, because of practices such as Microsoft's bundling of its own Web browser with its Windows operating system and its attempts to exclude other Web browsers (such as Navigator). In spite of Microsoft settling the lawsuit out-of-court and relenting to some of the government's demands designed to stop its monopolistic practices, Navigator nevertheless became a defunct product.

In contrast to Navigator's plight, Microsoft's Internet Explorer gained a continuously greater share of the Web browser market until it reached its peak of around 95 percent of user market share in 2003. However, because of competition from other Web browser application programs, Microsoft, though still dominant, saw its market share fall to just under two-thirds of the browser market by 2009. Version 10 is the latest version of Internet Explorer. Although early "Platform Reviews" were released in 2011, the final, completed version of Internet Explorer 10 was released in August 2012. In 2012, popular browsers also included Apple's Safari, Google Chrome, and Opera.

Online service providers offer proprietary packages that include browsers and search capabilities, but these have decreased in popularity as more people access the Web through high-speed cable and wireless networks. Because new sites are added to the World Wide Web nearly every second somewhere in the world, search engines are used widely to seek out sites that match the needs of Web surfers*. Search engines use a variety of ways to categorize information, depending on the engine. Many offer keyword searches and use Boolean operators* to make searches effective. Among the most popular international search engines are Google, Bing, and Yahoo! Baidu, China's most popular search engine, was the world's fourth most-used Web site in 2011. Metasearch sites, such as Dogpile or CNet's search.com and others, combine the resources of multiple search engines to answer a user's query for information.

The World Wide Web has influenced society in major ways. Businesses, individuals, schools, non-profit organizations, even churches, use Web sites to offer information to anyone who wants it. Classes and courses are available via the Internet, and people can use the World Wide Web to keep in touch with family who are away from home, via e-mail or personal Web pages, and meet new friends in countries they have never visited. It has become nearly impossible to have any contact with books, magazines, television, or radio and not be offered a Web address, also known as a Uniform Resource Locator (URL)*, to visit.

Widespread access to the Internet and the World Wide Web has created new issues in the areas of ethics, economics, privacy, and protection of individual rights. In many schools and public libraries, debate

* **Web surfers** people who "surf" (search) the Internet frequently

* **Boolean operators** fundamental logical operations (for example "and" and "or") expressed in a mathematical form

* **Uniform Resource Locator (URL)** a reference to a document or a document container using the Hypertext Transfer Protocol (HTTP); consists of a hostname and path to the document

Mosaic

Mosaic was the first popular graphical World Wide Web browser. It was released on the Internet in early 1993 by the National Center for Supercomputing Applications (NCSA) at the University of Illinois at Urbana-Champaign. Mosaic is distinguished from other early Web browsers by its ease of use and the addition of inline image to Web documents.

Yahoo!

David Filo and Jerry Yang developed the first online navigational guide to the Internet while attending Stanford University. They originally called it *Jerry's Guide to the World Wide Web.* The two students developed a means to bookmark and categorize their favorite Web sites, which eventually became known by the name Yahoo!, an acronym for *Yet Another Hierarchical Officious Oracle.* According to the company's own statistics, in 2011, Yahoo! Web sites were visited by nearly 700 million people times per month. Only Google, Facebook, and YouTube received more unique site visits in 2011.

continues over whether and how to restrict access to certain types of Web sites (such as those exhibiting pornographic content). The ease of sharing and reusing photos, graphics, text, music files, videos, movies, and other recorded media has led to concerns about copyright and protecting the rights of the creators of music, video, photographs, graphic art, and original documents. The cost of providing, maintaining, and updating online resources also has resulted in controversy about free access vs. paid subscriptions. As a medium for information, education, entertainment, and commerce, the World Wide Web is still expanding and improving.

▶ *See also* **Browsers • Hypermedia and Multimedia • Hypertext • Internet • Networks • Search Engines**

Resources

Books

Banks, Michael A., and Orson Scott Card. *On the Way to the Web: The Secret History of the Internet and Its Founders.* Berkeley, CA: Apress, 2008.

Web Sites

"Standards." *World Wide Web Consortium (W3C).* http://www.w3.org (accessed October 17, 2012).

Xerox Corporation

The roots of Xerox Corporation and its history of innovation started growing back in 1938. In October of that year, patent attorney Chester Carlson (1906–1968) invented the first xerographic image. Carlson believed that the world needed an easier and cheaper way to make copies of important documents. Previously, carbon paper, printing presses, or retyping were required to create a document copy.

However, it took nearly ten long years before Carlson could find a company that would develop his invention into a useful product. The Haloid Company, a small photo-paper maker in Rochester, New York, took on the challenge and promise of xerography. In 1949 Haloid introduced its first xerographic machine. Slow and messy, it required several steps to produce a readable copy—but it worked.

Birth of the Office Copier

Not until 1959, twenty-one years after Carlson invented xerography, was the first convenient plain-paper office copier unveiled. By that time, Haloid had changed its name to Haloid Xerox Inc. The Xerox 914 copier—so named because it could copy pages up to nine by fourteen inches—could make copies quickly at the touch of a button. It

Xerox headquarters in Norwalk, Connecticut. © *AP Images/Douglas Healey.*

was a phenomenal success. By 1962, some 10,000 copiers had been shipped. By 1963, Xerox Corporation had dropped the "Haloid" and had grown to a $22.5 million company, up from $2 million just four years earlier.

Xerox Corporation's inventive researchers and engineers went on to develop hundreds of industry-leading hardware and software products after the Xerox 914. By 2000 Xerox had become a $19 billion company selling document management equipment at almost every price and speed, including color and black-and-white digital copiers, network printers, fax machines, multifunction devices, and software. In October 2012, the company's assets stood at just slightly over $22 billion.

That first plain-paper office copier revolutionized the office—not only replacing carbon paper but also changing the way people used documents to communicate. The copier's transformation of business culture was so profound, and Xerox so associated with the process and machinery, that the company's name became colloquially synonymous with the word copy. To protect their tradename, Xerox ran a series of ads in business magazines that tepidly asked people not to refer to a copy as "a Xerox" or all brands of copiers as "Xerox machines."

Xerox's growing body of knowledge about office processes, as well as expertise in engineering, manufacturing, and technology, made Xerox the perfect breeding ground for new ideas about how to make the office—and office workers—operate better.

From Copiers to Computers

In 1970 Xerox gathered a team of world-class researchers to study the way that information was created, transported, and shared. Their mission was to create "the architecture of information." The scientists of the new

Inside the Copier

Xerography, invented by Chester Carlson, began the copying revolution. In xerography, an original image is transferred when light is projected onto an electrically charged surface. The image attracts oppositely charged toner particles, which are then fused into place on the copy paper, reproducing the original image.

The Xerox Alto

One of the world's first personal computers, the Xerox Alto, was born in 1973. The Alto was a prototype workstation, not an actual product that Xerox launched. But its development and technologies helped create the personal computer industry.

* **graphical user interface (GUI)** an interface that allows computers to be operated through pictures (icons) and mouse-clicks, rather than through text and typing

Palo Alto Research Center (PARC) in Palo Alto, California, were encouraged to dream, invent, and discover, as well as to push the outer limits of current technology. At the time, computers were still room-sized devices that only the most expert computer programmers could manage. But the PARC scientists' vision was to create simpler computers that could help people work together even more powerfully than a copier could.

By 1973 pioneering PARC researchers had changed the course of the computer industry and developed the world's first personal computer, known as the Alto. The Alto embodied several PARC innovations, including a graphical user interface (GUI), what-you-see-is-what-you-get (WYSIWYG) editing, overlapping "windows," and the first commercial mouse, so users could point-and-click their way through tasks. All of these features are standard components in Apple Macintosh and Microsoft Windows-based personal computers today.

PARC scientists also recognized a far more powerful role for computers to play. They networked, or connected, Altos via another PARC invention, the Ethernet, to further enhance people's ability to interact. Ethernet ultimately became a global standard for interconnecting computers on local area networks.

PARC also invented the laser printer, which was a natural extension of Xerox's expertise in putting marks onto paper. Laser printers allowed users of the Alto—and users of its successor, the Star, launched commercially in 1981—to simplify the procedure of printing out an exact copy of what they saw on their computer screens.

These, and dozens of other pioneering technologies from PARC, fundamentally changed the office—and the world. Xerox did not fully commercialize its personal computer technologies because at the time, the corporation remained focused on the core business from which it started: copiers. Instead, companies such as Apple Computer, Microsoft, and other Silicon Valley start-ups visited PARC's labs, licensed or replicated the technologies, and applied them to their own products and businesses.

PARC (formerly Xerox PARC) became an independent, wholly owned subsidiary in 2002. Innovation continues through its research centers in the 2010s, and PARC is regarded widely as one of the top corporate research facilities in the world. PARC scientists aggressively create new ways to improve user interfaces, build large scale electronic systems, and create ambient intelligence and ubiquitous computing systems.

 See also **Apple Computer, Inc. • Bell Labs • Intel Corporation • Microsoft Corporation • National Aeronautics and Space Administration (NASA)**

Resources

Books

Ellis, Charles D. *Joe Wilson and the Creation of Xerox.* Hoboken, N.J. John Wiley & Sons, 2006.

Lerner, Joshua. *The Architecture of Innovation: The Economics of Creative Organizations.* Boston: Harvard Business Review Press, 2012.

Owen, David. *Copies in Seconds: How a Lone Inventor and an Unknown Company Created the Biggest Communication Breakthrough since Gutenberg: Chester Carlson and the Birth of Xerox.* New York: Simon & Schuster, 2004.

Glossary

3D printing a manufacturing process in which machines lay down successive layers of materials to create three-dimensional products from digital information. Also known as additive manufacturing.

4G shorthand for fourth generation mobile communication and mobile Internet standards, including LTE and Mobile WiMAX networks.

abacus an ancient counting device that probably originated in Babylon around 2400 BCE.

acuity sharpness or keenness, especially when used to describe vision.

additive manufacturing an additive manufacturing process in which machines lay down successive layers of materials to create three-dimensional products from digital information. Also known as 3D printing.

address bus a collection of electrical signals used to transmit the address of a memory location or input/output port in a computer.

aerodynamics the science and engineering of systems that are capable of flight.

agents systems (software programs and/or computing machines) that can act on behalf of another, or on behalf of a human.

aggregate a numerical summation of multiple individual scores.

ailerons control surfaces on the trailing edges of the wings of an aircraft—used to manage roll control.

ALGOL a language developed by the ALGOL committee for scientific applications—acronym for ALGOrithmic Language.

algorithm a rule or procedure used to solve a mathematical problem—most often described as a sequence of steps.

all-points-addressable mode a technique for organizing graphics devices where all points (pixels) on the screen are individually accessible to a running program.

alpha beta pruning a technique that under certain conditions offers an optimal way to search through data structures called "trees."

alphanumeric a character set which is the union of the set of alphabetic characters and the set of single digit numbers.

ambient pertaining to the surrounding atmosphere or environment.

ambiguity the quality of doubtfulness or uncertainty; often subject to multiple interpretations.

amortized phasing out something in until it is gradually extinguished, like a mortgage loan.

amplitude the size or magnitude of an electrical signal.

analog a quantity (often an electrical signal) that is continuous in time and amplitude.

analogous a relationship of logical similarity between two or more objects.

analytic simulation modeling of systems by using mathematical equations (often differential equations) and programming a computer with them to simulate the behavior of the real system.

Analytical Engine Charles Babbage's vision of a programmable mechanical computer.

animatronics   the animation (movement) of something by the use of electronic motors, drives, and controls.

anthropomorphic   having human form, or generally resembling human appearance.

anti-aliasing   introducing shades of gray or other intermediate shades around an image to make the edge appear to be smoother.

app   short for application or application software, apps are software features designed to perform specific tasks or improve the user interface with Internet-based resources in a mobile operating system. Apps are common to smartphones, tablets, and other Internet-enabled portable devices.

applet   a program component that requires extra support at run time from a browser or run-time environment in order to execute.

approximation   an estimate.

arc tangent   the circular trigonometric function that is the inverse of the tangent function; values range from $-\prod/2$ to $\prod/2$.

artificial intelligence (AI)   a branch of computer science dealing with creating computer hardware and software to mimic the way people think and perform practical tasks.

ASCII   an acronym that stands for American Standard Code for Information Interchange; assigns a unique 8-bit binary number to every letter of the alphabet, the digits (0 to 9), and most keyboard symbols.

assembler   a program that translates human readable assembly language programs to machine readable instructions.

assembly language   the natural language of a central processing unit (CPU); often classed as a low level language.

asynchronous   events that have no systematic relationship to one another in time.

attenuation   the reduction in magnitude (size or amplitude) of a signal that makes a signal weaker.

authentication   the act of ensuring that an object or entity is what it is intended to be.

automata theory   the analytical (mathematical) treatment and study of automated systems.

automaton   an object or being that has a behavior that can be modeled or explained completely by using automata theory.

autonomous   self-governing, or being able to exist independently.

autonomy   the capability of acting in a self-governing manner; being able to exist independently or with some degree of independence.

axioms   statements that are taken to be true, the foundation of a theory.

Bakelite   an insulating material used in synthetic goods, including plastics and resins.

ballistics   the science and engineering of the motion of projectiles of various types, including bullets, bombs, and rockets.

bandwidth   a measure of the frequency component of a signal or the capacity of a communication channel to carry signals.

bar code   a graphical number representation system where alphanumeric characters are represented by vertical black and white lines of varying width.

base-2   a number system in which each place represents a power of 2 larger than the place to its right (binary).

base-8   a number system in which each place represents a power of 8 larger than the place to its right (octal).

base-10   a number system in which each place represents a power of 10 larger than the place to its right (decimal).

base-16 a number system in which each place represents a power of 16 larger than the place to its right (hexadecimal).

batch processing an approach to computer utilization that queues non-interactive programs and runs them one after another.

Bayesian networks structures that describe systems in which there is a degree of uncertainty; used in automated decision making.

Bernoulli numbers the sums of powers of consecutive integers; named after Swiss mathematician Jacques Bernoulli (1654–1705).

binary existing in only two states, such as "on" or "off," "one" or "zero."

binary code a representation of information that permits only two states, such as "on" or "off," "one" or "zero."

binary coded decimal (BCD) an ANSI/ISO standard encoding of the digits 0 to 9 using 4 binary bits; the encoding only uses 10 of the available 16 4-bit combinations.

binary digit a single bit, 1 or 0.

binary number system a number system in which each place represents a power of 2 larger than the place on its right (base-2).

binary system a machine or abstraction that uses binary codes.

binomial theorem a theorem giving the procedure by which a binomial expression may be raised to any power without using successive multiplications.

bit a single binary digit, 1 or 0—a contraction of Binary digIT; the smallest unit for storing data in a computer.

bit mapped display a computer display that uses a table of binary bits in memory to represent the image that is projected onto the screen.

bit maps images comprised of bit descriptions of the image, in black and white or color, such that the colors can be represented by the two values of a binary bit.

bit rate the rate at which binary bits can be processed or transferred per unit time, in a system (often a computer communications system).

bit serial mode a method of transferring binary bits one after another in a sequence or serial stream.

bitstream a serialized collection of bits; usually used in transfer of bits from one system to another.

Boolean algebra a system developed by George Boole that deals with the theorems of undefined symbols and axioms concerning those symbols.

Boolean logic a system, developed by George Boole, which treats abstract objects (such as sets or classes) as algebraic quantities; Boole applied his mathematical system to the study of classical logic.

Boolean operators fundamental logical operations (for example "and" and "or") expressed in a mathematical form.

broadband access a term given to denote high bandwidth services.

browsers programs that permit a user to view and navigate through documents, most often hypertext documents.

bugs errors in program source code.

bus a group of related signals that form an interconnecting pathway between two or more electronic devices.

bus topology a particular arrangement of buses that constitutes a designed set of pathways for information transfer within a computer.

byte a group of eight binary digits; represents a single character of text.

C a programming language developed for the UNIX operating system; it is designed to run on most machines and with most operating systems.

cache a small sample of a larger set of objects, stored in a way that makes them accessible.

calculus a method of dealing mathematically with variables that may be changing continuously with respect to each other.

Callback modems security techniques that collect telephone numbers from authorized users on calls and then dial the users to establish the connections.

capacitates fundamental electrical components used for storing electrical charges.

capacitive touch one of the two primary types of touch screen technology, it detects touches utilizing the conductive electrical properties of human skin. This systems, common on many popular smartphones, allows for user control of the device with very light touches.

capacitor a fundamental electrical component used for storing electrical charge.

carpal tunnel syndrome a repetitive stress injury that can lead to pain, numbness, tingling, and loss of muscle control in the hands and wrists.

cartography map-making.

cathode ray tube (CRT) a glass enclosure that projects images by directing a beam of electrons onto the back of a screen.

cellular automata a collection or array of objects that are programmed identically to interact with one another.

cellular neural networks (CNN) a neural network topology that uses multidimensional array structures comprised of cells that work together in localized groups.

central processing unit (CPU) the part of a computer that performs computations and controls and coordinates other parts of the computer.

certificate a unique electronic document that is used to assist authentication.

chaos theory a branch of mathematics dealing with differential equations having solutions which are very sensitive to initial conditions.

checksum a number that is derived from adding together parts of an electronic message before it is dispatched; it can be used at the receiver to check against message corruption.

chromatic dispersion the natural distortion of pulses of light as they move through an optical network; it results in data corruption.

cipher a code or encryption method.

client a program or computer often managed by a human user, that makes requests to another computer for information.

client/server technology computer systems that are structured using clients (usually human-driven computers) to access information stored (often remotely) on other computers known as servers.

cloud computing the use over a network of remote hardware and software computing resources.

cloud storage a remote network of computing resources accessible over the Internet that hosts user files. Also called a cyberlocker or file hosting service and popular as a location for remote computer back-ups or storing media, cloud storage allows users to access files stored "in the cloud" from other computers, tablets, or smartphones.

coaxial cable a cable with an inner conducting core, a dielectric material and an outer sheath that is designed for high frequency signal transmission.

cognitive pertaining to the concepts of knowing or perceiving.

collocation   the act of placing elements or objects in a specific order.

commodity   raw material or service marketed prior to being used.

compiled   a program that is translated from human-readable code to binary code that a central processing unit (CPU) can understand.

compiled executable code   the binary code that a central processing unit (CPU) can understand; the product of the compilation process.

compilers   programs that translate human-readable high-level computer languages to machine-readable code.

computer-aided design (CAD)   the use of computers to replace traditional drawing instruments and tools for engineering or architectural design.

computer-assisted tomography   the use of computers in assisting with the management of X-ray images.

computer peripheral   a device that is connected to a computer to support its operation; for example, a keyboard or a disk drive unit.

concatenates   the joining together of two elements or objects; for example, words are formed by concatenating letters.

concentric circles   circles that have coincident centers.

conceptualization   a creative process that is directed at envisaging a structure or collection of relationships within components of a complex system.

concurrency control   the management and coordination of several actions that occur simultaneously; for example, several computer programs running at once.

concurrent   pertaining to simultaneous activities, for example simultaneous execution of many computer programs.

configuration files   special disk files containing information that can be used to tell running programs about system settings.

cookie   a small text file that a Web site can place on a computer's hard drive to collect information about a user's browsing activities or to activate an online shopping cart to keep track of purchases.

copyrights   the legal rules and regulations concerning the copying and redistribution of documents.

cord cutting   a term that refers to forging traditional cable and satellite-based television subscription services in favor of online streaming media.

cosine   a trigonometric function of an angle, defined as the ratio of the length of the adjacent side of a right-angled triangle divided by the length of its hypotenuse.

counterfeiting   the act of knowingly producing non-genuine objects, especially in relation to currency.

crawls   severe weather warnings that are broadcast on the bottom of TV screens.

creative commons licensing   a free, easy-to-understand, rights management scheme that allows creators to reserve or waive some of their intellectual property rights in the interest of sharing and using works in public forums such as the Internet.

cross-platform   pertaining to a program that can run on many different computer types (often called hardware platforms).

CRT   the acronym for cathode ray tube, which is a glass enclosure that projects images by directing a beam of electrons onto the back of a screen.

cryptanalysis   the act of attempting to discover the algorithm used to encrypt a message.

cryptanalyst a person or agent who attempts to discover the algorithm used to encrypt a message.

cryptography the science of understanding codes and ciphers and their application.

cryptosystem a system or mechanism that is used to automate the processes of encryption and decryption.

cuneiform in the shape of a wedge.

cybercafe a shop, cafe, or meeting place where users can rent a computer for a short time to access the Internet.

cybernetics a unified approach to understanding the behavior of machines and animals developed by Norbert Wiener (1894–1964).

cycloids pertaining to circles, in either a static way or in a way that involves movement.

dark fiber a fiber optic network that exists but is not actively in service, hence the darkness.

data mining a technique of automatically obtaining information from databases that is normally hidden or not obvious.

data partitioning a technique applied to databases (but not restricted to them) which organizes data objects into related groups.

data reduction technique an approach to simplifying data, e.g. summarization.

data warehousing to implement an informational database used to store shared data.

de facto as is.

de jure strictly according to the law.

debug the act of trying to trace, identify, and then remove errors in program source code.

decimal system a number system in which each place represents a power of 10 larger than the place to its right (base-10).

decision trees classifiers in which a sequence of tests are made to decide the class label to assign to an unknown data item; the sequence of.

deformations mechanical systems where a structure is physically misshapen, e.g., dented.

degrade to reduce quality or performance of a system.

delimiters special symbols that mark the beginnings and/or endings of other groups of symbols (for example to mark out comments in program source code).

demographics the study of the statistical data pertaining to a population.

densities measures of the density of a material; defined as the mass of a sample of material, divided by its volume.

deregulation the lowering of restrictions, rules, or regulations pertaining to an activity or operation (often commercial).

die the silicon chip that is the heart of integrated circuit fabrication; the die is encased in a ceramic or plastic package to make the completed integrated circuit (IC).

dielectric a material that exhibits insulating properties, as opposed to conducting properties.

Difference Engine a mechanical calculator designed by Charles Babbage that automated the production of mathematical tables by using the method of differences.

differential analyzer a computer constructed in the early 1930s by Vannevar Bush at Massachusetts Institute of Technology (MIT); it solved differential equations by mechanical integration.

digital a quantity that can exist only at distinct levels, not having values in between these levels (for example, binary).

digital certificates certificates used in authentication that contain encrypted digital identification information.

digital divide imaginary line separating those who can access digital information from those who cannot.

digital library distributed access to collections of digital information.

digital media receiver any device that connects to a network to locate, download, or stream digital media files from a server so that users can broadcast them to their television. They are also known as media streaming devices or digital media hubs.

digital signature identifier used to authenticate the sender of an electronic message or the signer of an electronic document.

digital subscriber line (DSL) a technology that permits high speed voice and data communications over public telephone networks; it requires the use of a DSL modem.

digital subscriber loop (DSL) the enabling of high-speed digital data transfer over standard telephone cables and systems in conjunction with normal telephone speech data.

digital watermarks special data structures permanently embedded into a program or other file type, which contain information about the author and the program.

digitizes converts analog information into a digital form for processing by a computer.

diode a semiconductor device that forces current flow in a conductor to be in one direction only, also known as a rectifier.

diode tube an obsolete form of diode that was made of metal elements in a sealed and evacuated glass tube.

direction buttons buttons on a program with a graphical user interface that provide

a way of navigating through information or documents.

discrete composed of distinct elements.

disintermediation a change in business practice whereby consumers elect to cut out intermediary agencies and deal directly with a provider or vendor.

distance learning the form of education where the instructor and students are separated by either location or time (or both), usually mediated by some electronic communication mechanism.

distributed denial of service (DDoS) an attack in which large numbers of messages are directed to send network traffic to a target computer, overloading it or its network connection; typically, the attacking computers have been subverted.

distributed systems computer systems comprising many individual computers that are interconnected and act in concert to complete operations.

documentation literature in a human readable form that is referred to in support of using a computer or computer system.

domain a region in which a particular element or object exists or has influence; (math) the inputs to a function or relation.

doping a step used in the production of semiconductor materials where charged particles are embedded into the device so as to tailor its operational characteristics.

dot.com a common term used to describe an Internet-based commercial company or organization.

dragged to have been moved by the application of an external pulling force; quite often occurring in graphical user interfaces when objects are moved with a mouse.

DRAM the acronym for Dynamic Random Access Memory; high density, low cost and low speed memory devices used in most computer systems.

driver a special program that manages the sequential execution of several other programs; a part of an operating system that handles input/output devices.

drop-down menu a menu on a program with a graphical user interface that produces a vertical list of items when activated.

dumb terminal a keyboard and screen connected to a distant computer without any processing capability.

duplex simultaneous two-directional communication over a single communication channel.

dynamic changing; possessing volatility.

dynamic links logical connections between two objects that can be modified if the objects themselves move or change state.

EBCDIC the acronym for Extended Binary Coded Decimal Interchange Code, which assigns a unique 8-bit binary number to every letter of the alphabet, the digits (0-9), and most keyboard symbols.

e-books short for electronic books; books available for downloading onto an e-book reader.

e-reader an electronic device that displays and stores books and other texts.

egress to move out of an object, system, or environment.

electromagnetic a piece of metal that becomes magnetic only when electricity is applied to it; in general, the more electricity applied to metal, the stronger its magnetism.

electromagnetic relays switches that have a high current carrying capacity, which are opened and closed by an electromagnet.

electromagnetic spectrum a range of frequencies over which electromagnetic radiation can be generated, transmitted, and received.

embedded computers computers that do not have human user orientated I/O devices; they are directly contained within other machines.

embedded systems another term for "embedded computers"; computers that do not have human user orientated input/output devices; they are directly contained within other machines.

emoticons symbols or key combinations used in electronic correspondence to convey emotions.

enciphered encrypted or encoded; a mathematical process that disguises the content of messages transmitted.

encryption also known as encoding; a mathematical process that disguises the content of messages transmitted.

end-effector the end piece of a robotic arm that can receive various types of grippers and tools.

end users computer users.

enterprise information system a system of client and server computers that can be used to manage all of the tasks required to manage and run a large organization.

entropy a measure of the state of disorder or randomness in a system.

ephemeris a record showing positions of astronomical objects and artificial satellites in a time-ordered sequence.

ergonomic being of suitable geometry and structure to permit effective or optimal human user interaction with machines.

esoteric relating to a specialized field of endeavor that is characterized by its restricted size.

ether a highly volatile liquid solvent; also, the far regions of outer space.

ethernets a networking technology for mini and microcomputer systems consisting of network interface cards and interconnecting coaxial cables; invented in the 1970s by Xerox corporation.

Euclidean geometry the study of points, lines, angles, polygons, and curves confined to a plane.

expert system a computer system that uses a collection of rules to exhibit behavior which mimics the behavior of a human expert in some area.

fiber optics transmission technology using long, thin strands of glass fiber; internal reflections in the fiber assure that light entering one end is transmitted to the other end with only small losses in intensity; used widely in transmitting digital information.

field searching a strategy in which a search is limited to a particular field; in a search engine, a search may be limited to a particular domain name or date, narrowing the scope of searchable items and helping to eliminate the chance of retrieving irrelevant data.

file transfer protocol (FTP) a communications protocol used to transfer files.

filter queries queries used to select subsets from a data collection, e.g., all documents with a creation date later than 01/01/2013.

firewall a special purpose network computer or software that is used to ensure that no access is permitted to a sub-network unless authenticated and authorized.

firing tables precalculated tables that can give an artillery gunner the correct allowances for wind conditions and distance by dictating the elevation and deflection of a gun.

flashdrive a small, typically portable, solid state drive (SSD) utilizing flash memory for storing or transferring computer data.

floating point operations numerical operations involving real numbers where in achieving a result, the number of digits to the left or right of the decimal point can change.

flowcharts techniques for graphically describing the sequencing and structure of program source code.

fluid dynamics the science and engineering of the motion of gases and liquids.

Freedom of Information Act (FOIA) permits individuals to gain access to records and documents that are in the possession of the government.

freon hydrocarbon based gases used as refrigerants and as pressurants in aerosols.

frequency bands ranges of signal frequencies that are of particular interest in a given application.

frequency modulation a technique whereby a signal is transformed so that it is represented by another signal with a frequency that varies in a way related to the original signal.

full-text indexing a search engine feature in which every word in a document, significant or insignificant, is indexed and retrievable through a search.

fuzzy logic models human reasoning by permitting elements to have partial membership to a set; derived from fuzzy set theory.

gallium arsenide a chemical used in the production of semiconductor devices; chemical symbol GaAs.

gates fundamental building blocks of digital and computer based electric circuits that perform logical operations; for example logical AND, logical OR.

Gaussian classifiers classifiers constructed on the assumption that the feature values of data will follow a Gaussian distribution.

gbps acronym for gigabits per second; a binary data transfer rate that corresponds to a thousand million (billion, or 109) bits per second.

Geographic Information Systems (GIS) computing systems that capture, compare, create, analyze, organize, and display geographical data in a searchable and visually useful ways.

geometric relating to the principles of geometry, a branch of mathematics related to the properties and relationships of points, lines, angles, surfaces, planes, and solids.

germanium a chemical often used as a high performance semiconductor material; chemical symbol Ge.

gestural interface technologies designed to use mathematical algorithms to interpret or respond to human gestures.

GIF animation a technique using Graphic Interchange Format where many images are overlaid on one another and cycled through a sequence to produce an animation.

GIF image the acronym for Graphic Interchange Format where a static image is represented by binary bits in a data file.

gigabit networking the construction and use of a computer network that is capable of transferring information at rates in the gigahertz range.

gigabytes units of measure equivalent to a thousand million (billion, or 109) bytes.

gigahertz (GHz) a unit or measure of frequency, equivalent to a thousand million (billion, or 109) hertz, or cycles per second.

Global Positioning System (GPS) a method of locating a point on the Earth's surface that uses received signals transmitted from satellites to accurately calculate position.

granularity a description of the level of precision that can be achieved in making measurements of a quantity; for example coarse granularity means inexpensive but imprecise measurements.

graphical user interface (GUI) an interface that allows computers to be operated through pictures (icons) and mouse-clicks, rather than through text and typing.

groupware a software technology common in client/server systems whereby many users can access and process data at the same time.

gyros a contraction of gyroscopes; a mechanical device that uses one or more spinning discs which resist changes to their position in space.

half tones black and white dots of certain sizes, which provide a perception of shades of gray.

ham radio a legal (or licensed) amateur radio.

haptic pertaining to the sense of touch.

Harvard Cyclotron a specialized machine (cyclotron) developed in 1948 at Harvard University; it is used to carry out experiments in sub-atomic physics and medicine.

head-mounted displays (HMD) helmets worn by a virtual reality (VR) participant that include speakers and screens for each eye, which display three-dimensional images.

hertz (Hz) a unit of measurement of frequency, equal to one cycle per second; named in honor of German physicist Heinrich Hertz.

heuristic a procedure that serves to guide investigation but that has not been proven.

hexadecimal a number system in which each place represents a power of 16 larger than the place to its right (base-16).

high-bandwidth a communication channel that permits many signals of differing frequencies to be transmitted simultaneously.

high precision/high recall a phenomenon that occurs during a search when all the relevant documents are retrieved with no unwanted ones.

high precision/low recall a phenomenon that occurs when a search yields a small set of hits; although each one may be highly relevant to the search topic, some relevant documents are missed.

high-speed data links digital communications systems that permit digital data to be reliably transferred at high speed.

hoaxes false claims or assertions, sometimes made unlawfully in order to extort money.

holistic looking at the entire system, rather than just its parts.

hydraulic motion being powered by a pressurized liquid (such as water or oil), supplied through tubes or pipes.

hydrologic relating to water.

hyperlinks connections between electronic documents that permit automatic browsing transfer at the point of the link.

Hypertext Markup Language (HTML) an encoding scheme for text data that uses special tags in the text to signify properties to the viewing program (browser) like links to other documents or document parts.

Hypertext Transfer Protocol (HTTP) a simple connectionless communications protocol developed for the electronic transfer (serving) of HTML documents.

I/O the acronym for input/output; used to describe devices that can accept input data to a computer and to other devices that can produce output.

I/O devices devices that can accept "input" data to a computer and to other devices that can produce "output."

icon a small image that is used to signify a program or operation to a user.

illiquid lacking in liquid assets; or something that is not easily transferable into currency.

ImmersaDesks large 4 x 5 foot screens that allow for stereoscopic visualization; the 3-D computer graphics create the illusion of a virtual environment.

ImmersaWalls large-scale, flat screen visualization environments that include passive and active multi-projector displays of 3-D images.

immersive involved in something totally.

in-band pertaining to elements or objects that are within the limits of a certain Local Area Network (LAN).

inference a suggestion or implication of something based on other known related facts and conclusions.

information theory a branch of mathematics and engineering that deals with the encoding, transmission, reception, and decoding of information.

infrared (IR) waves radiation in a band of the electromagnetic spectrum within the infrared range.

infrastructure the foundation or permanent installation necessary for a structure or system to operate.

ingot a formed block of metal (often cast) used to facilitate bulk handling and transportation.

ingress the act of entering a system or object.

init method a special function in an object oriented program that is automatically called to initialize the elements of an object when it is created.

input/output (I/O) used to describe devices that can accept input data to a computer and to other devices that can produce output.

Inquisition the establishment of a religious court (1478–1834) where Christians as well as non-Christians were prosecuted for heresy.

intangible   a concept to which it is difficult to apply any form of analysis; something which is not perceived by the sense of touch.

integrated circuit   a circuit with the transistors, resistors, and other circuit elements etched into the surface of a single chip of semiconducting material, usually silicon.

integrated modem   a modem device that is built into a computer, rather than being attached as a separate peripheral.

intellectual property   the acknowledgement that an individual's creativity and innovation can be owned in the same way as physical property.

interconnectivity   the ability of more than one physical computer to operate with one or more other physical computers; interconnectivity is usually accomplished by means of network wiring, cable, or telephone lines.

interface   a boundary or border between two or more objects or systems; also a point of access.

Internet Protocol (IP)   a method of organizing information transfer between computers; the IP was specifically designed to offer low-level support to Transmission Control Protocol (TCP).

Internet Service Provider (ISP)   a commercial enterprise which offers paying subscribers access to the Internet (usually via modem) for a fee.

interpolation   estimating data values between known points but the values in between are not and are therefore estimated.

intranet   an interconnected network of computers that operates like the Internet, but is restricted in size to a company or organization.

ionosphere   a region of the upper atmosphere (above about 60,000 meters or 196,850 feet) where the air molecules are affected by the sun's radiation and influence electromagnetic wave propagation.

isosceles triangle   a triangle that has two sides of equivalent length (and therefore two angles of the same size).

iterative   a procedure that involves repetitive operations before being completed.

Jacquard's Loom   a weaving loom, developed by Joseph-Marie Jacquard ((1752–1834), controlled by punched cards; identified as one of the earliest examples of programming automation.

Java applets   applets written in the Java programming language and executed with the support of a Java Virtual Machine (JVM) or a Java enabled browser.

joysticks   the main controlling levers of small aircraft; models of these can be connected to computers to facilitate playing interactive games.

JPEG (Joint Photographic Experts Group)   organization that developed a standard for encoding image data in a compressed format to save space.

k-nearest neighbors   a classifier that assigns a class label for an unknown data item by looking at the class labels of the nearest items in the training data.

Kbps   a measure of digital data transfer per unit time—one thousand (kilo, K) bits per second.

keywords   words that are significant in some context or topic (often used in searching).

kilohertz (kHz)   a unit or measure of frequency, equivalent to a thousand (or 103) hertz, or cycles per second.

kinematics   a branch of physics and mechanical engineering that involves the study of moving bodies and particles.

kinetics   a branch of physics or chemistry concerned with the rate of change in chemical or physical systems.

labeled data   a data item whose class assignment is known independent of the classifier being constructed.

lambda calculus important in the development of programming languages, a specialized logic using substitutions that was developed by Alonzo Church (1903–1995).

LEDs the acronym for Light Emitting Diode; a diode that emits light when passing a current and used as an indicating lamp.

lexical analyzer a portion of a compiler that is responsible for checking the program source code produced by a programmer for proper words and symbols.

Library of Congress Classification the scheme by which the Library of Congress organizes classes of books and documents.

light-emitting diode (LED) a discrete electronic component that emits visible light when permitting current to flow in a certain direction; often used as an indicating lamp.

linear pertaining to a type of system that has a relationship between its outputs and its inputs that can be graphed as a straight line.

Linux operating system an open source UNIX operating system that was originally created by Linus Torvalds in the early 1990s.

liquid crystal display (LCD) a type of crystal that changes its level of transparency when subjected to an electric current; used as an output device on a computer.

local area network (LAN) a high-speed computer network that is designed for users who are located near each other.

logarithm the power to which a certain number called the base is to be raised to produce a particular number.

logic a branch of philosophy and mathematics that uses provable rules to apply deductive reasoning.

lossy a nonreversible way of compressing digital images; making images take up less space

by permanently removing parts that cannot be easily seen anyway.

low precision/high recall a phenomenon that occurs during a search when a large set of results are retrieved, including many relevant and irrelevant documents.

lumens a unit of measure of light intensity.

magnetic tape a way of storing programs and data from computers; tapes are generally slow and prone to deterioration over time but are inexpensive.

mainframe large computer used by businesses and government agencies to process massive amounts of data; generally faster and more powerful than desktop computers but usually requiring specialized software.

malicious code program instructions that are intended to carry out malicious or hostile actions; e.g., deleting a user's files.

mammogram an X-ray image of the breast, used to detect signs of possible cancer.

Manhattan Project the U.S. project designed to create the world's first atomic bomb.

mass spectrometers instruments that can identify elemental particles in a sample by examining the frequencies of the particles that comprise the sample.

mass spectrometry the process of identifying the compounds or elemental particles within a substance.

media streaming device a device that enables users to connect to a network or server and view digital media files on their television; also known as a digital media receiver or digital media hub.

megahertz (MHz) a unit or measure of frequency, equivalent to a million (or 10^6) hertz, or cycles per second.

memex a device that can be used to store personal information, notes, and records that permits managed access at high speed; a hypothetical creation of Vannevar Bush.

menu label the text or icon on a menu item in a program with a graphical user interface.

metadata data about data, such as the date and time created.

meteorologists people who have studied the science of weather and weather forecasting.

metropolitan area network (MAN) a high-speed interconnected network of computers spanning entire cities.

microampere a unit of measure of electrical current that is one-millionth (10^{-6}) amperes.

microchip a common term for a semiconductor integrated circuit device.

microcomputer a computer that is small enough to be used and managed by one person alone; often called a personal computer.

microprocessor the principle element in a computer; the component that understands how to carry out operations under the direction of the running program (CPU).

millisecond a time measurement indicating one-thousandth (or 10^{-3}) of a second.

milliwatt a power measurement indicating one-thousandth (or 10^{-3}) of a watt.

minicomputers computers midway in size between a desktop computer and a mainframe computer; most modern desktops are much more powerful than the older minicomputers.

minimax algorithm an approach to developing an optimal solution to a game or contest where two opposing systems are aiming at mutually exclusive goals.

Minitel network used in France that preceded the Internet, connecting most French homes, businesses, cultural organizations, and government offices.

mnemonic a device or process that aids one's memory.

Mobile device management (MDM) software that aids in standardizing settings, managing programs, protecting confidential information, and securing mobile devices.

mobile operating system (MOS) the software that allows smartphones, tablets, other portable devices to run programs and apps.

modalities classifications of the truth of a logical proposition or statement, or characteristics of an object or entity.

modem the contraction of MOdulator DEModulator; a device which converts digital signals into signals suitable for transmission over analog channels, like telephone lines.

modulation a technique whereby signals are translated to analog so that the resultant signal can be more easily transmitted and received by other elements in a communication system.

modules a generic term that is applied to small elements or components that can be used in combination to build an operational system.

molecular modeling a technique that uses high performance computer graphics to represent the structure of chemical compounds.

motherboard the part of the computer that holds vital hardware, such as the processors, memory, expansion slots, and circuitry.

MPEG (Motion Picture Coding Experts Group) an encoding scheme for data files that contain motion pictures—it is lossy in the same way as JPEG (Joint Photographic Experts Group) encoding.

multiplexes   operations in ATM communications whereby data cells are blended into one continuous stream at the transmitter and then separated again at the receiver.

multiplexor   a complex device that acts as a multi-way switch for analog or digital signals.

multitasking   the ability of a computer system to execute more than one program at the same time; also known as multiprogramming.

mylar   a synthetic film, invented by the DuPont corporation, used in photographic printing and production processes, as well as disks and tapes.

nanocomputing   the science and engineering of building mechanical machines at the atomic level.

nanometers   one-thousand-millionth (one billionth, or 10^{-9}) of a meter.

nanosecond   one-thousand-millionth (one billionth, or 10^{-9}) of a second.

nanotechnology   the design and construction of machines at the atomic or molecular level.

narrowband   a general term in communication systems pertaining to a signal that has a small collection of differing frequency components (as opposed to broadband which has many frequency components).

National Computer Security Center (NCSC)   a branch of the National Security Agency responsible for evaluating secure computing systems; the Trusted Computer Systems Evaluation Criteria (TCSEC) were developed by the NCSC.

Network Control Protocol (NCP)   a host-to-host protocol originally developed in the early 1970s to support the Internet, which was then a research project.

network packet switching   the act of routing and transferring packets (or small sections) of a carrier signal that conveys digital information.

neural modeling   the mathematical study and the construction of elements that mimic the behavior of the brain cell (neuron).

neural networks   pattern recognition systems whose structure and operation are loosely inspired by analogy to neurons in the human brain.

Newtonian view   an approach to the study of mechanics that obeys the rules of Newtonian physics, as opposed to relativistic mechanics; named after Sir Isaac Newton (1643–1727).

nonlinear   a system that has relationships between outputs and inputs which cannot be expressed in the form of a straight line.

O-rings   37-foot (11-meter) rubber circles (rings) that seal the joints between the space shuttle's rocket booster segments.

OEM   the acronym for Original Equipment Manufacturer; a manufacturer of computer components.

offline   the mode of operation of a computer that applies when it is completely disconnected from other computers and peripherals (like printers).

Open Systems Interconnections (OSI)   a communications standard developed by the International Organization for Standardization (ISO) to facilitate compatible network systems.

operands   when a computer is executing instructions in a program, the elements on which it performs the instructions are known as the.

operating system   a set of programs which control all the hardware of a computer and provide user and device input/output functions.

optical character recognition   the science and engineering of creating programs that can recognize and interpret printed characters.

optical computing   a proposed computing technology which would operate on particles of light, rather than electric currents.

optophone a system that uses artificial intelligence techniques to convert images of text into audible sound.

orthogonal elements or objects that are perpendicular to one another; in a logical sense this means that changes in one have no effect on the other.

oscillator an electronic component that produces a precise waveform of a fixed known frequency; this can be used as a time base (clock) signal to other devices.

oscilloscopes measuring instruments for electrical circuitry; connected to circuits under test using probes on leads and having small screens that display the signal waveforms.

out-of-band pertaining to elements or objects that are external to the limits of a certain local area network (LAN).

overhead the expense or cost involved in carrying out a particular operation.

packet-switched network a network based on digital communications systems whereby packets of data are dispatched to receivers based on addresses that they contain.

packet-switching an operation used in digital communications systems whereby packets (collections) of data are dispatched to receivers based on addresses contained in the packets.

packets collections of digital data elements that are part of a complete message or signal; packets contain their destination addresses to enable reassembly of the message or signal.

paradigm an example, pattern, or way of thinking.

parallel debugging specialized approaches to locating and correcting errors in computer programs that are to be executed on parallel computing machine architectures.

parallel processing the presence of more than one central processing unit (CPU) in a computer, which enables the true execution of more than one program.

parametric modeling a system using variables or parameters that can be observed to change as the system operates.

parity a method of introducing error checking on binary data by adding a redundant bit and using that to enable consistency checks.

pattern recognition a process used by some artificial-intelligence systems to identify a variety of patterns, including visual patterns, information patterns buried in a noisy signal, and word patterns imbedded in text.

PDF the acronym for Portable Document Format, developed by Adobe Corporation to facilitate the storage and transfer of electronic documents.

peer-to-peer services the ways in which computers on the same logical level can interoperate in a structured network hierarchy.

permutations significant changes or rearrangement.

personal area networking the interconnectivity of personal productivity devices such as computers, mobile telephones, and personal organizers.

personal digital assistants (PDA) small-scale hand-held computers that can be used in place of diaries and appointment books.

phosphor a coating applied to the back of a glass screen on a cathode ray tube (CRT) that emits light when a beam of electrons strikes its surface.

photolithography the process of transferring an image from a film to a metal surface for etching, often used in the production of printed circuit boards.

photonic switching the technology that is centered on routing and managing optical packets of digital data.

photons the smallest fundamental units of electromagnetic radiation in the visible spectrum—light.

photosensitive describes any material that will change its properties in some way if subjected to visible light, such as photographic film.

picoseconds one-millionth of a millionth of a second (one-trillionth, or 10^{12}).

piezoelectric crystal an electronic component that when subjected to a current will produce a waveform signal at a precise rate, which can then be used as a clock signal in a computer.

PIN (personal identification number) a password, usually numeric, used in conjunction with a cryptographic token, smart card, or bank card, to ensure that only an authorized user can activate an account governed by the token or card.

ping sweeps technique that identifies properties belonging to a server computer, by sending it collections of "ping" packets and examining the responses from the server.

piracy the unlawful copying and redistribution of computer software, ignoring the copyright and ownership rights of the publisher.

pixel a single picture element on a video screen; one of the individual dots making up a picture on a video screen or digital image.

pixilation the process of generating animation, frame by frame.

plug-in a term used to describe the way that hardware and software modules can be added to a computer system, if they possess interfaces that have been built to a documented standard.

pneumatic powered by pressurized air, supplied through tubes or pipes.

polarity the positive (+) or negative (–) state of an object, which dictates how it will react to forces such as magnetism or electricity.

polarizer a translucent sheet that permits only plane-polarized light to pass through, blocking all other light.

polygon a many-sided, closed, geometrical figure.

polynomial an expression with more than one term.

polypeptide the product of many amino acid molecules bonded together.

population inversion used in quantum mechanics to describe when the number of atoms at higher energy levels is greater than the number at lower energy levels—a condition needed for photons (light) to be emitted.

port logical input/output points on computers that exist in a network.

port scans operations whereby ports are probed so that information about their status can be collected.

potentiometer an element in an electrical circuit that resists current flow (a resistor) but the value of the resistance can be mechanically adjusted (a variable resistor).

predicate calculus a branch of logic that uses individuals and predicates, or elements and classes, and the existential and universal quantifiers, all and some, to represent statements.

privatized to convert a service traditionally offered by a government or public agency into a service provided by a private corporation or other private entity.

progenitor the direct parent of something or someone.

propositional calculus a branch of logic that uses expressions such as "If … then …" to make statements and deductions.

proprietary a process or technology developed and owned by an individual or company, and not published openly.

proprietary software software created by an individual or company that is sold under a license that dictates use and distribution.

protocol an agreed understanding for the sub-operations that make up a transaction, usually found in the specification of inter-computer communications.

prototype a working model or experimental investigation of proposed systems under development.

proxy server a server, system, or application in a computer network that acts as an intermediary for clients needing to mask a computer's location or identity on the network, get around network access restrictions, or that otherwise cannot access information on other servers directly.

pseudocode a language-neutral, structural description of the algorithms that are to be used in a program.

public key information certain status and identification information that pertains to a particular public key (i.e., a key available for public use in encryption).

public key infrastructure (PKI) the supporting programs and protocols that act together to enable public key encryption/decryption.

punched card a paper card with punched holes which give instructions to a computer in order to encode program instructions and data.

quadtrees data structures resembling trees, which have four branches at every node (rather than two as with a binary tree); used in the construction of complex databases.

quality-of-service (QoS) a set of performance criteria that a system is designed to guarantee and support as a minimum.

quantification to quantify (or measure) something.

quantum-dot cellular automata (QCA) the theory of automata as applied to quantum dot architectures, which are a proposed approach for the development of computers at nano-technology scales.

quantum mechanical something influenced by the set of rules that govern the energy and wave behavior of subatomic particles on the scale of sizes that are comparable to the particles themselves.

queue the ordering of elements or objects such that they are processed in turn; first-in, first-out.

radar the acronym for RAdio Direction And Ranging; a technique developed in the 1930s that uses frequency shifts in reflected radio waves to measure distance and speed of a target.

radio telescopes telescopes used for astronomical observation that operate on collecting electromagnetic radiation in frequency bands above the visible spectrum.

random access memory (RAM) a type of memory device that supports the nonpermanent storage of programs and data; so called because various locations can be accessed in any order (as if at random), rather than in a sequence (like a tape memory device).

raster a line traced out by a beam of electrons as they strike a cathode ray tube (CRT).

raster scan pattern a sequence of raster lines drawn on a cathode ray tube such that an image or text can be made to appear.

read-only memory (ROM) a type of memory device that supports permanent storage of programs.

real-time a system, often computer based, that ensures the rates at which it inputs, processes, and outputs information meet the timing requirements of another system.

recursive operations expressed and implemented in a way that requires them to invoke themselves.

recursive functions functions expressed and implemented in a way that requires them to call themselves.

relational database a collection of records that permits logical and business relationships to be developed between themselves and their contents.

relay contact systems systems constructed to carry out logic functions, implemented in relays (electromechanical switches) rather than semiconductor devices.

resistive touch one of the two primary types of touch screen technology, it detects variously applied pressure as device-controlling touches.

resistors electrical components that slow the flow of current.

retinal scan a scan of the retina of the eye, which contains a unique pattern for each individual, in order to identify (or authenticate) someone.

robotics the scicnce and engineering of building electromechanical machines that aim to serve as replacements for human laborers.

routers network devices that direct packets to the next network device or to the final destination.

routing the operation that involves collecting and forwarding packets of information by way of address.

satellite an object that orbits a planet.

scalar a quantity that has magnitude (size) only; there is no associated direction or bearing.

scalar processor a processor designed for high-speed computation of scalar values.

schematic a diagrammatic representation of a system, showing logical structure without regard to physical constraints.

scripting languages modern high level programming languages that are interpreted rather than compiled; they are usually cross-platform and support rapid application development.

search engine optimization (SEO) takes advantage of the way search engines crawl and index the Internet to increase visibility and prominence of a Web site among search engine results.

Secure Sockets Layer (SSL) a technology that supports encryption, authentication, and other facilities and is built into standard UNIX communication protocols (sockets over TCP/IP).

semantics the study of how words acquire meaning and how those meanings change over time.

semiconductor solid material that possesses electrical conductivity characteristics that are similar to those of metals under certain conditions, but can also exhibit insulating qualities under other conditions.

semiconductor diode laser a diode that emits electromagnetic radiation at wavelengths above about 630 nanometers, creating a laser beam for industrial applications.

sensors devices that can record and transmit data regarding the altitude, flight path, attitude, etc., so that they can enter into the system's calculations.

sequentially operations occurring in order, one after another.

server a computer that does not deal directly with human users, but instead handles requests from other computers for services to be performed.

SGML the acronym for Standard Generalized Markup Language, an international standard for structuring electronic documents.

shadow mask a metal sheet behind the glass screen of a cathode ray tube (CRT) that ensures the correct color phosphor elements are struck by the electron beams.

shareware a software distribution technique, whereby the author shares copies of his programs at no cost, in the expectation that users will later pay a fee of some sort.

Sherman Antitrust Act the act of the U.S. Congress in 1890 that is the foundation for all American anti-monopoly laws.

signaling protocols protocols used in the management of integrated data networks that convey a mix of audio, video, and data packets.

SIGs short for "Special Interest Group," SIGs concentrate their energies on specific categories of computer science, such as programming languages or computer architecture.

silica silicon oxide; found in sand and some forms of rock.

silicon a chemical element with symbol Si; the most abundant element in the Earth's crust and the most commonly used semiconductor material.

silicon chip a common term for a semiconductor integrated circuit device.

Silicon Valley an area in California near San Francisco, which has been the home location of many of the most significant information technology-related companies and universities.

silver halide a photosensitive product that has been used in traditional cameras to record an image.

simplex uni-directional communication over a single communication channel.

simputers simple to use computers that take on the functionality of personal computers, but are mobile and act as personal assistants and information organizers.

sine wave a wave traced by a point on the circumference of a circle when the point starts at height zero (amplitude zero) and goes through one full revolution.

single-chip a computer system that is constructed so that it contains just one integrated circuit device.

slide rule invented by Scotsman John Napier (1550–1617), it permits the mechanical automation of calculations using logarithms.

smart card a credit-card style card that has a microcomputer embedded within it; it carries more information to assist the owner or user.

smart devices devices and appliances that host an embedded computer system that offers greater control and flexibility.

smart matter materials, machines, and systems whose physical properties depend on the computing that is embedded within them.

smartphone an Internet-enabled cellular phone with computing ability that utilizes a mobile operating system and apps.

social informatics a field of study that centers on the social aspects of computing technology.

social media online sites or communities—such as Facebook or Twitter—where users share information, photos, video, music, and other media with other users.

softlifting the act of stealing software, usually for personal use (piracy).

software-defined networks (SDNs) the same as virtual private networks (VPNs), where the subscriber can set up and maintain a communications system using management software, on a public network.

solid-state drive (SSD) a data storage device without moving mechanical parts that utilizes an array of circuit assemblies as memory.

sonar the science and engineering of sound propagation in water.

SONET the acronym for Synchronous Optical NETwork, a published standard for networks based on fiber optic communications technology.

sound card a plug-in card for a computer that contains hardware devices for sound processing, conversion, and generation.

source code the human-readable programs that are compiled or interpreted so that they can be executed by a computing machine.

speech recognition the science and engineering of decoding and interpreting audible speech, usually using a computer system.

spider a computer program that travels the Internet to locate Web documents and FTP resources, then indexes the documents in a database, which are then searched using software the search engine provides.

spreadsheet an accounting or business tool that details numerical data in columns for tabulation purposes.

static without movement; stationary.

stellar pertaining to the stars.

streaming media audio or video that are viewable without delay or completely downloading because they are received over the Internet or other computer network by the user as a constant stream of data packets.

streaming media media such a music, videos, movies, and television shows available over the Internet.

subnet a logical section of a large network that simplifies the management of machine addresses.

supercomputer a very high performance computer, usually comprised of many processors and used for modeling and simulation of complex phenomena, like meteorology.

superconductivity the property of a material to pass an electric current with almost no losses; most metals are superconductive only at temperatures near absolute zero.

swap files files used by an operating system to support a virtual memory system, in which the user appears to have access to more memory than is physically available.

syllogistic statements the essential tenets of western philosophical thought, based on hypotheses and categories.

synchronization the time domain ordering of events; often applied when events repeatedly occur simultaneously.

synchronized events occurring at specific points in time with respect to one another.

synchronous synchronized behavior.

synergistic relating to synergism, which is the phenomenon whereby the action of a group of elements is greater than their individual actions.

syntactic analyzer a part of a compiler that scans program source code ensuring that the code meets essential language rules with regard to structure or organization.

syntax a set of rules that a computing language incorporates regarding structure, punctuation, and formatting.

T1 digital circuitry a type of digital network technology that can handle separate voice and/ or digital communications lines.

tablet (or tablet computer) is an Internet-enabled portable computing device with a touch screen user interface.

tangible of a nature that is real, as opposed to something that is imaginary or abstract.

task partitioning the act of dividing up work to be done so that it can be separated into distinct tasks, processes, or phases.

taxonomy the classification of elements or objects based on their characteristics.

TCP the acronym for Transmission Control Protocol; a fundamental protocol used in the networks that support the Internet (ARPANET).

TCP/IP networks interconnected computer networks that use Transmission Control Protocol/Internet Protocol.

TCP/IP protocol suite Transmission Control Protocol/Internet Protocol; a range of functions that can be used to facilitate applications working on the Internet.

telegraph a communication channel that uses cables to convey encoded low bandwidth electrical signals.

telemedicine the technology that permits remote diagnosis and treatment of patients by a medical practitioner; usually interactive bi-directional audio and video signals.

telemetry the science of taking measurements of something and transmitting the data to a distant receiver.

teleoperation any operation that can be carried out remotely by a communications system that enables interactive audio and video signals.

teletype a machine that sends and receives telephonic signals.

terabyte one million million (one trillion, or 1012) bytes.

thermal ignition the combustion of a substance caused by heating it to the point that its particles have enough energy to commence burning without an externally applied flame.

thermodynamic relating to heat energy.

three-body problem an intractable problem in mechanics that involves the attempts to predict the behavior of three bodies under gravitational effects.

thumbnail an image which is a scaled down copy of a much larger image; used to assist in the management of a large catalog of images.

time lapse mode to show a sequence of events occurring at a higher than natural speed so it looks like it is happening rapidly rather than in real time.

title bar the top horizontal border of a rectangular region owned by a program running in a graphical user interface (GUI); it usually contains the program name and can be used to move the region around.

tomography the process of capturing and analyzing X-ray images.

topographic pertaining to the features of a terrain or surface.

topology a method of describing the structure of a system that emphasizes its logical nature rather than its physical characteristics.

touch screen an interface that allows users to control the computing device by touching its screen.

trademark rights a trademark is a name, symbol, or phrase that identifies a trading organization and is owned by that organization.

trafficking transporting and selling; especially with regard to illegal merchandise.

training data data used in the creation of a classifier.

transaction processing operations between client and server computers that are made up of many small exchanges that must all be completed for the transaction to proceed.

transducers devices that sense a physical quantity, such as temperature or pressure, and convert that measurement into an electrical signal.

transistor a contraction of TRANSfer resISTOR; a semiconductor device, invented by John Bardeen, Walter Brattain, and William

Shockley, which has three terminals; can be used for switching and amplifying electrical signals.

translational bridges special network devices that convert low-level protocols from one type to another.

Transmission Control Protocol (TCP) a stream-orientated protocol that uses Internet Protocol (IP); it is responsible for splitting data into packets, transferring it, and reassembling it at the receiver.

transmutation the act of converting one thing into another.

trigonometry a branch of mathematics founded upon the geometry of triangles.

triodes nearly obsolete electronic devices constructed of sealed glass tubes containing metal elements in a vacuum; triodes were used to control electrical signals.

Trojan horse potentially destructive computer program that masquerades as something benign; named after the wooden horse employed by the Acheans to conquer Troy.

tunneling a way of handling different communication protocols, by taking packets of a foreign protocol and changing them so that they.

Turing machine a proposed type of computing machine that takes inputs off paper tape and then moves through a sequence of states under the control of an algorithm; identified by Alan Turing (1912–1954).

twisted pair an inexpensive, medium bandwidth communication channel commonly used in local area networks.

ubiquitous to be commonly available everywhere.

ultrasonic the transmission and reception of sound waves that are at frequencies higher than those audible to humans.

Uniform Resource Locator (URL) a reference to a document or a document container using the Hypertext Transfer Protocol (HTTP); consists of a hostname and path to the document.

Universal Product Code (UPC) the first barcode standard developed in 1973 and adopted widely since.

UNIX operating system that was originally developed at Bell Laboratories in the early 1970s.

uplinks connections from a client machine to a large network; frequently when information is being sent to a communications satellite.

vacuum tube an electronic device constructed of a sealed glass tube containing metal elements in a vacuum; used to control electrical signals.

valence a measure of the reactive nature of a chemical element or compound in relation to hydrogen.

variable a symbol, such as a string of letters, which may assume any one of a set of values known as the domain.

vector graphics graphics output systems whereby pairs of coordinates are passed to the graphics controller, which are interpreted as end points of vectors to be drawn on the screen.

vector processing an approach to computing machine architecture that involves the manipulation of vectors (sequences of numbers) in single steps, rather than one number at a time.

vector supercomputer a highly optimized computing machine that provides high performance using a vector processing architecture.

velocities vector quantities that have a magnitude or speed and a direction.

Venn diagrams diagrams used to demonstrate the relationships between sets of objects, named after John Venn, a British logician.

venture capitalists   persons or agencies that speculate by providing financial resources to enable product development, in the expectation of larger returns with product maturity.

video capture cards   plug-in cards for a computer that accepts video input from devices like televisions and video cameras, allowing the user to record video data onto the computer.

video compression algorithms   special algorithms applied to remove certain unnecessary parts of video images in an attempt to reduce their storage size.

virtual channel connection   an abstraction of a physical connection between two or more elements (or computers); the complex details of the physical connection are hidden.

virtual circuit   like a virtual channel connection, a virtual circuit appears to be a direct path between two elements, but is actually a managed collection of physical connections.

Virtual Private Networks (VPNs)   a commercial approach to network management where privately owned voice and data networks are set up on public network infrastructure.

virtual reality (VR)   the use of elaborate input/output devices to create the illusion that the user is in a different environment.

virtualization   as if it were real; making something seem real, e.g., a virtual environment.

visible speech   a set of symbols, comprising an alphabet, that "spell" sounds instead of words.

visualization   a technique whereby complex systems are portrayed in a meaningful way using sophisticated computer graphics systems; e.g., chemical molecules.

voice over Internet protocol (VoIP)   communication technology that delivers telephone calls, video calls, and voice communications via Internet Protocol.

volatile   subject to rapid change; describes the character of data when current no longer flows to a device (that is, electrical power is switched off).

waveform   an abstraction used in the physical sciences to model energy transmission in the form of longitudinal or transverse waves.

Web surfers   people who "surf" (search) the Internet frequently.

wide area network (WAN)   an interconnected network of computers that spans upward from several buildings to whole cities or entire countries and across countries.

wireless lavaliere microphones   small microphones worn around the speakers' necks, which attach to their shirts.

wireless local area network (WLAN)   an interconnected network of computers that uses radio and/or infrared communication channels, rather than cables.

workstations   computers (usually within a network) that interact directly with human users (much the same as "client computers").

xerography   a printing process that uses electrostatic elements derived from a photographic image to deposit the ink.

XML   the acronym for eXtensible Markup Language; a method of applying structure to data so that documents can be represented.

Directory of Computer Sciences Organizations

A

Apple, Inc.
1 Infinite Loop
Cupertino, CA, 95014
USA
Telephone: (408) 996-1010
Email: media.help@apple.com
Web site: www.apple.com

Argonne National Laboratory:
Mathematics and Computer
Science Division
9700 South Cass Avenue,
Building 240
Argonne, IL, 60439-4844
USA
Telephone: (630) 252-8808
Web site: http://www.mcs.anl.gov

Association for the Advancement
of Artificial Intelligence
2275 East Bayshore Road, Suite 160
Palo Alto, CA, 94303
USA
Telephone: (650) 328-3123
Fax: (650) 321-4457
Web site: http://www.aaai.org

Association for Computer
Machinery
2 Penn Plaza, Suite 701
New York, NY, 10121-0701
USA
Telephone: (800) 342-6626
Email: acmhelp@acm.org
Web site: http://www.acm.org

Association for Information
Systems
PO Box 2712
Atlanta, GA, 30301-2712
USA
Telephone: (404) 413-7445
Email: onestop@aisnet.org
Web site: https://ais.site-ym.com

B

Bell Laboratories
600-700 Mountain Avenue
Murray Hill, NJ, 07974
USA
Telephone: (908) 508-8080
Email: execoffice@alcatel-lucent.com
Web site: http://www.alcatel-lucent.
com/belllabs

Bletchley Park
The Mansion, Bletchley Park
Milton Keynes, MK3 6EB
UK
Telephone: +44 (0) 1908 640404
Fax: +44 (0) 1908 274381
Email: info@bletchleypark.org.uk
Web site: http://www.bletchleypark.
org.uk

C

Cisco Systems, Inc.
170 West Tasman Drive
San Jose, CA, 95134
USA
Telephone: (408) 526 4000
Web site: www.cisco.com

Computer History Museum
1401 North Shoreline Boulevard
Mountain View, CA, 94043
USA
Telephone: (650) 810-1010
Fax: (650) 810-1055
Web site: http://www.computerhistory.
org

Computing and Information
Technology Interactive Digital
Educational Library (CITADEL)
Web site: http://citidel.villanova.edu

Cray, Inc.
901 Fifth Avenue, Suite 1000
Seattle, WA, 98164
USA
Telephone: (206) 701-2000
Fax: (206) 701-2500
Email: crayinfo@cray.com
Web site: www.cray.com

D

Defense Advanced Research
Projects Agency
675 North Randolph Street
Arlington, VA, 22203-2114
USA
Telephone: (703) 526-6630
Email: outreach@darpa.mil
Web site: http://www.darpa.mil

E

Electronic Frontier Foundation
454 Shotwell Street
San Francisco, CA, 9411-1914
USA
Telephone: (415) 436-9333
Fax: (415) 436-9993
Email: info@eff.org
Web site: https://www.eff.org

G

GE Global Research
1 Research Circle
Niskayuna, NY, 12309
USA
Telephone: (518) 387-7914
Web site: http://gc.geglobalresearch.
com

Google Developers Academy
Web site: https://developers.google.
com/academy/

Google, Inc.
1600 Amphitheatre Parkway
Mountain View, CA, 94043
USA

Telephone: (650) 253-0000
Fax: (650) 253-0001
Web site: www.google.com/about/
company

H

Hewlett-Packard Co.
3000 Hanover St.
Palo Alto, CA, 94304
USA
Telephone: (650) 857-1501
Fax: (650) 857-5518
Web site: www.hp.com

**Hon Hai Precision Industry Co.,
Ltd. (Foxconn)**
105 S. Puente Street
Brea, CA, 92821
USA
Telephone: (714) 626-6900
Fax: (714) 626-6901
Email: foxconn-service@foxconn.
com
Web site: www.foxconnchannel.com

I

**Institute of Electrical and
Electronics Engineers (IEEE)
Computer Society**
2001 L Street NW, Suite 700
Washington, DC, 20036-4928
USA
Telephone: (202) 371-0101
Fax: (202) 728-9614
Email: help@computer.org
Web site: http://www.computer.org

Intel Corp.
2200 Mission College Boulevard
Santa Clara, CA, 95952
USA
Telephone: (408) 765-8080
Web site: www.intel.com

**International Business Machines
Corp.**
1 New Orchard Road
Armonk, NY, 10504
USA
Telephone: (800) 426-4968
Web site: www.ibm.com

**International Standards
Organization**
1, ch. de la Voie-Creuse, CP 56
Geneva, CH-1211 Geneva 20
Switzerland
Telephone: +41 22 749 01 11
Email: central@iso.org
Web site: http://www.iso.org

Internet Society
1775 Wiehle Avenue, Suite 201
Reston, VA, 20190-5108
USA
Telephone: (703) 439-2120
Fax: (703) 326-9881
Email: isoc@isoc.org
Web site: https://www.internetsociety.
org

L

Los Alamos National Laboratory
PO Box 1663
Los Alamos, NM, 87545
USA
Telephone: (505) 667-7000
Email: community@lanl.gov
Web site: http://www.lanl.gov

M

**Massachusetts Institute of
Technology (MIT) Computer
Science and Artificial Intelligence
Laboratory (CSAIL)**
The Strata Center, Building 32,
32 Vassar Street
Cambridge, MA, 02139
USA
Telephone: (617) 253-5851
Fax: (617) 258-8682
Web site: http://www.csail.mit.edu

Microsoft Corp.
1 Microsoft Way
Redmond, WA, 98052
USA
Telephone: (425) 882-8080
Web site: www.microsoft.com

Microsoft Research (MSR)
1 Microsoft Way
Redmond, WA, 98052
USA

Telephone: (800) 642-7676
Web site: http://research.microsoft.
com

N

**NASA Advanced Supercomputing
(NAS) Division**
Ames Research Center
Moffett Field, CA, 94035
USA
Telephone: (650) 604-4377
Email: contact-nas@nas.nasa.gov
Web site: http://www.nas.nasa.gov

**National Center for
Supercomputing Applications**
1205 West Clark Street, Room 1008
Urbana, IL, 61801
USA
Telephone: (217) 244-0710
Email: help@ncsa.illinois.edu
Web site: http://ncsa.illinois.edu

**The National Museum of
Computing**
Block H, Bletchley Park
Milton Keynes, MK3 6EB
UK
Telephone: +44 (0)1908 374708
Email: lin.jones@tnmoc.org
Web site: http://www.tnmoc.org

O

**Oak Ridge Leadership Computing
Facility**
PO Box 2008
Oak Ridge, TN, 37831-6161
USA
Telephone: (865) 241-6536
Fax: (865) 241-2850
Email: help@olcf.ornl.gov
Web site: http://www.olcf.ornl.gov

Oracle Corp.
500 Oracle Parkway
Redwood Shores, CA, 94065
USA
Telephone: (650) 506-7000
Web site: www.oracle.com

P

Palo Alto Research Center (PARC)
3333 Coyote Hill Road
Palo Alto, CA, 94304
USA
Telephone: (650) 812-4000
Web site: www.parc.com

S

Samsung Electronics Co., Ltd.
85 Challenger Road
Ridgefield Park, NJ, 07660
USA
Telephone: (800) 726-7864
Fax: (864) 752-1632
Web site: www.samsung.com

SAP
3999 West Chester Pike
Newton Square, PA, 19073
USA
Telephone: (610) 661-1000
Web site: www.sap.com

SRI International
333 Ravenswood Ave.
Menlo Park, CA, 94025
USA
Telephone: (650) 859-2000
Web site: www.sri.com

T

Texas Instruments, Inc.
12500 TI Boulevard
Dallas, TX, 75243
USA

Telephone: (972) 995-2011
Web site: www.ti.com

Thomas J. Watson Research Center
1101 Kitchawan Road
Yorktown Heights, NY, 10598
USA
Telephone: (914) 945-3000
Web site: http://www.research.ibm.com/labs/watson

W

World Wide Web Consortium (W3C)
32 Vassar Street, Room 32-G515
Cambridge, MA, 02139
USA
Telephone: (617) 253-2613
Web site: http://www.w3.org

Cumulative Index

Page numbers referring to illustrations are in *italic* type. Volume numbers are included.
Bold page numbers refer to the main entry on the subject.

A

A. M. Turing Award, 1:24, 25, 248, 251

AALs (ATM adaptation layers), 2:14–15, 4:20, 22–23

Abacuses, 1:**1–2**, *2*, 49–50

ABR (available bit rate) service, 2:14

Abu Ghraib prison, 4:86

Acceptor impurities, 1:243, 244

Access motion time, 2:242

Accessibility technology. *See* Assistive computer technology for persons with disabilities

Accounting software, 3:**1–4**, *2*, 5

Accounts payable software, 3:1

Accounts receivable software, 3:1–2

ACM. *See* Association for Computing Machinery (ACM)

Acrobat Reader, 3:130

Activation of software, 3:225

Active matrix liquid crystal displays, 2:82–84

ADA (Americans with Disabilities Act), 4:13–14, 18

Ada computer language, 1:153, 2:198–199

Adams, Michael, 3:45

Adaptive technology. *See* Assistive computer technology for persons with disabilities

Adding machines, 1:2, 3

Additive sound synthesis, 3:171

Address buses, 2:10

Addressing protocols, 2:47, 150
    See also Internet Protocol (IP); TCP/IP (Transmission Control Protocol/Internet Protocol)

Adleman, Leonard, 1:221, 4:58

Administrative factors, scaling, 2:215

Adobe Systems
    Flash plug-in, 1:15, 2:237
    founding, 3:244
    PDF file format, 2:135, 3:130, 4:102

    PhotoShop software, 3:22, 4:232
    Postscript page description language, 3:82, 85, 243, 244

ADS-B (automatic dependent surveillance-broadcast), 3:11

ADSLs (asymmetric digital subscriber lines), 2:59, 4:29

Advance phase, hacking, 3:122

Advanced Encryption Standard algorithms, 4:57

Advanced mobile phone system (AMPS), 2:39–40

Advanced Networks and Services (ANS), 4:175

Advanced Research Projects Agency Network. *See* ARPANET

Advanced Video Coding (AVC), 2:121

Adventure video games, 1:15

Advertising
    cookies and, 4:46
    data mining and, 4:65–66
    e-commerce, 1:70, 71
    fast-forwarding through commercials, 2:262
    free e-mail providers, 1:73, 74–75
    journalism Web sites, 4:202
    search engines, 4:243

AEA (Aerial Experiment Association), 2:24

AECL (Atomic Energy of Canada Limited), 4:119

Aerial Experiment Association (AEA), 2:24

AFCS (Automated Facer Cancelor System), 1:*197*

AFNOR (Association Francais de Normalization), 1:120

Africa
    abacuses, 1:1
    digital divide, 4:162

Agents, 1:136–137, 4:**1–3**, 12, 156

Agents on the Web (online column), 4:3

Agreement on Trade Related Aspects of Intellectual Property Rights (TRIPS), 4:228–229

Agriculture, 3:*4*, **4–8**

AI. *See* Artificial intelligence (AI)

AIEE (American Institute of Electrical Engineers), 1:122

Aiken, Howard, 1:54, 62, 66, 268, 2:283, 3:253

AIM (AOL Instant Messenger), 4:169

Aircrack network security program, 3:214

Aircraft flight control, 3:*8*, **8–12**

Aircraft navigation systems, 3:173–175, 176–177

Aircraft traffic management, 3:*12*, **12–15**

Airline reservation systems (ARSs), 1:33, 3:*16*, **16–19**

AirPlay mirroring, 1:19

AirPort technology, 1:144

AITP (Association for Information Technology Professionals), 4:118, 119

Akers, John, 1:110

Al Jazeera network, 3:221

al-Khowarizmi, Mohammed, 2:4

Alcatel-Lucent, 1:34

Alcatel-Lucent Bell Labs, 1:*32*, 2:*226*

Alcom, Al, 1:79

Aldus Publishing, 3:82, 85, 242

Algol-60 Report, 2:**1–3**

Algol programming language, 2:1–3, 194–195, 3:187, 188

Algorithms, 2:*4*, **4–6**
    Algol programming language, 2:1–2
    encryption, 4:55–56, 57
    music composition, 3:170
    parallel processing, 2:173–174, 175
    programming, 2:201, 202
    Turing Machine, 1:251

Alife. *See* Artificial life

Allen, George, 4:234

Allen, Paul, 1:84, 169, 172, 4:112

Alliance for Telecommunications Industry Solutions (ATIS), 1:120

Alpha beta pruning, 3:44

Altair computers, 1:84, 169, 4:112

Asynchronous transfer mode (ATM), 4:**19–23**, *20, 22t*
  See also ATM transmission
Atanasoff-Berry Computer (ABC), 1:55–56, 63, 66
Atanasoff, John V., 1:50, 55–56, 62–63, 66, 2:90–91
Atari, Inc.
  early video games, 1:82, 2:95–96
  founding, 1:79, 4:154
  Jobs, Steve employment, 1:142
  video game development, 1:15
ATIS (Alliance for Telecommunications Industry Solutions), 1:120
Atlantis (space shuttle), 3:229
ATM adaptation layers (AALs), 2:14–15, 4:20, 22–23
ATM Forum, 2:14
ATM layers, 4:20, 22
ATM machines (automated teller machines), 2:253, 3:*29*, **29–32**
ATM transmission, 1:194–195, 2:12, **13–15**, 4:173
Atomic bomb development. *See* Manhattan Project
Atomic Energy of Canada Limited (AECL), 4:119
AT&T
  Bell Labs, 1:31–32, 33–34
  frequency division multiplexing, 3:41
  software-defined networks, 2:270
  as top-tier backbone, 4:176
AT&T Labs, 1:33–34
Attenuation, fiber optics, 2:93
Auction sites, 4:108
  See also eBay
AUDEO voice synthesizer, 3:*234*
Audio books, 4:97
Audio files, 2:121, 3:113–114
Audio oscillators, 3:126
Audio synthesis. *See* Music, computer
Audiometer invention, 2:24
Augment interactive multimedia system, 1:105
Authentication, 4:**24–26**
  digital signatures, 4:86–89, *87, 88*
  distributed, 1:222
  e-banking, 4:93
  e-commerce, 4:99
  e-journals, 4:101, 102
  FTP, 4:133
  with HTTPS, 1:67

password protection, 1:220
security software processes, 1:219, 2:221
tokens, 2:217–218, 4:25, 107
Authorization, 1:219, 2:221
Auto-pilots, 3:9–11
Auto-Tune audio processor, 2:144
AutoCAD, 3:22
AutoDesk 3D Studio Viz, 3:22
AutoDesk Inc., 3:22
AutoDesSys Inc., 3:22
Automata (short story), 4:126–127
Automata theory, 1:32
Automated Facer Cancelor System (AFCS), 1:*197*
Automated teller machines (ATMs), 2:253, 3:*29*, 29–32
Automatic data processing, 2:85
  See also Data processing; Document processing
Automatic dependent surveillance-broadcast (ADS-B), 3:11
Automation, 3:*194*, 194–197
Automatons, 1:212–213, 4:126–127, 143, 144
  See also Robotics
Automobile industry
  driverless vehicles projects, 4:44
  onboard navigation systems, 3:176
  robotics use, 1:213, 214, 3:62–63
Autonomous Systems (ASs), 4:173–174
Autonomous vehicles, 4:44
Available bit rate (ABR) service, 2:14
Avatar (film), 4:8
AVC (Advanced Video Coding), 2:121
Aviation simulation. *See* Flight simulation
Aztec abacuses, 1:1

B

Babbage, Charles, 1:*29*, **29–31**
  analytical engines, 1:6–7, 20, 29–30, 50, 181, 182, 184, 3:191
  funding sources, 1:95–96
  King, Ada Byron collaboration, 1:30, 96, 151
  music applications, 1:184, 2:143
  printer concept, 2:191
  Royal Astronomical Society medal, 3:26–27
  Zuse, Konrad connection, 2:283
Baby Bells, 1:33

Backbone, Internet, 4:172–176, 186
Backgrounds, animation, 1:9, 10
Backlighting, LCDs, 2:83–84
Backpropagation, 3:180–181
BackTrack network security program, 3:214
Backup devices
  cloud storage, 2:113, 244
  magnetic disks, 2:241–243
  tape drives, 1:158, 2:113, 241
Backus, John, 2:2, 157, 193–194, 195
Backus-Naur form (BNF), 2:2
Bacteria research, 3:34–35
Bacteriorhodopsin, 3:166
Baer, Ralph, 1:79
Ballard, Robert, 3:136
Ballistics charts. *See* Artillery firing charts
Ballmer, Steve, 1:85, 170, 172, 2:*238*
Bandwidth, 1:155, 156, 2:92, 93–94, 4:**27–30**, *28*
  See also Data rates
Bandwidth regulation and restriction, 2:**17–20**
Banking, online. *See* E-banking
Bar codes, 2:167, 203–204, 207, 3:206
Baran, Paul, 4:184
Barbera, Joseph, 1:13
Bardeen, John, 2:**20–22**
  Bell Labs involvement, 1:34, 2:20
  superconductivity research, 1:128
  transistor invention, 1:66, 88, 125, 126, 241, 2:20
Barnes & Noble Nook e-reader, 4:95–96
Bartik, Jean Jennings, 1:66
Base-2 number system, 1:34
  See also Binary number system
Base-8 number system, 1:50, 91
Base-10 number system, 1:34, 35, 36, 50
Base-16 number system, 1:35, 36
Base stations, cellular networks, 3:40–41
Base terminals, transistors, 1:126, 245
Base+offset addressing, 2:*263*, 264, 265, *265,* 266
Basic Input Output System (BIOS), 1:161
BASIC programming language
  Algol origins, 2:2
  Gates, Bill contributions, 1:84, 169, 4:112

Canon, 4:75, 229

Canonic And-Or implementation, 2:77

CANs (controller area networks), 3:6

Capacitive touch screens, 2:185, 255

Capacitors, 1:160

Capek, Karel, 1:216, 3:24–25

CAPP (computer-aided process planning), 3:63–64

Carbon nanotubes, 3:49

Card readers
  ATMs, 3:30
  punched cards, 1:55, 58, 2:114

Card, Stuart, 4:221

Careers
  computer professionals, 3:54–57
  distance learning, 3:91
  multimedia development, 2:106
  system analysts, 2:248
  systems designers, 2:251

Carlson, Chester, 1:276, 278

Carnegie Institute of Technology, 3:79

Carnegie Mellon University, 3:90, 4:81, 185

Carpal tunnel syndrome, 1:66, 149–150

Carter, Thomas ("Tom"), 2:38–39

Case-based design tools, architecture, 3:22

Cash, digital, 1:69, 4:107

CAT scans, 3:65–67, 134

Catalog servers, 2:227
  See also Servers

Cataloging, electronic, 3:152

Catastrophe insurance market, 4:108–109

Catastrophe Risk Exchange (CATEX), 4:109

Cathode ray tube (CRT) displays, 1:255, 2:78–81, 254–255

Cathodes, in vacuum tubes, 1:253, 255

CATV (Community Antenna Television) systems, 1:239

Cave Automated Virtual Environments (CAVEs), 1:256, 257–258

The Caves of Steel (Asimov), 3:25, 4:127

CB radio, 3:118

CBR (constant bit rate) service, 2:14

CC (Creative Commons) licensing, 4:51–52

CCDs (charge-coupled devices), 4:231

CCTV (closed circuit television) systems, 4:141

CD drives, 3:131

CD-R (compact disk-recordable) technology, 2:244

CD-ROM (compact disk-read only memory), 1:171, 2:243–244

CD-RW (compact disk-rewritable) technology, 2:244

CDC. *See* Control Data Corporation (CDC); U.S. Centers for Disease Control and Prevention (CDC)

CDC 160/160-A minicomputers, 1:175

CDC 6600 supercomputer, 3:68

CDC 7600 supercomputer, 3:68

CDMA (Code Division Multiple Access) networks, 1:119, 3:41, 42

CDMA2000/WCDMA technologies, 3:41, 4:209

CDPD (cellular digital packet data) service, 2:281

CDS2000F Enterprise Server, 4:5

CDV (cell delay variation), 2:15

Cedeno, Judy, 4:115

Cel animation, 1:9–10

Cell Delay Variation (CDV), 2:15

Cell header generation/extraction, 4:22

Cell Loss Priority (CLP), 4:20

Cell multiplex and demultiplex function, 4:22

Cell phone towers, 2:*38*

Cell phones, 3:*40*, **40–42**
  authentication functions, 4:26
  e-mail capabilities, 4:168
  encryption needs, 4:58
  history, 2:38–41, 3:40–42
  phreaker hackers, 4:148
  social media access, 3:216, 217
  telephone system interactions, 3:246–247
  touch screens, 2:*254*

Cells (data packets), 4:19, 20

Cells, spreadsheets, 3:236–238, *237*

Cells, virtual circuits, 2:13–14

Cellular automata, 4:11, 13

Cellular digital packet data (CDPD) service, 2:281

Cellular networks
  base stations, 3:40–41
  generations of, 1:240
  increasing data transmission capabilities, 2:59
  overview, 1:238
  varying standards, 1:119

Cellular neural networks (CNNs), 4:217

Cellular technology, 2:**37–42,** *38*

Censorship: national, international, 4:**35–37,** *36*
  Arab Spring Internet blockage, 3:219–220
  Internet control and, 4:178–179
  social media protests, 3:222

Census Bureau, 1:**39–42,** *40,* 96, 100, 101, 107, 4:236

Centaur Records, 1:185

Center for Democracy and Technology, 4:37

CENTRal EXchange (CENTREX) service, 2:270

Central processing units (CPUs), 2:**42–45,** *43*
  assembly language and architecture, 2:7–9
  cache memory, 2:35–37, *36*
  mainframes, 1:155, 156, 157
  security measures, 2:217
  supercomputers, 1:232, 233
  vector processing, 1:233–234, 3:68
  See also Microprocessors; Parallel processing

Centronics connectors, 2:224

Century Optics, 4:74

CenturyLink, 4:176

Cerf, Vinton, 1:25, 4:260

CERN (European Council for Nuclear Research), 3:193, 4:32, 111

CERT (Computer Emergency Response Team), 4:87–88, 185

Certificate Authority (CA), 1:67–68, 2:270, 4:25, 99

Challenge-response password systems, 1:222

Challenger (space shuttle), 3:228, 4:125

Character-based interfaces, 3:249

Character codes. *See* Codes

Charge-coupled devices (CCDs), 4:231

Chat servers, 2:227
  See also Servers

Check out (e-commerce), 1:68

Checks, digital, 4:109

Checksums, 2:151

Chemistry, 4:**37–41,** *38*

Chemometrics, 4:40

Chen, Steve, 3:69

Chess, computer, 1:83

Database servers, 2:227
See also Servers
The Day the Earth Stood Still (film), 4:128
DB-25 connectors, 2:224
DDL (Data Definition Language), 2:238
DDoS (distributed denial of service), 1:224, 2:118, 3:213, 4:180–181
De facto standards, 1:119
De Forest, Lee, 1:86, 253
De jure standards, 1:119
De Morgan, Augustus, 1:151
Deafness, assistive technology, 4:16–17, 18
"Death Race" (video game), 1:81
Debit cards, 3:31
Debugging
    origin of term, 1:60, 101, 255
    project management, 3:204–205
DEC (Digital Equipment Corporation), 1:15, 44, 176
Decibel (unit), 2:24
Decideability problem, 1:251
Decimal number system. *See* Base-10 number system
Decision support systems (DSSs), 3:**79–81**
    agriculture needs, 3:5–6
    geographic information systems and, 3:115, 116
    overview, 2:109
    in programming, 2:201
    systems design, 2:250–251
Decision trees, 2:178, 4:68
Decrypted values, 1:67
Dede, Chris, 1:257–258
Deep Blue chess competition, 1:83, 111, 3:44–45
Deep Fritz chess program, 3:45
Defense Advanced Research Projects Agency. *See* DARPA (Defense Advanced Research Projects Agency)
Defense Meteorological Satellite Program (DMSP) Operational Linescan System, 3:*210*
Definiteness, in algorithms, 2:5
Defragmentation tools, 3:129
Delagi, Greg, 2:*262*
Delay-line storage, 1:58
Dell laptops, 2:*104*
DeMarco, Tom, 2:251

Demodulation of signals, 2:57–58
DENDRAL, 3:102–103, 144
Denial of service cybersecurity attacks, 1:224, 2:118, 3:213, 4:180–181
Denning, Peter J., 4:145
Derivatives, 1:4
DES (Data Encryption Standard), 4:57
Desargues, Girard, 1:207
Descartes, René, 1:207–208
Descendants, in object-oriented programming, 2:159–160
Descriptive markup, 2:131, 3:85–86
See also Markup languages
Design tools, 2:28–29, **69–72,** *70, 71, 72*
Desktop publishing, 3:**82–86**
    journalism use, 4:200–201
    office automation systems, 1:197
    productivity software, 3:199–200
    technology, 3:241–245
    word processing *vs.*, 3:82, 262
Desktop-style windows interface, 1:270
Desktop videoconferencing, 1:198
Destroy method (Java applets), 4:192
DETC (Distance Education and Training Council), 3:88
Deterministic models, political events, 4:237
Dethloff, Jürgen, 2:205
Deutsch Institute fur Normung (DIN), 1:120
Developer's office suite software, 3:137
Developing nations, information access, 4:161–162
Device managers, in operating systems, 2:162, 163
Devol, George C., Jr., 1:213
DFDs (data flow diagrams), 2:251
Dialects, of programming languages, 2:193
DIALOG information service, 1:114
Dialog-oriented systems, 1:133
Dick Tracy comic book series, 3:119
Dictation systems, 3:234–236, 4:16
Difference Engine, 1:20, 29–30, 95, 151, 152, 2:191, 3:191
Differential analyzers, 1:4, 53, 3:191
Differential equations, 1:4, 5
Differential GPS measurements, 4:137
Diffie, Whitfield, 4:58
Digital backs (cameras), 4:230
Digital cameras. *See* Cameras

Digital cash, 1:69, 4:107
Digital cellular systems, 2:40
Digital certificates. *See* Certificate Authority (CA)
Digital checks, 4:109
Digital computing, 1:**49–51**
    abacuses, 1:1–2, 49–50
    analog computing *vs.,* 1:2–3, 4–5
    mixed systems, 1:49
    physics applications, 3:192, 193
    speed *vs.* accuracy, 1:50, 51
Digital divide, 4:159–162
Digital Equipment Corporation (DEC), 1:15, 44, 176
Digital filmmaking, 4:*73,* **73–76**
Digital images, 4:**76–78**
Digital integrated circuits, 1:126–127
Digital Landfill (art Web site), 4:8
Digital libraries, 3:152–153, 4:*79,* **79–83**
Digital Library Federation (DLF), 4:79
Digital Living Network Alliance (DLNA), 2:148
Digital logic design, 2:*73,* **73–78,** *74, 75, 76, 78t*
Digital Millennium Copyright Act (DMCA), 3:225, 4:50
Digital music synthesis, 1:184
Digital photography, 4:*83,* **83–86, 229–232**
Digital rights management (DRM), 4:50
Digital signatures, 1:221, 4:58, **86–89,** *87, 88*
Digital single lens reflex (DSLR) cameras, 4:75
Digital subscriber line. *See* DSL (digital subscriber line)
Digital telephony, 1:237–238
    See also Telephone networks
Digital-to-analog conversion
    chip-based, 1:51
    for mixed systems, 1:49
    music synthesis, 1:184, 2:142–145
    time lags, 1:50–51
Digital versatile disks. *See* DVDs (digital versatile disks)
Digital wallets, 1:69, 4:109
Digitizing tablets, 2:254
Dijkstra, Edsger W., 2:201
DIN (Deutsch Institute fur Normung), 1:120

Education *(continued)*
 Open Source Education project, 3:*184*
 Organick, Elliot contributions, 3:*187–188*
 virtual reality use, 1:*256, 256–260, 257*
 See also Colleges and universities
Educational software, 3:**95–98**
EDVAC (Electronic Discrete Variable Automatic Computer), 1:58–59, 63, 66, 87, 2:90, 91
edX online course platform, 3:90, 4:106
EEPROM (Electronic erasable programmable read-only memory), 1:161
EGP (Exterior Gateway Protocol), 4:173
Egress/ingress (radio waves), 2:257
Egypt
 Arab Spring protests, 3:219–220
 cybersecurity attacks, 4:150
EIA (Engineering Industries Association), 1:120
Eich, Brendan, 4:198
8-bit code
 black and white display, 1:36
 color display, 1:37
800 telephone numbers, 3:246
Einstein, Albert, 2:277, 3:141
Eisenhower, Dwight, 1:87
Electrically alterable programmable read-only memory (EAPROM), 2:138
Electro-acoustic music, 1:184
Electroluminescent panels, 2:83
Electromagnetic relays, 1:65
Electromagnetic spectrum, 2:279–280
Electromechanical mouse, 1:181–182, 2:183
Electron guns, 1:255, 2:79
Electronic books. *See* E-books
Electronic calendars, 3:150
Electronic campuses, 4:**103–106**
Electronic cash (E-cash), 1:69, 222, 4:107
Electronic checks, 4:109
Electronic Data Interchange (EDI) protocol, 1:67
Electronic Delay Storage Automatic Calculator (EDSAC), 1:50, 59–60, 65, 87
Electronic Discrete Variable Automatic Computer (EDVAC), 1:58–59, 63, 66, 87, 2:90, 91

Electronic erasable programmable read-only memory (EEPROM), 1:161
Electronic Frontier Foundation, 4:37, 57, 186–187
Electronic journals. *See* E-journals and e-publishing
Electronic libraries. *See* Digital libraries
Electronic mail. *See* E-mail
Electronic markets, 4:**106–110**
 See also E-commerce
Electronic meeting rooms, 3:59–60
Electronic Numerical Integrator and Computer. *See* ENIAC (Electronic Numerical Integrator and Computer)
Electronic Performance Support Systems (EPSSs), 3:52–53
Electronic purses. *See* Stored value cards
Electronic Signatures in Global and National Commerce (E-Signature) Act, 4:87
Electronic tally systems, 4:105
Electronic Visualization Laboratory (University of Illinois), 3:212
Electronic *vs.* digital signatures, 4:87
Electronic wallets, 1:69, 4:109
Elements (Euclid), 2:6
Ellison, Harlan, 4:127
Elographics, 2:254
Elxsi, Ltd., 4:5
Embedded computers, 3:62, 63
Embedded technology (ubiquitous computing), 1:136–137, 3:**98–102,** 160–161
Embedding, objects, 3:138–139
Emirati Louvre museum, 3:*20*
Emitter terminals, of transistors, 1:126, 245
Emoticons, 1:74, 4:187
Encapsulation, in object-oriented programming, 2:158–159
Encoding
 information, 4:167
 keyboards, 1:147–148
 sound data, 2:234–235
Encryption. *See* Cryptography
Encyclopedias, multimedia, 3:130–131
End-effectors, 2:208
End-to-end architecture concept, 4:259
Enemy of the State (film), 4:127
Engelbart, Douglas, 1:104–105, 180–181, 2:186
Engelberger, Joseph, 1:213, 215

Engineering Industries Association (EIA), 1:120
England, Gary, 3:257
Enhanced Data rates for GSM Evolution (EDGE), 4:209
ENIAC (Electronic Numerical Integrator and Computer)
 creation, 1:87, 2:89–90, 3:71, 72
 ENIAC-on-a-chip, 1:254
 general-purpose nature, 1:6, 50
 history, 1:57–58, 63–64
 programming, 1:65–66
 security measures, 1:219
 vacuum tubes in, 1:254–255
Enigma (cryptographic machine), 1:56
Enigma (rotor machine), 4:57
Enquire software program, 4:111
Enterprise information systems, 4:3
Enterprise networks, defined, 1:195
 See also Wide area networks (WANs)
Entrepreneurs, 4:*110,* **110–118**
Entscheidungsproblem, 1:250, 251
Enumeration phase, hacking, 3:122
Environmental sciences, 3:35–36, 80, 124
EPC (European Patent Convention), 4:227–228
EPO (European Patent Office), 4:228
EPROM (erasable programmable read-only memory), 1:161, 2:138
EPSSs (Electronic Performance Support Systems), 3:52–53
Equation engines, 4:38
Erasable programmable read-only memory (EPROM), 1:161, 2:138
Eraserhead pointing devices, 2:186
Ergonomic keyboards, 1:149–150
Ergonomics, 1:**76–78,** 149–150, 3:251–252, 4:155–157
Ericsson smartphones, 2:180
Error correcting codes, 2:55–56, 55*t,* 56*t,* 150
Erwise (browser), 4:33
ESA (European Space Agency), 1:168
ESNET (Energy Sciences Network), 4:174, 176
Estridge, Phil, 1:110
Ethernet networks, 1:195, 278, 4:184
Ethics, 1:23, 27, 4:**118–121**
Euclid, 2:5, 6
Euclid's algorithm, 2:5

Gaming servers, 2:227
See also Servers
GAMS (General Algebraic Modeling System), 3:94
Gamut, of printers, 2:189–190
Gantt charts, 3:*203,* 204
GarageBand music software, 3:169
Garrison, Bruce, 4:202
Gates Foundation, 1:85–86, 172, 4:113
Gates, logic, 1:126–127, 2:73
Gates, Melinda French, 1:85, 86
Gates, William Henry ("Bill"), 1:*84,* **84–86,** 169, 172, 4:112–113, 146
Gateways, 2:33–34
Gattaca (film), 4:211
Gaussian classifiers, 2:178
GB (gigabyte), defined, 1:162
Gbps (gigabits per second), 2:17
Gemini Program, 3:227–228
Genachowski, Julius, 2:*18*
Gene sequencing, 3:34–35
Gene therapy, 3:165
General Algebraic Modeling System (GAMS), 3:94
General Electric, 3:188
General ledger accounting software, 3:1
General Motors (GM), 1:213
General Public License (GPL), 3:183–184
General purpose registers, 2:8
See also Registers
Generations, cellular networks, 1:240
Generations, computers, 1:**86–90**
See also Early computers
Generations, languages, 1:**91–95**
Generative computer-aided processing planning, 3:64
Generative systems, architecture, 3:22
Generic Flow Control (GFC), 4:20
Genetic sequences, 4:211–212
Genetics, computer-assisted research, 3:163–164
GEO (geostationary earth orbit), 2:211, 258–259, 4:139–140
Geographic information systems (GISs), 3:5, 6, **115–117,** 4:140
Geographical factors, scaling, 2:215
Geostationary earth orbit (GEO), 2:211, 258–259, 4:139–140
Geostationary Operational Environmental Satellites (GOES), 2:212

Germanium, as semiconductor, 1:125, 165
Gerrity, Tom, 3:79
Gerstner, Louis V., Jr., 1:110–111
GERTY (fictional robot), 4:128
Gery, Gloria, 3:52
GET command, 4:134
GFC (Generic Flow Control), 4:20
G.hn standard, 2:148
Ghonim, Wael, 3:220
GhostNet, 1:224
Giant magnetoresistance, 1:162, 2:139
Gibson, William, 1:261, 4:128
GIF animation, 1:8, 14
GIF images, 1:8, 14, 4:77
Gigabits per second (Gbps), 2:17, 4:28
Gigabyte (GB), defined, 1:162
Gigaflops (billions of floating-point operations per second), 1:233
Gilliam, Terry, 1:10
Giotto (space probe), 3:229
GISs. *See* Geographic information systems (GISs)
Glenn, John, 3:227
Global Positioning Systems (GPSs), 4:**135–138,** *136*
agriculture applications, 3:5, 6
development, 3:175–176
driverless cars, 4:44
overview, 2:213–214
PDA and smartphones receivers, 2:180–181
surveillance use, 4:140–141
Global surveillance, 4:**139–142**
Global System for Mobile (GSM) networks, 1:119, 3:41
Globalscape, 4:263
GLOSNASS global positioning system, 4:138
Gloves, data, 2:67, 105, 273
Glushkov, Victor M., 4:**142–144**
Gnomons, 3:173–174
Go to statements, 2:2
Goals, Operators, Methods, and Selection (GOMS) system, 4:221
Goddard Scientific Visualization Studio, 3:212
GOES (Geostationary Operational Environmental Satellites), 2:212
Goldberg, Emmanuel, 2:166
Goldfarb, Charles, 2:132

GOMS system (Goals, Operators, Methods, and Selection), 4:221
Google, 4:*242*
driverless cars, 4:44
Fiber for Communities project, 2:59
founding, 4:115–116
personalized information services, 4:164–165
search engine approach, 4:244–245
Google Books, 2:168
Google Chrome, 1:274, 2:225, 4:31–32, 225
Google Docs, 2:168, 3:199
Google Drive, 2:168, 3:199
Gopher protocol, 3:137, 4:186
Gordon, George (Lord Byron), 1:150–151, 153
Gore, Al, 4:237
Gort (fictional robot), 4:128
Gosling, James, 4:145
Gould, Chester, 3:119
Government funding, research, 1:**95–97,** 188–193
GPL (General Public License), 3:183–184
GPO (U.S. Government Printing Office), 4:89
GPSs. *See* Global Positioning Systems (GPSs)
Gramm-Leach-Blilely Act of 1999, 1:211
Grammar, in programming, 2:2–3
Granholm, Jackson, 4:144
Graph theory, for network topologies, 2:154
Graphic devices, 2:**99–101,** 3:192–193
See also Display devices
Graphic Interchange Format (GIF), 1:8, 14, 4:77
Graphical primitives, 3:211
Graphical user interfaces (GUIs)
character-based interfaces *vs.,* 3:249
evolution, 1:133, 3:250
introduction, 1:18
operating systems, 1:84, 2:163–164
Graphics cards, 1:15, 2:99, 3:114
Graphics tablets, 2:186
Gray, Elisha, 2:23, 24
Grayscale display, 1:36–37
Grosch, H. R. J., 4:145
Grosch's Law, 4:145

Gross, Alfred J., 3:**117–119**
Gross Electronics, 3:118, 119
Grötrupp, Helmut, 2:205
Groupware
    computer supported cooperative
      work and, 3:58–60
    for electronic collaboration, 1:198
    productivity software, 3:200–201
Groupware servers, 2:227
    See also Servers
Grove, Andy, 1:128, 130, 131
Groves, Leslie, 2:277, 4:125
Groves, Robert Martin, 1:41
GSM (Global System for Mobile)
  networks, 1:119, 3:41
Guardbands, 4:27
GUIs. *See* Graphical user interfaces
  (GUIs)
Gulliver's Travels (Swift), 4:125–126
"Gunfight" (video game), 1:80
Guns, analog-computer controlled, 1:4
Gunter, Edmund, 1:230, 231
Gurus, 4:**144–146**
Gyros (gyroscopes), 3:9

H

H. L. Hunley (submarine), 3:39
Hackers, 4:**147–151,** *148*
Hacking, 3:**121–125**
    ATMs, 3:31–32
    cookiejacking, 4:47
    Palin, Sarah e-mail, 1:75
    timeline of cybersecurity attacks,
      1:220–225
    See also Internet control and
      cyberwarfare
Haddock, Jon, 4:9
HAL (fictional computer), 4:127
Half-duplex radio systems, 2:38
Haloid Company, 1:276
Hamilton, Edmond, 4:126
Hamming code, 2:55–56, 56t
Hamming, Richard ("Dick"), 1:34, 2:55
Hand-drawn animation, 1:9–10
Hand-held video game units, 1:82
Handheld scanners, 2:168
    See also Scanners
Handoff, in cellular communications,
  2:39, 3:41
Handshakes, Telnet use, 4:264
Handwriting recognition, 2:167, 186
Hanging chads, 4:237

Hankey, Rosalie, 4:265
Hanna, William, 1:13
Hard copies, defined, 2:86
Hard-disk loading, 3:224
Hard drives, 2:106, 241–242, 243
Hardware authentication tokens,
  2:217–218
Hardware engineering, careers, 3:54, 55
Hardware representation, in
  programming languages, 2:1
Hart, Michael, 3:151
Harvard Cyclotron, 3:66
Harvard Mark I/II/III/IV computers,
  1:54–55, 60, 62, 101, 102, 108, 268,
  3:253–254
Harvard University
    edX online course platform, 3:90,
      4:106
    Facebook launch, 3:216, 263–264,
      4:117
    Zuckerberg, Mark affiliation, 3:263
Hashtags, 3:217
Hazen, Harold Locke, 1:53
HDLC (High-level Data Link Control),
  2:12
Head crashes, 2:243
Head-mounted displays (HMDs)
    early developments, 2:272–273
    educational use, 1:257, 259
    wearable computing, 3:100
Header data, in virtual circuits, 2:13–14
Header Error Control (HEC), 4:20,
  21–22
Headers, of packets, 2:151
Heal, Laird, 1:258
Health care. *See* Medical systems
Hearing impairments, assistive
  technology, 4:16–17, 18
Heath Robinson (cryptographic
  machine), 1:56–57
Hebb, Donald O., 3:180
HEC (Header Error Control), 4:20,
  21–22
HECC (High-End Computing
  Capability Project), 1:191
Heilig, Mort, 2:272
Hellman, Martin, 4:58
Help systems, application wizards,
  1:271–272
Henry, Joseph, 2:141
HEPNET, 4:174
Hertz, Heinrich, 2:279, 4:205

Heuristics
    artificial intelligence development,
      1:22
    defined, 1:22
    inference engines, 3:104
    knowledge-based systems, 3:143,
      144
Hewlett-Packard Company, 2:62,
  3:125–126, 4:115, *216*
Hewlett, William, 3:*125,* **125–127,**
  4:113–114
Hexadecimal number system, 1:35,
  36, 91
HIARCS (higher intelligence auto-
  response chess system), 3:46
Hidden Markov Models (HMMs),
  3:233–234
Hidden surface removal, 2:100–101
Higgs boson, 3:193
High definition television (HDTV),
  2:82, 4:153–154
High-definition video, 3:111, 114,
  4:74–75
High-End Computing Capability
  Project (HECC), 1:191
High-level Data Link Control (HDLC),
  2:12
High and low pressure areas (weather),
  3:258
High Order Language Working Group
  (HOLWG), 2:199
High order languages, 2:157–158, 199
High Performance Computing and
  Communications (HPCC) program,
  2:171
High precision/high recall search results,
  4:244
High precision/low recall search results,
  4:244
High-speed trains, 3:208
Higher intelligence auto-response chess
  system (HIARCS), 3:46
Hilbert, David, 1:251
Hiller, Lejaren, 1:185, 3:168
Hillis, W. Daniel, 2:200
Histograms, 3:75
History of computers. *See* Early
  computers; Early pioneers;
  Generations, computers
Hitachi, 1:109, 155
HMDs. *See* Head-mounted displays
  (HMDs)

HMMs (Hidden Markov Models), 3:233–234

Hodges, Larry, 2:274–275

Hoff, Marcian ("Ted"), 1:129

Hoffman, E. T. A., 4:126

Holberton, Frances Snyder, 1:66

Holey Optochip, 1:165–166

Holler, F. James, 4:40

Hollerith codes, 2:114

Hollerith, Herman, 1:39, 96, *99,* **99–101,** 107, 2:114

Hollerith tabulating machines, 1:99–101, *100,* 3:71

Holograms, 3:147

HOLWG (High Order Language Working Group), 2:199

Home entertainment, 4:*152,* **152–155**

Home location registers, 3:246–247

Home servers, 2:227
See also Servers

Home system software, 3:**128–132,** 137

Home theater systems, 4:*152*

HomePlug Powerline Alliance, 2:147–148

Honeywell, 2:90–91

Hopfield, John J., 3:180

Hopkins Beast, 1:213

Hopper, Grace, 1:60, **101–103,** *102*

Horty, John, 3:149

Host-based databases, 2:238

Host-based intrusion detection systems, 3:213–214

Host blocking, 4:36

Hounsfield, Godfrey Newbold, 3:*65,* **65–67**

HPCC (High Performance Computing and Communications) program, 2:171

HTC smartphones, 1:240, 2:181

HTML editors, 3:129

HTML (Hypertext Markup Language)
Berners-Lee, Tim contributions, 4:111, 145
browser use, 1:274, 4:31, 32
defined, 1:73
e-banking applications, 4:92
e-journal format, 4:102
e-mail use, 1:72
Java applets and, 4:191–192
JavaScript embedded programs, 4:194–199
overview, 2:*133,* 133–134

source code documentation, 2:160
XHTML development, 2:134–135

HTTP (Hypertext Transport Protocol)
Berners-Lee, Tim contributions, 4:32–33, 111, 145
browser use, 4:30–32
cookies, 4:45–47
defined, 1:67

HTTPS (Hypertext Transport Protocol with Security extension)
defined, 1:67
e-banking use, 4:93
e-commerce use, 1:67–68

Hughes, Chris, 4:117

Human brain research, 4:63

Human-computer interaction. *See* User interfaces

Human factors, user interfaces, 4:**155–157,** 256

Human Rights Watch, 4:36

Human *vs.* computer strengths, 1:76–77

Hurst, George Samuel, 2:254

Hybrid digital-analog music production, 2:142

Hydra chess computer, 3:45

HyperCard, 1:105

Hyperlinks
dynamic links, 4:100
hypertext and, 4:34
integrated software, 3:139
search engine results, 4:242, 243
sponsored links, 4:243

Hypermedia and multimedia, 1:*104,* 2:**103–107,** *104*
documents, 2:86
encyclopedias, 3:130–131
history, 1:104–105, 2:105
indexing speech recognition applications, 3:235, 236
office automation systems, 1:199
realism, 4:157
user interfaces, 3:250–251

Hypertext, 1:**103–105,** 4:32–33, 34, 111

Hypertext Markup Language. *See* HTML (Hypertext Markup Language)

Hypertext Transport Protocol. *See* HTTP (Hypertext Transport Protocol)

Hypertext Transport Protocol with Security extension (HTTPS). *See* HTTPS (Hypertext Transport Protocol with Security extension)

I

I Have No Mouth, and I Must Scream (Ellison), 4:127

I Love You virus (2000), 1:223

i-Minitel, 1:179

I/O controllers, 2:66

I/O (input/output) devices. *See* Input/output (I/O) devices

I, Robot (Asimov), 1:216, 4:127

I, Robot (film), 4:127

I, Robot (game), 1:15

IBM Corporation, 1:**107–112,** *108*
701 computer, 1:88, 108, 4:4
704 computer, 4:4
7090 computer, 1:33, 88
Amdahl, Gene Myron involvement, 4:4
Blue Gene P supercomputer, 3:46
C-T-R origins, 1:101, 107, 268
carbon nanotube development, 3:49
character code developments, 2:52
CHRISTMAS.EXE worm, 1:263
collaboration in industry, 1:170, 171, 2:62, 4:113
computer assisted instruction development, 3:50
Deep Blue chess competition, 1:83, 111, 3:44–45
flash drives, 2:243
FORTRAN association, 2:193, 194
Harvard Mark I involvement, 1:54–55, 108
Internet backbone connections, 4:175
intranet, 4:189
Lotus acquisition, 3:240
Magnetic Tape Selectric Typewriter, 3:259, 262
microcomputer development, 1:168
optical microchip development, 1:165–166
patents, 4:229
PDA introduction, 2:180
RAMAC 305 computer, 1:108
RS/4000 computer, 4:173
SGML development, 2:132
space program computers, 3:227–228
supercomputer development, 1:235, 2:175

Laser technology, 3:**145–148,** *146*
Laserwriter printers, 3:82, 85, 243
Lasseter, John, 1:14
LastPass, 4:114
Lathrop, George Parsons, 4:126
Latitude lines, 3:173
Lawrence Livermore National
 Laboratory, 4:149
LCD. *See* Liquid crystal display (LCD)
LDP (Linux Documentation Project),
 3:186
Learning Company, 3:97
Learning disabilities, assistive
 technology, 4:17
Learning, machine, 3:180–181
Learning Management Systems (LMSs),
 3:51–52, 53, 95–97
Least significant numbers, 1:3
Lebanon, cybersecurity attacks, 4:150
Lederberg, Joshua, 3:144
LEDs. *See* Light emitting diodes (LEDs)
Legal cases
 malicious software, 2:118
 software patent protection, 4:228,
  229
 Sperry-Rand lawsuit, 2:90–91
 See also Antitrust litigation
Legal systems, 3:**148–151**
Legislation
 computer fraud, 1:42–46
 disabilities, 4:13–14, 18
 driverless cars, 4:44
 hacking, 3:124
 Internet regulation, 3:222, 4:178, 179
 piracy, 3:225, 226
 privacy concerns, 1:210, 211
 telecommunications, 4:186, 246
LEGO-Logo, 2:128
Lego Mindstorms system, 2:128
Leibniz, Gottfried Wilhem von, 1:20,
 4:62, 254
Leibowitz, Joe, 4:*225*
Leica (dog), 2:214
Lenses, video cameras, 4:74, 75
LEO (low earth orbit), 2:211, 258–259,
 4:139–140
Level 3 Communications, 4:176
Levin, Ira, 4:126
Lex (lexical analyzer), 2:2
Lexical analyzers, 2:2, 63
LEXIS-NEXIS information service,
 1:114, 3:149

Libraries, digital, 4:*79,* 79–83
Library applications, 3:**151–153,**
 4:233–234
Library of Congress, 4:81
Libya, Arab Spring effects, 3:221
Licensing agreements, software,
 3:223–224
Licklider, Joseph, 4:183–184
LIDAR (LIght Detection And
 Ranging), 4:44
Life cycle methods (Java applets), 4:192
Light emitting diodes (LEDs)
 fiber optics development, 1:202, 2:91
 infrared radiation communications,
  2:259
 joysticks, 2:97
 optical mice, 1:182, 2:184
Light pens, 2:113, 186
"Like" feature, 3:264
Line printers, mainframes, 1:158
Linear encoding, 2:234
Linear integrated circuits, 1:126
Linear interpolation, 1:11
Linear Pulse Coding Modulation
 (LPCM), 2:234
Linear regression, data mining, 4:67
Link, Edwin, 1:226–227
Link layer, OSI Reference Model, 2:151
Linking, objects, 3:138–139
Links, hypertext, 1:105
Links, in networks, 1:193–194, 2:154
Linux Documentation Project (LDP),
 3:186
Linux operating system
 development, 2:164–165
 documentation project, 3:186
 mobile applications, 4:209
 open source concept and, 3:185
 scalability, 2:216, 4:145
Lipstick Enigma (artwork), 4:8
Liquid crystal display (LCD)
 CRTs *vs.,* 1:255, 2:84
 overview, 2:81–82
 projection technology, 4:104
 touch screens, 2:254–255
LISP (LISt Processing), 2:**123–125**
List servers, 2:227
 See also Servers
Live Free or Die Hard (film), 4:128
Live Messenger, 4:169
Live streaming technology, 2:237
LivePerson, Inc., 4:189

LiveScript. *See* JavaScript
LMDS (local multipoint distribution
 service), 2:281
LMSs (Learning Management Systems),
 3:51–52, 53, 95–97
Local area networks (LANs)
 bandwidth measurement, 2:17
 bridging devices, 2:*31,* 31–34
 computer supported cooperative
  work and, 3:57–60
 Internet backbone connections,
  4:173
 mainframe connection, 1:158
 network design considerations,
  2:147–149
 in office automation systems, 1:197
 origins, 1:239, 4:184
 overview, 1:195
 peer to peer networking and,
  1:138–139
 twisted pairs, 1:194, 2:257
 wireless, 2:281
Local/asynchronous distance learning,
 3:90
Local direct connection, mainframes,
 1:158
Local loops, 4:28
Local multipoint distribution service
 (LMDS), 2:281
Local/synchronous distance learning,
 3:89
Location aware mobile computing,
 4:209
LOCI (calculator), 3:254
LOCK (Logical Coprocessing Kernel),
 2:217
Locking, for concurrency control, 2:239
Lodge, Oliver Joseph, 4:205
Logarithms
 analog computer calculations, 1:4
 defined, 1:3
 Napier, John development, 1:230,
  231
 slide rule calculations, 1:3, 230, 231
Logic
 artificial intelligence development,
  1:21
 Boolean, 1:114–115, 116,
  2:25–30, 4:245
 digital computing use of, 1:49
 query languages, 1:94
 Turing, Alan work, 1:251

Logic gates, 1:126–127, 2:73

Logic Theorem Machine, 4:220, 253

Logical Coprocessing Kernel (LOCK), 2:217

Logical diagrams. *See* Flowcharts

Logicon, Inc., 2:203

Logo (programming language), 2:*125–126,* **125–130,** *129*

London Grand Prix simulator, 1:*227*

Long, Edward, 1:211

Long term evolution (LTE) technology, 1:240, 2:59, 4:209

Long-term memory, 1:133–134

Longitude determination, 3:173, 174

Looping, in programming, 2:201

Loosely typed languages, 4:197

LORAN (long range navigation), 3:10–11, 175

Lorraine Motel (artwork), 4:9

Los Alamos National Laboratory, 1:235, 2:175

Lossy compression, 2:120, 235, 4:77

Lost update problem, 2:239

Lotus 1-2-3, 3:137, 239, 4:114

Lotus Corporation, 4:114

Lotus Freelance Graphics, 3:200

Lotus Notes, 3:201

Lotus Smartsuite 97, 3:138

Lovebug virus (2000), 1:223

Lovelace, Ada King (countess). *See* King, Ada Byron

LoveLetter worm, 2:118

Low earth orbit (LEO), 2:211, 258–259, 4:139–140

Low precision/high recall search results, 4:243

LPCM (Linear Pulse Coding Modulation), 2:234

LSI. *See* Large-scale integrated (LSI) circuits

LTE (Long Term Evolution) technology, 1:240, 2:59, 4:209

Lucas, George, 1:18, 4:74

Lucent Technologies, 1:33, 34

Lynx (browser), 4:33

M

MacBook laptop series, 1:19, 146, 2:*79*

Machine language, 1:91, 2:9, 64

Machine Readable Cataloging (MARC), 3:152

The Machine Stops (Forster), 4:126

Macintosh operating systems, 1:18, 19, 171, 2:265–266

Macintosh personal computers
desktop publishing development, 3:82, 85
innovations, 1:144–145
introduction, 1:18, 144
Microsoft Excel, 3:239–240
virus attacks, 1:263
as WIMP system, 1:133, 272

Macro viruses, 1:262–263
See also Viruses

Macromedia, 1:14–15

MAD (Michigan Algorithm Decoder), 3:188

MAE (Metropolitan Area Exchange), 4:175

Magic mouse, 1:183

Magnavox, 1:80

Magnetic cores, 1:60, 2:136

Magnetic disks
information retrieval systems, 1:113
optical storage *vs.,* 1:204
second generation computer use, 1:88
as storage device, 1:160, 2:241–243
virtual memory, 1:161

Magnetic drums, 2:241

Magnetic ink character recognition (MICR), 2:114, 167–168

Magnetic resonance imaging (MRI), 3:135

Magnetic stripe cards, 2:113, **3:155–157,** *156, 157*

Magnetic tape
information retrieval systems, 1:113
as input device, 2:113
optical storage *vs.,* 1:204
second generation computer use, 1:88
as storage device, 1:160, 2:241
UNIVAC use, 1:88
videotape technology, 3:110–111

Magnetic Tape Selectric Typewriter, 3:259, 262

Magnetospirilllum magneticum, 4:212

Magnification programs, 4:15

Mail trap doors, 1:221

Main memory. *See* Memory; Random access memory (RAM)

Mainframes, 1:**155–159,** *156*
Amdahl corporation, 4:4
Andor Systems, 4:5
communication devices, 2:56
defined, 1:18, 79
early networks, 1:239
first video games, 1:79
IBM, 1:88, 108–109, 155–156, 2:45, 52, 4:4, 5, 6
journalism use, 4:200
minicomputers *vs.,* 1:173, 174

Major search engines, 4:244–245

Malaria, computer modeling, 3:36

Malaysia, cybercafes, 4:61

Malware. *See* Invasive programs; Trojan horses; Viruses; Worms

Management information systems (MISs), 2:109, 110, 3:79–81

Manchester Mark I, 1:59, 64–65

Mandelbrot, Benoit B., 3:159

Mandelbrot sets, 3:159

Manhattan Project
Feynman, Richard involvement, 4:123–124, 125
Kemeny, John G. involvement, 3:141
Organick, Elliot involvement, 3:187
von Neumann, John involvement, 2:276, 277

Manipulators (robot arms), 1:215, 2:208, 3:63

MANs (metropolitan area networks), 1:195, 2:147–149

Manufacturing
automation, 3:*194,* 194–197
chips, 3:*47,* 47–50
computer-aided, 3:38–39, 60–65, 4:255
computer-integrated, 3:64
decision support systems, 3:80
expert systems, 3:103
nanoscale technology, 4:217
process control, 3:*194,* 194–197
robotics use, 1:213, 214, 215, 2:207–208

Map overlay operations, 3:116

Map reclassification operations, 3:116

Maps
computer generated, 3:*174*
data visualization, 3:73
weather, 3:257
See also Geographic information systems (GISs)

Microchips, 1:*163,* **163–166**

Microcomputers, 1:77, **166–169,** 173
See also Personal computers (PCs)

Microfilm, 2:191

Micromarketing, 1:210

Micropayments, 1:69

Microphones, wireless, 4:103

Microprocessors
analog-to-digital and digital-to-analog conversion, 1:51
Apple products, 1:17, 18, 19
in auto-pilots, 3:10
computer science research, 1:47
fourth generation computer use, 1:89–90
in game controllers, 2:98
invention, 1:129, 167
manufacturing, 3:*47,* 47–50
multiple, 1:47
video editing needs, 3:114
video game use, 1:80, 82
See also Intel microprocessors; Parallel processing

Microsoft Access database software, 3:77

Microsoft Active Accessibility (MSAA), 4:18

Microsoft Corporation, 1:**169–173,** *170*
Apple agreement, 1:18
compatibility priorities, 2:62
flight simulation game, 4:157
founding, 1:84, 169, 4:146
history, 1:84–86, 169–173
IBM collaboration, 1:18, 110
Live Messenger, 4:169
mobile computing operating systems, 4:208
MS-DOS operating system, 1:84, 170, 171, 2:163, 4:267
video game development, 1:82
Visual Basic development, 4:267–268
Windows Media Player, 2:237
See also Windows operating system

Microsoft Excel, 1:171, 3:239–240

Microsoft Exchange Server, 3:201

Microsoft Flight Simulator (MSFS), 2:231–232

Microsoft Information Interchange Server (IIS), 2:225

Microsoft Kinect, 2:98

Microsoft Office, 1:171, 3:128, 137–138

Microsoft Outlook, 3:201, 4:169

Microsoft PowerPoint, 1:171, 3:200

Microsoft Publisher, 3:82

Microsoft SharePoint, 3:201

Microsoft Surface tablet computer, 1:*170,* 172

Microsoft Word, 1:171, 3:82, 262

Microsoft Xbox, 1:82, 4:154

Microwave Communications Inc., 4:175

Microwave transmission, 2:258, 4:28–29

MicroWorlds, 2:127

MIDI (Musical Instrument Digital Interface), 1:185, 2:235, 3:169, 170

Military
Ada computer language, 1:153, 2:198–199
computer assisted instruction, 3:50, 51
cryptography applications, 4:56–57
educational virtual reality use, 1:259
virtual reality training, 2:274
See also U.S. Department of Defense (DoD)

Millennium bug (Y2K scare), 3:124, 4:5

Miller, Joan E., 2:144

Million Book Project, 4:81

MIMD (Multiple Instruction, Multiple Data), 2:173

MIME (Multipurpose Internet Mail Extensions), 4:168–169

Mind over Matter (artwork), 4:7–8

Minicomputers, 1:44, **173–177,** *174,* 239, 3:206

Minimax algorithm, 3:44

Minimum attribute standards, 1:118

Minimum spanning trees, 2:155

Minitel, 1:**177–180,** *178,* 4:61

Minix operating system, 2:164, 3:185

Minsky, Marvin, 4:220

MISD (Multiple Instruction, Single Data), 2:173

MISs (management information systems), 2:109, 110, 3:79–81

Missile defense systems, 4:120

MIT (Massachusetts Institute of Technology)
decision support systems development, 3:79
e-journals, 4:102

edX online course platform, 3:90, 4:106
flight simulation project, 1:227
Kerberos authentication scheme, 4:101
Multics system, 1:221, 3:188
space program computers, 3:228
video game development, 1:79
X-Windows development, 1:272

MITS (Micro Instrumentation and Telemetry Systems), 1:169, 4:112

Miyamoto, Shigeru, 2:*96*

MMOGs (Massively Multiplayer Online Games), 1:16

Mnemonics, 1:91, 2:9

Mobile agents, 4:2

Mobile computing, 4:*207,* **207–210**
See also Cell phones; Laptop computers; Personal digital assistants (PDAs); Tablet computers

Mobile phone system (MPS), 2:38–39

Mobile phones. *See* Cell phones; Smartphones

Mobile robotics, 1:215, 2:209
See also Robots

Mobile switching centers, 3:41

Mobile virtual private networks (mVPNs), 2:271

Mobility management, 3:41

Modeling
animation, 1:9, 10
cosmological research, 3:28
molecular, 4:39
system analysis, 2:247

Modems
cable, 2:58
callback, 1:222
origin of term, 2:57
telephone, 2:57–58, 4:28
wireless, 2:258

Moderation, of discussion groups, 1:73–74

Modes, in fiber optics, 2:92

Modular engineering, 4:3

Modulation
lasers, 3:147
signals, 2:57–58

Modules, in programming, 2:201–202

Molecular biology, 3:**163–167,** *164*

Molecular computing, 3:166, 4:128, *210,* **210–213,** 217

Phosphorous, in semiconductors, 1:125–126

Photo diodes, 3:147

Photo-resist, 1:243, 244

Photo restoration, 4:*83*

Photocopiers, 1:276–277

Photography, 4:**229–232**
    See also Digital photography

Photolithography, 1:242, 243–244

Photomasks, 3:48

Photonic switching, 2:95

Photons
    fiber optics, 2:92, 95
    laser technology, 3:145, 146, 147

Photophone invention, 2:23

Photosensitivity, 4:41

PhotoShop image editing software, 3:22, 4:232

Phreakers, 4:148

Physical addressing, 2:*263,* 264, *264,* 265–266

Physical ergonomics, 1:76

Physical layer
    ATM transmission, 4:21–22
    network connections, 4:130
    OSI Reference Model, 2:151

Physical modeling synthesis (PhM), 3:171

Physics, 3:**191–194**

Picture lock (video editing), 3:113

Pierce, John, 2:144

Pigment-based inks, 2:190

Ping sweeps, 3:122

PINs (personal identification numbers), 2:218, 3:32, 4:25

Pioneers. *See* Early pioneers

PIPA (Protect IP Act), 3:222, 4:179

Piracy
    hackers and, 4:149
    Jacquard's loom punch cards, 1:142
    online gaming, 2:98
    peer-to-peer networking and, 4:171
    software, 3:223–226, *224*
    SOPA and PIPA acts, 3:222
    See also Intellectual property

Pittsburgh Supercomputing Center, 4:172, 185

Pixar, Inc., 1:13, 18, 144, 4:128

Pixels
    defined, 1:36, 4:76
    digital camera resolutions, 4:231
    dots per inch of printers *vs.,* 2:188
    LCDs, 2:81, 82

PKIs (public key infrastructures), 2:219, 4:88

Plan position indicators (PPIs), 3:13, 14

Plane polarized light, 2:81

Playing with Infinity: Mathematical Explorations and Excursion (Péter), 3:189, 190

Playstation, 1:82, 4:154

PLCs (programmable logic controllers), 3:6

Pleiades supercomputer, 1:191

Plessey Telecommunications, 2:203

Plotters, 2:191

Plummer, R. P., 3:188

Pocket Fritz 4 chess program, 3:46

Pointing cursors, 2:183

Pointing devices, 2:*182,* **182–187,** 253, 3:146

Points of interest (POIs), 3:*74,* 74–75

The Poison Dress (article), 4:265

Polar orbits, 2:211

Polarizers, in liquid crystal displays, 2:81–82

Police radio, 2:37–38

Political applications, 4:*233,* **233–237**

Political campaigns, 4:234–235, 236

Political information, computerization, 4:233–234

Polling, political, 4:236

Polonius security system, 2:217, 218

Polyalphabetic ciphers, 4:56

Polyalphabetic substitution systems, 4:57

Polymorphic viruses and worms, 1:264

Polymorphism, object-oriented programming, 2:160

Polynomials, 1:20

"Pong" (video game), 1:79–80, 83, 4:154

Pop-up dialog boxes, 4:*195,* 196

Population inversions, 3:145

Port IDs, 4:131, 132

Port scans, 3:122

Portability, of software, 2:62

Portable computing. *See* Mobile computing

Portable Document Format (PDF), 2:135, 3:130, 4:102

Position indicator cursors, 2:183

Positional notation, 1:35

Positioning sensors, for joysticks, 2:97

Positive Train Control (PTC) project, 3:208

Post, E. L., 2:2

Postscript page description language, 3:82, 85, 243, 244

Poulson Itanium processor, 2:37

Power transistors, 1:*242*

PowerMac series, 1:144

PPIs (plan position indicators), 3:13, 14

Pre-processors, image, 4:42–43

Precision, in information retrieval, 1:115, 4:164, 243–244

Predicate calculus, 1:21

Predicate logic inference engines, 3:105

Prefixes, metric, 2:95, 4:28

Prendergast, James ("Jim"), 1:122

Prescription drugs database management systems, 3:162

Presentation layer, OSI Reference Model, 2:152

Presentation software
    in office automation systems, 1:199
    political applications, 4:235
    in productivity software, 1:171, 3:200
    scientific visualization *vs.,* 3:211

President's Critical Infrastructure Protection Board, 1:224

Pressure measurement, 1:208

Pressure sensitive touch screens, 2:255

Pretty Good Privacy (PGP), 1:223

Preventing Real Online Threats to Economic Creativity and Theft of Intellectual Property Act (PIPA), 3:222, 4:179

Price, Mark, 4:69

Primary storage. *See* Memory; Random access memory (RAM)

Priming, 1:134

Primitives
    graphical, 3:38, 211
    Logo syntax, 2:127

Princeton University, 2:276, 4:172, 185

Print servers, 2:227
    See also Servers

Printing devices, 2:*187,* **187–192**
    3D, 3:62
    desktop publishing, 3:242–244
    mainframe connections, 1:158
    resolution, 4:76
    See also Laser printers

Printing press invention, 3:83

System/390, 1:109, 155

System analysis, 2:**245–249,** 250

System design, 2:246

System for the Mechanical Analysis and Retrieval of Text (SMART), 1:115, 2:109

System-in-package (SiP), 1:128

System-on-a-chip (SoC), 1:127

Systems design, 2:**249–252**

T

T1 circuits, 4:223

T1 leased lines, 4:29, 173

T3 leased lines, 4:29, 173

Tablet computers
  e-reader capability, 4:96
  encryption needs, 4:58
  GPSs, 3:176
  handwriting recognition, 2:167
  iPads, 1:19, 146
  Microsoft products, 1:*170,* 172

Tabulating Machine Company, 1:100–101, 107

Tabulating machines, 1:*100*
  Census Bureau use, 1:39, 96, 100, 101, 107
  Hollerith, Herman contributions, 1:39, 96, 99–101, 107

Tank, David W., 3:180

Tape cartridges, 2:113, 241

Tape drives, 1:158, 2:113, 241

Tapella, Robert C., 4:89

Tarski, Alfred, 1:21

Tartan Racing team, 4:44

Tax software, 2:283, 3:*2,* 201

TB (terabyte), defined, 1:162

TCP/IP (Transmission Control Protocol/Internet Protocol), 4:**259–262**
  firewalls, 4:130–132
  history, 4:184–185, 260–261
  Internet backbone connections, 4:173, 175
  intranets, 4:188
  OSI Reference Model *vs.,* 2:152–153
  overview, 1:195
  popularity, 2:149
  scalability, 2:216

TCP port numbers, 4:260

tcpdump network security program, 3:214

TCSEC (Trusted Computer Systems Evaluation Criteria). *See* Orange Book

TCST (thin client/server technology), 2:49

TDMA (Time Division Multiple Access) standard, 3:42

Technicolor, 1:12

Technology of desktop publishing, 3:**241–245**

tekGear, 2:101

Telcordia, 1:33

Telecommunication Standardization Sector of the International Telecommunications Union (ITU-T), 1:119–120

Telecommunications, 1:**237–241,** *238*
  document processing, 2:86–87
  information technology standards, 1:119
  legal applications, 3:151
  service providers, 4:246–249

Telecommunications Acts (1995/1996), 4:186, 246

Telecommuting, 1:199, 4:256

Teleconferencing, 1:198–199, 2:262

Telegraph systems
  codes, 2:50–51
  cryptography applications, 4:56–57
  history, 1:237, 2:141–142, 4:222
  railroad use, 3:205–206
  wireless, 2:257, 279, 4:205–206

Telemedicine, 3:162–163

Teleoperation, 1:213, 215

Telephone communication satellites, 2:212

Telephone networks
  analog to digital conversion, 4:28
  bandwidth capacity, 4:27, 28
  copper cabling, 1:194
  DSL development, 2:58–59
  history, 1:237
  packet switching *vs.,* 1:139
  phreaker hackers, 4:148
  video games, 1:82

Telephone relays, 1:65, 2:282

Telephone switching systems, 1:33, 53–54, 237–238, 3:41

Telephony, 3:**245–248**
  e-mail *vs.,* 1:74
  invention, 2:23
  TTYs, 4:17, 18

Teleprinters, 2:51, 57–58

Telerobotics, 1:215

Teletype machines, 2:57, 58

Television
  Apple TV, 1:19
  evolution from broadcast to cable, 1:239
  high definition, 2:82
  home entertainment use, 4:153–154
  interactive, 3:88, 4:105
  newsroom computer use, 4:200–202
  satellite broadcast, 2:212
  scanning lines, 2:82
  transition to digital, 2:261, 4:*87*
  weather forecasting, 3:*255,* 255–258

Telnet, 4:134, **262–264**

Telstar satellite, 2:212

Ten-Second Film Challenge, 4:*73*

Tenenbaum, Ehud, 3:123

Terabits per second (Tbps), 4:28

Terabyte (TB), defined, 1:162

Teraflops, 2:174

Term weighting, information retrieval, 1:115, 116

Terminal symbols, 2:2

Terminals, dumb. *See* Dumb terminals

Terminating resistors, 2:66

Terrorism
  airline passenger screening, 3:18
  anthrax scare, 3:36
  cyberwarfare, 4:179–182
  September 11 attacks, 3:18, 4:157, 266
  See also Bioterrorism

Tetrodes, 1:253

Tevatron particle collider, 3:193

Texas Instruments, 1:88, 126, 2:44

Text editing, 3:261

Text entry, 3:261

Text formatting, 3:261

Text messaging, 2:41–42

Text Retrieval Evaluation Conference (TREC), 1:116

Text telephones (TTYs), 4:17, 18

Text translation, urban myths, 4:265

Tfxidf values, 1:115

Thacker, Charles P., 1:251

Thakkar, Umesh, 1:258

Thematic mapping, 3:116

Therac-25 radiation therapy machine, 4:119

Voice-driven applications, 4:169

Voice mail, 1:74, 198

Voice-over-Internet-protocol (VoIP), 3:247, 4:248

Voice recognition. *See* Speech recognition

Volatility of RAM, 1:160

Volume software licenses, 3:223–224

von Neumann, John, 2:**275–277**, *276*
    artificial life model, 4:11
    EDVAC development, 1:58–59, 66, 2:90, 91
    Kemeny, John G. collaboration, 3:141
    stored-program concept development, 1:87
    Turing, Alan collaboration, 1:248

von Neumann machines, 1:58–59, 87

Voting, data processing, 4:236, 237

Voting districts, data processing, 4:235

Voyager (space probe), 3:231, 232

VPCs (virtual path connections), 4:21

VPI (Virtual Path Identifier), 4:20–21, 22, 23

VPNs (virtual private networks), 2:268–271

VR. *See* Virtual reality (VR)

VRML (Virtual Reality Modeling Language), 1:10, 11

Vulnerabilities, security software and, 2:220, 3:124

W

W3C. *See* World Wide Web Consortium (W3C)

WAAS (Wide Area Augmentation System), 4:137–138

Wafer-scale integration (WSI), 1:128

Wafers, 3:48

Wal-Mart, 4:69

Walkie-talkies, 3:117, 118

WALL-E (film), 4:128

Wallace and Gromit (animated characters), 1:10

Walt Disney Studios, 1:12–13, 14, 3:126

Walters, Grey, 1:213

Wang, An, 3:**253–255**, 262

Wang, Charles, 4:115

Wang Computer System, 3:262

Wang Laboratories, 3:253, 254

Wang Word Processing System, 3:254, 259, 262

Wannabes (hackers), 4:148

WANs. *See* Wide area networks (WANs)

"Warcraft" (simulation game), 1:83

Warez Dudez (hackers), 4:149

WarGames (film), 4:128

Warnock, John, 3:243–244

Waterfall paradigm, 2:249, 251

Watson (IBM computer), 1:23

Watson, James, 4:39

Watson, Thomas A., 1:240, 2:23

Watson, Thomas J., Jr., 1:108, 109–110, 268

Watson, Thomas J., Sr., 1:107–108, *267*, **267–269**

Wave interruption touch screens, 2:255

Wave table synthesis, 2:235

Wavelength division multiplexing (WDM), 1:202, 2:93

Wearable computing, 2:101, 3:100, 101

Weather forecasting, 3:210, *255*, **255–259**

Weather monitoring, 2:212, 3:119

Web. *See* World Wide Web

Web animation, 1:14–15

Web browsers. *See* Browsers

Web servers, 2:225, 227, 4:30–31, 188

Webb, Jim, 4:234

Webphone, 1:179

Web sites
    as art, 4:8
    intranets, 1:67, 195, 4:188–190
    journalism, 4:202
    political applications, 4:233, 234, 235

WebStar server program, 2:225

Wei, Pei, 4:33

Weighted information retrieval, 1:115, 116

Weiser, Mark, 3:101

Wells, H.G., 3:24, 25

Werbos, Paul J., 3:180

Wergo Records, 1:185

West Publishing Company, 3:149

Western Electric Company (WECo), 1:31–32, 33

Western Music Notation, 3:168

Westlaw, 3:149

Westworld (film), 4:128

What-if analysis, 3:201, 238

Wheatstone, Charles, 1:152, 2:113, 114

While Rome Burns (Woollcott), 4:265

Whirlpool project, 3:20

Whirlwind computer, 1:60

White Hat hackers, 4:148

Whiteboards, interactive, 4:104, 105

Wi-Fi (Wireless Fidelity), 4:209

Wide Area Augmentation System (WAAS), 4:137–138

Wide area networks (WANs)
    Internet backbone connections, 4:172–173
    mainframe connection, 1:158
    network design considerations, 2:147–149
    origins, 1:239
    overview, 1:195
    VPNs *vs.*, 2:268

Wiener, Norbert, 4:62–63

Wii, 1:*80*, 2:*96*, 98

Wilkes, Maurice V., 1:50, 59, 64, 65, 87, 249

Williams, Evan, 3:217

Williams, John, 4:69

Williams, R. Stanley, 4:*210*

Williams, Sir Frederic, 1:59, 64–65

Wily Hacker attack (1986), 1:223

WIMP (windows, icon, menu, and pointer) systems, 1:133, 3:241
    See also Graphical user interfaces (GUIs)

Window interfaces, 1:*269*, **269–273**, 2:86

Window manager functionality, 1:134

Windows Media Player, 2:237

Windows operating system
    accessibility utilities, 4:18
    creation, 1:84
    encryption abilities, 4:58
    GUIs, 2:163–164
    Internet Explorer bundle, 1:85, 274, 4:172
    introduction, 1:171
    Microsoft Excel performance, 3:240
    multitasking capabilities, 1:171
    Visual Basic programming, 4:268
    windows interfaces, 1:272

Windows Phone mobile operating system, 4:208

Windows technology, 1:95

Winklevoss, Cameron, 3:263

Winklevoss, Tyler, 3:263

WIPO (World Intellectual Property Organization) Copyright Treaty, 3:225